The Story of a
Pilgrim Family

From the Mayflower to the present time; with
autobiography, recollections, letters, incidents,
and genealogy of the author, Rev. John Alden,
in his 83d year

John Alden

Alpha Editions

This edition published in 2020

ISBN : 9789354029530

Design and Setting By
Alpha Editions
email - alphaedis@gmail.com

THE STORY OF A PILGRIM FAMILY.

FROM THE MAYFLOWER TO THE PRESENT TIME;

WITH AUTOBIOGRAPHY, RECOLLECTIONS,

LETTERS, INCIDENTS, AND

GENEALOGY OF THE AUTHOR

REV. JOHN ALDEN,

IN HIS 83d YEAR.

INTRODUCTION BY

REV. FREDERICK DENISON

1620-1889

BOSTON

J. H. EARLE

1890

PREFACE.

———o———

The name of Alden has, for more than two centuries, been familiar to every son and daughter of New England. The Pilgrim John, who first brought it to these shores, was a man of whom his numerous descendants are justly proud; not for his high station, great wealth or colossal intellect, but for his rectitude of character, fidelity to duty, and his eminently pious, practical and useful life.

It is my privilege to bear his name, and it has been my pleasure, in addition to my own personal experiences and recollections, to give in these pages a sketch of this ancient family from 1620 to the present time. I have also added a History of the Pilgrims; their rise in England; their life in Holland; their migration to America and their subsequent trials, sufferings and victories. It is a large subject, and one of absorbing interest, especially to those who trace their ancestry back to Plymouth Rock.

For much of the material used in preparing this history, I am indebted to " Bradford's Journal," "Morton's Memorial," Justin Winsor's "History of Duxbury," Judge Davis' "History of Plymouth," "Alden's Memorial," and the recent valuable contribution of John Goodwin's " The Pilgrim Republic," through the courtesy of his son, Wm. Bradford Goodwin; also to Hamilton A. Hill for facts in his little

5

brochure on some charter members of the "Old South Church."

I also acknowledge the kindness of Messrs. Houghton, Mifflin & Co., in granting the use of Longfellow's "Court-ship of Miles Standish;" J. S. Tilton, for the picture representing "Priscilla's Wedding Journey," and A. S. Burbank, of Plymouth, for the view of Leyden street in 1622; to Mrs. Agnes Gormley for "Alden's Epitaphs," and to J. Dutch Lord, Historian, for preparing Genealogy.

This is, without doubt, my last work. It was undertaken at the earnest solicitation of my friends, that many facts of and incidents of personal history might be preserved in permanent form. By the valuable aid of my wife I have been enabled to accomplish the task, and I now submit it to the public hoping that a perusal of its contents may please and profit all.

JOHN ALDEN.

PROVIDENCE, R. I., 1888.

TABLE OF CONTENTS.

——o——

I.

CHILDHOOD AND YOUTH.

II.

COLLEGE LIFE.

III.

TEACHING.

7

IX.

SILVER WEDDING OF SON.

PART II.

ANECDOTES AND REMINISCENCES.

X.

STORIES FOR WINTER EVENINGS.

XI.

STATESMEN OF MY DAY.

XII.

RELIGIOUS ANECDOTES.

XIII.

CELEBRATED DIVINES.

XIV.

FUNERAL SERMON OF JOHN LELAND.

XV.

EXCITING AND TRAGIC STORIES.

XVI.

STORIES FOR SABBATH SCHOOLS.

XVII.

TRIBUTE TO MY WIFE.

PART III.

PILGRIM HISTORY.

XVIII.

THE PILGRIM FATHERS.

PAGE.

XIX.

MAYFLOWER PASSENGERS.

XX.

PILGRIM LEADERS.

XXI.

JOHN ALDEN.

XXII.

DESCENDANTS OF THE ALDEN FAMILY.

XXIII.

REV. TIMOTHY ALDEN, A. M., PRESIDENT OF ALLEGHANY COLLEGE.

XXIV.

MILES STANDISH.

XXV.

THE AUTHOR'S LINE OF ANCESTRY.

XXVI.

PLYMOUTH—1888.

LIST OF ILLUSTRATIONS.

————o————

15

INTRODUCTION.

———o———

THIS volume, like a charming natural picture of rare scenery, is sure in the end to introduce itself. Worth is its own revelation. Well written and felicitously arranged autobiographies possess peculiar attractions, and contain large value in that they present the real instead of the theoretical, the *terra firma* rather than the nebulous and fanciful. They are the substantial and suggestive material for real history, which has been truly styled condensed biographies, the story of human lives brought together. The mass is only what the parts and elements make it. To understand history we must comprehend men. Aside from divinity there is no higher study than that of mankind, and practical divinity includes it.

Autobiographies are life pictures and inspiring object lessons ; like snatches and real photographic catches from the actual world, such that, though local and limited, they have in them the lines and tints, the power and potency of the general and universal. Whoever sees one mountain of a region, as of New England or the United States, sees the substantial features of the mountain range. In a truly represented life that is in any measure typical, may be seen vital parts of the great philosophy and economy of Divine Providence in our world. He who traces a mountain stream from its fountain to its destiny, will become acquainted with gorge and valley, ravine and plain, river and ocean. Our splendid charts of the ocean currents have been constructed from the daybooks of sailors.

Alas ! how many devour works of fiction to the neglect of biographies, travels, natural science and histories, wherein real life and the laws of the world may be found. A little soda water may be good on occasion, but wholesome food must not be omitted if we would develop strength. Athletes are not fed on confectionary and alcoholic drinks. Even poetic imagination, one of the highest gifts of the human soul, must keep its feet on the earth. The auto-biography here given presents the life of a gifted, favored and conspicuous actor during a period of eighty years, covering events from 1806 to 1888, — a period intensely engaging in all its aspects. A great American epoch, when large questions and interests of church and state, of province and nation, and of world-wide consequence have been hotly discussed by tongue and pen and sword. Great educational, moral and political battles having been fought, and marvellous victories having been won. In respect to intellectual and religious liberty, missionary enterprises, founding states and institutions, temperance reforms, the advancement of national relations and the overthrow of slavery on our continent, it may truly be said that the epoch here spanned has been the real heroic age of our country. In these great advances the writer of this book has been a keen-eyed witness and an influential participant.

A few words should be said of the good actor who reveals himself and his associates : unusually endowed by nature ; inheriting indeed some of the best blood that trod the deck of the Mayflower ; liberally educated ; imbued with the spirit and doctrines of Roger Williams ; a spiritual Christian ; an experienced teacher ; a distinguished preacher ; an ardent patriot ; a poet in fact, as well as in spirit ; a representative of a great freedom-pledged denomination ; a man who has travelled broadly, observed wisely, studied carefully, wielding a chaste and vigorous pen. His story from his remarkable memory and his charitable heart, cannot fail to be alike pleasing and informing. He presents his apples of gold on a groundwork of silver. Perhaps his excellent wife, to whom he owes more than words may express, may have aided him in polishing the metal. His gifted son has added charms to the volume by its illustrations.

As a mirror in which to study New England life during the present century, this book will be eagerly perused, and will be more and more prized as the years roll our nation onward into the great future which will be a child of the noble past. But the reader must not be detained from the banquet.

F. DENISON.

PROVIDENCE, R. I.

AUTOBIOGRAPHY

OF

REV. JOHN ALDEN.

———o———

CHAPTER I.

CHILDHOOD AND YOUTH.

 WAS born in Ashfield, Mass., Franklin County, in 1806, and am directly descended from John Alden, who came over in the Mayflower. A genealogical sketch will be found in Part III., together with other interesting facts concerning the Alden family.

Regarding my family relatives, I will quote from a letter, written by Rev. Dr. J. Taylor, for my Golden Wedding, in 1883.

"Mr. Alden belongs to a family of twelve children, most of whom lived to a mature age and filled posts of influence. He was trained amid the hallowed influences of religion. It would be rare to find a house that disbursed a more generous hospitality. His father's house was a house of prayer, where not only the children, but all the laborers, in doors and out, were assembled around the altar of prayer. His father, and one of his brothers, like himself, were ministers of the gospel. By his father's second marriage, to the widow of Rev. Mr. Gillette of Bloomfield, Conn., he had two excellent step-sisters, Abigail and Sarah, and a worthy step-brother, Hon. Francis Gillette, once a United States Senator, from Hartford, Conn."

My father was born in Bridgewater, Mass., in 1761.

My grandfather was one of the earliest settlers in Ashfield. He went from Bridgewater, Mass., and fortunately selected one of the pleasantest and best farms in the town, embracing a rich intervale on both sides of the Bear river. He built a log house, the style of that day, in a sunny place, protected from the winds. I have often visited the spot, with peculiar feelings. The house had gone to decay. The well only remained. A good two-story house was erected a little south of the spot, where my grandparents lived and died, and where their twelve grandchildren were born. Oh, what charming thoughts ever cluster around the old homestead. My grandfather moved his wife and three children, and then on horseback, went to Bridgewater, and put my father, then eight years old, on the horse behind him, and thus they rode nearly one hundred and forty miles, to the wilderness home, well stocked with bears, wolves, catamounts and Indians. My grandparents were very decided Congregationalists. They had two miles to go, he riding on a saddle, and she on a pillion behind him. Below is a copy of an epitaph on his tombstone :

> " Tender were his feelings,
>   The Christian was his friend,
> Honest were his dealings
>   And happy was his end."

My memory reaches back to the time my grandfather died. I was then two and a half years old. I very distinctly recollect seeing him chopping wood, sitting on a log in the pile of wood.

This same year, a Rev. Jesse Hartwell, a very eloquent man, visited my father. Notice was given that he would preach in our house, and it was full. His text was, " Zacheus, come down." He repeated his text often, bringing down his chair with force to make it the more emphatic.

An aunt has since told me that I sat in my little chair, eyeing him closely and constantly. The next day, she said I kept repeating portions of the sermon, and then the text, bringing my chair down with a rush. " Your father," said she, "said, ' I should not wonder if that impression should lead that boy into the ministry if he is ever converted.'"

Before I was three years old, I went to live for a time with my sister, Mrs. Betsey Ranney, wife of William Ranney, who gave me a little whip attached to a handle. One day I came running into the house, saying, "Betsey! Betsey! I saw a snake in the yard." "You don't know what a snake is, John." "Yes, I do." "How did it look?" " It was long like this whip." "What did you do to it?" " I whipped it." " What did the snake do?" " Look here"—thrusting my tongue in and out, —"that is what he did." " Then what did you do?" " I whipped! and I whipped him very harder! and he went quilliqurm — quilliqurm." How quilliqurm came into my head I do not understand, for I do not know of such a word in the English language. Yet my sister has always said I used that word.

There was a family by the name of Fiske that lived very near. Mrs. Fiske was very fond of children. On a visit to my sister, finding me a little chatterbox, she wanted me to go home with her. Soon I came back, saying, " Isn't Mrs. Fiske a real good woman? She gave me this bread and butter with wasupper's nest on it." I think I had never seen the honey in the comb before. She said, " Come again, John; we keep honey here." Being very fond of sweet things I went often. My sister said, "You must not go so often," and locked the gate. After a little while my prattle ceased, and soon I came to the gate eating bread and butter covered with honeycomb.

"John," said she, " how did you get over the fence?" " I didn't get over the fence." " I locked you in the yard, now you are in the road; how did you get over the fence?" "I didn't get over the fence, Betsey!" " You don't understand me. You was here and now you are there. How did you get there?" " Oh! I crawled under the gate like our Skip." My brother Ranney, I called Uncle Bill. One of his barns was about one hundred rods from his house. He was threshing in it. I went up to it and said, "Uncle Bill, I want you to tell me a story." He laid down his flail and sat in the doorway and said, " I will tell a story if you will tell one." " I can't think of any," said I. " You tell one and then I will if I can think of one." He told one and then called on me. I told him to put both hands over his eyes and shut them very tight. All was silent, and when he uncovered them I was many rods from the barn in full run for the house. In telling it since, I have heard him say he was never so completely fooled by any-one, old or young, in all his life. He finally said he would not tell me another story till I told one ; driven to it, I let slide the first story I ever told. "I went out toward the north woods, and looked, but did not see anything ; went farther and looked and looked, but saw nothing. I went on to the knoll near the woods, but saw nothing, but felt as though I was going to see a great black bear."

At the age of eight I trust I was converted. Ever after I longed to be a preacher, and many a time I would go into the woods, where the water poured over a dam, take a text and preach all I could from it, looking carefully that no one heard me. During a revival in Conway, several miles from my home, I went among the anxious to be prayed for. All others were adults. They were asked to pray for them-selves. I was in agony for my soul, and wanted to say, " God be merciful to me a sinner," but could not speak. On my return home in a cold winter night, I went to the barn and prayed, till the burden of sin was removed, and I loved to pray, and I have loved to pray ever since. Though I loved prayer, loved Christians and the Bible, hated and mourned over sin, and wanted to serve God, I feared I had not sufficient evidence to profess him. Then, more than seventy years ago, no children were taken into the church on profession of their faith. I was constantly anxious to know whether I was a true Christian. My father inherited a good farm, and kept us four sons at work on it. Once when working alone and seeing a cloud about to flit under the sun, I prayed it might go over the sun if I was a true Christian. It did not, and I still doubted. At another time I took shelter in the woods from a shower under a leaning hollow tree. I prayed if I was a Christian that the rain might be hurled into the hollow of the tree. Of course it was not. I thought God could do this and assure me, and no one be harmed. I was a child and did not realize that God never gave such evidences. I had little love for those pleasures in which youth delight. I used no profane language, and was in my element whenever there was a revival. I had one of the best of praying mothers, who used to take her children alone, and talk and pray with them.

> " Oh, who can tell the power of prayer
> For us and those for whom we care !
> Whate'er may be the outward form,
> If with the heart's affection warm,
> Though but a trembling, broken sigh,
> 'Twill surely win its way on high
> And bring a mother's blessing down
> The struggles of a life to crown."

My mother died when I was young, and her happy death had much to do with my conversion. My mind at this time was much exercised in regard to my hope in Christ — and here I would say, had my pastor been faithful in looking after my soul's interests, and helped me in the examination of the true state of my religious feelings, so many years might not have elapsed, humanly speaking, ere I publicly professed my faith in the Saviour.

When I was four or five years old, I was my grandmother's pet waiter boy, and often took my meals with her. She was a very pious woman, and told me a great many pious, practical stories. All who knew her called her a person of very superior talents and memory. I loved her dearly, and as a general thing, was faithful to all her wants. She lived in an L part of our building. All the care of getting her wood and water devolved on me. One cold winter evening, as I was about getting her wood for the night, two schoolboys of my class came along with their sleds, saying, " John, it is first-rate coasting ; get your sled and come with us." I said, " I must first prepare wood for my grandmother." " We can't wait a moment, for we want to get a good safe place to slide before it is too dark." "Tell me where it is, and I will find you when I get my chores done." " We do not know exactly, and you may not find us." " Come right along," said one, " I wouldn't lose all my fun for my grandmother's sake." Fearing I might not find the place, and thinking she would not suffer, for the little time I should be gone, I went with them. Finding the sliding splendid, I staid longer than I intended. When I returned, she had suffered with the cold, which caused a serious fit of sickness. The bitter tears I shed, and the agony I felt, I can never forget.

Around my delightful home wound a charming trout brook. My grandmother obtained a rod and line, tied a pin hook to it, dug some bait, went with me to the brook, which was only a few rods from the house. She caught a trout and thus showed me how to do it. That was enough to fire me up for a long life. " When you catch five," said she, " we will have a fine fry."

As quick as it dawned, I might have been seen upon the run for the brook, and I generally caught five or more before breakfast, as they were at that time very plenty. Trouting has been my chief recreation through life. With a little help I made a dam in this brook, and had a water-wheel going, and stocked the pond with trout. On this pond was a small raft. When I was five years old, I saw for the first time a person immersed. I had a young sister three years old, now the mother of several excellent children and the good wife of Edward Miner, Esq., of Illinois. She was ever with me as a general thing, in the water or out. I said, " Sophia, don't you want to be baptized?" She answered, " Yes," not knowing its import. It was a very warm day in July. I led her into the water of suffi-

BIRTHPLACE OF JOHN ALDEN.

cient depth, and went through with the ceremony. She was very angry. It was no saving ordinance to her. I made her promise not to tell our parents, and she remembered her promise.

When I was six years old, my father employed Miss Mary Lyon as a teacher in our family. After some years, she became the noted principal of the celebrated Mt. Holyoke Female Seminary, South Hadley. She was one of the best scholars I ever knew, and by far the most thorough teacher I ever had. She had the lessons repeated over and over again, so that we should not forget them. Much of that instruction is still fresh in my memory, and I shall ever cherish her teachings with profound gratitude, both in a moral and scientific point of view.

An event in my life at the age of fourteen, fully illustrates the maxim, that our natures have a hidden reserved force, which can only be called out in great emergencies. On the Fourth of July, a little past midnight, a messenger came to our chamber, crying, "The house is on fire!" I sprang up, and an older brother with me. The room was light as day. Our carriage he some twenty feet from the dwelling house, was on fire at the opposite end from the house. The neighbors rushed to the rescue. I had piled up cord wood to the top of the house next to our dwelling, which helped in saving it. The cry was, "Clear the house; the roof is on fire!" I sprang to the desk where my father kept his money and notes, broke the lock, wrapped a towel round the drawer, hastened out a back way, crossed a brook, and hid it and covered it with leaves. On returning, I saw the fire near the top of the house, burning briskly. There was an L part in the rear with a very flat roof, coming near to the eaves of the two-story part, which had a very steep roof. I had often tried with others to run up this roof, and some feet ere we reached it, we slid back. A permanent ladder stood by the roof of the L part. I seized a small pail filled with water, went up on the flat roof, determined to ascend, as that only would save the dear old homestead, where the whole eleven of us were cradled. I reached the top, poured on the water, and thus extinguished the flames. It caught again, and I put it out in the same way. I tried after that, but could not reach the top of the two-story house. I heard my father mourning the loss of his notes and money. I took him aside, and told him I had buried his talents in the woods. "Thoughtful boy, you have greatly relieved me, and saved our home."

I began to teach in the district schools before I was seventeen years of age. The first school I taught was located on the bank of the Deerfield river, opposite to where I taught an academy some dozen years after. The scholars had been allowed to take a stone boat and wide planks and slide down *en masse* a steep hill by the school-house. The parents had tried in vain for years to have the teacher stop it. I determined to keep good order without corporeal punishment. I told the school if any scholar was hurt, I should forbid such dangerous coasting. One boy was badly hurt. I then forbid all such sliding on penalty of punishment. For a week or so, they obeyed. But when I was coming from my boarding-house, I met my whole school, nearly fifty, coming in a rapid manner on boat and planks. I went to the school-house and awaited their return. I then told them I had said all should be punished who broke the rule. I had about twenty adults in school, several of them older than myself. I gave my rule to one of the oldest scholars, and told him to punish the one next to him, calling him out upon the floor. The whole school were thus punished by each other. The punishment was, three strokes of the ruler, put on according to the estimated guilt of the parties. When it came to the little children, the blows would not injure a humming bird. It proved effectual, and stopped all this kind of sliding.

In Belchertown, some ten miles from Amherst, the scholars had turned out one or two teachers. The committeeman asked Prof. Hitchcock if he could find a student in college who could govern their schools. He recommended me. It was in my senior year, and I did not wish to teach. The man said, "Do you think you can govern our school?" I answered, "I have no fear." "Well," he said, "if you can, I will give you double wages."

I engaged. I told the scholars I came to do them good, and would meet them five nights in the week, for school work, and try to have them make up lost time. All went well the first week. Soon the ringleader of all the mis-chief stuck a pin into the arm of a scholar next to him. I saw the young man start. I asked him the cause, and he told me. I requested the offender to stop after school. He did, but showed no penitence, and would make no promise of good conduct. He did the same thing the next day, and I stopped him, with the same result. I then told him if he disturbed the school again, I should either exclude him, or punish him, probably the latter, as he was a backward scholar. There were eight young men, I think, who had been engaged in putting out the former teachers. He told them what I said to him, and tried to get their promise to aid him if I punished him. All but one said, "This teacher is trying to do us good, and we will not do it." As the other young man was large and strong like himself, he concluded to make a trial of forces.

A few days after this, as the school was seated, he came from the tailor's shop with about twenty yards of lasting wound around his knee, and sat down on the children's seat, uttering at the time a low groan. I stepped up before him and asked why he had done it? With a saucy look and tone, he said, "Because I chose to do it." I demanded a reason. "If you must know, it is on account of a hole in my pants." I ordered him to take the listing off. He was a very long time in doing it; and then putting his thumbs each side of a hole about the size of a pea, he looked up in a triumphant and saucy way, and said, "Do you see that, sir?" He was a large and fleshy young man. I brought my ruler down on the fleshy part of his limb with a telling stroke as he sat before me. He sprang up with an oath, and with his fist struck at me, but hit only the ruler. He said, " Come on, and help." His help did not come. I said, " Sit down, or I will knock you down." He sat down. I commenced a talk of some length, till he began to weep, and many of the scholars and the teacher, too.

It was now time for recess. It was a cold day, yet his associates gathered around him. I was some anxious to know for what purpose. I let them stay out till they chose to come in. I positioned myself by the side of the fire-place, with a long iron shovel behind me, and my book and rule in my lap. They all stood in a circle by the fire, and then all but the offender left for their seats. He approached me in tears and said, " I ask your pardon for my abusive conduct this winter." " Will you ask that of the school also ? " " Yes," he said. The pardon was granted with tears of joy. I found that his associates did not leave him till he promised to do as he did. I said, "Orlando, I will promise to do all I can to help you in your studies." After that I had not a better friend in my school. He circulated a paper, with success, for lengthening out the school.

BIRTHPLACE OF MRS. ALDEN, CAMBRIDGE, MASS.

CHAPTER II.

COLLEGE LIFE.

EW, I think, have met with as many casualties as I have and survived them. At the age of nine years I was riding a furious horse, to harrow out corn. The horse became unmanageable, ran for home, the harrow bounding behind him. As he came to the top of a very steep hill, the harrow parted and left the whippletree and chains. As he ran down the hill, I was thrown off, and one of my limbs was caught in the chain, and I was drawn many rods, my head striking stones till I became senseless. Fortunately, ere I came to a high pair of bars, the chain came off. The horse leaped the bars and ran into his stall.

After a few weeks, I was able to work again. When a little older, I was standing on a bridge that was undergoing repairs. The bridge was within a few feet of a deep mill pond. A peculiar gearing, by which a string piece was being swung on to the bridge, gave way. A friend said, "Jump instantly into the pond." Had I not, I should have been thrown among the rocks and instantly killed. When a young man, I was knocked down by the falling of a tree, which left me for a time in an unconscious state. At another time, the lightning passed just over my head, and shattered a tree before me, prostrating me with the shock.

When young, I had unusual physical strength. I could out-do most men in lifting, working, jumping and wrestling. In my native town, there were two military companies. After training was over, the companies for years chal-

35

lenged each other for a game of wrestling. There was a family of two brothers who were for a long time victors in wrestling. They were in the opposite company in which I had just begun to train. They were among the stoutest men since the days of Samson. It is said of one of them, he was seen to lift a barrel of cider over a cart wheel into the cart. They swung their opponents in the air, and turned them over on the back. I was early desired to wrestle with one of them, but declined, saying I did not desire to be swung between the heavens and the earth until I was found guilty. Being constantly importuned, saying, "You understand all the ways admissable, and by them you have thrown the bullies of other towns ; just try him." He swung me round three times, but was unable to turn me. As he was fixing for another onslaught, I approached him suddenly, struck my heel on the back side of his knee joint, threw my breast against him with all my might, and over he went, and over him I went, making a complete somersault. I rushed up to him, giving my hand, saying, "Shall I help you up?" "Not fair," said he. Hundreds from both companies shouted, "Fair on your back, thank God, once in your life." I said, "Fellow citizens, I have forever done with wrestling." If Mr. —— had held on to me, he might have broken my neck. I am glad so savage a practice is so nearly at an end.

When I was about nineteen years of age, I commenced fitting for college with several others. Our teacher was the Rev. B. F. Clark, pastor of the Congregationalist Church in Buckland. He was a very thorough, good teacher. My mind at that time was deeply affected on the subject of religion. Mr. Clark gave me good advice, and said, "You will never find a more convenient time than now to attend to the interests of your soul." I could not put the subject off any longer. I spent many hours in secret prayer. If ever I was converted in my childhood, I felt that now I needed a more thorough conversion. It so affected me that for some days I could not study. I went home to seek my parents' counsel and prayers. It was a delightful home. On a pleasant October evening, I walked out on the pleasant section of our farm, resolved to give my heart wholly to God ere I returned. About midnight I went to my chamber in agony of soul. I felt that I could do no more. I was hedged up by the law, had gone the length of my chain, and was driven to Christ alone for mercy. I fell on my knees and cried, " Lord, save me, or I perish!" He heard that contrite prayer. The terrible burden left me, and I felt indescribably happy. As I began to think of God's boundless love, I was lost in wonder, love and praise. I was so overwhelmed, it seemed like trying to catch the waters of the mighty Niagara in a little cup. I went back to my studies, and for months had scarce a trouble, doubt or fear. It was not unlike the feelings of my childhood, only it was far greater in degree. I then felt it my duty to profess Christ. It was my choice to join the Congregationalist Church. That church was, and ever has been, very dear to me. I wanted to join it if I could make *baptiso* mean anything but immersion. I was then familiar with the Greek, but could not find that *baptiso* ever meant to pour or to sprinkle. I read church history and found that immersion only was practised for the first three hundred years after Christ. The sixth chapter of Romans showed me definitely the object of baptism. I united finally with the Baptist Church. I finished my fitting for college at the Amherst Academy. The graduating class from the academy had parts assigned them for the annual exhibition. My part was a tragedy. The scene was laid in Greece. It was in the time of the Grecian and Turkish war, which so moved the civilized world. The tragedy ended by the combat of the Grecian and Turkish generals. The war to be settled like a case in Roman history. The nation of the slain general was to be the conquered one. I had the part of the Grecian general, and slew the Turkish general on the stage, amid the deafening applause of the auditors. The precep-

tor of the academy at this time was Elijah Paine of Ashfield, an excellent and much beloved teacher.

From there I entered Amherst College, and graduated in
1831. I have ever looked back on my four years of college
life with great pleasure. Rev. Dr. H. Humphrey was one
of the best presidents a college ever had. He was an able
preacher, ever kind, watchful and pleasant. The college
had six professors, all pious, able men. The whole faculty, most of whom were preachers, sought the good of the
soul as well as that of the intellect.

They have all gone to reap eternally the harvest, for
which they faithfully sowed. The college was blest, while
I was connected with it, with two general revivals. In one
of the revivals, for days, in nearly every hall-way, the voice
of prayer was heard at all reasonable hours, in nearly every
room. Horatio B. Hackett, probably the ablest student
the college ever graduated, afterwards a famous professor
in Brown University, also a theological professor of great
worth, was so wrought upon by the convicting influences
of the Holy Spirit, that, by the advice of the faculty, he
did not study a lesson for three weeks. He finally gave
his heart to Christ and became a very happy, devoted
Christian. A large number of the students were at that
time converted. The influence of the prayer-meetings in
our class I feel yet. My class sent out about thirty ministers from its sixty graduates. The Congregationalist
Sabbath-school sought some teachers from the college.
Being requested as one, I asked the advice of one of our
professors what class to take. He said the most charming
class he ever taught was one where their ages ranged from
three to five years. I selected such a class of little girls
from the families of some of the professors and others.
None of them could read very well, being generally about
four years of age. I selected good Bible stories, telling
them to the children without giving the names of the
parties. I gave a card to each scholar on which was
written the book and chapter where the story could be

found, so that their friends could post them, and then had them tell me all they could remember the next Sabbath.

For illustration : "Children, I am going to tell you about the little boy who *minded* every time. His parents were very good, pious people, and they wanted him to be the best boy in all Israel; so they had him live with their minister. He had gone to his little bed when he heard his name called. He minded, arose and went to the minister, and asked him what he wanted. He told him he did not call him, and told him to go back to his bed. He minded. Soon he heard his name called again. He minded, and went to the minister's room. The minister perceived that it was God who called him, and he told the boy if he heard the voice again, to say, " Speak, Lord, for thy servant heareth." He minded. I suppose he said it over and over again and then said it as the minister told him. God loved that boy, and made a godly man of him, and he is almost the only one whose name and history are given in the Bible of whom no fault is recorded."

The next Sabbath I would ask the class to give the name of that boy, the names of his parents, and that of the minister. It was a luxury to hear these little girls tell the story so perfectly ; if one left out anything, up would come a lot of little hands to correct it. They surrounded me so that I should be sure to see their raised hands. Rain or shine, if well, they would be present. I never had a more interesting class. Years after I left college, I have been invited to visit them at their homes. In my college days I often went out to preach. The first sermon I ever preached was in North Leverett, in my freshman year. It was the means, under God, of the conversion of six interesting persons, which was the beginning of a revival that brought over thirty into that church. I spent much of my time in vacations, in addressing Sabbath-schools in various towns.

President Humphrey was accustomed to give lectures to the senior class, and often enforced them with an anecdote.

In selecting a wife, he said, " Select one well versed in domestic duties, for when you come to the table from professional toil and care, a well cooked dinner will be more desirable than a tune on the piano. Never marry for *money alone ;* it may not be an objection if all other things are right. I knew a man not a hundred miles from here, who married late in life solely for money. He was a rich farmer, and his farm joined one of great value owned by a maiden lady. He tried a long time in vain to marry her. One day he visited her, and said, ' My dear Sarah, do not fear or distrust me; for I do love you most dearly, so ardently that I love the *very ground you live on.*' ' That is what I fear ! ' But in the sequel he married her. The next thing was to get rid of her. She lived high, and was corpulent. He put her on very plain fare which only made her more healthy. He persuaded her to ride horseback, promising to lead the horse. When they came beside a precipice, he struck the horse in the flank, which caused him to throw his wife down upon the rocks and break a limb, and so harm her, that it cost him some hundred dollars, and she lives to torment him yet."

The town of Amherst, Mass., is a healthy and very moral town, with a large, neat, charming village, in which the college buildings are located. The view of the mountains in the distance is truly grand and imposing, and very beautiful when the foliage is brilliant with autumn's tinted hues. Few places can be found so well fitted for a college. It has, and ever had, a very able faculty. No college in the land has been more richly blest of God, with a wholesome moral influence. Parents may truly rejoice that they can place their children where they will be so thoroughly educated and tenderly cared for ; and where there are comparatively so few temptations. In behalf of the alumni, I venture to say we are all proud of our Alma Mater.

When digging a well near Main street, in Amherst, in 1829, the workmen found a live frog, seven feet below the surface. A stone came out at the side of the hole where the frog was, leaving a very small place, not sufficiently large for him to escape, yet exposing him to view. I found the gravel too hard to enlarge the hole with my fingers, showing there could be no trickery in the exhibit. Multitudes viewed him for the space of three days, when he died from exposure to the air. He was of a medium size. How came he there? and how came others found alive in the solid rock? To me, there is only one true theory. On personal examination of the Mt. Holyoke range, I am ready to indorse the opinion of many scientific men who have investigated the little ravines and pot holes on the top of Mt. Holyoke range, a thousand feet above the Connecticut valley, that once there was a vast lake extending up into Vermont, and that there was a mighty fall between Mt. Tom and Holyoke mountain. That would have put Amherst many feet under water. As the rocky barrier gave way, in time, the water barely swept over Amherst. The waves, urged on by the winds, might have buried that frog deeper and deeper under the gravel. This theory, too, might explain what we saw when they dug the foundation for the third college building. There were different kinds of stones formed together, some of which were evidently made smooth by water power.

When in college I was blest with an excellent, pious room-mate, by the name of French. He was a very talented man, and a thorough Calvinist. I said something that made him say, "That borders on Armenianism." "Are you a Calvinist," said he? "I think so, though I have not investigated the subject much." "Do you believe in the doctrine of election?" "Surely," I replied, "I believe God has elected all that accept of salvation." That led to a protracted discussion for many a night, and was a life-long benefit to me. "Then you believe that election depends on the volition or will of the subject, do you?" "That is the way I have heard it argued, I said." "When are saints chosen?" he asked. "From the beginning hath

God chosen you to salvation" (Thes. 2 : 3). "Is God unchangeable?" "Yes. If the Lord change not, did he determine to save the sinner when or at the moment he repented, then he always did or else he changed his mind, did he not? Could God see anything good in a heart entirely destitute of holiness, whereby he should choose him?" "No," I said, but I still hung on the free moral agency of man. These verses came before me: "Thy people shall be willing in the day of thy power" (Ps. 110:2). "The gifts and callings of God are without repentance" (Rom. 11 : 27). "Elect according to the foreknowledge of God through sanctification of the spirit and belief of the truth" (1 Peter 1 : 2). I found the point he pressed was the true one, for it was the scriptural one. Man by nature hates God and holiness, is "dead in trespasses and sins." "The carnal mind is enmity toward God" his Word declares. Hence God says, "Ye have not chosen me but I have chosen you" (John 15 : 16). He took me from the horrible pit and miry clay and established my goings. The more a man struggles in the pit of miry clay the deeper he sinks. So is he spiritually, in his own strength. When all human aid fails, he will cry, "Lord, save, or I perish." Yet every man acts free, free to hate, free to love. "Christ died for all." Salvation is freely offered to all. All refuse. So to save some he hath mercy on whom he will have mercy, and leaves others to their free choice, just as much as if there was no election. It harms none, but saves some. He does not bless all alike in talent, in their bodies or positions, and yet he blesses all more than they deserve. If men will choose darkness rather than light, it is not God's fault. I am fully satisfied that what is called the Calvinistic, properly understood — or the doctrine of free grace, I rather call it,— is consistent with itself and the Bible. I think that and the perseverance of the saints, really converted or born of the Spirit, are both clearly taught in Romans 8 : 29, 30.

The following extract of a letter was written in college

days (May, 1830) by classmate Sabine (afterward Rev. Dr. Sabine), alluding to the character and death of the beloved classmate French :

" I cannot forbear making allusion to a melancholy event, which probably has been disclosed to you before this, and which, while it is extremely sorrowful to me, must be doubly so to you. French is gone. Intelligence of this gloomy fact met my eye in the *Recorder*. Nothing could have surprised me more. Yes, he has left us. The class-mate whose memory is still cherished by us in all its fresh-ness and purity ; whose life comes up familiarly before us for an example ; whose faithful attendance upon daily duties makes him still seem as one of our number ; whose voice was heard often in support of order and justice, but espe-cially in prayer ; this classmate has left his seat among us vacant ; but may we not trust he has found a seat in a better community, where the voice of supplication is exchanged forever for the songs of triumph over tribulation and death. I am inclined to hope this sad occurrence will have a salutary influence over the class. It seems to stand forth prominently as a striking memento of our frailty."

A THRILLING EVENT IN COLLEGE DAYS.

Not a mile distant from Amherst College was an artificial pond, which some twenty of us, classmates, were often happy to visit on Saturday, and have a good swimming time. It had in the middle of the pond a stone butment, the relic of a bridge ere the pond was made. Any one could wade out to it, but if he stepped off, he would go into the water some ten feet deep. We had a classmate, Garvin by name, not quite seven feet tall, who could not swim, but was in the water wading about. We told him not to go to the butment, but he said if Polliphemus could wade the Ægean Sea, he could wade any pond in Amherst. He stepped off the butment and screamed. A Mr. Case, one of the best swimmers in the class, ran from the shore and plunged into the water and caught him as he rose, but they were so clasped that they both sank together. I sprang into the water, saying, "Hold on to my left hand and form a chain to the shore." I waded and swam so as to catch one of them by the arm just as they were sinking the second time I said, "Draw us all ashore." Garvin soon began to tell his thoughts while in the water. We were all astonished at the recital, and could scarcely have believed him had we not known him to be a man of truth. He thought first of the feelings of his parents over his death, then of this and that relative and neighbor, the funeral, the text, its effect on the class and college, etc. What a tremendous engine of Omnipotence is the mind and soul of man when roused to its utmost tension !

A DUEL OVERRULED.

There was a student, a member of the Freshmen class in Amherst college, challenged a classmate to fight a duel. He answered, "It is not proper or legal in New England to fight a duel" The student said, "It is tolerated where I live, and I will shoot you in secret if you do not accept the challenge." Fearing that he might do it, he consulted two shrewd classmates. They told him to write the challenger a letter, claiming the right to choose the seconds, the weapons, the time, the place and the distance. He accepted it. Then one of the seconds went to the challenger and said, "Do you know what kind of a man you have challenged? He is called the best shooter in Massachusetts. Are you a good shooter with the rifle?" "No; I always use a shot gun." Then you stand at a fearful difference." "I cannot help it. Men where I live never back down." "Well, I will do what I can for you," The next day, the other second met him, saying, "I thank you for the honor of acting as second in this bloody affray. Do you know what a marksman you have challenged? I never knew him miss. I have seen him kill a hawk while sailing high in the air, with his rifle. You may kill him, but he will certainly kill you. We have heard your father preach. He was an excellent man. What other family friends have you?" "I have one of the best mothers on earth, and nine brothers and sisters." "Are they all professors of religion?" "Yes, all but myself." "I hope you will pre-pare to meet your God if you persist in going on with this duel." "Men of my region never back down." "I will try to help you. We have decided that the weapons shall be rifles; the place, the college gymnasium; the time, 12 o'clock at night. The rifles are at our rooms, and you are to meet us there at 10 o'clock P. M."

The seconds charged both rifles with powder and wad only. The challenged student came in first, and was found by his opponent reading a newspaper and humming a tune. The challenger walked the room with downcast looks for some time. Finally he says, "Brother, can't we settle this in some other way?" "That will depend upon the spirit that you show; you have greatly insulted me." "What, my dear brother, would satisfy you?" "That you say you are sorry that you have treated me so ungentlemanly and meanly." "Oh! I never can say that, — I never can say that!" "Then expect sure I shall take your heart's blood to-night at twelve o'clock," and turned to reading his news-paper. The challenged student at about 11 o'clock said to the second, "Bring on your rifles. Are they sure fire?" "Yes; we snapped twelve caps consecutively." "Take your choice; a rifle is a rifle with me." "Are they both charged alike?" "Yes." The challenger continued to walk the room. He said, "I think your terms are rather hard" (weeping). "I shall give you no better terms." The seconds said, "It is time to go to the grove, that we may be there in season." The challenger walked slowly and sadly, following his opponent to the place selected.

They were placed back to back, and directed to march twelve paces, keeping time with the bell, and then to turn and fire at each other. When they had marched six paces, the challenger said, "Stop, brother!" and ran up to him, saying, "If I must say it, I must. I am sorry I have treated you so ungentlemanly and meanly." "Oh, all right; it is now settled."

One Saturday afternoon, some half-dozen of us, seniors, concluded to go to School Meadows and fish for pickerel. As it was a little out of town, the college law required that we should have leave from some of the faculty. They had all left town. We concluded to risk it, and ask leave when we returned. I was carrying a large string of pickerel, as we met Prof. Solomon Peck and wife in a carriage. My classmates said, "You are the oldest one; get us excused." The professor met us with a smile, saying, "Gentlemen, you have had fine luck." I then said, "Professor Peck, the law that students should not leave town without permission, we concluded, like the higher law, was made for the lawless and disobedient, and not for such honest fellows as we are; nevertheless, to make the thing sure, we tried to find some of the faculty, who ventured to leave town without consulting us, and we concluded to follow their example as they are excellent men, and leave without consulting them. Now if you think we need any excuse, please give it."

With a smile he said, "You are all excused," while his wife was convulsed with laughter, and the professor, too.

Between Amherst and Hadley was a large meadow that in the January thaw was filled with water. When frozen over it made a fine skating rink of about half a mile in length. To this, one Saturday, as we had no studies on that day, about a score of us classmates decided to go. One of my class had a patent pair of skates like mine, which gave us both vantage ground. About half way down the meadow, was a fence frozen in with three or four rails above the ice. I boastingly said, " I challenge you all to catch me e're we get to the end of the meadow." The student with patent skates, was the only one who kept

NEWTON SEMINARY AND AMHERST COLLEGE.

near me. We both jumped the fence, and as I came near the lower end of the meadow, I saw two large brush heaps, a little ways apart, and in making an effort to skate between them, the ice broke through, and plunged me into the brush heap. My classmate, coming with lightning speed at a little different angle, broke through the ice, and came against me, driving me still farther into the rotten brush heap. I tore the iron out of one of my skates when I fell. We lay there laughing, and the rest in the rear set up a shouting; we were so full of mirth we did not rise immediately. "Are you hurt?" was the cry. "No, but we have spoiled the farmer's brush heap for him." Taking up my broken skate, I said "Good afternoon, gentlemen, so much for bragging and racing." "Where are you going?" said they. "Back to college to discipline my imagination in reviewing logarithms and conic sections."

In 1831, I entered Newton Theological Seminary. In my first year there I superintended a Baptist Sabbath-school in Watertown, Mass. At the same time teaching a Bible class, and acting as a pastor as far as I could. We students were not allowed then to preach oftener than once in three weeks. The Sabbath-school was greatly enlarged, and a revival commenced in my Bible class, and extended into the parish, which brought a goodly number into the church. In making efforts to enlarge the Sabbath-school I caught a severe cold which so settled on my lungs, that I was obliged to go home for a little season. The parish sent a man with horse and carriage to carry me home. I announced the Sabbath when I would bid the Sabbath-school adieu. By an arrangement the Sabbath-school had made, on giving the parting hand to teachers and scholars, each one dropped a piece of silver in my hand. On approaching the Bible class I had given me a purse of near twenty dollars. All the presents amounted to very near one hundred dollars. With this were presented the following lines, dated March 4, 1833, from one of the Bible class :

Farewell, Alden, thou dost leave us,
  Nevermore perhaps to meet.
Other places soon shall know the
  Other friends thy presence greet;
Heav'n protect thee all thy days.

Heav'nly breezes gently fan thee,
  Stars of glory cheer thy way.
Saviour deign to guard him safely
  To the realms of endless day.

Alden, take our hearts' best wishes,
  Take our thanks for all thy care,
That our God for this may bless thee,
  Shall be our unceasing prayer,
Oh, reward him with thy smiles forevermore.

Farewell, Alden, must we utter
  That sad word, farewell, once more?
But through grace we hope to meet thee
  On that happy peaceful shore.
Farewell, Christian, God protect thee
  Till we meet to part no more.

FROM A MEMBER OF THE BIBLE CLASS.

I returned in about three months with improved health, and was happy to resume my labors again. The last year in Newton, I was located, with two others, to supply the church in East Cambridge. Newton Theological Seminary is located in one of the pleasantest places in New England. The city of Newton that surrounds it, is a very neat, charming place. The teachers, when I was there, were Professors Chase, Ripley, Ball and Knowles. They were all excellent men and very thorough in their teaching. Of nearly twenty students in my class, two of us only are living. Rev. Mr. Massey, formerly of Bellingham, now a resident in Virginia. Father Grafton was then pastor of the Baptist Church.

Three associations in Massachusetts united their contributions and built an academy at Shelburne Falls, Mass., and named it the Franklin Academy. I was desired to take the charge of it as Principal, with the understanding I

was to preach in the chapel. I commenced in the spring
of 1833 with thirty pupils, and closed the year with one
hundred and thirty-five. I taught and preached there six
years. A Baptist church was formed, of six members, in
the fall of 1833. I then was ordained as pastor, and served
them seven years. The sermon at the ordination was
preached by Abial Fisher. We had six revivals in the
academy, reaching more or less into the village. About
two hundred of my pupils experienced religion, a large

FRANKLIN ACADEMY.

number of whom became ministers. The church was
increased to over one hundred members, and in the meantime built a nice meeting-house on the banks of the Deerfield river. I employed Otis Fisher as one of my assistants, who was a very pious man and a good preacher. I
retained him some years. He was a great help to me, as
well as many other assistants, especially Rev. Mr. Felton
and Shepardson. When there were indications of a

revival, we had extra meetings, but kept the studies up as usual, ordering the chapel door closed at 9 o'clock, P. M. In one of these revivals the power of God was displayed in a wonderful manner. Sixteen of my pupils, most of them young men of great promise, were thought to have experienced religion in one evening. They all spoke of their great peace and joy.

It was difficult that night to close on time. At half past nine I saw the hall emptied, and went home worn down with labor and anxiety. At eleven I was awaked by three of my students, who were desired to ask me to come back to the chapel. I hastened there, and found nearly a hundred, seated as far apart as they could well be, many of whom were in tears. All were silent and solemn, save here and there a sob. I said, "It is always safe to pray ; let all kneel who wish to, for a few moments of silent prayer." I think all knelt. When I arose, I said, "Will all who desire to give their hearts to God, and desire prayer, come to the forward settees?" Three sceptics, who had opposed the revival, came first, followed by many others. I said to the first, "Are you here, Mr. G ——— , as a sincere seeker after God?" "I am," he said, weeping so loud, he might have been heard at quite a distance. The others were in tears. These sceptics each found themselves truly happy servants of God that night, and a number of others. Two of them became eminent ministers of Christ. One of them became pastor of the Baptist Church in Providence, and continued his pastorate for over twenty years. The third became an eminent lawyer in Worcester, Mass., and mayor of the city. This mayor said to me some twenty years after this, "I can never forget that night in the Franklin Academy. It was the making of me, and shaped my destiny for time and eternity. We had over two thousand attendances during the six years, mostly adults. Twelve states were thus represented, and some foreign countries. Its members have filled important positions in church and state and as missionaries abroad.

An extract of a letter from Rev. William Crowell, one of the earliest pupils of Franklin Academy, written while a member of Brown University, afterward an efficient editor of the *Christian Watchman* for several years:

REV. AND DEAR BROTHER:

I am happy that an opportunity occurs of fulfilling the promise which I made to you at parting.

The remembrance of the happy hours which glided away so agreeably at my beloved Shelburne Falls, while under your instruction, be assured, dear sir, is still fresh and lively. My thoughts often revert to that sweet romantic spot with an interest which seems to unite the past with the present. I often place myself in one of those environs which command such a beautiful view of the academy and village, mountains on either side rising in silent majesty, while the lovely Deerfield, the emblem of health and cheerfulness, pours its clear waters along their base. I hear the well-known sound of the bell calling to early devotion. Then I descend and proceeding up the familiar walk I arrive at the Mansion House, where everything bespeaks order, neatness and industry, while temperance and exercise unite to render health, activity and cheerfulness the characteristics of its inmates.

More is the joy to me of every recollection, associated as it is with the glorious intelligence that the Father of Mercy has been pleased once more to make such rich displays of his grace in calling souls from the ruins of sin, to taste his pardoning love. I trust my cold heart did rejoice, but how great must have been your joy! If we rejoice, let it be that success has been given to the cause of truth, and that God is thereby glorified. It is a glorious thought that mortal men are permitted to be workers with God, to assist in carrying out his grand designs. I rejoice in your prosperity, and hope you may receive a more than corresponding increase of faith and personal holiness.

I shall ever thank God for giving me this field of labor, where I saw so many rich displays of his love and power. The first year of my residence at Shelburne Falls, I was married to Ann Maria Chamberlain, of Cambridgeport,

Mass.   While there I had two children, Augustus Ephraim
Alden and Francis Howard Alden.   My wife was a great
help to me, both in teaching and painting in the academy,
and as a laborer in the church and Sabbath-school.   I have

BAPTIST CHURCH, SHELBURNE FALLS.

wondered in looking back upon the six years of double
labor that it did not ruin my health. Either was enough
for any one man. The frequent revivals, though they
greatly added to my labors, both comforted and strengthened me. We had a weekly meeting of all the pious stu-

dents, very much like the Methodist class-meeting, in which each one was asked to express his or her religious state of feeling. The greatest number of professors of religion at any one time was one hundred and twelve. I often think of those precious seasons with delight. The religious element aided me very much in the discipline of the academy. I had more trouble with a printed law of the school, viz. : " The sexes are required to walk by themselves," than from any other source. Two of my best students had violated the law. I had been told they had said they would not submit to it. I called on them, and after a pleasant interview, I said, "Young gentlemen, are you members of a temperance society?" "Yes," they answered. "When you signed the constitution, you felt bound to keep the pledge, did you not?" "Certainly." "You could not blame the society for disciplining you if you broke the pledge, could you?" "No." "How does this apply to institutions of learning, where the students have signed the constitution?" They both burst out laughing, saying, "You have truly caught us. We will not do it again." As my students were nearly all adults, and the sexes about equal in number, I had but little trouble in the discipline.

Our mode of instruction was on the inductive plan. When teaching my class in intellectual philosophy, we came to the subject of ghosts. I had about forty in that class. I asked all to raise the hand who believed in ghosts. A few only raised the hand. I said, "Please give us your proof." They told some exciting stories that looked rather unanswerable. I often satirized an error when I could. I said, "I will tell a ghost story, and thereby give you my opinion. It was said a room in a certain hotel was haunted. It was supposed a peddler was robbed and murdered in that room. If any one lodged there, in the dead of night a man would enter the room with his throat cut and approach the bed, and the occupant would leave in a fright. A clergyman called and wished to spend the night in said hotel. The

landlord told him he had no room but the haunted one.
The clergyman said, 'I do not believe in ghosts, I will
sleep there. Give me a Bible and hymn-book.' He read
and sang till the guests retired, determined to keep awake.
So he laid down undressed in bed, Bible in hand. Soon he
heard stealthy steps up the chamber stairs. The door
opened and a man approached the bed with his throat cut.
'What do you want?' said the minister. 'I am glad you
inquire,' said the spectre, 'all others that I approach flee
from me. I was murdered by this landlord, in this room,
and robbed of a thousand dollars. Follow me and I will
show you where he buried me. This may help convict him.'
He arose and followed the ghost into a smooth plain back
of the hotel, and pointing down, the ghost said, 'There lie
my bones.' He felt around for something to put there
that he might find the place in the morning. He found a
short stub. He put his hand in his pocket for his knife,
but he had left it on the stand where he had snuffed the
candle. Soon he began to gnaw the stub, and as he had a
sore tooth, he awoke gnawing the headboard."

About one hundred of my pupils boarded in Commons.
Deacon Benjamine Maxwell was our good steward and
manager of the farm connected with the Academy. He
was a man of good judgment and talents, ardently pious;
truly a generous, reliable man. He was a great aid to me
in all my labors in the Academy and the church. He was
the first deacon at the formation of the church. His wife
Clarrissa, was a devoted Christian, an excellent manager,
a lovely peacemaker, and filled well the place of that
excellent Mrs. Crouch, the first stewardess of the
Commons.

The church at its formation was very few in number.
Deacon B. Maxwell and wife, and three families by the
name of Apollos, Jarvis and Ralph Bardwell and their
wives were the early pillars, a charming nucleus, around
which the church grew wonderfully, as they were persons
of sterling character, universally beloved and respected.

The church now is, I suppose, the largest and strongest in the Franklin Association.

Two pupils, nephews of mine, are lawyers. Of one, Luke Ranney by name, I glean from a printed history of .his life-work, a few facts I am happy to record. He fitted in part with me for college, when I had a good opportunity to learn his superior talents. For a time he was a very successful teacher in a public school in Troopsville and Port Byron, in New York. He taught also in Christian County, Kentucky. He there saw the evils of slavery and labored ardently for its overthrow. I quote a few words from one of his lectures. " When I see the vast amount of evil that emanates from slavery, I shudder at the future consequences. The day of future doom may be distant, but it is sure to come. I may not live to see it, but the fatal seed is sown, and when the harvest comes, it will be one of death and desolation."

He did much in his public lectures on temperance. He removed to Elbridge, N. Y., in 1832. He was soon chosen supervisor of the town, and was chosen for a considerable time to represent in the legislature the first district of Onondago County. The bill creating the State Assessors, was written by him, and his influence contributed largely to its passage. His speech on the personal liberty bill, gave him a State reputation as one of the best debaters in the Assembly."

Mr. Ranney proved to a demonstration that an important corporation paid $265,000 to buy votes. I quote a portion of his scathing speech, not too severe for the crime. " What shall I say to those, if such there are, who have received the money of this corporation as a reward of their betrayal of their constituency, for surrendering up their rights for personal gain."

" Remember Judas Iscariot betrayed his Lord and Master for thirty pieces of silver ; and for that act has been held up for desecration, scorn and contempt, wherever the banner of the cross has been unfurled, even to the utmost

bounds of Christian civilization.   Turn your minds, gentlemen, within, and behold yourselves as in a glass, and see a
villain whose company you are obliged to keep, and from
whose vile companionship there is no escape.   Dishonored,
scorned and condemned by yourself, seeking through life a
hiding-place from the goadings of conscience, dying while
you are living, praying for the rocks and mountains to fall
on you and hide you from the righteous indignation of a
constituency you have betrayed, from a legislature you
have demoralized, from a State you have dishonored, and a
Republic you have disgraced."   He has freely given his
services in every important campaign since 1855.

A just tribute is due to the other nephew alluded to,
Hon. George Alden.   He was once a member of the
Franklin Academy.   He was an excellent scholar, and was
educated in Colby College, studied law and commenced
practice in Buffalo, N. Y.   He speedily rose to eminence
in his profession.   Here he married in 1855, Susan A.
Boss, daughter of Philip Boss, portrait painter, of Rochester, N. Y.   In 1857, they removed to Henry County,
Illinois, where he lived until the breaking out of the war.

In August, 1862, he helped to raise a company which
with seven other companies from that county and two
from Stark County, formed the 112th Illinois Volunteer
Infantry.   He was elected quarter-master of the regiment,
and served through the war.   In May, 1864, he, with
others, was taken prisoner in northern Georgia, by a band of
Wheeler's Cavalry, and taken to Macon, and as Sherman's
army advanced to the sea they were removed to Augusta,
Savannah, Charleston, Columbia, and so on North, until in
March, 1865, they reached Wilmington, Del., where they
were exchanged, and after a short furlough rejoined their
regiment and remained to the close of the war.

While in prison he was forced to lie for weeks on the wet
ground, where he came near perishing.   When in Charleston, as the shells came singing into the city, he and his
companions sang " Yankee Doodle " and other Union

songs. To prevent their influence on others, they were removed to the belfry of an exposed church; but this could not eradicate the spirit of patriotism which animated them, and as the shells flamed by, tearing the city to pieces, they would thrust out their heads and shout, "Hail Columbia" and "Yankee Doodle" for a chorus. As they did the Southern cause more harm in the belfry, they were returned to their former quarters.

In 1868, while residing in Galesburg, he received an appointment as special agent of the Treasury Department, and remained in the Government service nearly eight years. At the close of this important work, he resumed his law practice in Galesburg, where he was appointed judge, and was considered one of the very ablest advocates in the West. In 1884 he removed with his family to Fort Collins, Col., where he is at present engaged in ranching.

Another nephew, Henry M. Puffer, is a practising lawyer in Shelburne Falls, and a reporter for the County paper. He is doing a good business there. Of his talents and wit, let his speech at my golden wedding in 1883, bespeak it.

He, with his two brothers, Samuel and Charles, were graduated in Rochester University together, and the last two are active business men in the West. They were all sons of Dr. Puffer of Shelburne Falls.

My brother Willard removed when he commenced business in early life, to Cassadaga, N. Y., and there became an industrious and wealthy farmer. He was a good and kind husband and father.

Of my seven sisters all but one were pious and blest with excellent husbands and children. I have ever felt to bless God for such talented and lovely family relations. All my brothers and five sisters have left us. I have only two sisters left. Mrs. Dr. Puffer of Shelburne Falls, and Mrs. E. G. Miner of Illinois. They are pious, excellent women, whom I have ever loved dearly.

CHAPTER III.

TEACHING.

WHEN teaching the Shelburne Falls Academy, I was often called to give a course of chemical lectures in the adjacent towns. I had a good chemical apparatus, and I enjoyed the using of it. One lecture was on Caloric. By searching the chemistrys of Europe and America, I found out twenty-three ways of producing visible flame, without raising the temperature above summer heat, or seventy degrees Fahrenheit. For those who want to see a few mysterious exhibits, I give a few of them.

I. Put a little piece of phosphorous in a mortar with oscimuriat of potash, strike it with a pestle, and a loud report is heard.

II. Put a little phosphorous in the centre of a tumbler of water, pour strong sulphuric acid or nitric acid on the phosphorous, through a glass tube, and the phosphorous will burn splendidly in the water.

III. Put equal parts of gun powder and fine white sugar together, draw a thread dipped in strong sulphuric acid over it, and it bursts into a flame.

IV. Drop a piece of phosphide of calcium into a tumbler of water, the size of a pea, and more than a hundred flashes of flame, with a slight report, will be seen and heard on the surface of the water.

V. Put a little potassium on gun powder and touch it with an icicle, or a drop of water, and it bursts into a flame.

VI. Drop copper filings or bismuth into clorine gas and it takes fire.

VII. Drop hot turpentine into clorine gas and it takes fire.

The other experiments are more complicated and I will not give them here.

The question in the Lyceum connected with the Academy had been discussed: "Are the talents of the sexes equal?" Some of the members of my chemistry class asked my opinion. I said, "As there are twenty ladies and twenty gentlemen in this class, you may decide it, by seeing which will search out the most resemblances between the animal and vegetable kingdoms. You may report to me weekly." They entered upon it with much interest. Some weeks the ladies reported the most, some weeks the gentlemen. At the close of the term, they reported two hundred and seventy resemblances. What pleased and amused us all was, the parties came out just equal. They would not have found so many had they not worked so hard, philosophically and chemically.

In my natural philosophy class of some thirty adults, while dwelling on the wonderful power of hydrostatic pressure, I said I did not believe that two boards, twelve feet long, a foot wide, and an inch thick, could be placed standing upright, one inch apart, by any side appliances of wood so as to be filled with water. "How many think it can be done?" I had several young mechanics in the class ready to try it. I told them I would furnish all the materials, and if I failed I would pay them for their work, and if they failed they would only lose their labor. It was soon ready; a box twelve feet long, one foot wide, and one inch in diameter. I had the trial at noon, when all could see it. The box was placed in front of the Academy, to be filled from a second-story window. Before it was half-filled it began to form an oval shape, and ere it was filled the pressure pulled the boards apart in the middle.

A question was asked me: "How does water, one thou-

sand and thirty-three one-hundredths times heavier than
air, seventy degrees Fahrenheit, rise above the air?" I had
told my classes they might ask any questions, and if I
could answer them I would; if not, I would put them off for
a time. I told the class I could not then give the reason,
but no doubt there was a good one, and I would consider it.
I searched all the books I could get, asked many educated
men, but could get no aid. I was accustomed to give a
course of free lectures on chemistry, with experiments, each
fall term. When using the compound blow-pipe, which
will either melt or fuse all substances under its blaze, I put
some broken watch-springs under the blow-pipe. A little
globe of melted steel was seen at a white heat. I shook
this off, and put it under the chemical sink; and when my
audience left, took up the little ball full of small perfor-
ations where the heat went out, and found it a shell that
crumbled at the least pressure. Like Archimedes I
exclaimed, " *Eureka! Eureka!!* I have found it out." I
sent a heat second only to lightning into the melted steel,
and as heat is much lighter than air, of course it went
to the centre, where gravity is comparatively nothing.
So water composed of small round particles, which long
ago had been proved, receives the heat at the centre of
each particle and is thus made like a balloon, and ascends.
In a very warm day you can see the moisture ascend by a
glimmering in the air. This solves many a mystery in
nature; why an article will freeze nearly dry. The cold
forces the warm air into the centre of the particles of
water and carries them off. This explains why a very cold
day and a very warm one causes rain or snow. The heat
thus driven into the particles of fluid causes them to
ascend. Since then I have put this question to scores of
literary men, and have never found but one who gave an
immediate answer, and that was Dr. Baron Stowe of Boston:
" It is on the balloon principle, the heat entering the centre of the particles of water, carrying them up."

The only student of mine from abroad in the Franklin

Academy, who died at Shelburne Falls, was Richard Batten. He was a young Englishman of superior talent, a most excellent scholar and singer and a devoted Christian. He was intending to be a foreign missionary. He died at the Mansion House, then my home, with the rheumatic fever. Though a great sufferer, he would sing spiritual hymns, and seemed to triumph for a time over his sufferings. I can never forget his melodious strains as he sang :

> " Jerusalem, my happy home,
> Oh, how I long for thee!
> When will my sorrows have an end
> In joy, and peace, and thee ? "

The last words he uttered were, " Come, Lord Jesus, come quickly ! " This he uttered, looking up with a smile. The room was filled with his classmates and others. Several were converted by his happy death. It was the beginning of an extensive revival among the students. Shelburne Falls is one of the most romantic, neat, and charming villages in Massachusetts. The Deerfield river has here a fall of forty-five feet. When the river is low it has very attractive places. Large pot holes and channels, worn smooth in the granite rock, are a marvel. The mountains on both sides of the Deerfield river, over four hundred feet high, covered with variegated foliage, supported with here and there a frowning ledge, especially in time of autumnal scenery, beggars all description. The streets are regular and finely shaded. The Franklin Academy, the Arms Seminary, and four neat churches, are located here. The population, on both sides of the river, is about three thousand. When the Academy was built, in 1833, there were only eight houses in the village. It is soul-inspiring to hear the ceaseless thunderings of these falls, which are the deep-toned bass of the Creator.

Among the green hills of Shelburne, in a beautiful retired home, lived, some years ago, a much beloved father in Israel, Dea. David Long. He lived many years in the

service of the Saviour, and honored him in all the walks
of life.   The Sabbaths of the Lord were very dear to him.
Though several miles from Shelburne Falls, when able he
was at church, until he was nearly a hundred years old.   I
loved dearly to visit him and his son's family.   There
seemed a kind of holy inspiration surrounding the dwelling.
He was my very dear parishioner once.   A more amiable,
lovely man I never met.   A little time before his death he
said to Mrs. Alden, who visited him, "Now that I am dull
of hearing, and cannot distinctly hear the voices of those I
love, or listen to the sweet strains of sacred music that
once charmed and delighted me, and, above all, that my
sight is gone, and I cannot read or see my dear friends, but
sit in darkness, language cannot express how the comforting words of Jesus, that I committed to memory when
young, cheer and delight me.   Tell all Sabbath-school
children to commit to memory the Bible.   Now that I cannot see to read the Word of God, it is a great comfort to
repeat from memory so much of the precious Bible."   May
all the Bible and Sabbath-school classes treasure up this
important message from one whose pilgrimage then numbered ninety-nine years and six months.

"At the centennial celebration of Shelburne," says a
local paper, "the Rev. John Alden, former pastor of the
Baptist church in this village, and for several years principal of Franklin academy, responded as follows for the academy.   By some mistake the toast was not sent him, and
he had to imagine what it was."

All hail the joyous band, who come to greet
Each other on the track of life, and meet
From East and West, from North and South, to view
The cycles of a century.   All new
By reminiscences.   'Tis mine to speak
On one good theme ; let others nobly seek
To rouse a universe of thoughts, and give
The praise of those who died, and those who live
'Tis Academias Toast, to me unknown,
To which I must respond.   Thus am I thrown

Upon the waves of doubt, how best to meet
The sentiment proposed, and rightly treat
Its author. Will it show heroic toil
And sacrifice to place upon this soil,
Swept by the Deerfield, canopied by hills,
Watered around by thousand gushing rills,
A school to bless a needy world and raise
The low degraded heart to wisdom's ways?
This Institution rose through faith and prayer,
And scores of souls found life eternal there.
Or, will the Toast praise every one who taught?
Let him who led the van hear nothing aught
Of praise or blame. Truly enough, that he
Should carry on his heart the Franklin Academy.
Full many a teacher there deserves the praise
He richly earned in bygone halcyon days,
Or will it speak the honors of this town,
Foremost in morals, best of all renown;
Or, will it treat of noble pupils taught?
Then be it so. Yet some had scarcely aught
Of manhood in them; for to break the rules
And trample on the rights of all the schools.
Teach others to, seemed chiefly their delight;
Dream o'er their task by day, and visit girls by night.
Few such there were. A nobler band ne'er trod
The earth than most; true to their Maker God,
And true to man. Some grace the desk and bar
And hear the voice of praise both near and far;
Have gathered laurels on the field of fame,
And won for them a lasting, glorious name.
Some went to meet the Oriental Sun
And save the lost. Their work was bravely done.
Brighter than stars, in glory now they shine,
Who turned some souls from Moloch's direful shrine.
The Burmah convert and the Persian, too,
Saved by these youth, have now a heaven in view.
The light they struck, where darkness spreads its gloom
Will not go out till earth shall find a tomb.
Some sought the sunny South, to raise a race
From bonds and fetters—death and danger face;
Their work is done. Our country now is free.
Shout, nations, shout o'er this our jubilee.
Some went to California's golden plains,
To form a rising race to hold the reins
Of Knowledge, Truth, and Justice, too,—their names,
High on the roll of Honor, now are Fame's.
Some sought the prairie gardens of the West,
To preach, to teach, and make their country blest.

Thousands unborn will sing a grateful song,
And heaven and earth the melody prolong.
From half our favored states some here were trained
For earth and heaven. Some joyously have gained
Their high and heavenly home, and now look down
On this, their birthplace, from that holier ground.
Others who live on earth can ne'er forget
What joy was theirs when here in classes met.
Where e'er I go I find some happy son
To me most dear, a choice and favorite one
Who never can forget the days of yore,
When here he pored the works of science o'er.
Come, all ye living of that happy band,
Around this desk, and give the friendly hand.
Hail, Alma Mater of a favored race,
You are living still, to bless the world—the place.
Let not the parent die who reared such sons,
But ever live among fraternal ones.
As the pure streams from off our mountains flow
To fertilize and bless the plains below,
And swell the streams to aid the works of art,
And joy and gladness stir in every heart,
So this, our school, sent forth our happy youth
To fill our colleges and search for truth.
God bless our schools of high or low degree,
The glory of our land, which they keep free.
Baptize them all in heaven-directing Truth,
To be a safe resort for all our precious youth.

In the town of Coleraine, Mass., about five miles from Shelburne Falls, there were three good churches, Congregational, Baptist and Methodist. Rev. Jesse Purrington, a very able and devoted man, was the pastor of the Baptist church. He was a great help to us in the revival at Shelburne Falls, and one of the directors in our academy. Rev. Mr. Flagg, my teacher in the Sanderson Academy at Ashfield when young, was the pastor in the Congregational church, a very able and devoted man. There was a union prayer-meeting held in an outer district (I do not recollect the Methodist pastor), and a revival commenced there. The three denominations agreed to hold a union protracted meeting in the Baptist church, and requested me to do the preaching, limiting me to thirty minutes, which is long enough, I think, for any common sermon. I could only preach during my fall vacation. The meetings had been held some little time before I could go. When I saw on my approach that heavenly spirit in the prayer-meeting, and the house filled with solemn worshippers, I felt unfit to preach, and wished to be excused. This could not be. I went through the form without the power. My heart was anywhere but where it should be. I had been buried up in the classics, and worn down with care and labor. The spirit had almost left me. I had not watched and prayed as I should. I entered my carriage to go home and preach a thanksgiving sermon to my people, and return in the evening. I prayed and wept and agonized in spirit for a broken and contrite heart all my way home. I then went into my study, determined not to leave till I felt the full power of the Saviour's precious love. It came in its fulness. I had, the next day, a precious time preaching from the text, "He careth for thee." One of my great troubles has been to govern my imagination, which has built airy castles enough to overstock the universe. I longed to get back to Coleraine. I concluded to walk up half way, and ride with Brother Smith to Coleraine. Ere I came to his house, an elder son, a very influential man in the town, met me in tears of joy, saying, "I am the happiest man living. The subject last night was blest to me. I felt that I was lost, and continued to pray, 'Lord, save me or I perish!' till about midnight, when I found peace in believing. Oh, the precious love of Christ! why had I not sought it in faith before?" The love of Christ was all his theme on his way to the meeting. Whenever desired to aid in revival work, I made it a subject of special prayer, and did not consent until I gained an evidence that the Lord had a work for me to do, and then I tried to bring all my energy into action for its accomplishment. I usually spent most of the time out of meeting hours in visiting, conversing and praying from house to house. I requested that all the conversation should be religious, so far as it could be consistent with daily duties. I desired all to remind me if I violated the scripture injunction, "Let your conversation be as becometh the gospel of Christ." Like a good general, God generally works through the soldiers of his choice. He does this greatly through fervent prayer. We fully believe the prayer of faith is always heard. Nothing human can withstand it. The power of God was truly manifested from day to day. Two sermons were preached, one in the forenoon and one in the evening, preceded and followed by prayer-meetings. Every day witnessed several conversions. In the midst of the meetings we had two very rainy days and nights. Capt. Pierce, a man of great influence in the town, lived near the church. At the close of the forenoon meeting, he put his arm around me without saying a word, and started for his home. On the way he said, "You must not visit families till this severe storm is over." I had noticed him in tears during sermon time on exchanges there, and supposed him to be a Christian. I asked him if he thought himself a Christian. "I fear," said he, "I am not; but I have such a weakness when the love of Christ is preached that it often causes me to weep. It reminds me of a time, when twelve years of age, I used to go with several of my schoolmates during the intermission, and pray and sing." The house was filled in the forenoon service; and on our way with umbrella and lantern, I said, "What do you think, Captain, of an assembly in this rain?" "That house will be filled," he said. "According to thy faith be it unto thee!" I exclaimed. True enough, the house was full of hearers and the Holy Spirit. I then went with him to his house for the night. It rained most of the next day and evening. On our way to the evening meeting, I said, "Can it be that the house will be filled to-night?" The frost had come out of the ground, and the roads were fearful from mud and gullies. The captain raised the umbrella he held over me, and said, "That house will be filled. See the lanterns shining in all the roads to the church." It was indeed truly filled. Rev. Edward Davenport and Dr.

C. Puffer were exceedingly useful in this work. The Baptist church in those days had a large number of wealthy farmers.

There were two men of strong minds and wills at variance. The church strove in vain to settle the difficulty. Each had their relatives and strong friends. A little before this meeting a committee of one party called on me for advice. Knowing the men, who were dear friends of mine, I said, "*Pray.* I do not think men or angels can settle it. God only can do it." The same day a committee oft he other party called on me and I told them just as I did the other. Early in the meeting, the children of these men, who were talented and very interesting youth, asked their parents to pray for them. This brought both of them back to their Saviour, broken-hearted, penitent and humble. Now they could work together in faith and love. They lived near each other. Each started to confess, and they met in front of a little factory, in tears, sitting in their carriages, clasping each other by the hand, each one saying, " I am the one to blame; will you forgive me ? " The factory hands rushed into the street, many of them in tears, over the unexpected scene. That event carried the work in power into the factory. The other pastors asked Rev. Mr. Purrington to meet them and their deacons with his own, at a certain time and place. He said to me he hoped nothing would occur to break the charm of the heavenly union. " Fear not," I said ; " I do not think God will allow it." The announcement of their object only made us the happier. It was that we should try to pray in faith for the conversion of the whole town.

It was thought that over one hundred were savingly renewed. Every part of the town was blest more or less, and all the churches greatly enlarged. I heard of no difficulty in regard to the reception of the converts. I advised them all to take the Bible and decide the path of duty for themselves. By so doing they avoided all difficulties. Capt. Pierce and wife were both baptized by Rev. Mr. Purrington. They were nearly seventy years of age when they followed their Saviour in the ordinance of Baptism. I asked the pastor how Capt. Pierce was getting along? "Very happily," said he. "In the last two weeks he has grown more than his length. "That must be about seven feet, if I judge rightly," said I.

About this time I declined several calls where I was offered more salary than I was receiving, because I so loved this young church, which had been so sacrificing for Jesus. For a description of Shelburne, and Shelburne Falls, a part of it, I here quote from a dedication sermon preached in the Baptist church in 1836. Text, "I give thanks unto the Lord, for he is good." Finally, God's goodness is illustrated in the history of the town. Eighty-six years ago this town was unsettled. One vast wilderness covered these mountains, vales and glens, the covert of wild beasts, and the lonely retreat of the savage. No workman's tools broke the silence of the morning. All was much as the morning of creation left it. No happy feeling of civilized friendship ; no sound of the "church-going bell ;" no devout praise to God was here. Yet there was a praise less contaminate than the modern praises of men. It was not the horrid orgies of the savage; it was not the blood of victims offered to the Great Spirit; it was not the war-whoop, or the council fires. It was the praise of nature in her primeval grandeur ; it was the shriek of the eagle, unscared on his lofty crag ; it was the scream of the catamount echoing in the lonely wilderness ; the nightly howlings of the wolf and growlings of the bear ; it was the roaring of the winds around these "cloud-capt " mountains ; it was the vivid lightning athwart the heavens, and the deafening thunder peals ; it was the roaring of the Falls, nature's never-ceasing, solemn anthem. This beautiful region can no longer remain a wilderness. The savage can no longer prowl the forests ; the deadly beasts can no longer lie safe in their lairs, for the white man comes to inhabit these charming highlands. I find that the records of this town of Shelburne go no farther back than 1768, when it was incorporated. It was then called Deerfield, North West. The town took its present name from Lord Shelburne, of England, who gave the town a church bell.

This town, unlike many around it, had very little trouble from the aborigines. To the praise of our Puritan fathers, it was their first object to worship God. Messrs. Wyeth and Hotchkiss were their first preachers. The poverty of those times forbade expensive churches. They were content for many years to worship in a round log meeting-house, plastered so as to make it warm. They did nobly to foster education. The Congregational church was organized in 1770. The first pastor was Rev. Robert Hubbard, ordained October 20, 1773. He continued his labors till 1792. He was followed by Rev. Jesse Townsend. Rev. Theophilus Packard, D. D., was ordained February 20, 1797, and continued his labors as sole pastor till 1828, when his son, Theophilus, was chosen colleague. This church has had many revivals, and has done much good. In 1801, a revival added forty. In 1819, forty-six were added. In 1831 eighty were added. The present number is one hundred. In 1788, a Baptist church was formed. Rev. Mr. Green was the first pastor. In 1792, Rev. David Long became pastor, continuing forty years. In 1808, a revival added seventy-five. In 1831, thirty were added. This church was merged into the Baptist church in Shelburne Falls.

The Unitarian church was formed in 1828, of thirty members. Many more have since been added. The Franklin Academy was chartered in 1833. Both buildings were erected the same year. The Baptist church at Shelburne Falls was formed in 1834. When the water is low, the Falls is a very romantic place. The pot-holes of various sizes are a marvel. It is supposed that the river once ran on the Beechland side, from pot-holes high on the rocks. If so, there must have been a barrier below the Scots' bridge, which in time gave way, and thus changed the course of the Deerfield river. Logs have been found by well-diggers eighteen feet below the surface, in what is now the centre of the village. Stones also have been dug out below the surface, which show they have been smoothed by the power of water.

I accepted the call of the North Adams church, and settled with them April 1, 1840. The church at that time was sadly divided over the settlement of a former pastor. It was over six months before we could fully settle the difficulty. After the vote of settlement, which was harmonious, I asked for another vote, which was, never to speak of the difficulty again, and it was very faithfully kept. The church was strictly Calvinistic, some of them like the Indian's tree, straight and more too. The first year, by taking every street, and dividing them among the teachers, requesting each teacher to urge every child not belonging to a Sabbath-school to come to ours, we more than doubled the number of our school. I kept the names of the new scholars, and found in a revival, about three years after, over thirty were of the class just brought in. It was the custom in those days to have protracted meetings. My church was willing I should aid in such meetings when desired. During my pastorate in North Adams, I held such meetings in about half the churches in the Berkshire Association, and witnessed hundreds of conversions. I will give a description of two of these meetings, in the towns of Sandisfield and Tyringham. In the town of Sandisfield, Mass., there was a very good, harmonious Baptist church. They had an able, faithful pastor, Rev. John Higby. The parish had erected a fine church and parsonage. All was prosperous externally and they felt that a revival was the only thing needed, so they voted to hold a series of meetings, and sent for me to do the preaching. The first sermon was preached in the evening, and was blest to the conversion of a young man of great promise. He asked for prayers. The brethren prayed for him, until he found himself happy in a Saviour's love. The preaching was to be in the forenoon and at seven o'clock in the evening, preceded by a prayer-meeting. The meetings continued with a full house for one week, without another conversion. I felt greatly discouraged, fearing I was the cause, and went to my room, and continued in prayer, until the melting influences of the Holy Spirit filled my heart, and brought me humbly to seek for more love and faith. I started for the church with a strong travail of heart for the salvation of souls, but I could not fix my mind on a text. I tried to have some one of the ministers present preach. They were in the same dilemma. The house was filled, and I arose and told the assembly I could not select out of the scores of texts one for the occasion, and added, " Perhaps, brethren, God has some other work for us to do," and sat down. Deacon Jones, a very godly man, of consistent life, arose in tears, saying, " If we are in such a stupid condition, God's ministers cannot preach to us, I think we must repent, and do our first works." He began to confess, the last man who needed to do this. The confessions continued till after one o'clock in all parts of the house. Such a scene I scarcely ever witnessed. I said, " Brethren, I have a text now, and I long for evening to come to preach from it." From that hour the work went on gloriously, and it brought a large number of good Christians into the church. We had a sunrise prayer-meeting. It was in the choice days of autumn. Committees were appointed to visit through the town. I went, out of the meeting hours, from house to house, to converse and pray with the people. This was my usual way of working. More than a mile from the church, I found an old soldier of the Revolutionary war, walking with his crutches. I said, "Are you a soldier for Jesus?" "I fear not," he said. "Come up to the morning prayer-meeting at the church, and we will pray that you may be." He was very aged and infirm. "I don't go so far from home very often, but I will try to get there." He was there every morning for nearly two weeks. I asked him one morning to tell us his feelings. He arose and said, "When I was a boy, I went to an Indian prayer-meeting of the Stockbridge tribe, and heard an Indian woman speak very loud and feelingly, ' I love my Jesus.' Then she would speak in the Indian language, and ever and anon would exclaim, ' I love my Jesus,' in the English language." While relating this, the tears rolled down his venerable cheeks and he said, "*I* can now say, '*I love* my Jesus.' "

CHAPTER IV.

PREACHING.

THE Baptist church at Tyringham was divided by a lawsuit between prominent members. The pastor, a godly man, sought my aid. As I looked over the wide field I thought with Ezekiel, "Can these dry bones live?" I preached a week directly to Christians; that last ominous cloud passed away, and the Son of Righteousness, with his healing beams, melted cold hearts and fused them into one harmonious body. The day of confession and prayer will never be forgotten by many. Nothing like the love of Christ will harmonize the jarring elements of human hearts. There had been two dancing schools in the village and they had become divided among themselves. They voted one night to go to our meeting in a body. They came early, while we were holding a prayer-meeting, walking up the broad aisle, each seating his partner in the opposite pew, very gracefully, yet with here and there a sarcastic smile. The church were astonished at the unexpected sight.

I changed my text for the evening service, God having given me one for the occasion. We had a season of prayer, such as is seldom enjoyed. God was in that meeting of a truth. During the preaching all seemed serious and some were in tears. A young merchant, belonging to one of the best families in the place, a member of the dancing school, waited upon his betrothed to her home, and ere they parted, said, "Rhoda, had we not better be pious?" She looked upon him with tears on her face, "Edward, we

75

ought to be!" This was too much for him; they parted in tears. The next night found them, with many others, among the inquirers, and ere the meeting closed, they were united in a love purer and holier than any human love, a love never to be sundered. This Rhoda was a lady of great influence in the place, a teacher, and one of the best singers I ever heard. She was very useful in the precious revival that followed. When she sang, others often were silent. From this time the work went on with great power. I heard nothing more of dancing schools. They had what they enjoyed far better.

The preaching was forenoon and evening, preceded by a prayer-meeting. There was a paper mill a little distance from the meeting-house. I said to Brother Higby of Sand-isfield, who was with us, "Will you go with me to the paper mill, and let Brother Bush, the pastor, attend to the prayer-meeting? I feel impressed we have a duty to perform there." We went, and I asked the superintendent if we could converse with the operatives a few moments. He said, "Yes," and asked them all to come into the lower story. They stood in a circle, about fifty in number. They were all adults and an interesting group. I requested Brother Higby to commence at one side of the circle. I began also conversing on the other side, extending a friendly hand to each, which was accepted, until I met a lady of a proud look, using texts of Scripture as they occurred to me. She turned scornfully around, and I simply said, "The hand you refused me will soon be mould-ering in the grave, and your tongue locked in silence; pre-pare to meet thy God," and passed on. I soon saw her weeping. The random shot was the means of her conver-sion. We both spent a few moments in prayer, and invited them all to attend our meetings whenever they could. As I was leaving the mill, a portly, noble looking man, by the name of Bishop, gave me his trembling hand, and said, "I have long been an infidel, but I can be so no longer; pray for me, and call and see me." We left the mill and I entered

the pulpit and named my text, when Mr. Ogden, the superintendent, entered the church, beckoned to me, and
approached, saying, " God has stopped the mill, and they
wish you to come back there." To me it was a moment of
thrilling interest. I replied, "I think duty calls me here,"
and said to the pastor, Rev. Mr. Bush, " Will you please to
go up to the paper mill ?" He went, and all followed him
to the church, except Mr. Bishop, who could not leave the
engine. Mr. Bishop said, "Ask Christians to pray for me."
At the request of Mr. Bishop, I promised to see him at the
mill the next morning. As I approached he came hurriedly,
followed by a score or more of the hands, and with tears of
joy, he said, " I am the happiest man living. I think God
for Christ's sake has forgiven my sins."

He owned a beautiful cottage in the yard. I said, " Let
us go into your house, and thank God for it all." We went
in, and as many of the mill hands as could get in followed
us. We knelt together. After a few moments of prayer,
I asked him to follow me. I never heard such a prayer in
my life. He began by saying, "O God, teach me how to
pray! I cannot think of words good enough to address
thee." It was one of the most fervent, expressive, broken-
hearted prayers I ever heard. I rejoiced with him with
inexpressible joy. When God moves upon any of his
chosen ones, and puts forth his renewing, almighty power,
who can withstand it? A wicked, persecuting Saul is
prostrated at the feet of Sovereign Mercy, and made the
humble praying Paul. The conversion of Mr. Bishop is the
nearest, in all its bearings, to the conversion of Paul of any
I ever witnessed. All refuges of lies are swept away by
the power of God's word and irresistible Spirit. Though
pagan or infidel, the subject is made a new creature in
Christ Jesus. Paul well expresses it in Hebrews 4 : 12,
"For the word of God is quick, and powerful, and sharper
than any two-edged sword, piercing even to the dividing
asunder of soul and spirit, and of the joints and marrow,
and is a discerner of the thoughts and intents of the heart."

Oh, the wondrous power of God's love and mercy!
"Excuse me," said Mr. Bishop, "I want to tell Watson,
the Catholic in the mill, how I love Jesus." I soon followed him, and his divine eloquence was more than he
could withstand. He found him reading a Catholic paper;
he laid it down as tears were trickling down his cheeks. I
said to Mr. Bishop, "I want you to come to the evening
meeting, and just before I preach, I will ask you to tell us
what God has done for you."

He was a powerful orator, and was sought far and near
to speak in political meetings. He had a good voice and a
very commanding appearance. The news of his conversion
spread far and wide. The church was of olden style, very
large, with galleries on three sides, wide and capacious.
The church was packed, aisles and stairways. He arose in
front of the pulpit, a large and noble form, and began thus:
"*Brothers!*" and burst into tears. As he recovered from
his emotions he proceeded: "I ask the forgiveness of every
man, woman, and child in this house of God for the injury
I have done them by my intemperate and dissolute habits.
I hope God has forgiven and reformed me. I will now
give you some of my experience. I was born in England.
My father was a Baptist minister. He died when I was
young, yet I remember his leading me by my little hand to
the house of God. Being left an orphan, I sought various
employment, fell into bad company, and became intemperate. I came to America with a wife and four children, and
the cholera took away my wife and three children. I
became more intemperate, and sought the company of
sceptics to drown my troubles, but I made a dozen where
I drowned one.

"Since I have been in this town I have often gone to the
house of God, heard a sermon, went to my room, taking
some infidel associate and a jug of rum; and then with
Tom Paine's 'Age of Reason,' and 'Volney's Ruins,' we
tried to overthrow the truth preached. Last Sabbath forenoon, I went with the same purpose. The text Mr. Alden

used was, 'We shall all stand before the judgment seat of
Christ.' Rom. 14 : 10.   The first conviction was, *possibly*
there may be a day of judgment ; the next was *probably*
there will be a day of judgment ; and the next was, what
will be *my condition if there is ?*   I did not go to my room
and infidel books.   I went to the house of God in the afternoon.   The text was, 'Choose ye this day whom ye will
serve.'   The mere naming of that text was like a dagger
thrust through my heart.   Before the sermon closed, I felt
as though I should fall prostrate in the pew.   When I
arose for the last singing, I trembled under the mighty
power of that God I had so despised.   I went home in
agony of soul.   I spent a terrible night.   I was tempted to
commit suicide, but durst not do it.   On Monday night, I
cast myself at the footstool of Sovereign Grace and Mercy,
and cried, 'God, be merciful to me, a sinner.'   The burden
left me, and the love of Christ filled my heart with irrepres-
sible joy."   He then addressed the assembly, and gave
the most eloquent and affecting exhortation I ever heard.
Nearly the whole assembly were affected to tears.   To me,
it seemed the most eloquent preaching of any we had in the
whole month's meeting.   From that time the house was
crowded till the end of the meeting.   About a hundred
were probably converted.

About four years after this, Rev. Hervey Fitts, who so
faithfully served the Massachusetts Baptist State Convention for about thirty years, visited this church, and was desired to hold a series of meetings there.   He soon found a
most serious difficulty between the two influential brethren
spoken of before.   After trying in vain to settle the difficulty, the party said, "Mr. Alden was successful in settling
our former trouble, and we would like to have him come
and try to settle this."   The church voted to send for me.
Brother Fitts wrote me.   I was then pastor of the Central
Church, Westfield, and having some extra meetings, I
agreed to go, if he would fill my place.   He came to Westfield and told me all the particulars of the difficulty.   I

found I had a sermon, with a little alteration, that would nicely fit the case. I preached that sermon at Tyringham in the afternoon. The leading deacon asked the church to remain, saying that, "God in his providence has informed Brother Alden just what subject to take to settle this difficulty, and I think now is the time to do it." Others said, "How providential that such a subject should be given him." I asked the parties if they wished to have it settled. They said, "Yes," and agreed to meet me at ten o'clock, Monday, with the deacon. After about two hours of talk and prayer, it was all settled, and a good revival followed. I think in my second visit to this church, that I baptized a Congregational deacon and his wife, together with his three children, a complete household baptism.

While the blessing of God attended every effort abroad, I was for nearly two years greatly discouraged over my own dear church. The congregation was constantly increasing, which kept me somewhat encouraged.

One Sabbath I took for my text, Psalm 126: 6, "He that goeth forth and weepeth, bearing precious seed, shall doubtless come again rejoicing, bringing his sheaves with him." In my sermon I said, "God seems to bless the preaching of the truth to the salvation of souls everywhere but here. The fault is in me or you. It cannot be in God." I was about to severely blame the church, when God showed me where the fault was in an unlooked-for way. I repeated the text in part, "He that goeth forth and weepeth." Instantly the love of God seemed to overpower me, and I was in a flood of tears. This led me to say, "The early men of God watered the seed with their tears." As soon as I could control myself and see my congregation, I found the larger portion of them were in tears. All this was to show me I had not been tender-hearted enough in preaching. This was the beginning of a revival that brought many into the church.

From that time we had frequent additions. Sandford Blackinton and Rufus Wells, two very excellent business

men, who were wealthy manufacturers in what is now called
Blackinton, built a fine chapel for the accommodation of
the operatives and others. They invited the ministers of
North Adams to preach Sabbath evenings. There seemed
indications of a revival, and I was requested to hold a series
of meetings there. They continued three weeks, and fifty
or more were hopefully converted. At the close of said
meeting, I baptized the aforesaid gentlemen and their
wives, together with seventeen others, all of whom united
with the North Adams Baptist church. The Methodist
minister of North Adams baptized the same number, and
about the same number united with the Congregational
churches in North Adams and Williamstown. I then commenced preaching in the village, now the city of North
Adams, and held meetings thirteen consecutive weeks, and
preached over seventy extra sermons. This revival brought
seventy-eight into the church, forty-two of whom were
heads of families. Six merchants and manufacturers of
this number were men of wealth and influence. Rev. Dr.
Wescott aided me ten days in this revival. I shall never
forget the labors of Dea. Otis Blackinton, one of the best
men who ever lived, over seventy years of age, living more
than two miles from the church, who would come with
his team each morning, take me, and visit and pray till
the time of meeting. Dea. Duty S. Tyler, no less prominent and devoted, was greatly beloved, and exerted a powerful influence in and out of the church. Deacon Richmond also, by his counsel and prudent management, was a
valuable aid to the pastor, and did much toward the building up of the cause of our blessed Lord. Long will these
servants of God live in the memory of those who knew
them, together with many others, who, by their godly and
consistent lives, their sacrifices, and their love for Jesus,
will ever be gratefully remembered. Few men, if any, in
the business world, have ever lived who have been more respected for their energy, honesty, benevolence and kindness,
than Sandford Blackinton and Brother Rufus Wells, Dr.

Brayton, Duty S. Tyler, Dea. Samuel Ingalls, Rodman Wells, Salmon Burlingame, an early manufacturer, and Oliver Arnold. Their help respected and loved them, and some of them spent a long life in their service. For six years I visited their operatives, and I am happy to say I never heard the least word of complaint respecting either one of them. Their example and influence will go down to posterity, and be cherished in pleasing and grateful remembrance.

I will here quote a letter from Rev. A. C. Osborne, D. D., since then pastor of this church, written for my golden wedding, Dec. 5, 188

DEAR BROTHER:

The memory of your pastorate over this church from April 1, 1840, to April 1, 1846, is indeed most precious. God crowned your ministry with abundant blessings. You fed the church of God. You had souls for your hire. The goodly number of one hundred and ninety-eight united with the church during your pastorate, many of whom you led to Christ and into the church, became pillars, polished pillars, in the house of God. Some of them have gone up higher, to fill places in the house not made with hands, eternal in the heavens. Others are office-bearers in the church militant. In all the history of this church probably no pastorate has been more fruitful. No other six years brought into the church so many men of promise, who afterwards became officers of the church, making it a power in the community and among the churches of the Commonwealth. We thank God that you have lived to see prominent results from your labors here and elsewhere. We rejoice with you to-day ; not only with you, but with her, also, who fifty years ago chose to share the lot of one of God's servants, and without whose loving help and faithfulness and able co-operation those labors could not have been so fruitful and rich in blessing to the churches of our Lord. Some of your friends send with this a pecuniary token of esteem which we wish you to accept. If it was as large as the love to you which prompts it, you could not find room enough to receive it. Fraternally yours,

A. C. OSBORNE, Pastor.

FIRST BAPTIST CHURCH,

NORTH ADAMS, MASS.

REV. JOHN ALDEN, JR.,

PASTOR,

1840 TO 1847.

PASTORS OF THE CHURCH SINCE ITS

ORGANIZATION.

Rev. Geo. Witherell,   Dec. 1, 1808–Dec. 1, 1813
  "   Elisha F. Willey,   "   1, 1815–Apr. 1, 1817
  "   Hosea Wheeler,   Fall 1817–Summer 1818
  "   George Robinson,   "   1819–Spring 1820
  "   Samuel Savory,   Dec. 1, 1820–Feb. 3, 1829
  "   Charles B. Keyes, July 1, 1827–Apr. 1, 1834
  "   Asa H. Palmer,   Apr. 1, 1834–Apr. 1, 1836
  "   Samuel Covel,   May 1, 1836–Apr. 1, 1838
  "   Thomas Rogers,   Apr. 1, 1838–Apr. 1, 1840
  "   JOHN ALDEN, JR., Apr. 1, 1840–Apr. 1, 1846
  "   Horace T. Lowe, June 1, 1846–Apr. 1, 1852
  "   Miles Sandford, D. D.,
                    July 23, 1853–March 19, 1871
  "   Courtland W. Arable, D. D.,
                             March 17, 1872–1877
  "   A. C. Osborn, D. D.,   1877–1884
  "   Francis H. Rowley,   1884

Soon after my settlement in North Adams, I was asked, by some of my church if I had visited the widow Carpenter living on the side of the Green Mountains. As I had just been settled there, I had learned nothing of her history. "It will do you and her good to visit her." I went, and found the woman about seventy years of age, in a poor cottage. I asked her to give me her history. "It is a mournful one," said she. "I was married young, and had three sons. My husband became intemperate. He went at one time to the village and became intoxicated, and did not return home till the next morning. We picked over cotton for the mills, and put it round the room in racks to dry. I was called to aid a sick neighbor. I charged my oldest son not to light a candle while I was gone. As I was returning, I saw flames arise from my dwelling, and met my oldest son on his way to meet me, crying, 'Our house is on fire, and both my little brothers are burning in it.' I fainted and fell; but soon arose and hastened to my house, then on fire. I could see both of my dear boys in their trundle-bed, locked in each other's arms, with the flames around them. Had I not been held back by some neighbors, I should have rushed through the flames for them. In the morning, my husband came home. I hastened to him for sympathy, saying, 'Husband, our house is burned, and our two little boys are burned in it.' Crazed from his drunken revels, he said, with an oath, 'I wish you had been burned with them!' It so overcame me that it caused a fit of sickness. Some years after, we had two more sons. One, who was adopted, was riding in a cart; the oxen ran away, turned the cart over on him, and instantly killed him. We had a very charming boy we called Major. A clergyman from Bernardston, Mass., heard of him, called on us, and adopted him, and agreed to write to us often. He did so for a little time, but for weeks we heard nothing. I started on foot upon the frozen ground, a journey of over forty miles, and found he had fallen from the great beams of the barn, was killed, and had been buried three weeks. My husband grew more intemperate, and had rum sores on his limbs. I nursed him as well as I could, but many a time he has seized me by the hair of my head and hurled me against the wall until I was senseless. Soon he died cursing his God. I had one son left, and, like his father, he took to drink. He would work hard, and more than once he has come home crazed with drink, and broken almost everything in the house." Mrs. Carpenter was a talented woman, and a very humble, devout Christian. She was one of the best of singers. I sat in tears during the tragic narrative, and heard her sing a number of spiritual hymns, and joined with her in prayer. I left, I trust, a humbler, more thankful and better man. I had the pleasure of baptizing that son, who, so far as I know, lived a devoted life, and proved at last a great comfort to his godly mother.

My wife had a class of young ladies belonging to excellent families in the place. At the close of the sermon the inquirers were invited forward. The whole of the class, excepting an absent one, went in a group to the anxious seat. They went fully resolved not to leave the house of God until they gained an evidence that they loved the Saviour. In a former revival, they felt similarly; but finally said, " *Not now; not now.*" The assembly was dismissed, but they remained with their teacher, pastor, and some others. For more than an hour prayer was offered again and again, ere they fully gave their hearts to Christ. They could kneel and weep, but could not pray in faith. It was suggested, as it was getting late, that we leave the house of God. They began to weep and said, " Do not leave us; we cannot go home without making our final decision to give our hearts to the Saviour and to be forever on his side. We feel that if we say, 'Go thy way for this time,' we are eternally lost." They all uttered the contrite prayer that God in mercy heard. They arose praising God their Saviour, and in due time united with the Baptist church.

Such an unusual display of God's grace I seldom or

never witnessed. Both Mrs. Alden and myself could hardly believe it possible that all the class, save one, should so unitedly, and with one heart, give up all for Jesus. We felt that there was danger they might be deceived through sympathy one with another; but the future of their lives gave evidence of their true conversion. The one who was indifferent to her soul's interests at that time afterward yielded to the Saviour, and died trusting in God. Two others died in faith, and five are still living, and most, if not all, are active workers in the vineyard of our Lord.

I was called to pass through one of the greatest trials of my life, while pastor of the North Adams church, in the loss of a beloved child, Francis Howard Alden, aged five and a half years. I had taken much pains to tell him all the facts of the Bible adapted to his age. One cold winter evening he said, "Pa, you will not go out to make calls this evening, will you?" I said, "No." "Then I want you to tell me more about Jesus." I took him in my lap and went through the history of Christ's birth, death, and second coming as Judge. I found the child ran through the charming story from his remarks that he remembered much that I had told him before. He was in tears before I closed. He walked the room a little time, then came and asked me to go up in the study and pray that he might be prepared when Christ should come. On his return to the sitting-room he seemed very happy. He said, "How good Jesus is to die for sinners, and let little children come to him and be saved." From that time I let him follow me in family prayers. He used his own form of prayer. It was wonderful how he gained in expressing himself. His conversation seemed to run chiefly on religious subjects. He could not bear to see any one break the Sabbath, and often desired me to stop such offenders. If any of his mates used profane language in their plays, he would leave them, saying, "It makes me feel bad to hear you swear." "Come back, Francis; we won't swear." "You said so before, but you forget." I will here quote from an obituary of him

written at the time by Rev. Mr. Scarritt, who was living
with me, pursuing theological studies: " Francis, though
young, possessed a mind above mediocrity.   He often
evinced a readiness of mental perception and depth of
thought far beyond his years.   On one occasion, conversing with his mother respecting the Saviour's sufferings and
death, he remarked, 'You say that Christ is God, *where*
then, was *God* when *Christ died?*'   She tried to satisfy
his mind, but he seemed unhappy that he could not comprehend it, until she told him the Bible said that *God* and
Christ were *one*, and that he must believe the *Bible*.   He
then said, ' Ma, I will believe it, and make no further
query.'   He ever wanted all things demonstrated.   He
was of an ardent temperament, affectionate, dutiful and
conscientiously scrupulous about doing a wrong act."   He
died of dropsy on the brain.   Being asked if he was willing
to leave father, mother and friend, and go to be with Jesus in
Heaven, looking up, his eyes sparkling with joy, he said,
" Yes, and I will wait there till you come."   Though I had
thought God had converted him to be a minister or a missionary, yet I bless God that he gave me such a son to lose,
or take back to himself.

The funeral services were held on the Sabbath, and the
sermon, replete with excellent and comforting thoughts, was
preached by Rev. Robert Crawford, D. D., pastor of the
Congregational church, from the text, "The Lord gave,
and the Lord hath taken away ; blessed be the name of
the Lord."   His church and congregation united with us
in these solemnities.   At his funeral, the following verses
were pinned upon his shroud, and beheld by sympathizing
hundreds :

> " He sleeps in Jesus! blissful thought!
> He's freed from toil and pain,
> And in the resurrection morn,
> He'll wake to life again.
>
> In that blest morn, how bright he'll shine,
> Amid that dazzling throng,

As round the throne of God they bow,
   Redeeming grace the song."

The following lines were written by his father, and pub-
ished soon after his death :

Two sons to parents dear are blest
   Our cheerful, humble dome ;
But one is not, he's now at rest
   High in his heavenly home ;
Where all the angelic throng adore
He praises God forevermore.

Has Francis gone—forever fled ?
   In visions oft he's seen ;
We cannot make this loved one dead—
   His calm and manly mien,
His bounding step, his speaking eyes,
Before us daily, hourly rise.

His thousand tones, in word and song,
   Are echoing round our dome ;
For school he plods his way along,
   And now he's coming home ;
He's at my study door—with joy
I start to meet my coming boy.

Now from the sacred desk I view
   The pensive, solemn throng ;
My child is there, at worship, too—
   I'm tracing years along ;
Alas ! the joyous visions turn,
Lifeless—I see him in the urn.

Parents bereaved, has ever heart
   Like ours been made to bleed !
Is there no balm to heal the smart,
   No friend in time of need ?
Blest balm of Gilead : this alone
Can make us say, " Thy will be done."

One night this child—'twas not in vain—
   Climbed on my knee to say,
" Of Jesus Christ oh tell again
   Before you bow and pray."
His life, his death, his dying groans,
Were told in solemn, moving tones.

The tears rolled down; with heaving sigh
    He asked for me to pray,
That when the Judge of all draws nigh
    He might withstand the day,
And with the glorious Saviour rise
To dwell with him above the skies.

Prayer since that time has been his joy,
    And oft he'd leave his play;
Alone in tears we've found our boy
    Wishing with us to pray.
Sweet was the way before the throne
To bow to the Eternal One.

His bounds were set, one songster more
    Must join the eternal choir;
While lingering on this mortal shore,
    His thoughts were rising higher:
"I'd rather be with Christ at home,
And wait in heaven until you come." *

Oh, what a sad and solemn hour,
    When angels bore him hence.
He lives above; Death's lost his power,
    Nor would we call him thence,
An angel now amid the throng
Who sing the everlasting song.

With him I've roamed the forest wild,
    The crowded city walked,
The ocean beach, and taught my child,
    While God in thunder talked,
Of him whose wisdom shines above,
Beneath, around, a God of love.

O blissful thought! we yet may roam
    The Paradise above,
When all the ransomed throng get home,
    In purer, holier love ;
Wait, child, in heaven a few more days,
We'll join in everlasting praise.

While pastor in North Adams, I was called to part with my dear father. As a preacher he was sound in doctrine,

---

* Being asked whether he chose to live with his friends or die, he said he had rather die and be with Jesus in heaven, and wait there till we came.

and considered a very able preacher. A sermon from the text, "Who will show us any good?" I heard him preach in my college days so deeply affected me that I have often seemed listening to it still. He continued to preach until he was about eighty years old. He came to North Adams on a Saturday, at the age of eighty. I asked him if he felt that God had a message for him to deliver to us. "Yes," he said. A few years before this, he was thrown from his carriage, striking on his head, which somewhat injured his mind. I felt a little fearful, and told him so. "Well," said he, "appoint a meeting at five P. M."—it was then summer,—"and if I fail, they cannot blame you." I had an appointment for an out station at the same hour. On my return, I asked Captain Richmond, one of our senior deacons, how my father succeeded. "I was very much interested," said he, "I do not think you, or any minister in Berkshire County, could extemporaneously present such an array of Bible truth, and bring it so forcibly to illustrate the text." I remarked, "My father was called by many a 'living concordance.'" I never knew the man so fully acquainted with the Bible. He rarely found his equal in an argument. I have often sat, with much pleasure, and seen him use up a sceptic. When he got into an argument with me, and I saw he was likely to worst me, I either wound up with the Quaker's way, "You may think it is so, but I shall always think otherwise," or stop suddenly by saying, "It is wisely said, 'Never argue with a man over seventy years of age, expecting to get your case.'"

FROM A WESTERN PAPER.

"Died in Kewanee, Henry County, Ill., Nov. 24, 1865, Dea. David Alden, aged fifty-one years. A useful and eventful life, cut off so mysteriously and suddenly, deserves more than a passing notice. He was the son of Rev. John Alden, of Ashfield, Mass., and has a brother of the same name, widely and favorably known among the churches of

New England.   Mr. Alden experienced religion at the age
of seventeen, while fitting for college, at the Franklin Academy at Shelburne Falls, taught by his brother, who baptized him there.   He graduated at Brown University in
1837, and immediately engaged in teaching in Kalamazoo,
Mich., and thus laid the foundation of what is now a flourishing college.   The death of his wife, and his impaired
health, caused him to return, after two years of successful
labor, to Massachusetts.   Thinking then to enter the ministry, he entered Newton Theological Seminary.   Duty
seemed to call him from there to become the principal of
the Franklin Academy.   After two or three years of service there, the infirmities of an aged father called him to
the old homestead, to relieve the sufferings of his last
hours, often preaching where duty called.   It was here he
was called to bury his second wife, the daughter of Dea.
Otis Blackinton of North Adams.   Since then he has
been engaged mostly in agricultural pursuits in Southboro,
Mass., and Kewanee, Ill., teaching winters.   In both these
places he has served the church as deacon, and faithfully filled the office.   Very few can be found more honorable or praiseworthy in this relation.   As a Christian,
Brother Alden was intellectual and conscientious, of a calm,
cheerful, and happy temperament.   The church, in all her
interests, was very dear to him.   For her he was ever ready
to toil and sacrifice.   He was truly a burden-bearer in the
house of the Lord.   Throughout the whole community he
was regarded as an honorable man, a good citizen, and a
faithful, sincere Christian.   His family are bereft of a kind
father, and a faithful, confiding husband — a loss which
cannot be compensated by any earthly considerations.
Brother Alden's death was sudden.   When crossing a railroad, with horses and buggy, a train, that failed to blow the
whistle, unperceived by him till too late, threw him forty
feet.   He was taken up, and though he lingered thirty hours,
gave no signs of consciousness.   He leaves a wife, to whom
he was united in 1845, and four children, to mourn his

departure. The kindest sympathies of an afflicted church and community are tendered to them in their deep sorrow ; and they are specially commended to Him who is the refuge of His people."

FROM THE CHICAGO "HOME VISITOR."

" ' In the midst of life we are in death.' Four days ago the sun rose on as happy a family as this world contained. Nestled in a quiet home in one of the richest and wealth. iest prairies of the West, they were rejoicing that morning in a new treasure. A daughter had been added to their number, and the parents and trio of brothers were jubilant on the occasion. Their home was a model one. Intelligent industry had surrounded their home with comforts and luxury. Their library was well stored, as well as their larder, and daily mails posted them in all things secular and religious. They were surrounded with loving Christian friends. Even then the storm cloud was hovering, ready to burst upon them in deadly power. The father went forth from his home to be absent a few hours ; but alas ! it was to return no more alive. The guilty, reckless train had taken his life, almost in sight of his lovely home and charming family. Now you might have witnessed a touching scene. The coffined father, with classic features serenely beautiful in death, sealed with the smile of quiet satisfaction and confiding trust, was brought into the room, and placed by the couch of the heart-stricken mother and her unconscious infant, never to know a fond father's caresses. There sat the three dear brothers, feeling that much of their joy had departed forever. There, too, were weeping, sympathizing friends. That home once so joyous, now witnesses the widow's anguish and orphan's tears. Yea, more, it witnesses the power of Christian faith that says, ' Though He slay me, I will trust in Him.' "

During my pastorate here I lost a dear brother, Dea. Cyrus Alden, of the Shelburne Falls church. He had

long been a deacon in Ashfield, his native town. He was
extensively engaged in the manufacturing business. Next
to my father, he was my best earthly counsellor. When
some Gordian knot in theology came up, I often went to
him for solution. He could generally make that clear, but
his difficulty was farther ahead. He was sound in doctrine,
and much prized as a Bible-class teacher. He was a peace-
maker. For a time he labored under a delusion that he
could not speak in the conference meeting to any edifica-
tion. About this time, his native town chose him in the
place of an attorney to oppose a road the commissioners
put through the town. He plead their case in court, and
gained his point. The senior lawyer on the other side said
to me, " Your brother ought to have been a lawyer. I
never found a more shrewd or able opponent." I then
told him I hoped he would never fail to plead his Master's
cause before men. After that he tried to do his duty.
His disease caused him great suffering, yet he was cheerful and patient, and died in the triumphs of faith.

THE EARLY HISTORY OF NORTH ADAMS.

For my own gratification, and that of my friends, I have
spared no pains in searching out a correct history of a place
made dear to me from personal associations. I take as
reliable what is stated by W. F. Spear in an article on
North Adams, written in 1885, which greatly pleased and
aided me.

In June, 1762, a tract of land, seven miles by five miles,
was laid out, and named East Hoosac. It was what was
called North and South Adams. About this time nine
towns around were sold for sixteen thousand dollars. The
town was incorporated in 1778, and called Adams, in honor
of Samuel Adams, a leader in the Revolutionary War, and
Governor of Massachusetts. Less than one hundred and
fifty years ago, this beautiful city was a howling wilderness.
The eagle built his nest unscared, the fox burrowed undis-

turbed, and the bear and catamount sought their prey un-
molested. Capt. Ephraim Williams was the first pioneer, in
1750. The first settlers came from Connecticut. No town,
it was believed, was more patriotic in the state, or more generous in carrying on the War of the Revolution. Fort
Massachusetts was located in 1741, in a narrow part of the
valley leading towards Williamstown. Williams and his
hardy companions erected this fort with square timbers,
driven down into the ground, so as to make a strong fence,
mounted with a few swivels and made proof against musketry. The garrison had fifty men. It was rebuilt in 1747,
and garrisoned with one hundred men.

The fort was built as a protection against French and
Indian hostilities. Scouting parties were ranging the
woods in all directions to find the Indian trail, and prevent,
as far as possible, their murderous work. "Armed with
gun and hatchet and scalping knife, with provisions and
blankets on his back, the hardiest soldier scoured the woods
in quest of the savage. Every entangled thicket was the
place of ambush, and the tomahawk and scalping knife
were looked for in fear."

June 11, 1745, the enemy appeared, attacking a number
of men a little distance from the fort. They wounded two
men and captured one. Only one of the enemy was killed.
Aug. 20, 1746, an army of nine hundred French and
Indians, under Gen. De Vaudrew, made an attack on the
fort. Col. Hawks, the commander, had only twenty-two
effective men. This brave officer defended the fort twenty-
eight hours, against the Canadian general, with more
than forty times his number of men, and probably would
not have surrendered but for want of ammunition. Col.
Hawks lost but one man, while the enemy lost forty-five.
The fort was demolished by the French general. The
prisoners were marched to Canada, where twelve sickened
and died. A part of the prisoners were sent to Boston, a
few of whom came back. In May 25, 1747, the fort was
rebuilt. In August, 1748, Ephraim Williams, the founder

of William's College, was commander of the fort. A party
of three hundred Indians and thirty French attacked the
fort, and after receiving a vigorous fire for two hours, they
gave it up and withdrew with their dead and wounded.
The fort began to decay after the conquest of Canada, in
1748. The site of the fort is in the meadow owned by
Mrs. Bradford Harrison. Prof. A. L. Perry, and a few
students from William's College, planted an elm tree, in
1858, on the spot where the fort stood. Would it not be
well for a grateful posterity to erect a monument there, and
put on it some of the names of those brave defenders of our
rights? They did it long ago at Bloody Brook, and we
love to read the names of those who fell by the Indian foe.
It tells us what our liberties cost, and may stimulate those
who enjoy them, to perpetuate them.

Many relics of the war on the fort have been found near
where it stood. There are arrow heads, hundreds of bullets, a metallic tomahawk, several bomb shells, a large
round bowl, a silver spoon, and many rusty knives. Some
of these are preserved in the cabinet of William's College.
At first, the South Village was the largest; but soon the
superior advantage from the water power put the North
Village in the ascendant. The site of the North Village
was a pine forest intermingled with white oaks. The
Hoosac river then was much larger than now, and in earlier
times the lower part of the village was often flooded. The
clearing off of our forests, thus letting the sun shine on
the land, has greatly lessened our rivers by evaporation.
The principal land-holders at this time, 1795, in North
Adams, were Jeremiah Colgrove, Sr., Israel Jones, the first
justice of peace in the town, and serving in that office over
forty years, David Estis and David Darling.

In 1794, when Mr. Colgrove moved here, there were less
than a dozen houses in North Adams Village. All the
brooks at that time were swarming with trout. In early
times wolves and bears were troublesome. Deer and other
game were plentiful. The first store was fitted up in 1793.

Dea. Edward Richmond opened a store in 1825, on Main street, and kept it a long time. The same year, Ezra D. Whittaker, Esq., built a store, which he still owns on Main street. In 1727, J. Quinn Robinson & Son built a store on the corner of Main and Marshall streets. When Dea. Edward Richmond came here, in 1803, there were only two stores in the place. English calico then sold at from fifty to seventy-five cents a yard. Six yards then made a lady's dress! Wages were from eighty to one hundred dollars a year. Mechanics had one dollar a day, working early and late. Land out of the village was worth one dollar an acre. In 1799, the first cloth dressing was done by Roger Wing. In 1801, a carding machine was put into Capt. Colegrove's grist mill. The same year, David Estis threw a dam across the north branch, and put up a building for carding wool and dressing cloth. The first machine shop in the village, and probably in the county, was started by Mr. Giles Tinker, in 1811, and was run many years by him. He was an excellent man, of great energy and perseverance. In 1829, the population of the whole town was 2,500.

"In early times the study of grammar was considered a waste of time, and a knowledge of arithmetic was not thought necessary for the young girls of the school. The love of learning was a genteel name for laziness." But the standard of education rose rapidly.

DRURY ACADEMY.

Through the persevering efforts of Dr. E. S. Hawks and Dr. Isaac Hodges, Nathan Drury, Esq., of Florida, was induced to give three thousand dollars to build an academy in North Adams. It was erected on a beautiful eminence near the centre of the village. Dr. Hawks superintended the grading of the ground, and Dr. Hodges looked after the erection of the building. "The summit of the hill was lowered seventeen feet to give all needed conveniences. Many feet below the surface, there was found a tree fifteen inches in diameter, embedded in the gravel. The body of the tree was whole, and of hard wood. It had fallen to the south. The presumption is that the town of Stamford was once a lake, and that the bar was near the beaver mill. When it broke away, the rush of water caused the bluff, and buried the tree in the gravel." This theory may explain a number of similar bluffs in the valley. The academy has been greatly enlarged at the expense of about eighty thousand dollars.

CHURCHES.

There was a Congregational church formed in 1766, but owing to the poverty caused by the Revolutionary War, the church was given up. The Friends built a house in South Adams in 1781.

THE BAPTIST CHURCH.

After the failure of the Congregationalist church, no church was organized in North Adams until the present Baptist church was formed, which took place in 1808, constructed by Rev. Calvin Keys. In 1829, a brick church was erected, and remodelled in 1844. On the same spot, in 1848, a new church was built, ninety-four feet by sixty-three feet. In May, 1875, the church was badly burned, but was repaired and rededicated in 1880. The church, including all pertaining to it, is valued at one hundred thousand dollars. Present number of church members, 1071 ; number of Sabbath-school scholars, 1000.

THE UNIVERSALIST CHURCH.

This church was organized in 1842. In 1851, this parish erected a nice church on State street, with a good vestry.

THE METHODIST CHURCH.

The origin of this church dates back to 1823. Their first church was built on Central street. The house they now occupy is a fine edifice, valued at seventy-five thousand dollars. The number of church members is 750 ; number of Sabbath-school scholars, 555.

THE CONGREGATIONAL CHURCH.

This church was organized in 1827. The first meeting-house was built in 1828. Their present elegant church edifice was completed Sept. 6, 1865, at a cost of thirty-three thousand dollars. A bell, weighing 5135 pounds, hangs in the tower. It was a present from Samuel J. Whitten, at a cost of three thousand dollars. Number of church members, 510 ; number of Sabbath-school scholars, 360.

ST. JOHN'S EPISCOPAL CHURCH.

This church was organized in 1856. It is located on Summer street. In 1857, a church building was erected of wood, which was succeeded in 1869 by the present stone structure, valued, including ground, at twenty-six thousand dollars. The building was a gift to the society from Mrs. Hiram Sibley, of Rochester, N. Y. The society now has 160 communicants. The Sunday-school has 191 scholars, and fifteen officers and teachers.

THE UNION CHURCH.

The Blackinton Union church, located at Blackinton, was organized in 1843, with twenty members. The church building erected in 1871 is valued, including grounds, at twelve thousand five hundred dollars. There are now about 150 members. The pulpit is supplied by the pastors of the Baptist, Methodist and Congregational churches. The church building was erected by Sandford Blackinton, and donated to the village.

THE CATHOLIC CHURCH.

Their house of worship was dedicated July, 1869. Its 'ocation is on Eagle street. It has a chime of bells. The manufacturers and citizens of North Adams contributed towards these bells. The Catholic population is estimated at three thousand five hundred.

THE FRENCH CATHOLIC CHURCH.

The French Canadian church was formed in 1870. They commenced worship in their new edifice, on East Main treet, in 1874.

CHAPTER V.

PRIME OF LIFE.

N comparing North Adams as now existing with the past, I am constrained to say, "What hath God wrought!" Few places in New England have ever equalled it. Less than one hundred and fifty years ago, all that is beautiful in splendid public buildings, all that is tasteful and elegant in private residences, all that is rich in garden culture, all that is beautiful in streets and lanes, all that is charming and soul-elevating in civilized friendship and piety, was once entirely wanting here. In its stead, there was the primeval forest, the entangled morass, the howling wolf, the growling bear, and men more savage than they. If there was praise to God here then, it was the sighing winds among the lofty pines; it was the dead silence of nature in her wildness, or the lightning's blaze athwart the heavens, and the deafening thunder peals from mountain to mountain in nature's solemn anthem.

It is not so much a wonder that this place has become a pleasant, charming city, when we call to mind the list of the earlier business men of the place. Such are J. Colegrove, G. and E Tinker, S. and J. Blackinton, the Arnold brothers, Dea. D. S. Tyler, Col. Willmarth, Hon. H. Dawes, Dea. O. Blackinton, C. T. Sampson, C. Turner, the Ingrams, W. E. and S. Brayton, S. Johnson, E. Kingsley, O. Wells, D. Estes, A. Smith, E. D. Whitaker, Esq., Dea. E. Richmond, Hon. J. Robinson and father, J. G. Robinson and son, J. Jackson, S. Burlingame, Dea. S. Ingalls, R. Wells, George Millard, Deacon Wilber, Dr. T.

Brayton, Dr. E. Norman, Drs. Tyler and Phillips, E. S. Hawks, M. Babbit, S. N. Briggs, Brown and Harris, Deacons W. Gould, S. Gaylord and D. Rogers.

Most of these I knew, and appreciated their worth. A great number have gone to their rest; but we trust that the mantle of the ascended Elijahs has fallen on kindred Elishas, and that the work of patriotism, temperance, morality and piety will still move on successfully and gloriously. No language can express the pleasure I have enjoyed in most of the company above named, as well as many other kindred spirits. Such persons live on and will ever live in pleasing remembrance.

The condition of North Adams on the subject of temperance, in 1840, was anything but desirable. Fourteen stores sold intoxicating liquors. The friends of temperance felt it was high time to seek a reform. A Mr. Van Wagner, a very able lecturer, was hired to give ten lectures, which brought about a great change. He labored from house to house. Many hundreds were added to the temperance society. There was a unanimous vote in a full assembly to request our landlord not to sell alcoholic liquor at the bar, and their families voted with the throng. The year after, deeply impressed that we ought to begin the work with children, I made a public request for the children of the place to meet in the Baptist church, to form a juvenile temperance society. To my joy the church was well filled. The Rev. Dr. Crawford, the excellent pastor of the Congregational church, was heartily in the work. So, also, was the pastor of the Methodist church. The pledge was, "We pledge perpetual hate to all that can intoxicate." We began with a goodly number. At the second meeting, I introduced the following: "Resolved, that we will do all that we can consistently to get others to join." Before I put the question, I did all I could to rouse them to thorough action; and when I called for the vote, a large number jumped to their feet, and voted with both hands. "Call at my study to-morrow, and I will rig you out with as many

pledges as you want." I had work enough for that day. I
gave them a rule: "The one who obtained the signer first
should have him, as his only, on the list."

For many days I was met on every street. I travelled
with a show of signers. One very dark night, as I was
going to the post-office, I heard a boy say, "I have as good
a right to Tommy's pledge as you have." "No," said the
other, "I took it first, and by the rule, he is mine." I
stopped to listen. "That is Mr. Alden," said one of them.
"How do you know? We can't see one another." "It is
his step," he said in a low voice. I said, "What do you
wish, my boys?" "About Tommy. Who has a right to
him?" "The one who took his name first has the only
right to him," I answered. "I told you so," said the boy,
and off in the darkness they all ran. We had very many
interesting meetings. A few opposers said, "They are so
young, they do not know what they are about." At a meeting where many of their parents were present, I mentioned
this objection. One father arose instantly, and said, "I am
very happy to say, I have three boys in the society, the
youngest of whom is five years old. They have all been
trying to get Sammie, the youngest, to join, who is three
years old, saying, "Won't you join?" "No." "Why?"
"I want to go to Mr. Kingsley's cider mill, and suck cider
through a straw. He knows what he is about, I am quite
sure." On July 4, 1842, we had a Sabbath-school and juvenile temperance society celebration. A band marched up
about two thousand into a grove, where speeches of thrilling interest were made, and temperance songs were sung,
amid the waving of temperance banners, while the red,
white and blue, with their starry stripes, floated above and
around as if to cheer them in their brave resolves.

When pastor in North Adams, Rev. Dr. Crawford kindly
helped me to draw the gospel net for souls with good success. When we could not catch men, we occasionally
caught trout together. "Brother A——," says the doctor,
"a part of your parish and a part of mine live on the Stam-

ford hills. Let us go up in the morning with our fish tackle, visit in the forenoon, and fish the brook home that runs through Bear swamp." As we entered the little swamp, fed by cool springs, we found the beautiful speckled trout abundant. Aroused by the exciting sport, I was somewhat ahead. The doctor did not do things quite so fast, but enough more thorough to atone for it Though but a little in advance, I was hid from his sight by the dense shrubbery. He called to me in a loud, excited tone to come to him quick as possible. Thinking a catamount or bear had seized him, I pulled out the butt of my fish-rod and ran for him, dashing the alders and brush right and left, determined to die with him if I could not live with him. "Where are you? Where are you?" I cried. "Down here," he said. When I came in sight of him, he was gazing upon a large pine tree, which doubled my fears, if possible. "What beneath the skies," I said, "is up in that tree?" looking up into the green dense foliage, trembling in every nerve and muscle. "Nothing," said he," "only I caught my hook up in the tree, and could not get it down alone." "Why did you so frighten me with such loud and excited tones?" "Because you were fishing so furiously I feared no common tone would bring you back." I was trembling in fear one moment, and the next in joyful laughter.

Many pleasant interviews with this dear brother, Rev. Dr. Crawford, were spent, in company with my wife, at his home in North Adams. His most excellent companion, daughter of the noted President Griffin, of Williams College, was a lovely Christian lady. After their removal to Deerfield, Mass., we visited them at that place. I never shall forget the pleasant meeting of the family circle on a Sabbath evening, when Mrs. Crawford introduced, as one feature of their devotional exercises, the repeating of poetry particularly adapted to God's holy day. She had long continued the practice of repeating the following beautiful lines each evening hour of the Sabbath, and requested my wife and her sister, Miss E. Chamberlain, and myself to join her the same day and hour in our own home, and thus feel that we were mingling together our evening devotions :

"Farewell, sweet Sabbath of the Lord, farewell!
The sun's last beams are shed on mount and dell,
And dimly in the West
Day's rosy mantle only may be seen,
While stars gleam out its fluttering folds between.
Farewell, sweet day of rest!

"To-morrow earthly cares begin once more :
Thy hours of prayer, thy hours of peace, are o'er ;
The conflict and the strife,
The joys that tempt, the grief so hard to bear,
The rush of business and the weight of care,
Must come to darken life.

"Yet shall remembrance of thy calm repose,
Float round me oft like odors of the rose,
And peace and rest shall come,—
A Sabbath peace, e'en in the midst of strife,
A Sabbath rest amid the toils of life,
And make this heart their home.

"How like a fountain in the wilderness
To sinful man is such a day as this!
Or like the Sabbath's God,
The shadow of a rock in weary lands,
A refuge from the storms and burning sands,
An ark above the flood.

"Farewell, sweet Sabbath of the Lord, farewell!
The stars are shining now on mount and dell:
Thy dawning to my eyes
Seemed bright and heavenly as an angel's wings
When bending low before his God he sings
The song of Paradise.

"Farewell, once more! Accept my lowly lay
E'en now, as passing from the world away,
Thou passest with a smile,
And give me something of thine own repose,
And give me strength to bear life's weight of woes
E'en but a little while."

North Adams has ever been an interesting and enter-prising place. Two nice streams, the Hoosac coming from

the south with its transparent waters, flowing from the
thousands of springs of the Green Mountains that feed
them, running now this, and now that way, as if reluctant
to leave so charming a valley, and the North Branch coming from the Northern Mountains, fed by its many tributaries abounding with trout, meet with gladsome commin-
gling near the center of the village, waking life and industry into being, along its charming banks. The Greylock
Mountain on the west, towering up in magnificent splendor,
looks down on Williamstown, Adams and North Adams
from the highest land in Massachusetts, never tiring over
the grand panorama. The citizens of these flourishing
towns gaze in profound admiration at the grand scenery of
all the surrounding mountains, charming at any season of
the year, but when robed in their autumnal costumes made
indescribably beautiful by " September's many tinted pen-
cil."   They chime in with the language of the inspired
penman, "Great and marvellous are thy works, Lord God
Almighty!"   Who can behold God in all the grandeur of
nature, or his beneficence in Providence, or his infinite
love and mercy in Redemption, and not adore and love
Him? I can never forget the soul-enlarging and soul-
inspiring scenery of North Adams, or the noble men and
women who surrounded me, especially those for whom, and
with whom, I labored. The excellent members of the other
churches with whom I was acquainted, led by kind affectionate pastors, and the peculiar harmony among all Christians, has made this place ever dear to me.

From North Adams, I settled in Fayville, Southboro,
Worcester County, Mass., choosing a smaller church, I was
so worn down by former labors. The parish had just built
a nice house of worship, on which there was a debt. This I
removed by lecturing in towns adjacent, *versus* "Roman-
ism."   Under the labors of Rev. Mr. Haynes, a former pastor, there was a revival, lasting more than a year, numbering, as I was informed, nearly two hundred converts.
There were few unconverted ones left in the parish.   J

labored there two years, and we added but few to the
church.

The Rev. Hervey Fitts, agent of the Baptist State Convention, called on me, saying, " I want you to visit the
Center Baptist church in Westfield, Mass. I have sent
them many candidates, and those who would settle there
they do not want ; and those they wanted, did not choose to
become their pastor." Said he, " It is a beautiful village, of

WESTFIELD BAPTIST CHURCH.

about five thousand people. Westfield Academy is a
venerable, noble institution, with its many students. The
Normal school is located there, and is in a flourishing state.
As you have been a teacher, I think you are adapted to
that place, and ought to visit it." I said, " I do not want to
leave. I settled here in this farming church for life." He
said, " I will supply your place for a few Sabbaths if you

will go." I assented, and the first Sabbath I had fifty
hearers. I found the church discouraged. They had lost a
pastor, Rev. Mr. Perkins, of great influence and power. It
was in the time of winter that I visited Westfield church.
A friend kindly proposed to carry me in his sleigh to visit
every member of the church. The more I visited, the more
I became attached to the place and the church. The third
Sabbath I preached to about two hundred. They voted to
give me a call, said to be unanimous. I became more and
more interested as I visited the people, and finally accepted
the call. There was quite a debt on the house, and it
needed repairs. This debt we removed. We then fixed
over all the pews, put in a new pulpit, and frescoed the
house. Soon every pew was rented. In the autumn of
the second year, we had a precious revival. We had meetings every night for a number of weeks. I baptized at
noon, on the Sabbath, in the canal near the center of the
village, when the other churches could be witnesses of the
solemn ceremony. We had sometimes nearly a thousand
present. For five consecutive Sabbaths, the candidates were
just five in number each Sabbath. We had a revival the
next year, which brought twenty-six into the church. This
church has continued to prosper under the faithful labors of
other pastors. The present pastor is the Rev. Dr. Eaton,
an able man and excellent preacher, who has long been
their minister, and whose labors have been greatly blest.

At the close of the fifth year, I accepted the agency for
the Missionary Union for Northern New England. My
travel in my own conveyance greatly improved my health.
I enjoyed the work, except in the severity of winter. I
often rode in my sleigh many miles when the mercury was
twenty degrees below zero. Once I rode five miles when
the mercury was thirty-six below zero, and froze my face to
pay for my imprudence. During this agency, I formed
many interesting acquaintances, and passed through various
experiences. A few I will relate.

There were many who belonged to the Free Missionary

Society, on account of their anti-slavery views. I found a church of that stamp in Vermont. The pastor of the church, Rev. Mr. Pierce, an excellent man, who had been settled there twelve years, held the old church as a Free Mission church, but a portion in favor of the Missionary Union had seceded and built a new church, which then had no pastor. I asked the privilege of presenting the cause in the old church, and invite the other church to meet with us. He assented, on condition he might reply. I told him I so well understood the Free Mission view, I could present that also, and have two sets of papers circulated, one for each society, and if I did not answer his mind, I would like to have him reply. He said he was satisfied, and would not speak. It was an able and benevolent church. The contribution was large, and not a dollar's difference between the two collections. I was desired to preach in the afternoon, and feeling impressed that the two churches ought, and might be united, I took the love of Christ for my theme. The good old pastor sat weeping during a portion of the sermon, his heart full of the love of Christ; and at its close, he arose in tears, and said, "My dear brethren, we ought, all of us, to be united in one church." The feeling was general, and the meeting was appointed, and a happy union was consummated. This was followed by a precious revival. I continued there, and preached a few evenings.

Another event, to me quite interesting, occurred in Townsend, Vt. There was a large, rich, Baptist church there, whose pastor was Rev. Dr. Fletcher. I presented the cause of missions on the Sabbath, and, according to their custom, went forth on Monday for the collection. Brother Fletcher said, "The church is large, and covers a large extent of territory, and it has taken your predecessors three days to go over it." I said, "Such are my arrangements, I want to do it in two days." I did so, and raised more than the usual offering, by working early and late. He made me out a list. "As you go down Main street," said he, "you will come to a large hotel. The landlord is a sceptic, you had better not try him ; but his wife and two daughters are members of my church. Ring the bell at the rear door, and see them. Then a little farther down is a rich infidel, whose wife is a member of my church, and her husband has turned some agents out of his house, I would not go there." I came to the hotel, and not wishing to slight the landlord, I entered the bar-room and found him alone. He was a portly, interesting looking man. Having resolved not to spend over fifteen minutes there, I immediately introduced my business. He went to the chamber door, and said, "Wife, girls, come down here, there is a man who wants all our money for the foreign missions." I said, "No, my dear sir ; there are other good causes, and I would like to leave a nest egg, for another time, for a man who runs such a nice hotel and farm." We all went into the sitting-room, where he began his tirade against the missionary cause. I met it kindly, with the report in my hand ; and, when I could, I met him humorously, but plainly. This caused a pleasant state of feeling, and disarmed him of his opposition and prejudice. Seeing my time was about up, I said, "If every member of the Baptist church in our country, said to contain over two million of members, should give twenty-five cents each, we should raise more than we do for foreign missions." He said, "Wife, he is going to let us off lightly. Here is a dollar for us four." He remarked, "Don't be in a hurry, I want to see you more." "I must say, as the prophet said, 'The King's business demands haste.'" "Come and put up with me another year in welcome."

Having succeeded better than I expected, I thought I would try the infidel. He was rich, and had a splendid house and farm. I found him at home. I asked from him a glass of water, complimenting him for his fine place. I told him I admired the condition of his fruit trees. Having had some experience in that line, I asked him all the didactic questions I could. He seized on some of them as practical for himself. As I had resolved not to spend over

fifteen minutes there, I said, " Can we see all your farm
from that little eminence in the rear of your house?" He
answered, " Yes," and I hurried up with him, took a rapid
view, and hastened from it down to his house, and asked for
another glass of water. He asked, "Are you a doctor?"
"No." "Are you a lawyer?" "Only as I put the law
and gospel together. I am agent of the foreign missionary
cause, and if you would like to give to that cause, I would
receive it most thankfully." "Who sent you here?" "No
one." "I turned some agents out of my house," said he,
"who did not treat me to my liking; but when they treat
me as you have done, they are welcome here." Pointing to
his wife, he observed, " *There* is one who gives. What do
you want to give?" "Just what you please to give me,"
said the meek, quiet woman. He handed her a two-dollar
bill, and invited me to call again.

I will record only one more incident among the many I
might give. In Northern Vermont I presented the Missionary cause on the Sabbath, and Monday I sought a man
to get into my carriage, and guide me to the members of
the church. They recommended their senior deacon, a
man over eighty. He said he was so old and infirm, he did
not think any one would wish to see him. I was told he
had been very useful, and was still much beloved. After
much cheery argument he consented. I told him I was
accustomed, where it was proper, to spend a few moments
in prayer, that a blessing might rest on the gift and the
giver, and alternate with my guide. For a number of visits,
he wished to be excused. We came to a house where the
mother was recovering from a long fit of sickness. She
exclaimed, " O Deacon, I am right glad to see you." She
turned to me, and said, "I am ever glad to see the Missionary agent. She handed me a good offering. " Would
you like to have a little circle of prayer?" " Most surely,"
she replied. " Please follow me, and the Deacon follow us."
She was a very pious and talented woman. I rarely ever
heard a prayer that equalled it. The Deacon was in a

flood of tears, and prayed like a man used to it. After
that he was ever ready to alternate. Vermont has some
full-grown hills, and my horse was a little too anxious to
leave each hill to please the good Deacon. As she was
sure-footed, I had no fears. Thinking of the language of
the prophet, " The King's business demands haste," I was
willing to let her spin. So he reproved me in the following
verse :

> " Up the hill urge me not,
> Down the hill press me not,
> On the plain spare me not,
> In the stall forget me not."

As I am near his age, I now think it good advice to all.
The Deacon said, as I landed him safely home, " I feel like
a new man; I would like to accompany you to-morrow."

Westfield is one of the pleasantest villages in Massachusetts.   It is situated on the Westfield river, surrounded by
table-lands, with beautiful groves and glens, probably once
the shores of a lake.   The barrier rocks gave way in the
east part of the valley, and left a very fertile plain, of many
miles in extent, now the site of the village.   In early times
it was a great resort for the Indians, and many relics have
been found, even the stone oven where they cooked their
game. The town has ever been noted for its industry,
morality and intelligence.   During my pastorate, I made
the acquaintance of many eminent men, ranking among the
first in their profession.   The Rev. Dr. E. Davis was then
pastor of the Congregational church, and he and his intelligent and excellent wife were ever ready for any good work
that improved the mind or spiritualized the heart.   They,
and their rich, benevolent church, did much to aid the Baptist church, and seemed ever to rejoice in its prosperity.
I have ever been thankful for many personal favors received
from them.   My attachment to Doctor Davis, by our
mutual labors on the school committee, both in the examination of teachers and by visiting the schools together, was

very strong. Few men were his equal in kind and judicious management. The harmonious feeling between the churches, and in my own church, made my pastorate a very pleasant one. The many acquaintances formed in and out of my parish has ever made Westfield very dear to me. Few places, I am sure, had more intelligent and choice spirits in proportion to its inhabitants than this place.

I left the service of the Missionary Union, and accepted a call at Windsor, Vt. This is an old, venerable town, and in early times was quite as populous as Springfield or Hart. ford. Here is located the Vermont State-prison and the United States Court House. The place is noted for its shady dells and groves — one of which has long been called " Paradise "— and its splendid scenery of mountain ranges. The Connecticut river sweeps gracefully through it, in sight of most of the residences. The Baptist church here was one of the strongest in the State. Rev. E. Hutchinson, a beloved theological classmate, was long the faithful and successful pastor of this church. He had to resign in consequence of illness. For a time they had no pastor, and the church, once a power in the State, began to decline. There had not been a baptism for five years.

Soon after I came, I accepted the chaplaincy of the Vermont State-prison half of the time, the Congregational minister officiating the other half. We were obliged to preach a sermon every Sabbath afternoon after our own service, and visit the prisoners.

Our first labor in the church was to revive the Sabbath-school. Mrs. Alden was appointed associate superintendent, and she and her sister, Miss E. Chamberlain, and other faithful teachers, did much to increase the school. We nearly trebled the number the first year, and made good the library. Seeing the condition of the church, I preached one sermon every Sabbath till October, making over twenty, on the subject of Revivals. The last sermon was from the text found in Nehemiah 4 : 10, "There is much rubbish, so that we cannot build the wall." All the effect I had seen was, as Bunyan expresses it, " Ear-gate was open." Before preaching this sermon, I said, " If I see no symptoms of a revival, I intend to change my subject."

As the assembly was leaving, Dea. Perry Skinner, called one of the best deacons in Vermont by many, met Deacon Hopkins, another good old deacon, as they came into the porch, and said, in tears, as he held on to his hand, " I have nothing to give away; I take all that sermon to myself." Still holding each other by the hand, they confessed and wept, and were joined by some others. Very soon we found a Divine influence permeating the church. From that day a revival commenced that lasted till April of the next year. During most of the months I preached six times a week. That revival settled all old difficulties, and brought into the church a large number, some of marked influence in the town. The work went into the prison. Miss E. Chamberlain circulated tracts there, and one had the title " One Honest Effort," which was the means of the conversion of one prisoner. Ten, we thought, gave evidence of a saving change. Truly Christ preached there " to the spirits in prison." Miss Chamberlain found a father who would not let his children go to the Sabbathschool. As she tried him a second time, still refusing, she left the tract, " One Honest Effort." He read it, was convicted by it. He said to himself, "If that stranger cares so for my soul, I ought surely to care for it." He did. He came to our meetings, asked for prayers, and soon we heard his prayers, and saw him and all his together in church, and he a good member.

Near the close of our revival, Deacon Parker of the Congregational church, who had been a constant and very able worker in all our meetings, was taken sick with the pneumonia. It was a sad disappointment to us all, he was so devoted, affectionate and earnest. Soon as I heard of his illness, I hastened to his dwelling. I found him very sick, but very happy. He lived four days; I was with him more

or less every day. It was soul-inspiring to hear him talk,
and try to sing. I was there the night he died. Feeling
sure we must lose him, I asked him how the "dark valley
of the shadow of death" appeared. He raised both hands,
and with a heavenly smile I can never forget, exclaimed,
"It is not dark; it is light, all light," and tried to sing:

"Jerusalem, my happy home, oh, how I long for thee!"

But his voice failed, and he asked some others to sing it and
several other good hymns. He died happy in the full triumphs of faith. Of all such we may say, "O Death, where
is thy sting!"

Windsor, in years past, was proverbial for its intelligent
and Christian ladies. Ministers and teachers sought their
companions from this lovely vale nestled so closely between
the cultivated Cornish hills and the grand old Ascutney
proudly towering above it. Six or more of our best Baptist ministers found their wives in this delightful spot.
Among them was Drs. Stowe, Porter, Swaine, Day and
Gardner, and Rev. Mr. Hutchinson, all of blessed memory.
Drs. Gardner and Day still live. All were eminent and
successful workers in the vineyard of our God, and those
now living continue faithful and true to the cause of our
blessed Master. The Baptist church has continued to
prosper under the labors of able and successful pastors.

After my appointment as agent of the American and Foreign Bible Society for Southern New England, I removed
to Northampton, Mass. For a time I acted as an agent for
the female college in Worcester, and raised about twelve
thousand dollars. Rev. D. M. Crane was the able and successful pastor there. He was one of my early pupils in the
Franklin Academy at Shelburne Falls. I was his pastor,
and now he was mine. He was a very prudent and zealous
worker, and held on his way there many years, greatly
beloved by the church and community generally. The Insane Hospital is located there. They then had the pastors,
embracing me among them, for their chaplains. Out of

the three hundred patients, not over one hundred were
sober enough to worship in the chapel. There was one
man who gave the closest attention, reaching out his hand
for a handful of truth, and throwing it among the worshippers, and pointing out the ones he thought needed it, then
reached out for more.   Like many professed sane persons,
he took none for himself.   I was preaching, having heaven
for my theme, when an intelligent looking lady, on a front
seat, leaped up farther than I supposed a lady could jump,
exclaiming :

> " I'm ready, I'm ready, I'm ready to go ;
> One moment for heaven I'll leave all below."

She sat beside the superintendent lady, who, when she
came back to the earth, affectionately put her arm around
her. She looked up, meek and apparently happy as an
angel, and remained quiet. Generally there was good order
and attention.

The following is the strangest freak of humanity that I
ever saw, or heard of. A splendid looking man, dressed
richly, and, from his language, I judged a liberally educated
person, wished Dr. Prince, the head physician, to introduce
him to me, at the close of the service. I said to the man,
" Friend, how did you happen to find this splendid boarding-house ? "—it would not do to call it an " Insane Hospital"
to him, for the insane think the only sane persons in the
world are in these hospitals. " How do you like here ? "
said I. *"First rate, first rate.* I think Dr. Prince here is the
best man this side of heaven. You will find I know all
about heaven, if you have time to hear me through."
" Please proceed."   " Well, sir, I am very happy to tell you
that I have made here the greatest speculation, by a
thousand per cent. and more, that was ever made by any
mortal in this world." " Go on, my dear sir, I am very
anxious to hear about it."   " Not more than I am to tell
you. Now, sir, please give me the closest attention, and

see if I do not interest you more by far than you was ever interested. I want you to believe everything I tell you, for I can prove it all. I do not tell lies ; I never told but one in my life, and that was when I was young. I found out all liars would go to hell; and when I found out what an awful place it was, I put on the brakes to my tongue, and durst not tell another lie. It is easy enough to stop, if you put on the brakes in season. If you do not, there will be an awful wreck. Only think of it ! It will run you right straight into hell.

"Well, now, to begin, I was born out West, in the middle of the town of Ohio ! I cannot stop to tell you anything about my pedigree. I went into business when young, and drove it furiously night and day, determined to be a rich man. Almost before I could realize it, I found myself worth one hundred thousand dollars. Most men would be satisfied with that, but, with some, the more they get the more they want. That was my case. I wanted just two hundred thousand dollars, and I wanted, if possible, to make it quick. I spent most of one night planning, and finally it all came out clear. It was to get a contract of the Western States to remove all the mosquitoes. My plan was to make a very light pair of steel wings, and put them on to every mosquito, and when the high northern winds blew, it would send every tormenting bugler into the Gulf of Mexico. I wrote first to the Governor of Michigan, as I was acquainted with him. He wrote me he thought it a fine thing, and ordered five millions sent C. O. D. ; Wisconsin ordered four millions; Iowa, six millions, and Missouri ordered ten millions. It is a great State, and the mosquitoes proportionally large, which made them order so, I think. All said, 'Send soon as may be, C. O. D.' I figured it up, cost of help and material, so that I should make just one hundred thousand dollars. I had the wings all done before I sent off any. I sent to Michigan, C. O. D., and a note came the next mail. 'They are all right-side wings, and are not worth a cent.' On looking over the other packages, I found every one was just so, and instead of making one hundred thousand dollars, I had lost just so much, and was not worth a penny. Besides, I got a little bit of steel into one of my eyes, that no optician, or anyone, could remove. Elate with hope, I bore it bravely, but the terrible loss increased the inflammation, and nearly made me sick. I have a blessed, good wife, who inherited twenty-five thousand dollars, all in the bank. 'Now,' say she, 'my dear husband, it will do you good to travel a while, and here is five thousand dollars; go where you please.' This is the first place that fully satisfied me. Here is the beautiful Connecticut river, with its eight thousand acres of the richest meadow lands. Here towers up, one side, Mt. Holyoke with its pleasant house and grounds on its summit, carrying visitants up by steam. On the other side is Mt. Tom, thirteen hundred feet high, three hundred feet higher than Holyoke. In the rear are beautiful groves and glens and trout brooks, and then here are these splendid buildings, large enough to accommodate five thousand boarders, so I concluded to stop awhile."

"Well, what about the wonderful speculation?"

"Yes, yes; I am coming right to it. One night I lay planning about this steel in my eye. Just before daylight it came out, clear as amber, how I could do it. Get a piece of steel, and put it in the heel, and you can have a telegraph from head to foot, and know just the condition of your system. I submitted it all to Dr. Prince; he is my counsellor, and he is a good one. He said 'It must work well, and I will fix you out, and we will try it.' So first we telegraphed, 'What is the state of the blood, heart, and brain? 'All right,' was the reply. " Is there anything wrong?' 'There is a little redness about one of your eyes and a very little dark-colored mite there.' That showed us it was a perfect work. I then said, 'Doctor, I want to telegraph to God.' Said the doctor, 'I think you had better telegraph first to Gabriel.' So I did, and the response was quick, 'What is wanted, brother?' 'I want to know how many angels there are in heaven?' Here is the exact number," handing me a roll of seven sheets of foolscap paper, beginning with units, etc.

"Why," said I, "that is more in number than all the particles of solid and fluid in this world."

"I should not wonder," said the insane man; "but it is perfectly correct. Gabriel knows; and there are no liars in heaven. The Bible says there is nothing there that 'worketh abomination or maketh a lie.' Did you think there were so many angels there?" I did not know. "Well, you know now. I said, 'Doctor, I want to telegraph direct to God.' 'If you speak reverentially, it may not be wrong.' No sooner did I do it, than instantly there was a response, 'What is wanted, my son?' 'I want to know if such and such ones,' reading off a long list of departed ones, 'are in heaven?' 'Some are and some are not.' On taking the list, I found a number there whom I supposed would never get there, and some not there that I supposed would be. That settled it, for God knows. My great speculation is that I can know all that is transpiring in heaven, earth and hell. Oh, how happy it makes me! No language can describe it," leaping up for joy. "But after all there is a gloom over it all." "Ah! what is that?" "It is a fear that, when I am buried, that steel may get out of my heel. But I have given Dr. Prince the promise of three thousand dollars if he will follow me to the urn and see the steel is in; and he has promised to do it if he outlives me, and to put it in his will, directing his administrator to do it if I outlive him. So I am tolerably sure." "What do you want it in for?" said I. "Don't you know?" "Not surely." "Why, it is to be perfectly ready for the resurrection. When God wants me, I shall come up like a punctual, honest man, when he telegraphs for me."

In my twelve years' labor for the Missionary Union and the Bible Society, I made the acquaintance of many hundred very dear friends that I expect to meet in heaven, or I shall be one of the most disappointed mortals in existence. Most of them are in heaven now. Among the many homes I found to welcome and cheer me, I often think with much pleasure of Deacons Warren, Chapin, and Chase, and Dr. Lawson Long, all of Holyoke; Deacon Knowles and Deacon Ensign and W. Upson of Westfield; Deacon Foster and Dickenson of Springfield; Deacon Blake of Chicopee Falls, and others. I never knew a more able business man than the latter. He was the life of the Baptist church in Chicopee Falls, and the general agent for the factories there for twenty-seven years. He was the adopted father of my son's wife. He was ever cheerful and prompt; a man of wonderful executive ability. The operatives loved, respected and feared him. Why such men are called off in the midst of life and usefulness is a great mystery. But God knows best.

CHAPTER VI.

LATER PUBLIC WORK.

Y appointed field, as agent for the American and Foreign Bible Society, was Massachusetts, Connecticut and Rhode Island. My duty was to preach to as many churches as I could on the Sabbath, collect the offerings on the Sabbath, or take a list and collect from house to house. In some places, such as Providence, Newport, New London, and some other places, I could preach for three churches on the Sabbath. The work was laborious, but very pleasant. A hearty welcome in most places made it so. In some places there was a revival, and I was allowed to spend a few days there, if desired. I began the work in a given State, and went through the State, so that the churches the next year were visited nearly the same month, and day of the month, as in the former year. I was accustomed to gather together groups of youth and children, and tell them Bible and historical stories. I was asked in some cases, where there was a large family of children, to rise before light and tell them such facts as I thought would do them good. I never failed to visit the Sabbath-school on the Sabbath, and give them a cheery talk. It was a great pleasure to do it. I followed this manner of working through the States aforesaid for ten consecutive years, raising more and more each year. On the tenth year, the sum was over three times as much as the first year. At this time, the society was merged into the American Publication Society. I would gladly have worked longer, had not this union been formed. Before

I finished the ten years, I removed to Providence, R. I., as it was nearer the centre of my field.

After the death of my father-in-law, Ephraim Chamberlain, of Cambridgeport, a very worthy and benevolent man, Mrs. Anna Chamberlain, our good mother, spent the last fifteen years of her life with us. She was the daughter of Major Thomas Hovey, of Brighton, Mass., who brought up a very numerous family of excellent children; a family, I think, second to none in that region, in merit and influence. Mother Chamberlain was one of forty-six who formed the First Baptist church in Cambridgeport, and was ever a very prominent and useful member. She died, with us, in Northampton, at the age of seventy-five, a very peaceful and triumphant death. When I saw that we must part with her, I said, "My dear mother, you have been with us fifteen years, and in all that time no act or word of yours has hurt the tenderest feeling of my heart. Your pious, patient and cheerful demeanor has been a good example for us all. We would gladly have you one of our family still, but God is about to take you to your heavenly home. We will lead you affectionately down to the Jordan of death, and pass you into the care of escorting angels, and the God of angels, forever to be in his presence, to mingle with the loved ones gone before, and all the holy family of heaven." She looked up with a cheerful smile I can never forget, and said, "It seems as if I could see them as I never did before," and then her spirit took its joyful flight.

I cannot refrain from speaking of my wife's sister, Miss E. E. Chamberlain, who has been with us since the death of our dear mother, some twenty years since. She is one of the most self-sacrificing Christian women I have ever known, her whole life being devoted to good works. As Providence city missionary for ten years, she did excellent service; and since that time, as well as for many years previously, her work for temperance, and in the Sunday-school, has been one of the most successful and extensive of any woman in this country. For many years she has had

charge of the infant and primary department of the Broadway Baptist church in this city. During this time, over
ten thousand different children have been under her charge,
very many of whom she has gathered together in her missionary work. Truly may she be called the benefactress of
the poor, and a model Sabbath-school worker. May she
long live to continue in this blessed work.

RESIDENCE AT PROVIDENCE.

Myself and family have occupied the above residence
for the past twenty years, overlooking Dexter Common,
one of the most beautiful sites in the whole city. Here
several of my grandchildren were born, John Augustus
Alden and Edward Dana Alden, sons of A. E. Alden.
My son, Adoniram Judson Alden, had recently born in this
house, twins, John Alden and Miles Standish Alden, a great
family event !

In reviewing the scenes connected with the years spent in Providence, there comes before me, the Christian, self-sacrificing life of our cousin, Miss Eliza S. Forbes, who was a member of our family, more or less, for ten years. Her devotion, her steadfastness in the cause of Christ was seldom equalled. Her family associations were of high order, and her intimate friends were those of a literary and intellectual character. She was formerly a member of Mt. Holyoke Seminary, and afterward a teacher in the Institution at Charlestown, Mass. She was compelled from failing health to leave her public duties and to return to her home in Westboro, Mass. After months of suffering, she was given up to die ; but God had a work for her to do, and to the astonishment of her friends she was raised from that bed of sickness to comfortable health. But months of anxiety and years of watchfulness were in store for her, and she accepted without a murmur the appointment of her Heavenly Father, her home being her mission field. She felt that in this world, with all its brilliant prospects, her attainments in science and literature were just nothing in comparison with the approbation and smiles of Him who was all in all to her, the first and last in her heart's best affections.

> " Jesus, on thy breast reclining,
>   I wait thy holy will;
> Hushed be every sad repining,
>   Every anxious thought be still ;
>   Oh, how blessed
>   Here to wait thy loving will !

> " Well thou knowest my heart's deep craving,
>   Something in thy field to do,
> Where are whitened harvests waving,
>   And the laborers are few ;
>   Yet 'tis better
>   Here to wait thy loving will."

It was her privilege to administer to the wants of her beloved parents, who had ever sought the temporal and spiritual welfare of their dear children, and finally to be by their side as they passed to the better land. So one by one the dear family circle was broken, and she remained to be by their side as they neared the shining shore. Three gifted brothers and two lovely Christian sisters, both wives of devoted, efficient ministers, were called from fields of unusual usefulness to go up higher. The love she bore her Saviour, and her deep interest for the church with which, while with us, she was connected, many of the elder members of the Pilgrim Church can bear ample testimony. She highly appreciated the work of both pastor and people, and would often speak of the great privilege she was enjoying of sitting so pleasantly under the droppings of the sanctuary and listening to the words of wisdom from him * who was rich in the experience and knowledge of God's holy Word. She would often sit by the bedside of the sick and dying, and impart to them, through God's grace, that faith and holy trust which through her life helped her to say, " It is the Lord ; let him do what seemeth him good." Her work having been accomplished, the summons came, " Child, your Father calls, come home ! "

> Lord, the lights are gleaming from the distant shore,
> Where no billows threaten, where no tempests roar,
> Long beloved voices calling me I hear ;
> Oh, how sweet their summons fall upon my ear !
> Let me haste to join them ; may it not be so ?
> Loose the cable, let me go !

As I had been through the cities of New England in my missionary working, and though I found many of the cities very pleasant, I felt a preference for Providence on many accounts. My location here was nearest to the Central Baptist church, and I united, with my family, with said church. I have ever found it a very devoted, spiritual church. At that time, Rev. Dr. H. Lincoln was the pastor, and the deacons were Brethren Ham, Butler, Hartwell, Boyce and

---

* Rev. Dr. Laurie.

Hartshorn. I can never forget their fervent prayers, able exhortations and sweet songs of praise. The pastor, Dr. Lincoln, and the first four deacons, have gone to reap their faithful sowings. But they will ever live in endearing and hallowed remembrance from all who knew and loved them. This church has ever been wonderfully blest with excellent pastors. It would be difficult to find a church superior to this in harmony of action, talent and benevolence, or possessed of better officers and pastors. The departed ones were truly superior men, men of God greatly beloved, and ever to be remembered with gratitude. The former official Elijahs have gone up, but we trust their mantle has fallen on good and faithful Elishas, who will be equally kind, spiritual and watchful, and who will finally win as precious a record. The blessings of church relationship, with kind and affectionate leaders, all working in love and harmony, are inexpressible, a rich foretaste of the church triumphant. After completing my Bible agency, I accepted the Missionary agency of the Rhode Island Baptist State Convention. The *Christian Watchman* noticed it thus: "We are happy to learn that the Rhode Island Baptist State Convention have secured the services of Rev. John Alden as their missionary agent. He has been a faithful, successful agent for the Missionary Union for Northern New England, and for the last ten years agent for the American and Foreign Bible Society for Southern New England. From his large success as a pastor, prior to his agency, we trust he will be happy and useful in his present responsible position."

After about two years of toil, finding my health failing under the onerous load, I resigned, and preached as temporary supplies in various churches. Work in something good has ever been my delight. In later years, I have been busy with hands and brain caring for myself and others. About six months since I had a fall, that has hitherto prevented me from travelling, and I now am at work with the pen. If those who come after me find half the pleasure in reading my varied life that I do in living it over by writing, I shall not regret the laborious task.

While here, I was requested to be the poet of the day at the Centennial Celebration of Ashfield, Mass., my native town. Providence, that shapes the destiny of all things, so ordered that I could do it by laying me on a sick bed with a lung fever. Otherwise I might not have found the time. My physician would not let me write but one verse a day. After the doctor and my wife were out, I began courting the Muses, and they so inspired me, I took Spencerian measure, nine lines to a verse, in order to relieve me of the pressure as much as possible.

CENTENNIAL CELEBRATION, JUNE 2, 1865.

"At the east end of a plain, where the beautiful village of Ashfield, Franklin County, Mass., is situated, there was an arch, covered with evergreens and flowers, spanning the street, on the front of which was written, 'Sons and daughters of Ashfield, welcome home.' On the other side was written, 'Our country is free: the greatest year of the age.' On the west end of the village, a similar triumphant arch spanned the street, on which was written, 'June 21, 1765, and June, 1865. The year of jubilee is come. One hundred years old to-day.' A car containing thirty-six ladies, clad in white, and wearing red sashes, with crowns of evergreen, and a white flag in their hands, representing every state in the Union, and with a lady sitting in the centre, dressed in red, white and blue, representing Liberty. Following the car was a wagon with two negroes: one manacled, and named, "Liberty, 1765;" and the other, erect and free, labelled, "Liberty, 1865." After marching through the street, with good lively music, a large procession, under Hon. Henry Dawes, marshal of the occasion, was formed, and escorted by the Shelburne Falls band to a beautiful grove, a little distance north of the village. There was a spacious stand erected. In front of this was a side-hill, well shaded, where benches for many thousands were prepared, all of which were speedily occupied. The marshal called the vast throng to order, and after singing a good original hymn, a very appropriate prayer was offered by Rev. T. Shepard, D. D., of Bristol, R. I., a former beloved pastor in this town. Hon. H. Dawes then delivered an able and thrilling address of welcome. Rev. Dr. William P. Payne then gave the historical oration, a very thorough, able address. After music by the band, the Rev. John Alden of Providence, a native of the town, gave the Centennial poem.

"Mr. Alden, when called for, arose and said, 'Ladies and gentlemen, after listening to the very able address of Dr. Payne (which was an hour and forty minutes long), I think we need a little rest or change. I believe a good hearty general laugh would do us all good, if we can make a raise.' The following anecdote was then told :

"When President Edward Dorr Griffin, decidedly one of the ablest and most eloquent divines America ever had, was professor of Sacred Oratory in Andover Theological Seminary, it is said he called all the students into the rhetorical chamber on important business. They came He arose, a man nearly seven feet in height, of the most dignified and commanding address of any man I ever saw, Daniel Webster not excepted, and said, 'My dear young brethren, fearing the warm weather and your hard studies would make you gloomy dyspeptics, I felt it my imperious duty to call you all here for the remedial purpose of laughing one-half hour.' Calling upon one of the most sober students in the Seminary, saying, 'Brother Stevens, will you begin?' Taken by surprise, his utterance sounded more like a duck than a human being. Yet it struck the right note that vibrated *pro and con* for more than half an hour."

Having my man on the platform, Rev. Charles Porter, pastor of a Congregational church in Boston, an early classmate in the Sanderson Academy in Ashfield, always

ready for any good work, seated among scores of digni-
taries, I said, " Brother Porter, will you begin?" He
made such hearty burst it set the whole throng into convulsive laughter. The first strain was irregular. Mr.
Porter gave the second pitch — he was a fine singer, with
a stentorian voice — and it was followed by some ten thousand voices, more or less, like peals of charming thunder
rolling on thunder. I sat down and enjoyed it, repeated
nearly a dozen times. As I arose, a very corpulent man,
about the only one not standing then, rose slowly, a white-
headed old man, and as he stood erect, said, loud as he
could, " *Yeh, whah, whah, whah!*" That set the ball
rolling afresh, and I sat down again, and as there was a
lull, I arose, when a strong female voice laughed up the
scale to the eighth note, and her voice broke, and she
squalled some like a loon. This caused a humorous convul-
sion. I had to sit down again and laugh, for I could not
help it. Soon a man with a heavy bass voice laughed the
scale down, beginning where the woman left off. The
experiment proved a better success than I expected. That
laughing time so rested the assembly, and, together with
fiery patriotism of the times, saved me from a failure.
Most stood during the fifteen minutes I occupied, cheering
nearly every verse.

The Ashfield soldiers had that day returned from the war.
Seats next to the platform in front of the band were
reserved. They did not all get into the village in season to
march with the multitude. Just as we were seated, we
heard their music by the arm of the lake. The tune was
"Yankee Doodle," double quick, with a good base drum.
When they came in sight, the cheering beat all I ever heard.
It reverberated through the grove, and nearly drowned the
music of the soldiers. They were marched to the seats
reserved, a bronzed, broken band, about half that went to
battle. As I looked on the flag, torn and stained with
blood, and its staff scathed with minie balls or bayonets,
or both, and then beheld the heroes spared, many of them

I knew, I buried my face in my handkerchief and wept, for a long time, tears of joy.

The town had ordered the biggest tent that could be found, and we were to march to it and dine. As we were riding in the carriage for the tent, Mr. Dawes said, "Alden, I liked your poem, and I shall toast you in the tent." I simply replied, "Look out, or I shall shoot back." After the marshal had read many good toasts, he said, "The poet of the occasion — we see a man can be a good educator, a good minister, and a good poet!" It came so unexpectedly hot, for a moment I did not know how to reply. I cooly said, "There are two things I think it difficult for a man to decide as to himself: one is, when he is an *old man ;* and the other is, whether he is a *poet.*" When chaplain of the Vermont State-prison, I saw two boys, five or six years old, and one threw the other down in the mud and water near the prison. As he was some distance ahead of me, I ordered him to let the boy get up. As he did not heed me, I took him by his collar and set him on his feet instanter. He looked up boldly and said, 'Old man, you haven't any business.' Said I, 'Run for home, or I will make business and put both of you in prison.' They heeded me and ran. I was then about thirty-seven years old. As to the other point, Dionysius, called the tyrant of Syracuse, took it into his head to write poetry. After writing I know not how much, he sent for Diogenes, a philospher of his realm, and read it to him, and asked him what he thought of the poetry. He said he had rather not tell him. 'As your sovereign I demand it.' He was noted for his honesty. 'If I *must* answer you, I must honestly say I do not think it very good.' The king was so mad he shut the philosopher up in prison a week, and had him fed on bread and water. He then went to the prison, and told Diogenes to come with him to the palace, where he began again to read his verses. The philosopher took up his hat and cane, and was about to leave. 'Where are you going?' 'To prison if you are going on with that poetry.'" I then turned and said, "The Honorable Marshal of the day — I have not a doubt of his patriotism or oratory. But there is one great fault in the minds of many distinguished men, both sides of Mason's and Dixon's line, that they cannot correct. He remains firm as the everlasting mountains among which he was cradled. What is this fault? You look astonished. Do not be frightened. We are not to blame. What is the fault they find? It is simply this: Sink or swim, survive or perish, he is *determined to stick to the Union.* That is why he has been in Congress so long, and good, I hope and believe, for a few decades more."

THE CENTENNIAL POEM.

Hail, town that gave us birth! Loved Ashfield, hail!
You've summoned all your scattered sons afar,
Once in a hundred years, who on the scale
Of life remain, joyous without a jar,
To view once more their native hills and home,
Scathed by a thousand changes, yet the same
In form and feature,—the old fashioned dome
That tells a thousand tales of childhood's scenes,
From which no sterner acts the spirit ever weans.

A hundred years ago, how wild this town!
The bear, the wolf, the Indian, too, was here,
Who roamed the forests then, looked up or down
In trembling fear; above, around, his ear,
True to his safety, rouses many a fear.
How glorious the change! Forests depart,
All that was wild is gone. Joy starts the tear,
As o'er thy hills and vales we see where Art
Has done its thousand things to gladden every heart.

A hundred years! What scenes have come and gone
In those vast cycles! Thrice our land has shook
With thunder peals of war, the trumpet's tone,
The charge; the fiery chivalry to brook,
In every quarter, portion, lane and nook.
At last, now quailing low at every look
Of truth and justice, waving on our flag
That floats! And still will float o'er earth and sea,
Bright ægis of the land that ever shall be free!

A hundred years! and who have lived and died
In all thy borders in that round of years?
The rude forefathers, men all true and tried,
From earth have passed, 'mid doubts and fears;
The learned and honored, gray as holy seers,
Have gone their way; their venerable forms
Amid a thousand fancies live as yet,
And must forever live.   Their sun is set
But heaven and earth all gloriously have met.

Whoever lives to bless the world, enduring lives;
He starts a wave on mind forever on to roll,
Eliciting new thoughts; eternity then gives
Its endless sweep of thought o'er mind and soul.
So all the books piled high from pole to pole,
Could never treasure half the thoughts of one
Who's on the wave that never had a goal.
When sink the hills, the stars, the moon, the sun,
His swelling peal of everlasting joy is just begun.

Where now thy Porters, Sandersons, and Smiths,
And other heralds of the cross, who blessed
Their race in preaching gospel truths, not myths?
High in their heavenly home in peace they rest,
No wave of trouble more corrodes the breast;
They've gone to reap on the immortal shore,
And left on earth a priceless, rich bequest.
Now bending from their starry home, adore
God there, God here, God's working evermore.

" Full many a son, to fame and fortune known,"
On the long list of Time's retreating tide,
Are thine.   They graced the bar, the desk, have sown
On human hearts, to mould aright and guide.
Their work is done, and sleeping side by side
In the lone churchyard, honored by their names—
Which move the inmost heart and make it glide
Into the hallowed past, which stirs the soul,
By mingling with the loved, who've haply reached their goal.

Hail to the clergy! Sons, or adopted sons,
Who mingle at thy altars, or who preach
In other favored fields.   Ye gifted ones,
Ever rejoice.   Yours the great work to teach
A reckless world how it may safely reach
Peace here on earth, and peace above the skies.
Be faithful, then, and earnest, and beseech
The wayward to be wise, and seek that shore
Where saints and angels shout in bliss forevermore.

Hail, men of all professions, present, past,
Upon thy records, medicine, or law.
They've done their noble work, and now at last,
Ere a new hundred years began, we saw
It meet to praise them well, and thence to draw
From all their many virtues, light and lore,
Our own proud legacy for all coming time.
Thus garnered in fond memory's garnished store,
We'll praise the worthy, now, forever and forevermore.

Hail to our yeomanry ! a noble band,
Life of the town, who onward roll the car
To bless all ranks at home and through the land,
The glory of our nation near or far ;
True to our flag, who've gathered every star,
And thrown them to the breeze in every clime,
And firmly said, 'mid North and Southern foe,
God will avenge the oppressed, and in due time
Roll thunder bolts of wrath in woeful, direful chime.

Hail, teachers of the town ! Your work is great,
Never half prized, rarely rewarded right.
The lady teacher, is the call of late.
Let it be so; we'll ever keep in sight
What best enlightens, strengthens, gives delight.
Then rouse, ye maidens ! out and bless the race,
And ignorance drive to chaos and old night.
Be firm, unless some Jacob with a grace,
May want a private teacher so he'll give a better place.

Soldiers of Ashfield, hail ! a glorious band,
Who, when the traitors dared our rights invade,
And trail in dust the flag, the glory of our land,
And one bold stroke on old proud Sumter made,
Could not sit still and see a foe invade,
Cruel as death, with murder in his soul,
And rouse not for your country and repel the raid.
'Twas yours, ye braves, to hurry and enroll,
And meet the foe and back the tide of battle roll.

O where's the town that lost no soldier son
In fighting for our altars and our homes ?
They sleep in glory's grave.   Never shall one
Be overlooked, while in our now safe domes
We'll treasure up their names.   Thank God ! it comes
Of their proud valor; we've a country yet.
Thrice bought with blood, we'll prize the precious boon,
And on the records high inscribe their names
Who fought our battles through, forever to be Fame's.

Will e'er a band of tyrants ever dare
Again to draw the sword on this our land,
So doubly guarded by God's fostering care?
His heart shall fail, and palsied be the hand
Of one, or every nation, on earth's strand,
Who thinks to crush God's kingdom in the West.
As soon expect shall sink the solid land,
As God forsake us all at sin's behest.
Safe, then, beneath the Almighty arm eternally we'll rest.

Of all the crimes that ever cursed our world,
This century records the crowning one,
And yet it's only Slavery unfurled!
Grow wan, ye stars, and dark thou glorious sun,
While waves of sorrow roll around the world!
Our nation weeps, and must weep on the more
Because her noble leader fell—thus hurled
From glory by a stroke! His life is o'er—
God make his death chase traitor hordes from shore to shore.

We hail the dawn of a long prosperous day;
The shackles off, our country all is free:
Mind now on mind may have unbounded sway,
Light in God's light, all human kind may see,
O triumph of the world! O glorious day!
What of the future now can e'er be told,
In arts and sciences, no bard can say,
Beneath God's smile earth never can grow old,
But gives new light and joy, unfolding to unfold.

This day long severed friends in gladness meet;
This day they part to meet on earth no more.
O! it is heaven begun to feel we'll greet
Our ransomed friends upon the shining shore.
Others may view the heavens that curtained o'er
Our young life, and gaze in rapturous joy;
Others may climb the mountain tops and thread the vales,
Follow the streams, hear God in nature's voice,
And do as we did once, amid it all rejoice.

A hundred years, this day begins its dawn.
None here expects to live that period through,
We all shall pass away before the morn
Of that far distant day, to rise anew
We trust, and higher joys in heaven pursue;
Yet while on earth we stay, God help us all
To nobly act our part, be faithful, true,
To God and man, that when in death we fall,
Our works may follow us. read and approved by all.

"We cannot better portray the elastic and buoyant spirit of our classmate, Mr. Alden," says Rev. Dr. Sabin in the history of his college class, which he was appointed to write, "than by quoting from his response to a letter of invitation to him to attend a meeting of his college class at the thirty-fifth anniversary of their graduation.

"'REV. LEWIS SABIN, D. D.:

"'My dear brother classmate, and for two years my excellent roommate, it would give me great pleasure to meet our class again, but such are my official duties, I cannot consistently do so. I will write you simply to say, as Daniel Webster said, I *live*; live with Massachusetts, Connecticut and Rhode Island on my hands as agent of the American and Foreign Bible Society; live to write Centennial poems for my native town as often as the Fates roll the centuries from their spindles; live, enjoying life, with a prosperous family honorably settled around me; live, joyfully thinking of those beloved classmates of ours, the best the world ever produced, or ever can; live with enough to live on, yet wanting a little more; live without any of the peevishness incident to old age, but growing, I think, more cheerful and contented daily; live, rejoicing, my dear brother, that I did not get the valedictory from you, for whom I had too much love and respect to do any such thing; live trying to follow the golden rule of loving my neighbor as myself, so if he is apparently the most prosperous it makes no difference, it is all in the family. So I live, now sixty years old, and good, for aught I know, for a decade or two more.'

"Those of us who have been accustomed to meet Mr. Alden," says Mr. Sabin, "could not fail to see how his sunny and wholesome cheerfulness has kept him young and happy, bringing forth fruit of active usefulness, when, otherwise, feebleness and decay might be expected."

1833.   FIFTIETH   1883.

WEDDING ANNIVERSARY

OF THE

REV. MR. AND MRS. JOHN ALDEN,

AT THE

CENTRAL BAPTIST CHURCH,

Providence, R. I.,

WEDNESDAY EVE'NG DEC. 5, FROM 7 TO 10.

PROGRAMME.

ORGAN VOLUNTARY.

Reading, 23d Psalm,	Rev. J. W. Olmstead, D. D.
Invocation,	Rev. J. C. Stockbridge, D. D.
Singing,—"He Leadeth Me,"	
Introductory Remarks,	Rev. R. Montague.
Biographical Sketch,	Rev. J. Taylor, D. D.
"Old Oaken Bucket,"	Church Quartette.
Original Poem,	Rev. F. Dennison.
Reminiscences,	Rev. O. P. Gifford.
Hymn.—"Rock of Ages,"	
Missionary Labors,	Rev. H. M. Bixby, D. D.
Hymn.—"From Greenland's Icy Mountains,"	
Ceremony,	Rev. Richard Montague.
Prayer,	Rev. J. V. Osterhout.

CONGRATULATIONS.

College Life at Amherst,	Rt. Rev. Thomas M. Clark, D. D.

CHURCH QUARTETTE.

Letter Reading,	Dr. Bixby and Rev. B. S. Morse.
Reminiscences of Newton,	Rev. S. Field.

CHURCH QUARTETTE.

Letters from Churches, - - - - - - Individual and informal.
Remarks by Rev. J. T. Smith, D. D., H. M. Puffer, Esq., Rev. W. H. Eaton, Rev. J. V. Osterhout, and D. F. Crane, Esq.
Hymn.—"When Shall We All Meet Again, - - - - Church Quartette.
    BENEDICTION.—Rev. W. F. Armstrong.

EDITORIAL FROM PROVIDENCE JOURNAL, DEC. 6, 1883.

FIFTY WEDDED YEARS.— PLEASANT OBSERVANCE OF THE GOLDEN ANNI-
VERSARY OF REV. JOHN ALDEN AND WIFE AT CENTRAL BAPTIST
CHURCH.

The parlors of the Central Baptist church were filled with the relatives and friends of the Rev. John Alden, a noted instructor and preacher of the Baptist denomination, principally in Western Massachusetts, for the past forty years, and his estimable wife, assembled to tender their congratulations on the attainment of the golden anniversary of their marriage. The celebration was arranged by committees of the churches in Shelburne Falls, North Adams, and Westfield, in co-operation with the members of the family and friends of the Central Baptist church of this city, and a most interesting and entertaining programme was arranged. There were two sons, four grandchildren, and a picture of a great-grandchild present, the immediate family and a large representation of clergymen from Boston, and pastors of churches in this city and vicinity. The aged couple were well preserved and in the enjoyment of remarkably good health, entering most heartily into the festivities of the occasion.

The exercises opened with reading the twenty-third psalm by the Rev. Mr. Olmstead, of Boston, followed by prayer by Rev. Dr. Stockbridge. After singing by the choir, Rev. Mr. Montague, of the Central Baptist Church, made some appropriate remarks touching the significance of the occasion, and the Rev. J. Taylor, D. D., then read an interesting biographical sketch of Rev. Mr. Alden. It was learned that John Alden was a lineal descendant of the Pilgrims, and was born in the town of Ashfield, Mass., Jan. 10, 1806, and belonged to a family of twelve children, most of whom lived to a mature age and filled posts of influence. His father and one of his brothers, the youngest child in the family, were, like himself, preachers of the gospel. The family held an influential position in the region, on account of its wealth, intelligence, and social position. Young John was forced to surrender his hard physical toil on the farm, and became a student at Amherst in 1827. Mention was made of his diligent application to the enrichment of his mind, and his graduation in 1831. The late Dr. N. A. Fisher, of this city, and the Rev. Dr. Thatcher Thayer, of Newport, were among his classmates.

He entered Newton Theological Seminary, on leaving college, and remained there two years. Pleasant allusion was made to his courting period in Cambridgeport, and the joy at his home when the bride appeared. Attention was then directed to his entry upon the pastorate at Shelburne Falls, in his native county, and his taxing double service as principal of the Academy, both being sustained for seven years with eminent success. For six years he was pastor of the North Adams church; then, at Westfield, where he prepared a history of the village; then in Southboro, and afterwards chaplain of the State-prison at Windsor, Vt. He has also served the denomination to which he belongs as agent for mission and Bible work. Since 1867 he has resided in this city, and a few years since was the poet on the occasion of the centennial celebration of his native town. Of the three children born to Mr. and Mrs. Alden, one found an early grave. A little grandson of remarkable beauty and promise died in this city a few years ago. Most of the large family of sisters and brothers, of which Mr. Alden was so conspicuous a member, have gone to the home beyond.

An original poem, composed by the Rev. Frederick Dennison, was then read in his absence by the Rev. Mr. Montague, which gracefully and impressively commemorated the occasion, and met with pleasant recognition. The Rev. O. P. Gifford, of Boston, responded to the invitation to call up some interesting reminiscences. Aside from those contained in Dr. Taylor's biography, mention was made of his commencing teaching at the age of seventeen; his organization of what was afterwards known as Franklin Academy; his term of service in the academy, during which he had over two thousand pupils, more than two hundred of whom experienced religion, and fifty became ministers; his formation of the First Baptist church at Shelburne Falls, the result of seven years' labor being one hundred and fifty members, a new house of worship, and the strongest church in the Franklin association; his pastorate of six years at

North Adams, where he baptized more than two hundred, among them heads of families, six merchants and manufacturers, whose wealth was estimated at two million dollars; this church now has about nine hundred communicants; at Westfield he raised the debt and added some seventy members to the church in his six years' pastorate; and his agency for Southern New England of the American and Foreign Bible Society, which he held for ten years, doubling the contributions of former years. He is now, to use his own words, " in his seventy-eighth year, waiting patiently for the Master's summons." The address was enlivened by sparkling and witty anecdotes, which were duly appreciated. After singing "The Old Oaken Bucket," Rev. Dr. Bixby spoke in terms of the highest eulogy of Brother Alden's missionary work, which might be said to be the brightest, best, and most fruitful years of his remarkable ministerial life. Then the hymn, "From Greenland's Icy Mountains," was sung, and the nuptial ceremony was most impressively performed by the Rev. Mr. Montague, with eloquent reference to their happy married life for half a century, the closing prayer being offered by Rev. J. V. Osterhout, of the Broadway Baptist Church. Then came a season of congratulation from the assemblage, taking the form of cordial hand clasps, and the bestowal of substantial tokens of love and respect. Rt. Rev. Bishop Clarke was called upon to give some reminiscences of college life at Amherst, and he recalled many pleasant incidents in his associations with Mr. Alden, alluding humorously to his matrimonial entanglement and his memorable contest with Dr. Thatcher Thayer of Newport, as story tellers, which commenced at six o'clock in the evening and lasted till midnight, ending in a drawn game, no story to be waited for over a minute, under the conditions. He referred to the confidence and respect John Alden won from his classmates, and hoped that he would live to celebrate his diamond wedding. After a solo by Mrs. Chaffee, letters were read by Dr. Bixby from Dr. Thayer and Mr. J. A. Pratt of

Shelburne Falls, the latter having been a pupil of Principal Alden at Franklin Academy. Rev. Mr. Field read an interesting sketch of reminiscenes at Newton. After which letters from the following named gentlemen were read : Dr. J. A. Sherman, of New York, who mailed twenty five-dollar gold pieces ; Hon. Peter Parker, of Washington, D. C., who enclosed fifty gold dollars ; Rev. Messrs. Eaton, of Westfield, and Crane, of Shelburne Falls ; Dr. Osborne, of North Adams church, who inclosed a pecuniary token of esteem in behalf of the church; Rev. Geo. Felton, of Greenville, Mass. ; Hon. Henry L. Dawes, of Pittsfield, and others. The Rev. Dr. Smith followed with some interesting remarks, as also a nephew of Mr. Alden, H. M. Puffer, Esq., of Shelburne Falls.

Among the pleasing features of the gift-making was the presentation of a tiny picture of the great grand-child, born two months ago, by Miss Lena Hunt, in a verse or two of poetry, very prettily delivered ; also a large picture, in six parts, containing views of the birth-place of Mr. Alden, the churches over which he held pastorate, Franklin Academy, Amherst College and Newton Seminary, a most appropriate and acceptable gift from his son, A. E. Alden, of Boston. The employees of the Alden Photo Co., of Providence and Boston, gave a purse of gold. Joel Goldthwaite, of Boston, J. R. Rand and Addison Rand, of New York, and many other friends were among the list of contributors. Rev. Mr. Alden was called upon to make a response, and did so in some verses which conveyed his deep gratitude and appeciation of the efforts of all who had participated in the festival. The choir then sang " When shall we all meet again," and the company was dismissed with the benediction.

A RECOGNITION OF THE MARRIAGE CEREMONY BY REV. R. MONTAGUE.

Marriage is an ordinance of God, old as the family of man. It has been the basis of social order, the nourisher of domestic affections, the inspirer of noble and unselfish character in all the history of our race. Moses honored it; Christ enforced it; the Apostles commended it; God blessed it. The union brings together two congenial spirits, whose affections intertwine so lovingly as to express a common hope and purpose; yet the individuality, by its very distinctness, enriches the common fund of happiness. The wife becomes more manly, and the husband more womanly, and thus both are more perfected.

For fifty years, my friends, you have borne a common name, shared a common work, honored God and travelled toward a common heaven. For fifty years has the love that led to this union been ripening, growing in strength and purity, until you stand, not as you stood at first, to make your vows of marriage love, looking eagerly to the future, but now to recall the joys and sanctified sorrows of a rich and honored past. Fifty years ago you plighted troth, so long as you both should live. To-night the old vows rest easily and joyously upon you, and need no renewal. It is an hour for gratitude and praise. May God spare you, my brother and sister, to each other and your dear family, for years to come. May your life be so increasingly hallowed as daily to suggest that dear and indissoluble union between the Lord and his church, between Christ and his purchased body, that body whose servants you long have been, and whose members may you long continue to be. The Lord bless and keep you; the Lord make his face to shine upon you evermore. Amen.

PRESENTATION OF PHOTOGRAPHIC VIEWS.

MADE BY AUGUSTUS E. ALDEN TO HIS PARENTS, ON THE EVE OF THEIR GOLDEN WEDDING ANNIVERSARY AT THE CENTRAL BAPTIST CUHRCH, PROVIDENCE, R. I., DEC. 5, 1883, EMBRACING THEIR BIRTH- PLACES, CHURCHES, INSTITUTIONS OF LEARNING, WITH WHICH THEY ARE AND HAVE BEEN CONNECTED.

My dear father and mother, it is with pleasure that we meet you here this evening to congratulate you on this, your Golden Wedding anniversary. It is with deep, heart-felt gratitude to the Giver of all good and perfect gifts, that he in his tender mercy has spared you both to us so many years. But when I look on you, so advanced in life, I am reminded, ah, too well, that you are fast passing away; and it becomes us, your children, who owe a debt of gratitude that all children owe to parents, to gather around you now more closely, watch over and care for you and endeavor to make your last days your most pleasant and happy ones,—and may you yet be spared to us many years.

It seems quite fitting at this time to present to you a memento. The views presented will doubtless carry you back to the very early days of your childhood. Many of these memories are very pleasant, and some sad, and so on through your years of toil and usefulness. The different views herein presented will bring to your recollection many scenes of your life work. Please accept this frame of pictures, as a token of remembrance, from your son, Augustus E. Alden.

Rev. John Alden's Golden Wedding, Dec. 5, 1883

BY REV. F. DENNISON.

The Lord of old to Moses said,
  And bade it writ on holy page,
Rise up before the hoary head,
  And pay just reverence to age.

The ancient mandate still holds sway
  Since words of meetness never die;
No righteous rule shall fade away
  Until the stars forsake the sky.

To-day two veterans are named,
  The lines inlinked for fifty years,
For valor and for virtue famed,
  Triumphant over foes and fears.

They've seen the tide of conflict roll,
  And bravely acted in the strife;
They've steady pressed towards the goal
  And well-nigh reached the crown of life.

What though their annual ides have run
  Almost fourscore 'neath varying skies;
They greet to-day a golden sun,
  And view it with a sweet surprise.

Is this John Alden that we see?
  Yes, both of Pilgrim name and blood:
Nor has he shamed his pedigree,
  Or dwarfed the vein of brotherhood.

Obedient to the call of God,
  Accepting John the Baptist's view,
Himself has Jordan's waters trod,
  And led a thousand converts through.

A champion in his day of strength,
  The foes of truth, he fearless faced,
And won such victories at length
  As chroniclers have proudly traced.

Full high his hands have held the cross,
  Above all earthly honor prized;
What men call gain he counted loss
  To magnify the name of Christ.

Nor less devoted by his side,
  As helper in all works of grace,
The one selected as his bride,
  And ever worthy of her place.

The world from noble women still
  Receives its highest Christian charms,
As from their lips in worship thrill
  With sweetest notes, our holiest psalms.

There is no ministry on earth
  Like that of woman's changeless love,
Its beauty of celestial birth
  Reflecting that which reigns above.

This pair, like palms by Jordan's brink,
  Whereto unfading life is given,
While of waters here they drink,
  Lift up their fruited crowns to heaven.

So, brother, teacher, preacher, friend,
  Anew we hail thee and thy bride;
To both e'en to your journey's end,
  The pledge of heaven be verified.

We bring our debt of reverence,
　Far more than language of our lips,
And share in your sweet confidence
　Of everlasting fellowship.

MR. ALDEN'S RESPONSE.

Thanks, first, to *Him* enthroned above,
A God of majesty and love,
Seen in his image stamped on man,
The sexes two, a wondrous plan
To happy make the human race,
Sorrow divide and woes efface.
Thanks to the *donors* one and all,
Respondents to this final call.
Thanks to the *pastors*, true and kind,
Who tried in vain a way to find
To make the hymeneal knot more sure,
Bound once, forever to endure.
Thanks to the *singers*, whose sweet lays
Have won them everlasting praise.
Thanks for this *beauteous house of prayer*,
To meet our friends, and with them share
Congratulations, hearty, kind ;
Such joys on earth we seldom find.
Thanks to the *Marshal*,* ever true
To serve the dead and living too,
Whose usefulness can only be
Measured by an eternity.
Thanks to the *speakers*, whose rich strains
Have roused our hearts, and thrilled our brains ·
May their reward the treasure be,
To have one wife a century.

Would you have one wife fifty years
In world of death, of sighs and tears ?
Praise every worthy act, and she,
More ardently will love and be
Dear and more dear continually;
A priceless jewel, lustrous, bright,
A sun by day, a star by night.
Though God ordained the husband head,
If side by side they meekly tread
Life's stormy maze, nor strive for power,
Smoothly will life glide on each hour,

---

* Deacon Boyce, both deacon and sexton.

Let both feel wedded sure for life,
One husband only, one good wife.
'Tis God's own law, and happy they
Who tread the path and never stray.
The parties two, let man decide,
And far as may be please his bride,
The law obeyed, the victory 's won,
Two happiest souls beneath the sun,
Seeking each other's highest joy,
A boon complete without alloy.

Soon child and youth, and men of sterling worth,
Must parted be, and pass away from earth.
Then may we sink as sinks the evening star,
When lingering o'er the western hills afar,
With undiminished and unclouded light,
Still mild, still pure, still pleasant and still bright.
With no volcanic roar, convulsive throe,
Wild tumult or fierce blaze, she sinks below.
Then may we rise in heaven's unclouded light,
Eternally to praise in rapturous delight.

CHAPTER VII.

FIFTY WEDDED YEARS.

BIOGRAPHICAL STATEMENT BY JEREMIAH TAYLOR, D. D., A
RELATIVE OF REV. JOHN ALDEN.

EW names in New England have been more honored for over two centuries than that of John Alden. The pilgrim of this name has the traditionary honor of being the first person who leaped from the ship on to the *rock* of Plymouth harbor, from the company of pilgrims who landed there in 1620. He also has earned for himself a distinguished place among the illustrious men of the period, as one who spoke for himself at the suggestion of Priscilla Mullins, when commissioned to woo her heart and hand for another.

The descendents of John Alden, the pilgrim, have held in such veneration and high esteem the many virtues of their great-grandmother Priscilla, and have so admired her picture as delineated in art, and have been so enraptured by the recital of her praises in the songs of Longfellow, that they have never regretted, that, in the matter of courtship, their great ancestor was a little too smart for the noble Captain Standish.

Our friend, the worthy guest of this occasion, is a lineal descendent of the pilgrims, and we may reasonably suppose from the fact that he took his choice from the fair maidens of Cambridge, Mass., when he led Miss Ann Maria Chamberlain to the bridal altar, that he inherited not a little of the wooing spirit of his illustrious progenitor. Mr. Alden took the name of his father, and during all his early years, he was John Alden, Jr.

He was born in Ashfield, Mass., in 1806, and as the dates show, was of ripe age when he entered those matrimonial alliances which have held him for fifty years. The fact that his life has continued so far down toward the close of the century, with the commencement of which it began, speaks well for the tender love and fostering care which has attended these parties in the changing busy scenes of the family during all the matrimonial voyagement. It does not seem possible that the domestic machinery should have run on for so long a period with promise of remaining many years yet to come, unless at all times the running of the household gear was free from friction and in the best of order. In this bad age of so much domestic infelicity, surely those who have set so good an example of loving and patient continuence ought to wear a golden crown.

Mr. Alden belonged to a family of twelve children, most of whom lived to mature age, and filled posts of influence. He was reared among the hallowed influences of religion; and his home was open to ministers of the gospel, who came as they pleased, and stayed as long as they pleased, and departed with just as much money, if not a little more, than when they came. It would be rare to find a house that disbursed a more generous hospitality. His father's house was a house of prayer, where not only the children, but all the laborers, in doors and out, were gathered around the altar of family worship. His father and one of his brothers, the youngest child in the family, were, like himself, preachers of the gospel.

The first years of his life were spent at home on the farm. In 1825, he united with the Baptist church in Ashfield. Soon after, he commenced his preparatory studies for College in Amherst Academy, and graduated at Amherst College in 1831. It was my privilege, as his kinsman and resident in the family, to drive him back and forth over the twenty miles of distance between his home and the college. Many a time during the years constituting the term of study then, and much of the inspiration which carried me a student to the same institution a dozen years later, was derived from those pleasant drives and choice companionship by the way. Mr. Alden early sought to enrich his native town through the stores of knowledge which he had acquired. I doubt not he recalls, with great satisfaction, the address he gave in the school-room where he was once a learner, on the battle of New Orleans, under Gen. Jackson, in 1815. The lecture was illustrated with maps of his own drawing, and was so well prepared and

delineated as to gain him nearly as much praise as that
bestowed upon the old hero of the battle ; but it did not
bring him to the presidency of the United States, and I do
not really think he had any such aspirations when he prepared the lecture.   The late Dr. N. A. Fisher, of this city,
of pleasant memory, Rev. T. Thayer, D. D., of Newport,
and Bishop T. M. Clark and Hon. Peter Parker, of Washington, were his classmates.   On leaving college, he
entered Newton Theological Seminary, and while there
accepted the call to take charge of the Franklin Academy,
at Shelburne Falls, Mass., where he held the double relation of principal and pastor six years.

I well remember the scene in the old homestead at Ashfield, when the son and brother came back bringing his
bride with him.   There was unusual joy ; a new offering of
thanksgiving and praise was laid upon the family altar.   It
was an auspicious beginning of married life consecrated to
the service of God, and which now stands before us encir-
cled with the golden sheaves of fifty years.   Mr. Alden
entered upon his public professional life at Shelburne Falls,
his native county.   He undertook to do double service.
He became pastor of the church in that now thriving village, and also principal of the academy, which had just
been planted there.   Either field of labor was enough to
tax the energies of any young man; yet, during the six
years that he held these responsible situations, eminent
success attended his labors.   In all these duties, the young
wife was a burden-bearer by his side, a helpmeet such as
God makes for a man when he gives him a paradise complete.   This certainly was the most successful period in the
history of this institution.   Subsequently we find our
friend for six years pastor at the Baptist church in North
Adams, then at Southboro, then at Westfield, Mass., afterward at Windsor, Vt., where he was pastor of the Baptist
church and officiated as chaplain a part of the time at the
Vermont State-prison.   He has served his denomination as
the agent for foreign missions in Northern New England,
and for the Bible Society in Southern New England.
Since 1867, his home has been in this city.   When his
native town celebrated its hundredth anniversary, Mr.
Alden was the poet of the occasion.

This long life has not been devoid of bereavements.
Again and again they have been in situations which might
have led them to exclaim, "All thy waves and billows have

gone over me." But, to-day, they who travelled so far together, stand erect, trusting in God, and it does not become us to moisten the riper golden sheaves even with the dew of tears. Of their three children, one found an early grave; also a little grandson of remarkable beauty and promise died a few years ago in this city. Most of the large family of brothers and sisters, of which Mr. Alden was so conspicuous a member, have gone to the home beyond. Yours, truly,

J. Taylor.

LETTER FROM SENATOR H. L. DAWES.

PITTSFIELD, Nov. 29, 1883.

REV. J. ALDEN:

My dear sir, Mrs. Dawes and myself send you and Mrs. Alden our most hearty greetings and congratulations, on this anniversary, so laden with precious memories and gracious providences.

Your kind invitation takes us back over many years, when, in North Adams, strangers among a strange people, the hand of friendship was extended to us, and it has never been forgotten or withdrawn; looking back over those years, full of vicissitudes and rich reminiscences, how valuable such a friendship proffered when friends were most needed. To you, my dear friends, this must be an hour of supreme happiness, filled with gratitude to God for his manifold mercies, and to the friends he has gathered around your footsteps in the long journey he has permitted you to travel together. How precious to you must be the evidences multiplied on every hand of the love of those among whom you have lived. They are a tribute to your fidelity. May you be long descending together the western slope, with not a stone in your pathway, or a thorn by the wayside. And may this journey, full of years of usefulness, end only in the glory of a cloudless, golden sunset.

Most truly yours,

H. L. Dawes.

BLACKINTON, Nov. 20, 1883.

REV. AND MRS. JOHN ALDEN:

Dear friends, I congratulate you on the fiftieth anniversary of your marriage. May you live to see many more happy days. God is good to spare you to each other so many

years. I have not forgotten your labors in Blackinton thirty
years ago. Eternity only can reveal to us the blessings
of that revival. It was a miracle of grace to see business
men seeking the Saviour and humbly asking the prayers
of God's people. Most of that happy number are praising God in heaven. Soon, it may be very soon, we shall
join them there.

Sincerely yours,

C. BLACKINTON.

REMARKS BY REV. J. T. SMITH, D. D.

In occupying a few moments among all the pleasant
words of this interesting occasion, I very well know that it is
not that I have any special gift to interest an audience in a
little speech. This is asked of me because I, with her who
has stood with me beside this worthy couple, have been
their life-long friends.

My relations with Rev. Mr. Alden commenced while I
was a youth in my native town in Western Massachusetts.
The church of which I was a member had built a meeting-
house, and sent for Mr. Alden, then Principal of Shelburne
Falls Academy, to preach the dedication sermon. The
impression of that eloquent sermon still lingers among my
youthful memories. I can testify to the high reputation of
the Franklin Academy under his care, both educationally
and religiously.

Williams College was celebrated for its revivals. Not
less so was Franklin Academy at Shelburne Falls, Mass.
Not only was it understood that good scholars were turned
out there, but unconverted pupils left in a great many cases
truly devoted Christians. I can also testify in all his work,
as teacher and pastor. Mrs. Alden was ever his efficient
helpmeet, to whom he owed much of his large success. My
next point of contact with our brother was in connection
with North Adams. I had suggested to one of the deacons
that I thought Mr. Alden might be obtained as the pastor
of the North Adams church. The good deacon thought it
might be well to make the trial, and sent for him to supply
the church for a Sabbath. The experiment quickly resulted in a unanimous call, which was promptly accepted.
In that pastorate, at the opening of that great revival,
which brought such a company of the business men of
North Adams into the Baptist church, with all their

wealth and influence, I was with him as a fellow worker. The revival began in a special effort in a manufacturing village about two miles from the centre, completely sweeping it, and bringing in almost all the business men and their families. After this work, the effort was begun in North Adams Centre. I well remember the difficulties he had in securing the united co-operation of the church at its beginning, and the energy with which he said to me, "The meeting shall go on, though it requires the head of John the Baptist." It did go on, and the revival recommenced with mighty power. That revival settled the position of the Baptist church in that village, as the leading church in Western Massachusetts. During this period of his history, it was that I made a selection of, to me, the dearest and most lovable lamb of his flock as my very own, which in due time I received with his benediction. Ever since, while I have been her accepted minister, he has been her pastor. Perhaps to make it all plain, she had excellent reasons to feel an unusual and lasting attachment to him, as he was the instrument in the conversion of several of her brothers and sisters, at the time of the revival I have spoken of, most of whom were baptized by him. Besides, her honored father was the active co-operating deacon of the church at that time, and his intimacy in the family, and his ministrations with them in domestic joys and sorrows, established this tie, not easily sundered. In all subsequent changes, I have been his, and my wife has been her confiding friend. We have never been thrown so far apart but that a good degree of intimacy could be kept up. We rejoice with them in every token of honor and esteem which this happy occasion is bringing them. I am happy to declare, that among all contemporary ministers of any denomination, I know of none who have achieved a more honorable or enviable name, or record of labor and success, in different lines of public service, than Rev. John Alden.

Fraternally yours,

J. T. Smith.

LETTER FROM ROBERT CRAWFORD, D. D.

Champaign, Nov. 25, 1883.

Rev. John Alden and Mrs. Ann M. C. Alden:

Much esteemed friends, I thank you much for the kind remembrance on my own part and that of my children.

My beloved wife was included in this invitation, but for more than two years she has been with the blessed ones, where they "neither marry or are given in marriage." She and I cannot celebrate our Golden Wedding here, but I trust we may in the city where the streets are golden and the gates are pearl. You may be with us then. With warm and sincere affection, I congratulate you both, my dear friends, on the event you are anticipating as the crown of your married life of fifty years. I thank God on your behalf that you have been spared so long to each other, and that you have been permitted to see so much good and so little sorrow in your family life. May the good Lord bless you still, and spare you so long as it is best for you both, and if it is right for me to wish it, may your separation be short. But God knows best. Your kind invitation carries me back to the summer of 1840, when I first knew you as pastor of the North Adams church, when you kindly extended to me the right-hand of fellowship, as the pastor of the Congregational church of that place. I remember the cordial reception given by you both to my dear wife and me, who were strangers to almost all in the place. We were then, with trembling hearts, just entering the marriage relation and pastoral work. I remember distinctly the proposition you made, and to which I heartily assented, that as we were to be together pastors of churches near each other, but of different names, that we would try to work together for the upbuilding of Christ's kingdom, in love and harmony, preaching our sentiments to our own church, as duty seemed to dictate, but abstaining from any personal discussion between ourselves. I thought the agreement a wise one, and I am happy to say it was religiously observed by us both. I rejoice with a thankful heart in thinking over the unbroken and intimate Christian friendship and intercourse, and co-operation in Christian work in which we were united in all the years we were together in that busy place. There were two scenes and services of bereavement which brought us very near together in Christian affection and sympathy. I could wish truly to be with you on the evening of December 5th, but cannot, I am so far away from my home in Deerfield. Were my wife with me as in years gone by, I am sure we should be interested to be with you. We know not how much our departed Christian friends know of us. God cares for us. What deeply interests us of a spiritual nature interests him. I think we may cherish the thought that those whom we call *ours*, though he has taken them to himself, will still have an interest in us, and know something of our earthly affairs. It may be they know more and are more interested than we imagine. It is at least pleasant to think they are ours still, and that they remember us as being still theirs. I am pastor still of the Congregational church in Deerfield. I am now in my eightieth year. Wishing you a happy issue of your Golden Wedding, and the best of heaven's blessings now and evermore, I remain,

Yours in Christian love,

R. CRAWFORD.

LETTER FROM DR. THAYER.

NEWPORT, R. I., Nov. 3, 1883.

My DEAR BROTHER ALDEN :

The physician's orders keep me quite at home. Besides, a moment's thought should convince you that my advanced age utterly unfits me for a connubial frolic with such an extraordinary juvenile as you are. Once indeed I was considerably younger than you. But that was fifty years ago. Now, if I may judge from the neighings of your Pegasus, you must have wonderfully renewed your youth, and reversed our old relation. Nevertheless, I remember affectionately that old relation, your genial spirit, your kindly Christian interest in me, a boy. Amid the scenes and persons in college life, now growing dim, I recall distinctly your pleasant intercourse with your classmates, and the feeling of confidence with which they ever regard you. There are few of us left to testify this. But I will speak for all. Doubtless you will hear many pleasant things said to-day, but count not the least this testimony to the affection and esteem in which you are held by your college classmates. God bless you, my dear brother, and the faithful, loving wife of fifty years.

Affectionately and truly your classmate,

THATCHER THAYER.

LETTER FROM DR. PETER PARKER, WASHINGTON, D. C.

My DEAR BROTHER ALDEN :

Your affectionate letter, of November 5, was duly received. The state of my health explains my delay in an-

swering the letter. I have long suffered from spinal difficulties, rendering it impossible to express myself in writing.
Never before have I so realized my proximity to two
worlds. One is receding, and soon to be left ; and the other
in prospect, soon to be entered. How interesting the long
retrospect to both of us ! How inconceivable the eternal
prospect ! It does not appear what we shall be. Oh, the
divine assurance ! Fifty years you have lived with the wife
of your youth, and are now expecting a Golden Wedding.
I cannot be present, but I enclose, commemorative of the
fifty years, a corresponding number of golden dollars.

Affectionately yours,
PETER PARKER.

LETTER FROM REV. GEORGE D. FELTON.

EAST GRANVILLE, MASS., NOV. 17.

MR. AND MRS. ALDEN :

Precious dear old friends,— never more so than now.
God bless you, and cause his golden sun to shine bright
upon you on the fifth of December. For a bright day, a
cheery day, a golden day, we will fervently pray ; also that
many golden pieces and golden speeches may be made to
gladden your hearts. We assure you, dear friends, that
nothing would afford us more profound delight than to
mingle with the happy throng whose kindly greetings and
cheerful gifts will demonstrate the strong attachment felt
for the personal worth and abundant labors which we
know have brought their priceless reward. May that demonstration be so vivid that it shall never be effaced from
memory, and never cease to cheer, while the winter of old
age shall continue. This allusion brings vividly to mind
incidents and scenes of more than forty years ago, that
thrill my heart with gratitude,— the old Franklin Academy, the old Mansion house, those pleasant groves and
walks where I spent hours of heavenly converse, the
embowered path to the baptismal waters, so often trod by
obedient and rejoicing subjects, the old familiar hymn,
" Whither goest thou, pilgrim stranger ? " sung by inspiring
voices that vibrated through the grove, and the stream
itself. Bless God for the old Deerfield river, the baptistry
of Shelburne Falls. Then, too, that blessed revival, when
prayer-meetings in different rooms were frequent ; when
Christians were weeping over and praying for anxious ones,

and trying to rouse the careless ones to seek the Lord. Do you remember being sent for at about eleven o'clock at night, to come to the chapel, and converse and pray for many anxious ones, who felt that they could not go to their rooms until they had made their peace with God? Then, too, those morning prayer-meetings in the chapel at break of day,— there it was that the spirit of the Lord touched my heart and sent me to my room to devote the day to fasting and prayer, that the path of duty might be made plain before me, and I be willing to walk in it. The struggle of that day removed all my doubts as to what Jesus would have me do, and my soul was made joyful in the thought that it was my privilege to tread in the footsteps of my Divine pattern, enter the liquid grave and come up in the likeness of Christ's resurrection. Then came the first covenant meeting, and that joyful Sabbath when seventeen happy ones put on Christ by baptism, myself, I think, the happiest of them all.

Affectionately yours,

GEORGE D. FELTON.

LETTER FROM PROF. H A. PRATT, WHO WAS ONCE PRINCIPAL OF FRANKLIN ACADEMY.

SHELBURNE FALLS, Nov. 24, 1883.

REV. JOHN ALDEN :

Dear Brother, I sincerely regret that my work will prevent me from enjoying the pleasure of being present at the fiftieth anniversary of your wedding. It is not strange that I remember you with pleasing satisfaction, as your name is pleasantly associated with my first emerging from the public school to that higher institution of learning, called the Franklin Academy, of which you were the first honored principal. This was in the spring of 1835, when I was sixteen years old.

It was my great venture from home. I arrived at Shelburne Falls just as the organization of the term had commenced in the old chapel. Two more awe-inspiring men I had never seen than Messrs. Alden and his assistant, O. Fisher, who occupied the platform. I had never entertained the thought that I ever should attain to such dignity and power, or that I should ever occupy the same identical position, even without the dignity. It has, therefore, been my wont to regard you with profoundest respect. This was imposed at the first meeting, and the example of that term has influenced my life in all my subsequent career. Such is the influence of association and example, whether elevating or demoralizing. I am happy to say the impression made by the teachers during that term on my character, both as a scholar and Christian man, have never been effaced; and I feel that I owe to them, in a measure, whatever of success I have achieved in life. Allow me, then, to congratulate you on this golden occasion, which commemorates your happy and protracted domestic life. I have had the pleasure of but a slight acquaintance with your excellent wife, but I doubt not she has contributed a large share to your mutual happiness and success in life, and merits the first part in the well-earned congratulations of this happy occasion. May it please the good Father of us all still to grant you both many years of usefulness and honor.

Very truly yours,

H. A. PRATT.

REMARKS OF REV. THOMAS CLARK, D. D., BISHOP OF RHODE ISLAND.

It gives me great pleasure to be present on this joyous occasion. I have attended many golden weddings, but the large assembly present in this sanctuary, and the venerable speakers on this occasion, make this the most charming gathering of the kind I ever witnessed. I love to look over the space of more than half a century, and call to mind my dear college classmates. There is a strong tie that binds classmates together that time can never sunder. Among my classmates none were more respected and beloved than Dr. N. A. Fisher and John Alden, both now in Providence, and Rev. Thatcher Thayer, D. D., of Newport, R. I. Thayer and Alden were famous for story-telling in college days. A number of classmates, during a short vacation at Thanksgiving time, made a bet of a good supper, which of the above two would come out victors in story-telling. The parties were equal in number on a side. The conditions were, that the parties should alternate, and the one who could not commence a story one minute after the other ended, should be considered worsted. The place was Alden's room. The time to commence was six P. M. The umpire was L. Sabin, afterwards our valedictorian, Alden's roommate. They continued from six P. M. to twelve. The old chapel bell told the hour. They laid a blank paper before themselves, and when one was telling an anecdote, the other would write down a few words of a story, but I think neither had recourse to his manuscript. When midnight astonished us all, there was a cry, "*Enough!* They have enough on the paper to last all night, and we are almost dead with laughing. Let us all pay for a supper, one never earned in that way, and better than was ever eaten by mortals." As I call up the charming reminiscences of college days, and the toils and successes of Mr. Alden, I am happy to find him and his wife so vigorous and happy. May that peculiar harmony that has crowned the past still continue like the path of the just, that "shineth brighter and brighter till the perfect day," the day that will celebrate the eternal marriage of the Lamb to all the redeemed.

Truly yours,
T. M. CLARK.

FROM REV. A. M. CRANE, PASTOR OF SHELBURNE FALLS BAPTIST CHURCH.

SHELBURNE FALLS, Dec. 4, 1883.

REV. AND MRS. ALDEN:

The pastor, who after the lapse of fifty years follows in your footsteps, ventures to write you, and in behalf of the church to send congratulations upon the well-rounded period of fifty years of your married life. But few landmarks remain to tell us of the generation in which you moved. We have the same river running through the place, with its beautiful falls; the same mountains standing guard on either side of us; the same sun shines upon us, and the same God over all, in whom we put our trust. But the people who listened to your voice and felt the inspiration of your presence have passed away. Here and there I find one who was a contemporary with you here, whose memory bridges over the half century and brings to us pleasant remembrances of you and your work. They tell us how you came here with all the enthusiasm of youth, as a teacher, to give instruction in Shelburne Falls Academy, and as a preacher to lay the foundation of the church of Christ in this place. They tell us of your devotion to your work; of your self-sacrificing labor, and your wise plans for the future. But now the times have changed, and the few houses standing here in your day have increased to a thriving village. The church edifice, which you assisted in building by giving four hundred dollars, more than half of what you were then worth, has given place to a larger and more beautiful structure. The church itself has become a strong body, able to assist others.

If the greater part of those whom you led into the church have passed away, yet their children remain faithful to the doctrines you preached, and, with others, are now building upon the foundation you laid. Now, those of us whose fortune it is to hold the ground, gained in part by your labors, send to you both Christian salutation. May the same gospel which you preached in your youth be to you a support and consolation in old age, keeping the heart young in Christian love and fellowship, and dispelling all clouds that may obscure the visions of the future.

A. M. CRANE.

FROM MRS. SOPHA MINER LYON THICKSTON, PRINCIPAL OF
THE PELLA INSTITUTE, IOWA.

MY VERY DEAR UNCLE AND AUNT:

It is customary, on noted and pleasant anniversaries, to wish the parties many happy returns of the same. But I cannot truthfully wish you many returns of the golden fiftieth wedding. Long before you shall have reached the *first* one, you will both be inhabitants of the golden city, treading the golden streets, wearing the golden crown, and singing that new and wonderful song which none but the redeemed could learn. Allow me to present the united congratulations of my husband, self and family, on this memorable occasion.

My dear uncle, your beloved sister, Armilla Alden, lived with her husband, Aaron Lyon, Esq., fifty-three years. They were my beloved parents; born in New England, and married in New England. They have to-day three living children, who were born in their dear old New England home. One, Mrs. Lucy T. Lord, rests from her missionary labors in China, and her works there are following her. I wish, my dear uncle, to present a tribute of appreciation for your kindness to, and interest in the welfare of my two oldest sisters, who returned to New England for a more complete education. Alone, among strangers, you was to them as an older brother. I know they never forgot your kindness to them while under your instruction in the Shelburne Falls Academy, preparing for Mt. Holyoke Seminary. Five years ago, I spent a few months in New England, visited your family, became acquainted with my very dear aunt, and your loved ones, and renewed my acquaintance with you, my dear uncle, who had visited at my father's house when I was a child. Among other visits of great interest, I spent a day at Mt. Holyoke Seminary, where the last of my dear aunt Mary Lyon's teaching was done. I stood in silent awe in the room from which the angels carried her to paradise. I speak of this, as she was once a teacher in my grandfather Alden's house, and I know you all loved her and her work.

This was my first visit to New England, the home of our ancestors, and it has been to me a source of constant pleasure. Now, my dear uncle and aunt, I pray God's blessing to abide with you, as the sun is getting low, and the shadows are growing longer. May your sun of life set quietly in a serene sky, and your waking be glorious. With regrets that we cannot be present, and share in the festivities of the anniversary, I am, lovingly,

Your neice,

SOPHIA MINER LYON THICKSTON.

REMARKS OF HENRY M. PUFFER, ESQ., OF SHELBURNE
FALLS, MASS.

MR. CHAIRMAN AND ASSEMBLED FRIENDS:

It gives me great pleasure to be here to-night at this joyful Golden Wedding occasion. The fact that I travelled hundreds of miles to be here, attests my sincerity. This much loved uncle and aunt of mine have been intimately connected with childhood's joys and my manhood's experiences. They were frequent visitors at my happy home in Western Massachusetts. When seeking rest from his arduous labors in academic halls, or revival work, my uncle would hie himself to Colrain to visit his youngest sister, my dear mother, and fish and hunt with her wide-awake boys, and tell interesting anecdotes with the doctor, my honored father. It was this loved aunt, who, at every visit, would make this bashful nephew stand up in the middle of the old sitting-room and speak his little Sunday-school piece, or recite his district-school declamation. In all our pleasant interviews, I have only two things to complain of. First, that she encouraged me to write poetry in my early years. Second, that she would scent tobacco smoke the farthest of any person I ever knew,— washing and perfuming made no difference. When she did notice the taint of sinful indulgence upon the garments of the young collegian, her remarks were forcible and never to be forgotten. I think I felt some as Moses did when he heard the awful thunderings on Mt. Sinai. But she was a good aunt.

The memories of my honored uncle crowd on my mind's camera too fast for expression, when I think what he has been to me and my brothers. It was you who called us in the early morn to dig worms with which to entrap the golden speckled trout in the meadows, or in the fast running streams of the mountains. It was you who would keep us waiting in the hot sun, holding the horse, while you were soliciting subscriptions for the Bible or Home Missionary Societies. It was you who greatly rejoiced when you obtained the most game, or the greatest number of trout or pickerel, but always had some good excuse to offer when, by good luck, your nephews came off first best. It was you who called our attention to spiritual things and to the importance of laying up treasure in heaven. It was you who first encouraged us to pursue a collegiate course, and through the long years of educational and professional stud , aided us by friendly advice and much appreciated treasure. I can never forget the joyful times we had together in our vacations, while hunting on the hillsides, fishing in the blue waters of the Connecticut, or in the rapid old Deerfield, or in the noisy brooks. All these scenes form a luminous background for memory's page, exceedingly precious, and never to be forgotten. I go back to the time when, a young boy, I carried you and your brother David, both of whom were in college then, from my home to your old family homestead in Ashfield, and you appointed me a judge to decide which was the most learned. You spoke in Latin and he in Greek, as it was then stated to me. Since then I have made up my mind, that no Roman or Greek, had they heard the language you used, would ever have mistrusted that a dictionary of either language had ever been in the family. I well remember how awe-struck I was with the immensity of your understandings. It is that love of the humorous and relaxation that has kept you so vigorous and useful. The village in which I live owes its first academy and first church to your indefatigable efforts and liberal contributions and self-denial. The first of which I was an alumnus, and of the other a member. Your spiritual children and your students are scattered over all the country. They are honored and useful. Even their children are taught to revere your name. It has done my soul good to witness this celebration. I rejoice to see you surrounded with so many dear relatives and friends, classmates, and dear brothers and sisters in Christ. I heartily thank all who have added to the pleasure of this evening by their presence, their letters, their speeches and gifts. May we all be present at the great eternal celebration around the Golden Throne.

HENRY M. PUFFER.

HISTORY OF NEWTON THEOLOGICAL INSTITUTE, BY REV SAMUEL FIELD, D. D.

READ BY HIM AT THE GOLDEN WEDDING, DEC. 5, 1883.

We shall not on this special occasion, even with all the solemnities of a half century resting on it, adopt the mournful strains of the Roman arena, for the chime of fifty wedding bells is in the air, telling with their sweetest notes of joys that bring again the bride's blush of youthful happiness and the pride of the rejoicing bridegroom.

Newton Theological history is my part of this festive entertainment. I will endeavor to weave it with bright colors befitting the occasion. This institution was founded in earnest prayer, pious consecration, and love to God and man. The growth of the Baptist denomination, from its planting in this city of Roger Williams, demanded an institution of a high order. Wide fields for Christ were opening around this noble centre, by the rapid increase of our population, that spread itself over New England and the mighty West. The harvest was great, the laborers few. Our pioneer ministry had done a noble work; and it was in part the great success of their labors which created the necessity for more ministers, with such important qualifications as a Theological Institute could furnish. Therefore, on the 25th of May, 1825, at a large meeting of ministers and laymen, representing different sections of New England, it was decided to establish such an institution. Newton Centre, seven miles from Boston, was the place selected. A gentleman, by the name of Peck, had a fine estate on a hill commanding a wide and beautiful view, on which he had erected a spacious mansion, with a graded road adorned with trees. Reverses compelling the sale, it became the Theological Institute. A stranger riding by one day, asked Father Grafton, more than forty-eight years ago, if that large building on the hill was a mill? He replied he knew of one Peck who was ground out there. The gospel hopper has never lacked a yearly grist since.

One of the notable things in the founding and endowing of the institution at the beginning, was the marked liberality of some who commenced life in humble circumstances, and accumulated wealth for the purpose of devoting it to the service of God. Nath. R. Cobb, born in Maine, came to Boston in his youth, and found employment as a clerk. At twenty-one years of age he entered on business for himself. He possessed unusual business talent ; a man of great penetration and unconquerable perseverance. But he took God into his plans, resolving by his grace that he would never be worth more than $50,000 ; that he would give one-fourth of his profits to charitable purposes, if ever worth $20,000 ; if $30,000, three-fourths, and the whole after $50,000. Within thirteen years, under such self-imposed bonds, he gave away more than $40,000, of which Newton received $15,000. A lady from Boston established a store opposite Cambridge University. Prospering in her business, she employed a young clerk, Levi Farwell, who afterward became her partner in business, and though she was several years his senior, she took him as partner for life. Having no children, they adopted Newton Institute. Levi Farwell for eighteen years, till his death, was treasurer, and one of the public buildings is honored with his name, "Farwell Hall." Gardner Colby, born in Maine, came with his

widowed mother to Boston in his youth. He became a
very successful merchant and a devoted friend to Newton
Institute, and was treasurer, after the death of Levi Farwell, twenty-four years. His heart was so large that one
institution could not fill it, and so he took into it Waterville college of his own native State, by an endowment of
$50,000, and that institution now bears his honored name
as Colby University. The early history of Newton Institute
was the common one of such seminaries, but it struggled
successfully through all its difficulties, and now rests
by repeated endowments on a foundation which promises
for it a progress and prosperity never before known. The
institution was opened with Rev. Ira Chase its first instructor, with whom was associated, at the beginning of the
second year, Rev. Henry J. Ripley. These two constituted
the faculty for six years. In 1834, Rev. Mr. Knowles
entered the institution as one of the professors, and Rev.
Barnes Sears in 1836. In 1838, Prof. Knowles died, and
Prof. H —— was called. The institution graduated its first
class in 1826, consisting of two members, Eli B. Smith and
John E. Weston. In 1828, there were four graduates, of
which class was Barnes Sears. In 1829, there was a class
of nine; in 1830, eight; in 1831, nine; in 1832, seven; in
1833, fourteen; in 1834, nineteen, a large class, and, as
was proper, the name of John Alden led the rest.

Standing with our brother and his beloved companion
here to-night, as we look back over the last fifty years, how
crowded is its history of great events! What treasures of
wealth, what costly sacrifices of life and blood have been
offered up on the altar of our country! What victories for
Liberty! What progress in learning — institutions spring-
ing up all over our land, endowed by its treasures for ages
hidden, and kept in store for the necessities of coming
nations that would find here their home! What an increase
of churches and ministers and missionaries, and what wonderful success in preaching the gospel in heathen lands!
Never was the call more urgent for institutions and

churches and ministers in our land. It is a blessed sight for those who are passing from the labors of active life into the quiet shades of retirement, to live in such an age. Newton Theological Institute has sent forth for work in the gospel field nine hundred men. To calculate the influence of these nine hundred men is impossible. It is a wide spread and permanent power, which eternity only can make known. We can all with gratitude exclaim, by the review, "What hath God wrought!"

THE SUBSTANCE OF A SPEECH BY REV. DR. BIXBY, OF CRANSTON STREET BAPTIST CHURCH, PROVIDENCE, FORMERLY A VERY ABLE AND SUCCESSFUL MISSIONARY IN THE ORIENT.

DELIVERED AT THE GOLDEN WEDDING OF REV. JOHN ALDEN, IN THE CENTRAL BAPTIST CHURCH, PROVIDENCE, R. I.

Brother Alden for twelve years was most intimately connected with our missions in foreign lands, as agent of the Missionary Union two years, and of the American and Foreign Bible Society ten years. The latter society had its origin in connection with the work of Bible translation and distribution in Burmah, and during all its history it was an effective helper in the work of foreign missions. Mr. Alden's agency work for these societies in 1853 covered an auspicious period in the history of the Burmah missions.

In 1853, Southern Burmah came suddenly under British rule. The missionaries were sent at once into the populous centres, little Toungoo, Shwaygeen, Rangoon, Henthada, Prome and Bassein. The harvest that followed was truly wonderful. In Toungoo, within two years, thirty churches were planted, two thousand, one hundred and forty-four converts were baptized, and within ten years, one hundred and twenty-six churches were formed, with over six thousand converts. In Shwaygeen, five hundred and seventy-seven were baptized within the first year, and many more afterwards. In Henthada, under the labors of the devoted Thomas, fifty-six churches were formed within a few years,

with over two thousand members, and Bassein soon num
bered nearly or quite six thousand converts. The records
of this great onward movement were used by our brother
with thrilling effect in his appeals to the churches of New
England. They were stirred as they had never been
stirred before. There was a great demand for Bibles and
Testaments, especially among the newly-gathered Karen
converts. I remember that in many of the Christian villages, there was only one copy of the Scriptures in a
village, and that was kept in the chapel. It was largely
through the American and Foreign Bible Society that this
great demand for Bibles was met, and it was mainly with
New England money that the Bibles were supplied, and
largely through our brother's efforts, whose field was in
New England, that the money was secured. I had the
pleasure of hearing him between 1857 and 1860 in different
places, and especially in my own church, the Friendship
Street Baptist Church of Providence, and his appeals were
full of facts from mission fields, and full of pathos and
power.

I believe our dear Brother Alden did much in those
twelve years to develop the missionary character of the
New England churches, and thus he has become a perpetual
blessing to the cause of missions at home and abroad.

GOLDEN WEDDING EXTRACTS OF LETTERS FROM COLLEGE
CLASSMATES.

38 ROWLEY ST., ROCHESTER, N. Y., Nov. 9, 1883.

MY DEAR CLASSMATE ALDEN :

I think that I have seen less of you than of many others
of our class since we left our dear old Alma Mater. I am
sorry, for it has been my loss rather than yours. I have
been engaged wholly in the work of the ministry since I entered it, in 1838. I was in West Springfield nearly eleven
years ; in New York city eleven ; in Geneva, N. Y., thirteen ; and in Lyons nine. After I had reached the age of
seventy-one, I began to think that I might be excused from
the further duties of the pastorate, resigned my charge, and

removed to this city in August, 1882. We were led to come
here mainly by the fact that our oldest son resided here with
his family. We find great comfort in being near them. We
have two other sons. I am preaching occasionally almost
every Sabbath as it turns out, and I am delighted with the
work. I have had a very happy life. God has given me
four parishes, and nobody ever had better or more pleasant
ones. We have been blessed with revivals of religion in
every one. In Lyons, 1881, we received one hundred and
five into the church on profession at one time. But, dear
Alden, I did not mean to write about myself so much. I
am glad to learn that God has spared you and your dear
wife so long. May life and health be fully preserved and
prolonged to you both. I trust that the coming anniversary will be "golden" with God's own sunshine. The dear
old class of '31! How sadly the ranks are broken! Bliss,
Jewett, and Fisher, gone within these recent months! Who
of us next may follow, and how soon, we cannot tell. Be it
so. We would not live alway. It is better to be with the
Lord in heaven than on earth. I am looking "towards
sunset," but find very little to comfort me in anything that
I am, or have done. God is very good and very precious,
and beyond the earthly sunset I am hoping through my
Saviour to reach the dawning of a brighter day. With the
best of all good wishes and earnest prayer that the dear
Lord will have you both in his keeping, and enable you still
to bring forth fruit in old age, fulfilling his gracious promise that in the evening time it shall be light, I am, dear
brother, with all loving regards to you and yours,

Your old classmate,
A. A. WOOD.

CANTERBURY, N. H., Dec. 10, 1883.
MY DEAR CLASSMATE:
Your kind letter of Nov. 5, 1883, was duly received. I
often think of the days spent at Amherst with pleasant
recollections; but I would not, if I could, live the times over
again. I was then a full believer in the theology taught
there. But differences in religious beliefs have no influence
over my friendly relations with those with whom I come
in contact.

I have little cause to find fault with the share of happiness that has fallen to my lot. I have never enjoyed the

happiness, nor suffered the anxieties, resulting from the matrimonial relation, and cannot say that the review causes any regrets. It would have given me much pleasure to have met you and your friends at your Golden Wedding. But, instead, please accept the inclosed trifle. I would be glad to make it larger. With the best wishes for the happiness of yourself and wife, I am sincerely,

Your friend and classmate,
GALEN FOSTER.

BOSTON, MASS., HOTEL CLUNEY, Nov. 11, 1884.

REV. MR. ALDEN:

Dear Sir, your letter directed to Rev. J. Whitney was forwarded to me from Newton. My father fell asleep in Jesus, after great suffering, May 31, 1879, and we believe passed to his home in the heavenly mansions. The home at Newton Centre was broken up after the death of my parents. " The places that once knew them, now know them no more forever." With sincere regret that you had not before learned of the death of your old classmate and my father, I remain,

Yours, respectfully,
L. J. WHITNEY.

BROOKLINE, Nov. 6, 1883.

DEAR CLASSMATE AND FRIEND :

The receipt of your letter arouses the pleasant remembrance of former days in a way that has become very rare with me of late years. I almost never meet a classmate, and only occasionally hear of one. I regret to learn from your letter that Thatcher Thayer, the only survivor of the three in our class with whom I was most intimate, is in failing health. But we are all moving onward to join the great majority, and those of us who are left may reasonably expect the summons to come soon.

Our class of ninety was represented by Prof. Abbott and others as a very promising one—in its first year. I felt a great interest in the publication of the biographical sketch of the Amherst Alumni of the first half century, which has lately appeared. What I would wish, in such a publication, would be information in regard to intellectual and spiritual progress on the part of each member, but it would be vain to hope for that.

Do you remember Dan Weed, who was the best mathematician, and the soundest sleeper among us? I had quite lost sight of him for forty years, until the volume above mentioned spoke of him as in one of the departments in Washington. It is very unlikely that circumstances will allow me to be present at the very pleasant festival to which you kindly invite me. If I could be there, it would be very pleasant to meet yourself and those of our classmates who may join you. In any event, accept my hearty congratulations, and my best wishes for the successful issue of your festivity. So wishes your friend,

CHARLES K. WHIPPLE.

HAVERHILL, Nov. 16, 1883.

MY DEAR CLASSMATE:

I received your kind note and a very polite invitation to your Golden Wedding, which my health forbids me to accept. You recall the happy days we spent in Amherst College; they were truly so. Your dear face, as in college, is daguerreotyped on the tablet of my heart as clearly as though it was but yesterday I saw you. You say you have lived seventy-seven years; I shall arrive at that figure if I live till the fourth of February next, and I have lived in the same house forty-four years. You, like many of our class, as I learn by the late college record, have had a varied experience, doing much good in many places. But now our life's work is done. I have been on the retired list of my profession thirteen years, and am now waiting that better life which we may both expect from the character which we have garnered in this.

Truly and affectionately yours,

KENDALL FLINT.

CHAPTER VIII.

GOLDEN WEDDING LETTERS.

MIDDLEBOROUGH, Nov. 9, 1883.

MY DEAR CLASSMATE:

 RECEIVED a very kind and pleasant letter from you giving me an invitation to your Golden Wedding, but now I do not go away from home to remain even over night. Our classmates are going fast. I am sorry to hear of the illness of Drs. Thayer and Parker. I received a call from Dr. Thayer some ten years ago, and it was a very pleasant one, and that is the only time I have seen him since we graduated. I am nearly seventy-nine years of age; my health is good, but I have to take care of it. I remain, your friend and classmate, with good wishes for your future,

ELIAB WARD.

FROM REV. GEORGE WATERS.

CAMBRIDGE, MASS., Nov. 10, 1883.

MY DEAR CLASSMATE:

Your letter has been duly received. I have been a resident here for about six months, but consider that it will be my permanent home. My wife's relatives and friends reside here and in this vicinity. Our children are settled, one in Kingston, N. Y., one in New York city, and one in this State. All well, and doing well. I am not quite as old as you, being in my seventy-fourth year. We have been married a little more than forty-five years; have had many blessings, as well as many crosses and trials. It is but the common lot of our fellow-creatures. I congratulate you on your prolonged life, and especially the unusual continuance of your marriage state, for it is very rare that a Golden

171

Wedding can be celebrated. Hope you will have a joyful time, not only with hearty congratulations, but with something more substantial. I would gladly be present if I could, but circumstances will not afford me that pleasure now. With prayers that many blessings may still rest on you and yours, I remain very sincerely and fraternally,

Your old friend and classmate,

GEO. WATERS.

FROM REV. THOMAS BISCOE.

HOLLISTON, MASS., Nov. 23, 1883.

MY DEAR CLASSMATE ALDEN:

Your interesting letter was duly received. I congratulate in the fact that God has so kindly spared you and your dear wife each to the other for these fifty years, and that you are so soon to celebrate your Golden Wedding.

It was the privilege of myself and wife, together with our children and some of our grandchildren, to celebrate our Golden Wedding, in a very quiet, but very pleasant way, the second day of last September. Our own children, who yet survive, were all present, though not their wives. They gathered from this State, from New York, Ohio and Nebraska. So you see by the distances they came, that they made special efforts to gather under the paternal roof. To look back over the half century of our married life, it seems very short. Many events, pleasing and sad, have happened to us. But I believe I have enjoyed as much of life as any of my classmates, though many of them have occupied wider spheres as the result of their superior ability, and gained more notoriety in the world. But more than half of our class have passed over the river, to other scenes, and as you say, "we must soon follow them." I retired from the active work of the ministry in 1875. I hope you may have as pleasant and enjoyable a Golden Wedding as we had, and a large flock of golden eagles crowding your purse.

I remain, fraternally, yours,

T. C. BISCOE.

FROM PROFESSOR S. H. WALDO.

GENESEO, ILL., Nov. 8, 1883.

DEAR CLASSMATE:

Yours of the 5th inst. came to hand last evening, and

glad was I to receive it. My wife was not continued to me for a Golden Wedding. She died Nov. 15, 1881 ; but I have married again. You speak of desiring my history. It would be a long and variegated story. Oh, how strangely Divine Providence leads us! What scenes I have passed! God has given me opportunities of doing good. I hope they have been somewhat improved. My usual health has been good, and though I am now eighty-one, my friends think me a wonder for activity. I feel little of age. By a strange providence, during a few years last passed, I have been able to prepare an English Grammar, which is thought by many to be a remarkable production. I have no question that it surpasses any grammar of the kind, among some two or three thousands that have been published for the explanation of our mother tongue. It saves four-fifths of the time in the study of our language. May God bless you and your dear companion, giving you both many more happy days on earth and an eternity of unspeakable joy. I have seen little of our class in college since graduation, but oh, may God gather us all in heaven by and by! Should any of our class be present on that occasion, remember me to them with the best of wishes.

Yours, truly,
S. H. WALDO.

FROM PROFESSOR A. S. TALCOTT.

BANGOR THEOLOGICAL SEMINARY, NOV. 8, 1883.
DEAR CLASSMATE :

Your letter received this week interested me much. I wish very much that my own condition was such as to enable me to make some valuable contribution to you at your coming Golden Wedding.

More than two years ago, my throat became so severely affected that it was utterly impossible for me to continue my labors at the Seminary. I was obliged to resign my professorship, which I had held for forty-two years.

I have three children, all of them invalids. Their mother, one of the best of women, died nearly eighteen years since, having been for many of the best years of her life a constant sufferer. I have many, many mercies for which I should be thankful.

We are both of us, my brother, near the end of our course; may we meet in a better world.

Believe me, as ever, yours, affectionately,

A. S. TALCOTT.

FROM HON. THOMAS M. HOWELL, U. S. COMMISSIONER.

CANANDAIGUA, ONTARIO CO., N. Y.

DEAR OLD CLASSMATE :

The enclosed will notify you of the sad bereavement that has fallen upon me in my old age. The billows of desolation roll over me afresh this day; and my utter loneliness, only those who at threescore and ten years have lost what I have lost, can realize. The sympathy of a few of my old classmates has touched my sad heart. Pray write me a line.

Sincerely,

T. M. HOWELL.

CONGRATULATIONS OF RELATIVES AND FRIENDS.

LETTER FROM E. K. ALDEN, SECRETARY OF AMERICAN BOARD OF COMMISSIONERS FOR FOREIGN MISSIONS.

BOSTON, Dec. 3, 1883.

DEAR SIR :

Were my venerable father, who was called to his rest nearly three years ago, at the ripe age of almost ninety-three — thirteen years after he had celebrated his Golden Wedding, — now living, and were he able to respond to the kind invitation which I, as one of his sons, received a few days ago, to be present at the approaching Golden Wedding upon the fifth of December, I have no doubt that his salutation would take somewhat the following form:

"Eleaser, son of Dr. Ebenezer, son of Deacon Daniel, son of Daniel, sendeth greetings to Reverend John, son of Reverend John, son of David, son of Eleaser, younger brother of the aforesaid Daniel — these two brothers, Daniel and Eleaser, being both sons of Deacon Joseph, son of Joseph, son of John and Priscilla of the Mayflower, — with congratulations that you came straight from Plymouth Rock through the first three illustrious generations, John, Joseph, and Deacon Joseph, also that when the two brothers, Daniel and Eleaser, parted company so far as to become the founders of two family lines of posterity, they were wise enough to select for their wives two sisters, Abigail and Martha, daughters of Joseph Shaw, the supreme honor of the Shaw family, not forgetting the Chief Justice Lemuel. Congratulating you most of all that the goodly succession has continued down both lines to the present day, by those who have rejoiced, being identified with the sterling Christian faith and character of their pious ancestry."

I take great pleasure in transmitting this message in behalf of the line of the Daniels and the Ebenezers to the line of Eleaser, David and the Johns. Hoping that the present John now celebrating his Golden Wedding may emulate the example of the first John and live on in the service of his generation, certainly until his eighty-eighth year, I remain,

Respectfully yours,
E. K. ALDEN,
Son of Eleaser, son of Ebenezer, son of Daniel, son of Daniel, son of Joseph, son of Joseph, son of John the First.

EXTRACT FROM A LETTER BY REV. MR. BARBER, OF FAYVILLE, MASS.

DEAR BROTHER:

Please accept my congratulations on the occasion of this joyous anniversary of your marriage. While a half century must have brought to your experience many trials and sorrows, it cannot have failed to afford both you and yours many days of joy and gladness, which must at this anniversary season move your hearts with emotions of devout thankfulness and praise to the kind Source of all our benefits. I doubt not that duly appreciating the abounding goodness and grace of God our Saviour, from your home altar of worship has ascended the acceptable offering of thankful hearts. May the blessing of a loving Lord ever gladden and make golden your lives and home.

Fraternally yours,
J. BARBER.

EXTRACT FROM A LETTER BY REV. A. H. GRANGER, D. D.

BURRILLVILLE, Nov. 12, 1883.
MY DEAR SIR:

Your kind invitation came duly to hand. It will be fifty

years next April since I went to Shelburne Falls. If I were dropped down there to-day, I have no thought that I should know the place. The same heavens would stretch over me, and the same Deerfield river would flow by the village, but all else would be completely changed. I hope you will have a pleasant gathering on the fifth of December. I shall try to come and bring my offering ; but if I should not, you will know the reason. I remain,

Fraternally yours,
A. H. GRANGER.

EXTRACT FROM A LETTER BY A NEPHEW, PROFESSOR D. B. PURRINTON.

WEST VIRGINIA UNIVERSITY,
MORGANTOWN, Nov. 26, 1883.

Mother is in receipt of your kind invitation to the approaching anniversary celebration, as also the letter accompanying it, which forcibly reminds her of the pleasant days and scenes of long ago. ; and she wishes me to assure you, "that if she were in her accustomed health, she would gladly commit to paper some of the interesting reminiscences suggested by your approaching family reunion." My father, Rev. Jessa Purrinton, died in 1869. It was a very sad and gloomy time for us. But God has been very good to us all, better than our fears, and infinitely better than our deserts. He has given us greater prosperity than we had any reason to expect, for which we can never be too grateful. It is our prayer that he may grant us such supplies of grace as may be needful to discharge aright the duties devolving upon us, and finally to stand in his presence, redeemed and saved through Jesus Christ. I have for years been taught to love and revere you both, my uncle and aunt. It would be a great pleasure could I be permitted to see you yet in the flesh. If I could do anything to contribute however slightly to the interest of your celebration, it would most certainly be done. My mother, your neice, extends her hearty congratulations, with many thanks for your kind remembrance of her. We all join her in wishing you a most joyous anniversary, and a succession of returning years, pleasant in reminiscences, bright in prospect, and glorious with the presence and blessing of Almighty God.

Yours, very sincerely,
D. B. PURRINTON.

GALESBURY, Dec. 1, 1883.

DEAR UNCLE AND AUNT:

Enclosed you will please find New York draft for $ ——,
endorsed payable to your order. I desire the above
amount to be divided strictly in accordance with the laws
of Rhode Island, and that when thus divided, that no portion of it may be spent for any unlawful purposes, such as
buying tobacco, snuff, etc.

Had you postponed the first wedding thirty days, I might
possibly be present at the fiftieth anniversary, as I expect
to come East shortly.

Hoping you may both have a most pleasant, happy,
enjoyable and profitable time on the evening of the 5th
inst., and that the enclosed may be in time, as a token of
love and respect from Susan, George and Will, I am,

Your affectionate nephew,

GEORGE C. ALDEN.

WEST VIRGINIA UNIVERSITY,
MORGANTOWN, Nov. 26, 1883.

MY DEAR UNCLE:

It would give me great pleasure to unite with you and
your other friends in commemorating your fiftieth wedding
anniversary, but distance and professional duties render it
entirely impracticable. Accept our heartfelt congratulations, and our best wishes for your future happiness and
usefulness.

Your affectionate nephew,

FRANKLIN LYON.

PROVIDENCE, December, 1883.

MY DEAR BROTHER AND SISTER:

Please accept my congratulations on this fiftieth anniversary of your marriage. God bless you as you still go on
the downward path of life, and make the remainder of your
pilgrimage golden with service for the Master until life's
close. Then may you find your names recorded in the
Golden Records on high, and find an abundant entrance
into the Golden City, where the loved ones of the past and
present shall be reunited, no more to be severed.

Your loving sister,

ELIZABETH ESTHER CHAMBERLAIN.

OUR GREAT GRANDCHILD, HELEN RUTH CLARKE,

was born Nov. 15, 1883, about three weeks previous to the Golden Wedding. On the presentation of her picture to us, the following lines were repeated very impressively by Lena Hunt, nine years of age:

> This picture of your great-grandchild
>   We bring to you this night,—
> God keep her spirit undefiled,
>   A golden treasure bright.

> And when in after years
>   You see this face so dear,
> Oh, then bless God the treasure came
>   In golden month and year.

EXTRACT OF A LETTER FROM MISS THEODOSIA ALDEN.

CASSADAGA, Nov. 26, 1883.

MY DEAR UNCLE AND AUNT:

We very much regret that we cannot be with you at the gathering of relatives and friends on the fiftieth anniversary of your marriage. The ties of kindred are strong in my being, and the dear friends so widely scattered are ever remembered with love, and it is hard to forego the joy of seeing the dear faces that will be gathered under your roof. I often recall the interviews with friends in the days that are no more, so vividly, that they seem to fill the room like real voices, and bless anew and again with their happy memories.

We, as a race, are brave and hopeful; if perchance we are swept into the trough of the sea, and the cold billows run over us, we pop out with a laugh and a joke, full of courage for the next page in life's history, whether it brings sunshine or storm. This hopefulness we have inherited in full measure from our father, but from mother comes the power to reach out and take hold of the spiritual, bring it into every-day life, with its genial fructifying influences. How fast our kindred are gathering on the other shore! Aunt Eunice Alden Ranney, so lately with us, is now numbered with the dead. I love to think of those who have served so long and faithfully as being free from the trials and cares incident to earth. I have no sad or gloomy thoughts in regard to death, the deliverer, which introduces us into the real life of which this is but the shadow.

SHORT EXTRACT OF A LETTER FROM MISS SARAH C. ALDEN.

BELCHERTOWN, Dec. 24, 1883.

MR. AND MRS. ALDEN:

Dear friends, I write you at this time to thank you for your kindness in remembering me in connection with your Golden Wedding. When I received the invitation, I hoped I might be able to go to Providence, and there present my congratulations, but was unable to accomplish it. I learned from the Providence *Journal* that, on the evening of December 5th, you had a very interesting and enjoyable time, and one of great success. You well remember Mr. Thomas Sabine, some of whose children were your pupils when you taught school in this town. He was the father of your classmate, Rev. Lewis Sabine, D. D. He is still alive. The one hundredth anniversary of his birth was celebrated last Saturday, the 22d.

Very truly, your friend,
S. C. ALDEN.

SHORT EXTRACT OF A LETTER FROM BROTHER MINER.

WINCHESTER, ILL., Nov. 30, 1883.

REV. JOHN ALDEN AND WIFE:

Dear friends, your letter of invitation to attend Golden Wedding is received. I would be happy to be with you on the evening of December 5th, but the distance and season of the year, together with sickness in the family, will prevent us from being present. Enclosed please find draft ——. May the evening of your life be blessed with serenity, and in Heaven may you be rewarded.

Yours truly,
E. G. MINER.

FROM DR. J. A. SHERMAN.

RUPTURE CURE OFFICE, 251 BROADWAY,
NEW YORK, Dec. 4, 1883.

REV. JOHN ALDEN:

Dear Sir, I regret very much that, through press of business, I am unable to be present at the celebration of your fiftieth wedding anniversary. Allow me to tender you and yours my congratulations. I am proud to feel that I was a humble instrument in the hand of God of relieving you of a terrible hernia which was fast pressing you down to the grave, and restoring you to health, whereby you doubtless live to enjoy this happy event. May God in his goodness continue your felicitous days of union, so that when he calls you separately home, it may seem but a momentary transition of one preceding the other to the shores of endless bliss.

Yours, truly,

J. A. SHERMAN.

[I am happy to say I was completely cured by Dr. Sherman's treatment.—JOHN ALDEN.]

SHELBURNE FALLS, Nov. 27, 1883.

RESPECTED FRIENDS:

The invitation to your Golden Wedding, which was so kindly sent us, was received with much pleasure. Please accept our congratulations on the pleasant occasion, with the desire that you may enjoy many more anniversaries, and live to celebrate your Diamond Wedding.

With the best wishes of your friends,

MR. AND MRS. OZIAS LONG.

CAMBRIDGE, Dec. 2, 1883.

DEAR FRIENDS:

Please accept the enclosed sum from a few of your old friends, with kind wishes.

Yours, sincerely,

REV. MR. CHASE.
J. M. S. WILLIAMS.
DEACON J. HOLMES.
MRS. ABBY THORNDIKE.
MRS. H. M. DODGE.

WINCHENDON, MASS., Nov. 21, 1883.

REV. AND MRS. JOHN ALDEN:

Dear friends, we received your kind invitation to be present at your Golden Wedding. Please accept the enclosed coins with our best love, and the prayer that the kind Father in heaven may spare you to each other many years.

MRS. LEVI STEARNS.
MISS HARRIET BUTLER.

HAVERHILL, December, 1883.

DEAR COUSINS:

You will conclude our congratulations are rather late, but they are not the less sincere on that account. May your last days prove your best days, and after life's toils and trials are ended, may you both have an abundant entrance into the everlasting kingdom of our Lord and Saviour, Jesus Christ.

Your friend and cousin,

MRS. JULIA RUSSELL.

BOSTON, Dec. 3, 1883.

REV. AND MRS. JOHN ALDEN:

Dear friends, I am in receipt of an invitation to commemoration reception attending the fiftieth anniversary of your wedding, and I am much pleased to observe that so many friends are interested in celebrating such a rare and important event with appropriate ceremonies. I well remember many pleasant visits to your home, and I trust it may always be my privilege to address you as dear friends, and remember that "auld acquaintance" shall never be forgot.

Very truly yours,

JAMES LEWIS HOVEY,
U. S. Treasury.

NEW YORK, Nov. 22, 1883.

DEAR COUSINS:

The invitation to your fiftieth wedding anniversary is before me. My wife, Abby and Walter join me in congratulating you that so much of life and its varied experiences have fallen to your lot. We cannot be with you on the 5th of December, but hope that the day will be one of pleasure to you and yours. That no sorrow will cloud an hour of your remaining years is the earnest wish of us all.

Yours truly,

EMERY B. FAY.

BOSTON, Dec. 4, 1883.

MY DEAR COUSINS:

Your letter with invitation to attend your Golden Wedding duly received, for which I thank you. Fifty years compasses a multitude of experiences in the history of us mortals. In the history of the nation it embraces nearly one-half of its existence. It seems to me that no equal space of time since the creation has been so full of interest, and where life was worth so much to live. I feel to bless the Lord that he has cast our lot in this age of progress, and that whatever reverses or discipline he has seen fit to mingle in our cup, the blessings so much overshadow the opposite considerations, that we have abundant reason for thanksgiving and praise. May the future years of your earthly life be crowned with heaven's best blessings, and may we, when our earthly pilgrimage is over, join the host of dear ones gone before.

Affectionately yours,

S. C. FAY.

SHELBURNE FALLS, December, 1883.
DEAR BROTHER AND SISTER ALDEN :

Am very glad to hear of your pleasant wedding. It is true that here you have labored, and others have entered into your labors ; but you have the satisfaction of feeling that God blest you, and that it was his cause in which you toiled. Please accept the enclosed, with the very best wishes of

B. AND E. B. MAXWELL.

HILLSIDE COTTAGE, NORTH ADAMS, November, 1883.
REV. MR. AND MRS. ALDEN :

Kind friends, your invitation to your Golden Wedding came duly to hand, for which please accept our thanks. Nothing would give us more pleasure than to be present and participate in the joys of that happy event. We hope a large number of your many friends will be with you to give you joy, and make the occasion filled with many golden memories. With high regard and many kind wishes, we must ever remain filled with much love for you both.

Yours, truly,

MR. AND MRS. JOHN ARNOLD.

SHELBURNE FALLS, MASS., Dec. 4, 1883.
MY DEAR BROTHER AND SISTER :

I congratulate you on the fiftieth anniversary of your wedded life. The season of the year seems to forbid my presence with you at this time. Enclosed find my mite to help increase the larger. May Heaven's blessings continue to rest upon you. Eighty-two in a few days.

J. B. BARDWELL.

Over fifty-one years ago I used to mail letters weekly to Ann Maria C ——, of Cambridgeport, while you supposed no one knew the name of your intended.

J. B. B.

SHELBURNE FALLS, November, 1883.

DEAR UNCLE AND AUNT:

You have my hearty congratulations on this golden anniversary of your marriage! I do think it a fitting thing to celebrate, for any couple who have lived together fifty years, especially those who have been so useful and so much in public life. "The Lord bless thee and keep thee; the Lord make his face to shine upon thee, and give thee peace."

How strongly I am reminded to-day of one who would gladly have shared these festivities; but I trust he has gone up higher, and will give you a welcome at the marriage supper of the Lamb.

Your loving niece,

FLAVILLA ALDEN WHITNEY.

MERIDEN, CONN., Dec. 4, 1883.

REV. JOHN ALDEN AND WIFE:

Dear friends, it afforded me much pleasure to hear from you a few days ago, when I received an invitation to your Golden Wedding. It has been nearly thirty years since we met and parted in Westfield. I should enjoy it much if I could meet you again, and talk of the various scenes through which we have been led by an overruling Providence. The last ten years of my life have been years of sadness and misfortune, with only a glimpse of sunlight now and then; but I think I can say, "It is all for the best," when every event is ordered by a loving Father. I know that the words of instruction I heard from your lips in Westfield, when I was just commencing the Christian life, have been of use to me ever since. I should like very much to be with you, but it is impossible. My mother is feeble, but her mind is clear as ever. She is eighty-one years old. My father died three years ago. I will close, hoping that we may meet again, if not here, in the hereafter.

Yours, very truly,

JULIA A. OSBORN.

WESTFIELD, Dec. 3, 1883.

DEAR MR. AND MRS. ALDEN:

I received your kind invitation to your Golden Wedding. Should be very glad to be with you on that occasion. I remember you both with a great deal of pleasure, and your earnest work with us. I trust you will enjoy the gathering, and hope you may be spared to each other and your friends a little longer, and at last, that we may all meet as one great family, where parting is not known.

Yours.

MRS. N. INGERSOLL.

TO MY FRIENDS, THE REV. MR. AND MRS. ALDEN:

We regret exceedingly that we cannot be present at the fiftieth anniversary of your marriage, and nothing but sickness at home has prevented. May you long live to enjoy the blessings of earth, and when Jesus calls you home, may you find a golden harvest awaiting you above. The best wishes of your friends,

MR. AND MRS. T. D. HUDSON.

WORCESTER, Dec. 3, 1883.

REV. AND MRS. ALDEN:

We very much regret circumstances will not permit us to be present at the anniversary celebration. May God bless by many additional years of wedded bliss.

In Christian love and affection,

MR. AND MRS. P. G. SKINNER.

WESTFIELD. Dec. 4, 1883.

DEAR FRIENDS:

Many thanks for your kind invitation to be present at your fiftieth wedding anniversary. May it be a joyful one to you and yours. I have been reminded of earlier days, when you were living among us, and Mr. Alden was my pastor. I remember your kindly ministrations, and the time when I gave my heart to Christ; the baptism of myself with many others. There have been many changes since. The cause of the dear Saviour was never more precious to me than now; I want to be loyal to him.

Affectionately,

JANE E. THURSTON.

EXTRACT OF A LETTER FROM GEO. H. FELTON, M. D.

ST. PAUL, MINN., Nov. 20, 1883.

MR. AND MRS. ALDEN:

My very dear friends, my invitation to your Golden
Wedding reached me in my home here yesterday. I cannot
command the language to tell you of my congratulations
that your lives have been prolonged to enjoy this occasion, or to express the pleasure I take in recalling my own
acquaintance and friendship with you. Among my earliest
recollections are those of my visits to your home in Westfield, and of yours to my father's home in Granville; and
these occasions stand out prominently among the memories
of childhood, because they always gave me so much genuine pleasure. And no less prized have been the opportunities afforded me from time to time, since those early days
of renewing my intercourse with you. I sincerely wish it
were possible for me to be among those who will take your
hands on your anniversary, thanking God for all he has
done for you during these years that are fled, and asking
his blessing upon those that remain for you on earth, that
they may be many and peaceful, yet filled with joyful antic-
ipations of that life which shall not be measured by years.
Remember that I have always been, and am yet,

One of your boys,

G. H. FELTON.

PROVIDENCE, December, 1883.

MY DEAR FRIENDS:

We shall be most happy to accept your invitation to
your Golden Wedding, and allow us to congratulate you
that you have lived to see this golden day. May the few
remaining years that are left for you be blessed with peace.

Your friends,

MARY D. HOWARD.
PHEBE A. HOWARD.

ANDOVER, Nov. 20, 1883.

MY DEAR COUSINS:

We received your very kind invitation to be present at
the anniversary of your Golden Wedding. The time for
our Golden Wedding would have been January, 1882, but
we had lost so many of our dear family that we could not
make up our minds to celebrate it. The Lord has come
very near to us, once, and again, and again, and again, and

taken away our dear children whom we tenderly loved;
but we know that " He doeth all things well."

Your affectionate cousin,

Susan Stone.

80 Madison Avenue, New York.

My Dear Friends :

I must tell you how pleased my sister Lucy and I were
to receive your cards of invitation to your Golden Wedding. Instinctively our thoughts turned to the old days at
Westfield, and the picture came before my mind of my
father seated in his rocking-chair, my mother on the sofa,
and you, Mr. Alden, in another chair, genially whiling away
the hours by pleasant chat and story-telling! How pleasant to think of the contrast to the busy, driving, exhaust-
ing cares of business life in this city, is the picture! It is
certainly refreshing to think of so genial and pleasant a
life as yours coming to so pleasant a period in its journey
as the Golden Wedding. Our very pleasantest recollections are of the happy days of our life when you were
in Westfield, and your family and ours were neighbors.
Our heartiest wishes are for your continued health and
prosperity.

Faithfully yours,

Addison Rand.

240 Broadway, New York.

Dear Mr. and Mrs. Alden :

I received the invitation to attend the celebration of the
fiftieth anniversary of your marriage—your Golden Wedding. At Westfield, when I was a mere boy, I many times
made your house my home, and I do not forget the hearty
welcome and good cheer that always prevailed in your
house. My brother Addison unites with me in sending
herewith a small token of our remembrance of former days,
which please accept with our hearty congratulations and
best wishes.

Sincerely yours,

Jasper R. Rand.

Northampton, Mass., Dec. 4, 1883.

My Dear Mr. and Mrs. Alden :

I thank you for your kind invitation to be present at the
celebration of the fiftieth anniversary of your marriage. I

have delayed writing, hoping the way might be opened to manifest, by my presence, the love I cherish for you. Please accept the golden coin enclosed as a token of regard. I have not forgotten the many kindnesses received. I do not doubt that you will receive many cheering testimonials of love from many dear friends, the thoughts of which will brighten all your remaining days, and when done with earthly things, may we all have a glad reunion where our happiness will be without alloy.

Yours, in love,

CORDELIA SAWYER.

NORTH ADAMS, MASS., Nov. 30, 1883.
MY DEAR MR. AND MRS. ALDEN:

I received with many thanks your cards announcing your fiftieth wedding anniversary. Please accept the enclosed amount as a small reminder of my regard and esteem for your welfare and happiness. With the kindest regards, I remain,

Yours, truly,

EDWARD R. TINKER.

NORTH ADAMS, Dec. 3, 1883.
REV. AND MRS. JOHN ALDEN:

My dear friends, just at this time it seems almost impossible for me to leave my business, and much as I should have liked to be with you Wednesday evening next, I have had to bend to the necessity of remaining at home. Mrs. Whittaker unites with me in sending our congratulations, together with our best wishes and prayers that these years to come may be peaceful and happy and full of joy to you both.

Yours, very truly,

MR. AND MRS. V. A. WHITTAKER.

REV. AND MRS. ALDEN:

Dear friends, we received with pleasure the summons to your Golden Wedding, and regret that we cannot be present, feeling as we do that it will be a feast in the fullest sense of the word, and one which we can ill afford to lose. Although almost unknown to you, we feel that we can claim you as friends, for we know your hearts are this night, and ever, filled with love and good will to all your Heavenly Father's children. We feel our indebtedness to you as the dearly loved father and mother of a friend whom we esteem most highly, and never meet without pleasure. My husband joins with me in sending kindest greetings and wishes for your welfare, and if we meet not here, we will trust our heavenly Father for a meeting in his home.

Most respectfully yours,

EMMA M. METCALF.

MR. AND MRS. R. C. METCALF,
    Dec. 4, 1883.

TIVERTON, R. I., Dec. 1, 1883.

TO REV. AND MRS. JOHN ALDEN:

Dear friends, it is not consistent for us to accept your invitation for Wednesday evening, December 5th. But you will confer upon us the great pleasure of appropriating to your own use the accompanying check, which is presented as a slight token of the very high esteem in which you are held by us.

Very respectfully,

MR. AND MRS. WM. S. ROBERTSON.

AUBURNDALE, Dec. 3, 1883.

MR. AND MRS. ALDEN:

Dear friends, your kind invitation came while we were absent. It would give us great pleasure to be present, but convenience does not permit. We trust the occasion will be one of great pleasure and enjoyment. It is a matter of deep thankfulness that you have been allowed to tread a united path for so many years. May it continue to be bright until it passes the heavenly gate. With best wishes and many prayers,

Yours, cordially,

SUSAN C. JENNINGS.
ALICE C. JENNINGS.

EXTRACT OF A LETTER WRITTEN BY MRS. B. H. CRANE, WIFE OF THE LATE REV. D. M. CRANE, OF NORTHAMPTON.

My cross leans against a dark sky, and I learn some new meaning every day through that little word "alone." How I miss the strong arm and ready hands of him once at my side, in bearing the burdens, his counsel, encouragement, the morning and evening prayer for strength to do God's will, and in the hottest fire hold still. You speak of your sainted mother (Mrs. Anna Chamberlain), whose presence and prayers hallowed your charming home in this place. I remember her dear motherly face, gentle, quiet spirit, and loving heart, and often look at her picture, and think how precious the legacy of a Christian character.

Golden Weddings are rare events, and blessed occurrences; few ever reach them. After two score years and ten of tireless, devoted life in the holy bonds of matrimony, with profound respect and admiration we say, All hail! noble pair. The soft, solemn chime of far-off bells echoes the refrain, and starry eyes of loved ones gone before look down in benediction. I am glad this anniversary is to be fittingly commemorated. It will make you happy in many ways: in the renewed evidence of the affectionate regard of your children; in the friendships of your life, and the kind care of your heavenly Father, till he welcomes you home. Memory, lost to things near, now turns tenderly back through the drifts of years to that sweet oasis, the morning of life, when, at the dear home of the bride, in the presence of parents and friends, most of whom have gone to the silent land, the impressive ceremony was performed which forever blends two souls in the wondrous interlacings of sweet companionship. With light feet and joyful hearts you went boldly forth to pursue the path that leads to high noon, and when the steeps to be climbed became more rugged and difficult, you shared each other's fortune, smiled and wept together, inspiring each with new courage and enthusiasm, and grew stronger through trial. The silken cords of love which bound you became a band of polished silver, set with household jewels glowing in the love-light of home. Fifty years of married life passed as a shadow that returneth not. Here we have no continuing city. As servants of God, your lives have been one of ministry to the wants of others, your dear sister sharing with you the blessed reward of doing good; now may they be of reception, in the returning bread cast upon the waters. May the Divine Presence shed a halo of glory over the calm tranquil Indian summer of your lives.

Please accept this token of affectionate regard in response to your kind invitation.

Yours, truly,

B. H. CRANE.

New Haven, Conn., Dec. 3, 1883.
Rev. and Mrs. John Alden :

Dear friends, the invitation to your Golden Wedding was received in due time. We are happy to be able to tender our congratulation, both personally and in behalf of our father, who considered you a very dear friend. That your days, which have been so useful and honorable, may be continued for many years, is the sincere wish of

Yours, very truly,
J. L. Ensign.

West End Institute,
New Haven, Nov. 24, 1883.
My Dear Mr. and Mrs. Alden :

Thirty-three years ago, when I stood before you, I did not anticipate the honor or the pleasure of an invitation to your fiftieth anniversary ! How I should love to be present to present my congratulations and good wishes on that occasion, especially for the sake of my dear father and mother, who ever held you both in loving remembrance. Since this may not be, will you then, dear friends of the long ago, accept our sincerest love and most earnest prayer that you may find your last days to be really and truly your best days, and the promise verified that "the path of the just is as the shining light that shineth more and more unto perfect day."

I am, very affectionately yours,
Sarah L. Cady.

Beloved Christian Friends :

A card announcing you fiftieth wedding anniversary was received by Mr. Tillinghast in Columbus, O. He wrote me, if I attended, to give you his most hearty congratulations, and say to Mr. Alden, he remembered the first time he heard him preach, and of course his subsequent work in church and business — especially the big trout. May you live many years yet and reap a heavenly reward finally. Allow me to congratulate you here in thought and word. May your hearts be made glad by a golden harvest of appreciation, which you have earned by long years of Christian toil and steadfastness. May it also be your lot to do much of Christ's loving work for years to come.

Yours, respectfully,
Mrs. C. E. Tillinghast.

Hope Valley, R. I.

20 Cook St., Providence, R. I., Dec. 7, 1883.
Dear Mr. and Mrs. Alden :

I had fully expected to have the pleasure of extending to you, in person, my congratulations upon your happy anniversary, both for our own sakes, and our dear mother's,* who, were she still with us, would have so rejoiced in your joy. We want to offer you our congratulations that our dear Father has spared you so long to each other, and to the world. Our prayer is, that only a golden light may shine upon your path, till at the last you may walk the golden streets in the blessed land above.

Affectionately yours,
Harriet E. Stockwell.

Westfield, December, 1883.

Mr. and Mrs. Alden :

My dear friends, your invitation is received. Accept thanks. We would gladly be present and participate in the exercises. We have none but kindly remembrances of you and yours, and it would give us great pleasure to be with you on this, your anniversary. In connection with you, we always think of the loved ones in our family who have gone to their home in heaven. Mother unites with me in sending congratulations, and wishing you may spend many happy years together.

Yours, in love,
Mrs. M. Doane.
Eliza M. Doane.

EXTRACT OF A LETTER FROM LAWSON A. LONG, M. D.

53 West 26th St., New York, Dec. 17, 1883.
Very Dear Friends :

I learn from Sister Bell that you have recently enjoyed a Golden Wedding. I regret that I did not receive my invitation so that I could join with the rest of your friends in offering my sincere congratulations. Just before father's death, the last time I saw him alive, I told him that I would be his mouth-piece, and as long as I remained upon the earth he should be represented. So you may look upon this letter as in a measure inspired by him. I am sure that he would congratulate you with the same heartiness that I

---

* Mrs. Dr. Davis of Westfield.

do, and I have no doubt but that he would also say that
your present joy was of little moment compared with the
happiness in store for you on your arrival home.   My faith
makes that fact clear, but he has seen what God has in
store for those who love him, and if he could speak to us, he
would say, " Rejoice rather that your names are written in
the Book of life."

I remember well how you and your wife looked in 1836,
when you were young married folks, so I think I can safely
claim to be classed with your oldest friends.   I have often
thought of you, but when the snow and frost say good-bye
in the spring, and the trout brooks are free from surface
water, I always think of Brother Alden, and I have felt sure
if I was unable to attend to the trout, that he would.   I
have had some good interesting times since I have seen
you.   One beautiful May afternoon, after catching a dozen
trout from six to fourteen ounces each, I felt so happy that
I offered up a prayer of thanksgiving by the side of the
brook ; you can doubtless appreciate my feelings.   My
church relations here are very pleasant ; am a member of Dr.
McArthur's, of the Calvary Baptist church.   It is the finest
church in the world of our denomination, costing half a million of dollars, including grounds.   I am, as I can myself
see, a second edition of my father, as to zeal, steadfastness,
and faith.   There is room in my heart for but one desire,
and that is to be conformed to the image of Christ, and, like
him, do always those things that please God.   I am glad to
assure you I shall be happy to meet you where there will be
no more parting.

Your brother, in Christ,

L. A. LONG.

WESTFIELD, MASS., Nov. 28, 1883.

REV. JOHN ALDEN :

Dear friend, it would give me great pleasure to be present, if I could consistently with other duties, at the commemoration of the fiftieth anniversary of your wedding day,
to which you have so kindly invited me.   I had the privilege, a few weeks ago, of attending a like anniversary, that
of Mr. and Mrs. Blood of this town, old parishioners of
yours.   For two to have walked hand in hand to the golden
period, is of itself a mark of the Divine favor, and partici-
pating in such a commemoration seems like treading upon
holy ground   May the day be indeed a golden day to you

and your companion, and as you advance towards the sun-setting, may it brighten more and more into the perfect sunrising in the golden streets. I enclose a check, but a piece of paper to be sure, but it has a transmitting quality to a limited extent,—I could wish to a much greater extent. I rejoice to think that you have not only long known, but that you have also been enabled these many years to tell others the secret of transmitting all things into the true gold which perisheth not.

Yours, sincerely,

H. HOOKER.

CHAPTER IX.

SILVER WEDDING OF SON.

NE special event in my life of great interest to me and my family was the celebration of the twenty-fifth anniversary of the marriage of my son, Augustus E. and Ella B. Alden, on the evening of Nov. 21, 1884, at their residence in Stoneham, Mass. The following notice in regard to the event is from the *Independent*, published in Stoneham:

A SILVER WEDDING.

On the evening of November 21st, a large number of relatives and friends assembled at the residence of Mr. and Mrs. A. E. Alden, on Spring street, to celebrate the twenty-fifth anniversary of their wedding. The many beautiful and valuable remembrances from friends, present and absent, formed a center of attraction. Another matter of interest to all was the fact that there were present the representatives of four successive generations, viz. : Rev. John Alden, of Providence, and his wife (who celebrated their Golden Wedding about a year ago), the groom and bride of twenty-five years ago, their daughter and her husband, Mr. and Mrs. Clarke, of Providence, and their daughter, Helen Ruth, a year old.

After the delicately prepared collation had been partaken of, all assembled in the parlor to enjoy the literary feast which the occasion had prompted. Congratulatory remarks were made by Rev. A. J. Hovey ; interesting reminiscences and benediction were given in verse by Rev. John Alden. Among the several poems contributed was the following, (set to music), composed for the occasion, by Prof. D. B. Purrington, of West Virginia University (a relative of the family), and beautifully rendered by Mrs. Clarke and Miss Arnold :

CHIME ON, MARRIAGE BELLS.

BY D. B. PURRINGTON.

Words of friendship, songs of greeting,
　From the West land far away,
Eastward speeding, swiftly fleeting,
　Hail this happy wedding day.
Marriage bells, still gaily ringing
　Down the corridors of time,
Fragrant thoughts of love are winging
　On their sweet and silvery chime.

Ties of kindness fondly tracing
　Through the labyrinth of years,
Every soul in love embracing
　Who the name of " Alden " bears,
Many noble names we cherish
　From the stillness of the tomb,
But their deeds can never perish—
　Fadeless in immortal bloom.

Name renowned in sacred story—
　Name our Pilgrim Fathers knew,
Let this heritage of glory,
　Make us faithful, noble, true;
Sire to son the gift bequeathing,
　To the latest hour of time,
Joy and love and duty breathing
　Through each merry wedding chime.

In reunion fondly meeting,
　'Mid the mem'ries of the day
Pray receive this friendly greeting,
　Sent from kindred far away ;
May we all in sweet communion,
　When from earth our spirits fly,
Join at last the grand reunion
　Through the portals of the sky.

CHORUS.

Chime on, marriage bells,
           Chime on, sweetly on.
  In joyful melody,
           Sweetly chiming.
For the love of the years agone,
           Sweetly chiming.
  And of ages yet to be.

Rev. A. J. Hovey, pastor of the Stoneham Baptist church, was present, and addressed the parties in a very pleasant and happy manner. Congratulations and music followed. Mrs. Mattie A. Clarke and Miss Arnold played and sung an original piece of poetry and music, by Prof. Purrington, of West Virginia University, a son of Mrs. Nancy Purrington, whose father was the only brother of Miss Mary Lyon, the noted founder of Mt. Holyoke Female Seminary. Mrs. Purrington's mother (my beloved sister, Armilla Alden) was one of the mothers so rarely found who prayed earnestly for her children, that they might be found ready for the service of their Master when-ever and wherever he should call for them to labor in his vineyard, be it on foreign shores, in New England, or in any part of the mighty West; and when she heard the voice of Jesus, through her loving daughter, Lucy (after-ward the wife of Rev. Edward Lord of Ningpo, China), asking her consent to leave her native land, and labor for the benighted heathen, she answered, "For this I have prayed, and shall I now refuse? Go, my child; and the ben-ediction of Heaven go with and rest upon you." She was married to Rev. Edward Lord, and labored four years with him in China, returned to her native land, and died among her kindred, leaving a bright and faithful record of Chris-tian work. Again this dear sister was called to give up another dear child, Freelove, the second wife of Rev. E. Lord, who, after several years of toil and work in the mis-sionary field, died, and was buried in China.

To Mr. and Mrs. Augustus E. Alden, on the Evening of their Silver Wedding—Nov. 21, 1884,—Celebrated Dec. 5, 1884.

PROVIDENCE, December, 1884.

My Dear Children :

Twenty-five years have passed since you stood at the
altar in the house of God, and pledged your constancy and
love ; around you then were father, mother and dear grandmother, brother, Aunt Lizzie and loving friends, who cared
and prayed for your present and future good. Some of
them have passed to the other shore, and their faces here
you will see no more ; but do you forget them ? No,
never ! Their prayers, their counsels, their deeds of love,
will ever be remembered. Since then, changes have come.
Children, one, two, three and four have come to enliven and
cheer you amid the toils and cares of life ; the Angel of
Death has not taken from your home one of these loved
ones. Yea, more, God has given to one of the household
band a loving Christian companion, ready to share her joys
and sorrows ; and when the fiftieth anniversary of your
parents came, there was given you a golden treasure, a
jewel more precious than the jewelled crown of queens !

> " God keep her spirit undefiled,
> A golden treasure bright."

Accept, my dear children, this small silver offering on
this, your Silver Wedding anniversary. Be assured I never
shall forget your interest and care for your parents, so rapidly descending the hill of life. May your future be fraught,
not only with temporal, but great spiritual mercies. May
you live to lead the way to the cross of Christ, your children following in the narrow way to life eternal.

God grant that we may be an unbroken band in the
kingdom of our blest Redeemer, and finally join the unnum-
bered hosts in anthems of eternal praise.

Your loving mother,

Mrs. Ann M. C. Alden,

Dear Cousins of the Alden Tribe :

Please accept salutations and congratulations upon your
approaching anniversary on the 21st inst. May the benedic-

tion of John and Priscilla, of the ancient days, and of all the
goodly succession since, abide with you.

I remain, respectfully yours,

BOSTON, November 19th.   E. K. ALDEN.

PROVIDENCE, November, 1884.

DEAR AUGUSTUS AND ELLA:

Please accept this silver offering as a memorial of the
silver anniversary of your marriage.

Is it possible that twenty-five years have passed since,
at the altar, in the church of God, before many witnesses,
you were united in the sacred bonds of matrimony! Side
by side you stood in the bloom of youth, life seemed bright
before you, and you knew but little comparatively of the
cares and perplexities of life. Years passed, and young
immortals were committed to your care and training.
They have been preserved amid all the dangers of childhood. The Angel of Death has not crossed your threshold
to take one of your darlings from the home circle. All
have been spared. A new link has also been added.

"Another little wave
Upon the sea of life."

Truly you have reason to say, "Bless the Lord, O my
soul, and forget not all his benefits." "Who redeemeth
thy life from destruction; who crowneth thee with loving
kindness and tender mercies."

May your future life be useful and happy in each other,
happy in your children, and, above all, happy in the service
of your heavenly Father. Some of the loved ones who
were present twenty-five years since have passed away
from the scenes of this life, and are "safe within the vale."
Other dear parents are spared to an advanced age, and have
passed the golden anniversary of their wedded life. Their
pathway has been brightened by your true, filial devotion
to their interests. As years increase, trials and sorrows
come to darken life; but remember that

"Every cloud has a silver side,
Though dark the cloud may be."

"All things work together for good to those who love
God." Take God's word for your guide, and may you be
enabled henceforth to rejoice in its truths, heed its warn-

ings, obey its precepts, and trust in its promises. Thus
will you be prepared for the future duties and responsibilities of life, and for a home in our Father's home on high.
Yours, with best wishes,

AUNT LIZZIE.

1859.   MR. AND MRS. A. E. ALDEN.   1884.

WRITTEN FOR THEIR SILVER WEDDING BY E. E. CHAMBERLAIN.

Twenty-five years! a happy pair,
  In youthful beauty fair,
Stood side by side, with purpose true,
  Whatever might ensue,
To help each other in the strife
  With all the ills of life.

Twenty-five years have sped their course,
  As rivers from their source;
Each one with goodness crowned,
  Fresh mercies all around,
Call forth each day new songs of praise,
  With sweet and joyous lays.

Twenty-five years! four children dear
  Were given you to rear;
All have been spared to see this day,
  None have been called away,
But here this night together stand
  A happy household band.

Mattie, the first-born daughter fair,
  Eyes of blue, and flaxen hair;
With gentle mien and modest grace
  Depicted in her open face,
To lovely womanhood has grown
  And from the home-nest flown.

Lillie next, in spring-time coming,
  With golden ringlets waving,
With face so fair, and eyes so bright,
  Of home she was the light;
Childhood has passed — a Christian youth;
  Firm may she stand for truth.

John Alden, proud to bear the name
  Of one who cross'd the main;
A boy of spirit, wild with play,
  And every childish way;

A noble manly form he bears,—
God keep from sinful snares.

The household pet, your Eddie, dear,
Next came to bring you cheer;
His childish prattle, winning ways,
Brightened your cloudy days;
A merry-hearted boy to-day,
May he ne'er go astray.

Last year a little grandchild came,
Sweet Helen Ruth by name,
A priceless little treasure, given
To train for earth and heaven, —
God keep the darling in the way
That leads to endless day.

Twenty-five years! gone, gone for aye,
None can Time's current stay.
Oh, give to God the fleeting hours;
Serve him with all your powers;
Then may you, one unbroken band,
Dwell in that happy land.

CHICOPEE FALLS, Nov. 19, 1884.
MR. AND MRS. AUGUSTUS E. ALDEN :

My dear friends, allow me to congratulate you on the twenty-fifth anniversary of your marriage. It seems but yesterday since that night's great gathering at the church. I look back through the vista of years, and through all the lights and shadows and vicissitudes since 1859, and the scene of that evening reproduces itself before my eyes : a slight young man of good figure and costume, a most cheerful expression, and leaning on his arm, the graceful form of a young girl of eighteen with one of those faces of classic beauty and delicate sweetness, now so rarely seen,— these stood before me, facing the great assembly, and with a few brief words, followed by a prayerful benediction from your honored father, were joined in marriage till death should you part. How many loving eyes which looked on that joyous scene are now closed to all that is earthly! Your good father and mother yet linger (God bless them), and may it be your joy, as was lately theirs, to celebrate yet another wedding a quarter of a century hence. We shall not be here to greet you then, but let us hope your children will, like your fathers' and mothers' children, be there to rise up

and call you blessed. With many wishes for your mutual health and happiness, in which Mrs. Bellamy cordially joins, I remain, as ever, your old friend, long your pastor,

REV. R. K. BELLAMY.

FROM HENRY M. PUFFER, ATTORNEY AND COUNSELLOR AT LAW.

SHELBURNE FALLS, Nov. 19, 1884.

MY DEAR COUSINS :

Words cannot express my regret at not being able to attend your Silver Wedding anniversary on the twenty-first. How well I remember you both, when you were good looking and even too young to marry; now you are a staid old couple, and dignified, venerable grandparents, surrounded by wedded blossoms, holy tokens of the heaven-blessed union. How I should love to take you by the hand and say, God bless and ever make you happy and prosperous, while travelling the declining way of life. But keep the declination as nearly level as possible. Cross no bridges until you come to them. Never let go each other's hands, and avoid the water bars and ditches incident to life's great highway.

> Years are short, and cares are many,
> Soon you'll lay your burdens down;
> They who help the cross to carry
> Will be first to wear the crown.

I hope that next Friday will find you altogether replete with health, happiness, and merriment. I should love dearly to be with you all and see those Golden Wedding veterans, my highly prized uncle and aunt, together with yourselves, children and pet grandchild! May the stars of heaven look kindly down, and bountiful blessings ever be yours.

Affectionate cousin,

HENRY.

757 OAKWOOD BOULEVARD, CHICAGO, Nov. 19, 1884.

DEAR COUSINS AUGUSTUS AND ELLA :

Your card is received, and how am I to reply? What thoughts crowd through my mind of those twenty-five years! How utterly useless for me to attempt to put them on paper. It seems to me that one could hardly desire a

richer gift than is enjoyed by those who, hand in hand, lovingly travel earth's pilgrim ways, with mutual sympathy in
the trials which take so much courage to bear, and in the
exquisite joy of a love so tender that nothing else can even,
in ever so imperfect a degree, illustrate the soul joy of
union to Him who has declared that He is Love.

May such love continue to bless you, and your dear Ella,
very many more years, is the wish and prayer of

Your affectionate cousins,

ELBRIDGE AND MAY HOVEY.

NORTHAMPTON, MASS., Nov. 4, 1884.

Good boy to remember us! Can it be that you are a
married man, and twenty-five years at that? Why do you
by your dainty card of invitation so delicately remind me
of my patriarchal age? I am a young man, and yet you,
my boy of only a little while ago, have the audacity to
place before me a reminder of my rapidly approaching old
age! Well, it's all right, and I gratefully accept that fact,
and say, "Goodness and mercy have followed me along the
years." But, really, are you not joking? 1859 — 1884 — a
quarter of a century; and so it must be that you are no
longer a boy, but a full-grown man. Well, I bring you on
paper my heartfelt congratulations, and thank you sincerely
for your kind remembrance of us, and if we cannot be
present on that glad occasion, send you a benediction.
You will have a good time, I know, with the wide circle of
friends you have made; and may you, and the dear one who
bears your name, long live to bless each other and the
world.

Sincerely yours,

S. E. BRIDGMAN, for self and wife.

HAVERHILL, MASS., Nov. 18, 1884.

MR. A. E. AND MRS. ELLA B. ALDEN:

Dear friends, your beautiful card of a recent date was
duly received, for which please accept our thanks and kind
wishes. It would, indeed, give us very great pleasure to
meet you at the time and upon the interesting occasion
named in your card of invitation, and renew an old, long
and pleasant friendship, but we feel that we must deny ourselves that pleasure at the present time. Can it be it is
nearly twenty-five years since we saw you married one even-

ing in Chicopee Falls! Well, it may be, such is the flight of time. You know best about this. But what changes have taken place since. What a type of human life in this poor, perishing world do these changes represent! "Nothing human is abiding." How much of the past rushes upon the mind as we review the past; persons and events crowd upon the mind for consideration. But it is with the present and future, mainly, that we have now to do. The past has gone beyond recall, and if we can only profit by it, so as to make our little future the better, it will be well to do so.

We trust you will enjoy a very pleasant time on the occasion in near prospect, with your children, and such other friends as may meet with you, and may the good Lord greatly bless your future in this life, and abundantly fit you for the higher and more enduring joys of the life to come. To us all, the end of this brief life is nearing. May we be prepared for it. Please accept our kind regards and best wishes.

Yours, very truly,

WILLIAM THAYER.

70 WAKEMAN AVE., NEWARK, N. J., 1884.

DEAR MR. AND MRS. ALDEN:

Allow me, in the crowd of your friends surrounding you to-night, to tender my congratulations also, upon the arrival of the twenty-fifth anniversary of your marriage. A happy union, an unbroken family, mean so much. Doubtless you realize how great is your call for thankfulness, for blessings so few attain. Four children, all yet spared to you, giving you yet their presence and affection, — how rare the pleasure!

And then a grandchild also is given you, to fill your hearts afresh with love and tenderness. This blessing, too, I know by sweet experience. But alas, my first, my pet, went in early years to join the redeemed above. Your parents, too, beloved and revered, are still with you, to enter into all your enjoyments, to encourage, advise and aid you with their own extended experience. Thrice blessed are you truly.

I have remembered in gratitude the kindness of each of your family, parents, sons, and "Aunt Lizzie," towards myself and little ones while I was so ill, away from my friends and home. And have read with interest all mention of their names and doings which has come to my notice. With warm wishes for your enjoyment to-night, and all through the future of your way heavenward,

I remain, yours, very truly,

S. B. WILSON.

Of my two sons, Augustus and Judson, I wish to say a few words. Augustus, being the eldest, has always, from his early manhood, shown for his mother and myself most faithful and loving care, and now, in our declining years, is truly a staff on which to lean. Of a peculiarly affectionate and generous disposition, his attitude towards us has been one of constant and unvarying devotion.

Judson, affectionate and kind, has been called in his pursuits to live at a distance from us most of the time. Hence the filial duties have naturally fallen upon the eldest, who has constantly been with us until quite lately. I had hoped they would choose to follow some one of the professions, and to this end proposed each a college course ; but they decided in favor of a business life, for which my eldest son early showed great aptitude, and for several years stood among the leading men in his line of business. At the present time, although retaining his photograph rooms in Boston, he is engaged in advancing the interests of his spring property in Stoneham, Mass., where he now resides with his family, consisting of his estimable wife, Ella Blake, and three children, Lillie, John and Edward. Their home is very pleasant, being located only nine miles from the city, having a lovely surrounding country, picturesque and most healthful, the Cedar Park Springs, as the place is called, being on an elevated tableland two hundred and fifty feet above Boston, making it exceedingly desirable as a health resort, as I believe it is destined to become in the near future. My other son, Judson, also resides in Boston, and is engaged in the photograph business, and is considered a superior artist in portrait and landscape work, especially views of interior and exterior of buildings. In April, 1885, twin sons were born to him. In memory of the historic stories of Plymouth days, they were named by their grand· mother, respectively, John Alden and Miles Standish Alden. Near me, in Providence, lives my oldest grandchild, Mattie, the wife of Dea. Walter Clarke, an enterprising young man, and an earnest Christian worker. He is now connected with the city treasury department, is also an active mem· ber, as is his wife, of the Broadway Baptist Church. They have a beautiful home and two lovely children, Helen Ruth and Ronald Blake.

PART II.

—o—

CHAPTER X.

STORIES FOR WINTER EVENINGS.

ABOUT seventy years ago, a man from my native town, intemperate and quarrelsome, became unpopular, and moved to a new town, in Ohio, where some of his old cronies lived. In such cases the neighbors would turn out and build a log house for the new comer. This man, James Cobb, by name, went a little distance from his new log house, to put up one for a new settler. They finished it about dark, and Cobb shouldered his axe, and started alone for his home, singing, as whiskey pitches the tune. Near his path was a ravine, in which he heard one, as he thought, mimicking him. Thinking it one of the party trying to scare him, he stopped and addressed it, "You can't frighten this Cobb; there is pith in it," and went on. It followed him soon on the trees over his head. He ran for life. A hung-up coverlid was his only door. He rushed through it, and landed on all fours in the middle of his kitchen. His wife screamed, "What is the matter, Jimmie?" "The devil of a catamount is after me." They looked at the doorway, and saw a huge panther's paw move back the coverlid, and show a terrific head. As he saw the fire and heard their screams he retreated. Cobb boarded the doorway with strong timbers, and spent most of the night swearing he would have his heart's blood or die in the effort. He charged his rifle heavily. A light snow fell in the night. Going out with rifle and hatchet in his belt, he saw tracks around his house where the monster had been, and he then tracked him toward the ravine. As he came upon a little knoll, he saw the panther a few rods from him in a position for a leap, his head between his paws. But he was asleep. He fired his two balls at his head; one ball hit his head, the other paralyzed the silver cord of his neck. He sprang towards Cobb, who drew his hatchet, and, like Milton's Death, "delayed to strike." It was his final leap. He dragged him home, and he measured, as he said, over ten and one-half feet in length.

Near by this place another tragic event occurred. There were some thieving Indians in the region. Two white men lived side by side. One of them, who had considerable money, which was known to his neighbors, had to leave home for the day. He said, " I will reward you if you will watch my premises till I return, as my wife is alone." He promised to do so. About midday, an Indian, with the war paint on, knocked for entrance. The man's wife refused to let him in. He declared he would come down the chimney, if she would not let him in. The chimneys of such log houses are made very large, and the houses only one story. She told him if he came down thus it would be at the peril of his life. She had an axe in the room and a good fire burning. When she heard him well on his way, she set fire to her straw bed, placed beneath, and as he came tumbling down, strangled, with the axe she killed him. She then ran over to the neighbor, asking her to come and see what she had done. The man was not at home. The wife came, saying, "You are a brave woman, and you have served the Indian right. He meant to rob and perhaps kill you." They both stood stupefied over the horrid scene. " I am glad you did the deed, and saved your life and money. Your husband had quite a lot of it How glad he will be on his return." Said one of the women, " Did you ever see so mean an Indian, and his features so resemble a white man. Perhaps he is a half breed." "Why," says the neighbor, " he has stolen my husband's coat; I know it by a singular patch I put on it." They washed the paint from his face, and, lo! it was her husband.

During my agency for the Bible society, I had two weeks vacation each year, during which time I took two trips to the Maine lakes trouting. There are four lakes that make a chain of lakes, forty miles in length. Through these lakes, or from them, the Androscoggin river flows, abounding with speckled trout. The first is the Rangeley Lake, ten miles by five. The second is the Mooseluemaguntic, or, as the Indians named it, *Moose-heard-my-gun-tick.* This lake is eleven miles by four. Third, the Richardson Lake, ten miles by two. Lastly, the Umbagog Lake, about the same size. All these lakes, except the Umbagog, yield only speckled trout and dace, on which they feed. During my first trip, I took two amateur fishermen from North-ampton, Mass., with me. In five days we captured four hundred pounds of trout, in size from one to four pounds. In the next trip, four of us caught fifty-four pounds in one day; there were only twelve in number, thus averaging four and one-half pounds each. We fished in about fifteen feet of water, shoreward. When one of those furious fellows felt the hook, he would rush for the centre of the lake, making the reel sound like a lightning train of cars in the distance. He would not slacken his furious speed short of fifty feet. Then we would reel him in. It often took from twenty to thirty minutes. He would outdo old Euclid in making angles in speed, if not in number. It is rare that a real speckled trout is caught that weighs over twelve pounds. Dr. S. P. Hubbard, of Taunton, Mass., who was my family physician when I was settled in Westfield, was one of the party, and one of the best doctors in New England in catching trout or saving human life. I think my love of this sport has prolonged my life. When oppressed with toil and care, a good sweat, chasing the trout up and down the mountain streams, saved me, per-haps, from paralysis. Where I stand in this picture is at the head of a fall nearly seventy feet. I would not take my

oath that it was the roughest spot in the universe, for I have not travelled it all over. It was in this place my son, A. E. Alden, took this picture of me. His picture and his brother's are seen in this view.

All through the sublime mountain region there are hundreds of acres on which it is probable no white man ever climbed. It is the most romantic, clandestined, clancular place I ever saw. If I could think of any more expressive adjectives I would insert them, and then feel how weak is language to express the grandeur of this scenery. On firing a pistol we could hear half a dozen echoes.

The preceding cut represents a scene in one of my fishing trips. It is found near Capt. George M. Estey's Greenvale House, at the head of the Rangley Lakes, and is mentioned by Capt. C. A. J. Farrar in his illustrated Guide Book as follows:

"A short distance from the Greenvale House is a mountain stream, not only noted for its excellent fishing, but also for its fine scenery. Follow it up for quite a distance from the road, and you will come to a deep ravine, cut out of the solid rock by the powerful action of the water during the spring freshets. This ravine extends up the stream for a quarter of a mile, the brook being broken all through it by rapids, cascades and falls. Along its sides, where the water has washed out all the earth, huge crevices are found in the rocks, and from several of these, in the last of June, 1876, we took some splendid ice, many of the pieces being two to three pounds in weight. It is a wild and romantic place, and one which is eagerly sought after by lovers of nature. The dark rocks, the water flashing in the sunlight, the numerous natural bridges, caused by trees which have been uprooted by tempests, and have fallen across the ravine, the roar of the cataract, the grateful shade to be had under the old forest trees, are all congenial to one who wishes to walk in nature's solitudes, and who can appreciate such a wild country. When visiting the Greenvale House, by all means spare half a day to visit this brook, as we are confident you will be well satisfied with the time so spent."

Of all trout-fishing during my life experience, preference is decidedly in favor of the Androscoggin lakes and tributaries, although I have had some rare sport in the vicinity of Mt. Kineo House, Moosehead Lake, through the genial courtesy of Mr. Dennen, proprietor of Mt. Kineo, who is always wide awake to entertain and guide the sportsman to the favorite spot where the speckled beauties are "*always found.*" On the John Brown tract and in the Chateaugay lakes, I found the trout smaller and of inferior quality, as compared with those found in the Maine lakes, notwithstanding Mr. Murray's preferences and those of President Cleveland.

My last trip to the Androscoggin lakes was made during the summer of 1884, with my son, A. E. Alden, and his family. We made in to the lakes from Bethel, Me., first to the Umbagog, the lower lake of the Androscoggin chain, a most beautiful and romantic sheet of water, from there by steamer and carry, we arrived at Middle Dam and Richardson lakes, where we were entertained by Capt. C. A. J. Farrar at his camp. Capt. Farrar has been, and is, one of the most active workers in opening up this and the Andover route to and through the chain of lakes and their many large tributaries. His illustrated Guide Book is the most complete work of the kind ever published, and should be bought by the tourist and sportsman, and every one desiring to know about trout and game in the wilds of Maine, and the best routes to and from. After leaving Capt. Farrar, we took the steamer for Upper Dam, and there we were met by Mr. J. A. Straw, the active manager of the Union Water Power Company, of Lewiston, Me. Here has been erected a fine lodge, with all the modern improvements, yet wild in its location and general arrangement, and is under the charge of Supt. John Chadwick, a man every way capable of serving the public at this, the grand center of all the fishing grounds. Here the Union Water Power Company have erected one of their largest and most extensive and expensive dams to be found all through this chain of lakes, which water privilege they control. Their business in the transportation of logs and lumber is immense, and is entirely under the management of J. A. Straw, Esq., one of the most thorough engineers to be found, a man of push and brains.

From Upper Dam, we took the cosy little steamer owned and run by Capt. Fred Barker, one of the most competent and obliging men to be found in all the lake region. With him we steamed across the Mooselucmaguntic Lake to his camp under Bemis mountain, and near the outlet of Bemis stream, one of the best fishing points on the lakes. Capt. Barker's place is known as Camps Bemis, and consists of some twenty log cabins and cottages, built and arranged in a very attractive and romantic manner, on a knoll under the mountain, and overlooking the grand old lake, in keeping with the wild and mountainous scenery around; frontier life outside, but inside, splendid beds and all home comforts. It is truly the most wild, rustic camp I have ever seen.

From this point, after remaining two weeks, Capt. Barker took us up to Indian Rock or Camp Kenebago, at the junction of Kenebago and Rangeley streams. Here is where the Oquassoc Angling Association have spent so many hundreds of dollars in building and other improvements on their place. From Indian Rock, we followed up the Rangeley stream on foot, to the outlet of Rangeley Lake. Here we stopped at the Mountain View House, owned and kept by Mr. Henry T. Kimball. Beautifully located at the outlet of the Rangeley Lake, it is one of the best-built and best-kept hotels in the State of Maine, in many respects the best. At certain seasons of the year, this point is the favorite fishing ground in all the chain of lakes, especially for large trout. From here, the steamer takes us through the Rangeley lakes, the inlet near the Greenvale House, where Capt. Estey will give you good rooms and the best living in all the mountains and lakes of Maine. Never pass through

Rangeley without taking dinner with him. He knows how to cook trout in the daintiest manner to tickle the palate of the most fastidious epicure, and he, as well as Mr. Kimball, knows how to keep a hotel. On my last trip, I spent several days at this house, and took great pleasure in the sport afforded by the brooks and small lakes in the vicinity. From Greenvale, we make out of the lakes by way of Phillips and Farmington, a route full of romantic and delightful scenery. All who are fond of fishing sports cannot do better than to take a trip through the Androscoggin lake region.

Some thirty years since I visited my brother and brother-in-law, A. Lyon, Esq. They lived near each other in the village of Cassadaga, N. Y. I had not seen them for nearly twenty years. I called first on Brother Lyon in the evening. I said, "Brother Lyon, how shall I work it to be unrecognized by my brother Willard." "Let my son Ezra go and introduce you as a Mr. Longfellow." "No," said I, "he will see through that." He was a wealthy farmer. "What are farmers selling now?" "Wool," said he. "I have it now." Knowing, like Job, he was well stocked with sheep and had not sold his wool, I chose to go alone. I rung his bell. His little Theodosia opened the door. "Is there a man named Alden lives here?" "Yes," he replied, sitting at his desk posting his books. "Have you wool to sell, sir?" "Yes, in abundance." "Is it fine Merino and well cleansed?" "Yes. If you can find a Tory weed in a single place, I will give the fleece to you." "I would not buy it if there was." This was the first time I ever heard of a Tory weed. "How much have you?" "Two large chambers full." "What is your price, cash down?" He gave it. "You cannot expect to get that unless it is of very superior quality." "It is; come and look at it." "I fear it will be of no avail." "Have you bought any in this region?" "No, nor shall I at such prices." "We often sell to Massachusetts agents; are you from that State?" "I am." "From what town?" "Ashfield." "I used to live there." "Alden, Alden, I have met an Alden when teacher of Franklin Academy; is he any connection of yours?" "I have had two brothers who taught there, John and David." "I think it was John that I imperfectly knew, and I have seen David. Where is John now?" "He is pastor of a church in North Adams. Are you acquainted there?" "Some. It is quite a flourishing manufacturing place. There are about twenty factories there." I kept talking ever and anon of wool, lest he should suspect the joke. Thus I marched him three times over Ashfield and the adjacent towns. "Please throw off your wrapper and stop with me." "No, I thank you; I am pledged at another place." "Come, go up and look at the wool; I think we can make a trade." Thinking he might say it was evening, and he had not a fair chance for recognition, I went up with him to his chambers. He began to throw fleeces into the hall. Soon a full Merino fleece came out. "This will do. Will you warrant the whole lot will average half Merino?" "Yes, and much more." I took a lock of the full-blood Merino fleece, and held up a lock, saying, "Please hold up the lamp and let me look at it." Thus the lamp and the wool was between our faces, my tongue running on the subject of wool. "I wish you would stop with me; I want to inquire more about Massachusetts people. I think we can trade," and he fell considerable in the price, if I would take the wool from his house. "No, I shall not take it even at that price." "I wish you would call in the morning." I assented. I had filled his head so full of wool that I took him all over his native region again, much to my own delight. I then said, "I think I have carried the joke far enough." "Good heavens!" said he, throwing his arms around me, "is this John?" His wife, a little ill, was lying on a bed, and burst into laughter. She said she was pretty sure I was a brother from a resemblance to Deacon Alden, my brother, who recently visited them. On my return the question came quick, "Did you swoop him?" "Yes." "Well, you are the first man we ever knew who came off first best

with him." " Perhaps they did not have a ton of wool to
help them." Ezra, my nephew, went down to his house
and said, " Uncle, how did you make out with the Massa
chusetts wool agent ?" and he never said a word.

HAFED'S DREAM.

The wisdom and benevolence of God are richly displayed
in the immutable laws by which he governs the universe,
and the certain penalty that follows from breaking them.
The law that the same causes, under the same circumstances, always produces the same effects, is an indescribable blessing.   Were it not so, no sure advances could be
made in mechanics, philosophy, or the *materia medica.*
The opposite was very finely illustrated more than fifty
years ago by Rev. Dr. Todd, by what he called Hafed's
Dream.   I have not seen it for forty years.   It is practical,
and I shall try to reproduce it in my own words, perhaps
adding some and forgetting some.   Hafed had a beautiful
home at the base of the Himalaya mountains, where perpetual verdure smiles.   Every fine flower and shrub bloomed
around his splendid mansion.   He had a beautiful, lovely
wife, and three charming daughters.   Hafed felt happy.
But amid all these domestic joys, Hafed's wife took sick.
Medicine was soon ordered, and Hafed made a mistake and
gave her poison, which killed her.   He refused to be comforted.   A little while after, a portentous cloud hung in
mid heaven over his mansion.   His daughters were gazing
at the wonderful displays of the lightning, and listening to
the voice of God in the thunder peals.   The lightning
struck them all dead.   Hafed rebelled under the chastening
rod, and wished he could live in a chance world, where
poison would not certainly kill.   He laid himself down in
his desolate loneliness and fell asleep.   He awoke in a
chance world.   All things looked strangely.   Hafed walked
along between strange fences.   He saw on the fence a man
of enormous size, with but one great eye, so placed he had

to mount the fence to see. How is this? Do all in this
chance world have but one great eye? No; they sometimes
have a dozen, and sometimes none. Hafed walked on.
He saw apple trees bearing pumpkins and squashes. Soon
the sun failed to shine, and all was perfect darkness. All
at once it burst out in dazzling splendor, ten millions of
miles nearer the earth, with a scorching heat. "Alas!"
said a man near him, "for my great ox, that chanced to have
wool instead of hair, he must die now," and so he did. He
walked on, and next saw a man digging, who had dug down
twenty feet for potatoes. "How is this?" said Hafed.
"Well," said he, "potatoes are found sometimes near the
surface, sometimes twenty or thirty feet below, and sometimes we can never find them." He next saw two men
gleefully rowing a boat. All the water froze suddenly, and
the men froze to death in their boat. He hastened, through
fear of the cold, to a house. Just as he entered one, a gun
was discharged in a closet. "That gun," said the owner,
"I snapped at some game three days ago, and it chanced
just now to go off." Hafed was hungry, and ordered a dinner of toast and coffee. When a fire was kindled, all the
smoke came down and drove them out of the room. "We
must wait," said the host, "for sometimes the smoke goes
up, and sometimes it comes down." "I am sick of a chance
world," said Hafed. "I am weary and faint and hungry.
Let me have a couch on which to rest and sleep a little."
He slept, and awoke at home, thanking God he was not in
a chance world.

HOW TO SETTLE DIFFICULTIES.

I have lived over eighty-two years, and have never sued
or prosecuted any one, and was never so served by
others. Scarcely any thing has comforted me in all my
settlements more than the name of a peace-maker given
me. Where I have attempted, only a very few cases,
among the many, have turned out like the man's fiddle

that had only one string and played one tune, "'Tis as it was, and was as it is." In a very few instances the case was left to referees. I have a case or two laid over for the court of heaven, and I am quite sure if the parties do not settle it here, it will go hard with them at the highest chancery. This, like almost every subject, calls up one or more anecdotes. It called up a story of a young married Protestant Irishman in Connecticut, who bought a farm and attended the Congregational church. For a time he was punctual in his attendance and paid his pastor liberally. But as his family multiplied as by magic, he neglected every duty. His pastor, wishing the spiritual good of his soul, and that of his family, called on him, and tried to rouse him up to duty. He plead poverty. His pastor told him he thought he would get four-fold for all he gave him. He said, "Peggy, what do you think the minister said unto me this blessed day? He said if we gave to him, we should have four-fold." "Do you believe it, Patrick?" "Yes, surely I do. I never knew any of these good Connecticut ministers to tell lies. Now, my dear, we have but one cow, and four would be mighty better," and he gave up the cow. "I fear you have done too much." "Oh, no; for you said we should get four-fold." The cow was of a very affection-ate nature, and proud of the other sex, and she invited the four oxen of the pastor's to accompany her to the old home, and when the Irishman saw them all jubilant in his yard, he said, "Peggy, and what do you think now? As sure as there was a St. Patrick, the four-fold has come. And now, my honey, we will have bafe enough in the barrel." He sent for a butcher, and had the largest and fattest one slaughtered and hung him up in his barn. The minister sent over his boy to drive the herd home. The boy came back crying, and told his father that they had killed old Brady. Astonished and grieved, the parson took his cane and walked over to the Irishman's, and said, "What does this mean," suppressing his feelings as a Christian should, "that you have killed my darling ox?" "Indade, I thought

him all my very own. You know your reverence said unto
me, if I gave to you I should have four-fold, and verily, indade, as I knew you was a man of truth, I thought most
surely you had sent them." " I did not mean in this world."
"I am verily sure you said nothing of any other world."
" Well," said the good parson, "as you did not understand
me, I want to do right by you, and I will have the thing left
out to three of the best of men, and you may choose them
all." "Very well; if it is the other world you meant, I will
leave it to Abraham, Isaac and Jacob, three of the best men
in that good world, and to no other."

DOES GOD EVER GIVE PREMONITORY WARNING?

I will submit a fact or two. If he does, we should heed
it. The steamer Erie, that played between Buffalo and
Cleveland, was repaired and varnished over. It took fire in
the night, on its way to Cleveland, some thirty years since,
and was consumed, and many lives were lost. I have the
following story from a merchant of Cleveland, whose life
was saved by heeding premonitory warning. Riding with
him a short time after the sad event, he pointed the spot
out where the Erie took fire. " Please sit down and let me
tell you how I was spared. I left Cleveland in the morning
boat with two horses I hoped to sell in Buffalo. I told my
wife, a feeble, nervous woman, I should be back at night in
the Erie. I sold my horses hours before the boat was to
leave, and bought my ticket, and went for the boat. Some
time ere it was to start, I had a strong impression come
over me, 'Don't go up in the Erie to-night.' 'Why,' I
reasoned with myself, 'my business calls me, and my wife's
feebleness.' I tried to ward off the impression, but could
not. I walked on to the wharf, and then back on to the
boat. My conviction was so strong I nearly fainted under
it. It seemed to me a warning, and I left the boat, and quartered in a hotel in sight of the landing. About midnight I
was awakened by loud voices and heart-rending groans. I

hastened to the wharf, to see the Erie burnt down to the water's edge, with a score or more wretched sufferers burnt beyond all hope of recovery, some of whom said, 'Kill me, and prevent further agony.' Then I understood why I had the silent warning." He seemed to be a devoted Christian. "I took the morning boat, the boat that brought in the Erie the night before," he said, "and going to my house, I found my wife a raving maniac, rushing around the house, franti. cally exclaiming, 'My husband was burnt to death on the Erie.' I said, 'My dear, I am your husband, all safe.' 'Get out of my house! My husband was burnt on the Erie.' I went to my family physician, who could do nothing. I sought the advice of the Insane Hospital doctor. The advice was, 'Have her sit up late, till tired out, and when sound asleep, get into the bed without waking her.' In time she awoke and said, 'Who is here?' 'I am home, all safe.' At which expression she shouted for joy, saying, 'Is it so? Is it so?' and became perfectly rational.

Several years since, I read the following story in the *Christian Watchman*, which is very careful what it publishes. The full names of the parties were given and the town in New York where it occurred. I have forgotten the names, but the facts have ever been remembered. A rich widow lady, pious and benevolent, had a daughter living near her, who had an ungodly husband. She said to her daughter, "I think of giving quite a sum to a mission cause," which will account for the sequences. This good lady lived alone, some distance from the village. One day she visited friends in the village, and as she was about to leave the last one, she said, "I never felt so about going home." "Have you ever been molested?" "No. It is only a needless fear, I think," standing at the door. "Stop with me." "No; I must go home," putting her hand on the knob. "I feel strangely, and shrink from starting, and yet I must go." "Take Rover, our great watch-dog." Rover proudly escorted her home, and she paid him a supper in advance. As she retired, she put Rover on the foot of her bed. It was a dark, rainy night. She heard a crash in the lower story, at which Rover lifted his head. Then all was still. Soon the door opened, and Rover sprang and grappled with something. An instrument fell on the floor, and soon a heavy body fell, struggling a while, and all was still. Rover came back on the bed. She was too affrighted to light up. When it was light, behold, there on the floor lay her son-in-law, throttled to death by the faithful watch-dog, and by the door a butcher knife, that fell in the first grapple, with which he intended doubtless to murder his mother-in-law.

INDIANS.

I have travelled over nearly every Indian battlefield in New England. None have more interested me than that of Bloody Brook and Old Deerfield. It was in those places the Indians assembled in force to capture the first settlers. In Deerfield, they erected a strong fort by settling heavy timbers into the ground, standing up some fifteen feet above the ground, rudely covered. This fort, proof against tomahawk and bullets, would accommodate a large number of men and women ; arranged for all culinary purposes. The log-house by its side was another strong rendezvous. I was in this house before it was taken down. The logs were of white oak, and the doors were of very thick, white oak plank, with nails driven in, the heads as large as a cent-piece, touching each other. But the Indians dug a hole in the front door, and shot a man in the house. I saw where balls hit the ceiling. That door, I am told, is in the attic as the Indians left it.

Men that cultivated the soil kept their rifles near them, and a man to watch as a sentinel. This was in the time of the French and Indian war. The Indians came mostly from Canada, urged on by the French, who gave them a reward for every white man's scalp. They made an attack on the fort and block house in the night, in the winter,

when the crust would bear them. They halted near the
fort and put their ears on the crust, to find out if any were
up in the fort. Hearing no noise, they made a vigorous
effort to burn the house, but failed to harm the house or
fort. It is said the women put their churns on the scaffold
of the fort, pointed toward the foe, and they frightened
them away, as they had great fear of cannon. When the
weather became warm, the Indians made many attacks,
murdering all they could, and stealing in all directions.
This so roused the whites that they raised a company of
twenty-five brave men, armed with muskets, and furnished
with several days' rations. They were ordered to travel
north in search of the foe. The first trail they found was in
the northern part of Bernardston. They followed this trail
till they came to a valley, where eighteen Indians were
feasting on a deer. As they saw twenty-five men, all armed,
they pretended great friendship, leaped up and down, pointing to their muskets stacked against the trees. There was
one Indian who could talk English, and one white man who
could talk Indian tongue. The Indian said, "We be glad
to have white man come and help kill the wolves, bears and
catamounts. Catamount terrible, jump on Indian and tear
him to pieces." They wanted them to eat deer and smoke
with them. Some of the soldiers said, " These Indians are
friendly." The captain said, "They will kill us all before
morning if we don't take care of ourselves. You are all
put under me, and I wish you to go with me and seek a
place of safety. They sought a little eminence in the
woods, near a background of rocks. The captain ordered
them to cut down trees about the size of a man, and cut off
twenty-five logs about the length of a man. Then to pile
up logs, and set them on fire, by which to cook their supper. When they had eaten supper, he ordered them to
put the logs as men would lie around the fire, and put their
caps on the end of the logs on the opposite end from the
fire, and then hide among the rocks near by, and await the
result. If they fired on the foe, let those on the right fire

at those on the right. "Observe the strictest silence, and we shall soon see if they are our friends. Do not expect them till the fire goes down, and they think we are all asleep." Soon as the fire grew dim, a dark cloud seemed to be slowly and silently approaching. It was the eighteen Indians. They halted at the foot of the little hillock. A stalwart Indian came up with his musket cocked and pointed toward the fire. When he saw all asleep, as he thought, he put his musket down, and pointed his finger at every one when counting them, and withdrew. He went down to the chief and said, if I mistake not, "Quedando se son it, pluralibus que furassibus non serando Americani." "All are there—twenty-five Americans,—and all of them are fast asleep." Then another came up and counted them. Their chief told them to go up very silently, and as he gave the warwhoop to fire, and kill the rest with the tomahawk. They came up in the most careful manner. The waiting soldiers could hear them cock their muskets ere they came in sight of the fire, —*click, click, click.*

Instantly, as they came in full view of the logs, with living men's caps on, the warwhoop sounded, "Roundedando, furabile, quemsabilorum." I do not pledge perfect accuracy in giving the Indian language. It makes me think, when trying to call up the Indian dialect, what Lord Byron said of his college studies, "And where is all that Greek that I forgot!" Bang, bang, went every Indian's musket, and then they rushed on with the tomahawk, and as they struck on the headless cap, the captain said "*Fire,*" and every Indian fell dead. This gave great peace and safety to the Deerfield settlers.

BLOODY BROOK MASSACRE.

King Philip, son of good old King Massasoit —"the best friend the English ever had," said Edward Everett,—determined to destroy every white man in New England. For this purpose he visited every tribe, even the Mohawks in

New York. He could not make them act in unison. Had
he, the purpose had been accomplished, as they then out-
numbered the whites by many thousand. The early
settlers in Deerfield, Springfield, Westfield and other
places, had been so thinned by murders and robbing their
possessions, that they appealed to their friends in Eastern
Massachusetts for aid. Ninety-two men, under Capt.
Lothrop, called the flower of Essex, with lumber wagons
loaded with provisions and clothing, started to aid them.
They halted at Bloody Brook, now called South Deerfield,
to feed their horses and dine. They stacked their guns
against the trees. Fine grapes were hanging in rich fes-
toons on the trees which they climbed. Philip, with seven
hundred warriors, was on the trail. He gave the warwhoop,
and the Indians seized the guns of the white men, and shot
seventy-six of them. I have often read the names of those
slain on a fine monument a grateful posterity erected.

A thrilling fact was given me over thirty years ago,
when agent of the Missionary Union, in Northern New
England. It was given by Dea. J. Battis, of Manchester,
Vt. Up in a valley, among the Green mountains, eight miles
from Manchester, is a beautiful lake abounding with large
speckled trout. It was over three miles from any house.
An uncle of Deacon Battis, E. A. Jameson, and his friend,
James Hulett, started for this lake, with a rifle, axe and fish
tackle, to spend a time in trouting. They erected a cabin
on the bank of this lake, by putting down posts and rafters,
sloping it down to the bank. They covered it with large
strips of hemlock bark, and wove boughs of hemlock into
the sides, and made a bed of boughs. They then made a
pile of dry logs in front, to set on fire in the night. After
catching fish for their breakfast, they set the log heap on
fire and went into their cabin. Mr. Jameson lay down
with his rifle by his side, and was soon sound asleep. Mr.
Hulett, with his axe by his side, could not sleep. He was
not used to sleep with bears and catamounts for his neighbors. In the dead of the night, he heard stealthy steps

near the eaves of the shanty. Soon a huge panther jumped on the roof of the cabin, making the rude structure tremble. "Jameson! Jameson!" cried Hulett, "what on earth is on our cabin?" Looking up coolly, "Bark," he said. "Bark? there is something as heavy as you are just leaped on the roof." "I guess you have been dreaming." "I have not been asleep, nor shall I ever be, unless it is the final sleep." "Please be quiet that I may sleep, so as to enjoy the morrow," and lay down for it. While they talked Mr. Panther listened. When all was still he crawled up, and put one huge paw on the top plate. Jameson sprang up, rifle in hand. "Goodness!" said he, "it is a huge panther's claw." Hulett was raising his axe in great excitement. "Keep still, keep still!" said Jameson. While they talked the panther did not move, but as soon as silence reigned, the panther showed he meant business by putting up the other paw, and showing a huge, ugly head. "Keep still, Hulett." The light was brilliant, but the panther could not see his game until he brought his head over so that the light made his eyes look like balls of fire. Hulett could not be held back longer. He rushed forward with his axe and yelled as loud as he could, "Yah! catte, yah!" The panther leaped to the ground, and with a farewell scream went into the woods; and the two hunters went to stirring up the fire and watching the trees till daylight, and soon left the lake for home, and told the tragic tale. As they were men of truth, no one doubted their veracity. Those who had bear-traps set them near the lake.

J. Burrett and Johnson Burrett, great trappers, set their trap, putting a long, green toggle or pole through the ring of the chain. When they visited the place the trap was gone. They could see marks on the staddles, showing it had been drawn into the forest. As they proceeded cautiously along, Jared said, "See there!" "See what?" said the other. "I saw a terrible head and fiery eyes of a catamount just over those rocks." "I don't see any terrible head. I guess you had a spectral illusion." "As true

as there are any Green mountains in Vermont, I saw an
awful head of a live panther." As they stood gazing upon
the magic place, up came the terrible head, with the heavy
trap on a fore leg. "Let us go up on higher ground and
get a better view." The panther looked daggers at them
and tried to seize them, but was held fast by the trap.
Said Johnson to Jared, "You see that white spot in his
throat; cut his jugular vein for him." Soon as the ball
struck him, he sprang as far as he could, with a dismal
scream, the blood flowing in a stream from the pierced
artery. They dragged him home, and he measured nine
feet long. I wrote to the deacon and asked him if I had
remembered correctly. He replied, "You have it all right."
He adds:

"The panther was a huge animal. I saw him the next day
after he was killed. You have the measurement, nine feet,
correct. Hundreds came from far and near to see him. A
photograph of him was taken before he was stuffed. He
was sold to a museum for fifty dollars, and the brothers got
forty dollars bounty from the State. These brothers have
killed, in all, sixty-three bears. Your letter, dear brother,
gave us much pleasure by carrying us back to the time you
shared a night's stay with us, when engaged in the missionary work. Mrs. Battis wishes to be remembered kindly to
you.

"Cordially yours,
"J. BATTIS."

Some thirty years ago, a man in one of our Western
States told us the following tragic tale: "I was hunting, and,
being weary, I laid down in a little hollow and fell asleep,
with my rifle by my side. When I awoke I was covered up
with sticks and leaves. Knowing the habit of the catamount in search of food for her cubs, I trembled for my
fate. I carefully removed the covering, not knowing
whether the shrewd catamount was just leaving or returning. She was not in sight. Finding a rotten log about
the size of a man, I threw it down where I had lain, and
covered it as I was covered, and climbed up a tree in full

sight, awaiting the issue. Soon I saw a catamount coming from the woods with three cubs, which she hid in a secret place, with a peculiar purr, which meant, I suppose, 'Do not leave till I call for you.' She then approached carefully, sat a moment on her haunches, then sprang upon the covered log, which she tore to pieces, scattering the fragments in all directions. Seeing her failure, she looked in every direction, and just as her eyes fell on me, I sent a ball crashing through her head, which killed her. I reloaded my rifle, and went where the careful mother hid her kittens. I shot the three, neither of which made the least effort to escape." Thus the hunter saved his life by knowing the habits of the catamounts. Would that all children obeyed their parents as strictly as the lower order of animals do.

Some thirty years since, a man in Illinois was on his way to visit a friend. He was directed to go the main road, until he came to a hotel, there take the left, and when he came to a hill, take the right, a new road to save travel up the hill, and he would soon reach the village where his friend lived. The traveller was on horseback, and when he came to the hotel, he stopped to dine. "Ike," said the landlord to his son, "take good care of the horse." He had a pair of loaded pistols in his holsters, attached to the saddle, which he did not remove. The landlord seemed much pleased with his guest, offered him brandy, and hoped he would rest there awhile, and offered to board him cheap. "I am going to visit a friend, whom I hope to find to-day. Will you direct me?" The direction was as before given, except taking the right at the hill. "A bridge is gone, so you must go up the hill through a forest." On coming to the hill, he saw no tracks of travel up the hill, while the other road was different. He thought he would look to his pistols ; the priming holes were both spiked. He removed the spiking, withdrew the balls, and found the powder all right. He rode up into the woods. The landlord came into the road from a side road, saying, "I thought I would see you safely through." He suddenly turned his horse round, drew his pistol, and said, "Stranger, money I must have. Hand over." The traveller drew his pistol instantly, and sent a ball through his head. He fell from his horse a dead man. He dismounted, tied the landlord's horse, rode on and obtained help, and they carried the wretch to his home. But Ike and the horse were not to be found. His wife, said to be a good woman, expressed a fear that her husband had murdered persons in those woods, yet she had not dared to express it for fear of her own life. They searched, and found three new-made graves, with men in them who had been shot.

A few years ago, I fell in company with an honorable, excellent man, who made quite a fortune among the early gold diggers in California. "I spent," said he, "five years there, and killed twenty-five grizzly bears in the time." "Did you have any difficulty in so doing?" said I. "Only in one case," said he, "and I did not mean to with that huge monster. I generally shot them in the ear. This bear I saw about ten rods from me, going in a direction that would bring him no nearer. I thought best to let him go on, and stepped behind a small burr oak. He made a halt, looked towards me, and, with a snuffy grunt, made for me. I fired at him, but it only increased his speed. I climbed the burr oak. The thick limbs prevented his ascent, and he tried to bite them off. He left the limbs, and began to gnaw the body, but finally began digging up the tree. As the ground was soft, he made fearful head-way. I charged my rifle up in the tree, and when his head was in the right position, I put a ball in his ear. I wish you could have heard him roar. It was sideling, and he rolled over and over, throwing the leaves and dirt in all directions. I dressed him, and he weighed twelve hundred pounds, which I sold in San Francisco at one dollar a pound, and took one hundred dollars bounty for him. In those days meat and butter were one dollar per pound in San Francisco."

A TERRIBLE NIGHTLY RIDE OF BUSHHEAD, THE ROBBER.

In the early settlement of Minnesota as a State, a dry goods pedler, who made his headquarters in a hotel, was robbed of his goods. Suspicion rested on a tramp, called Bushhead, for that and other robberies in the region. He was often at the hotel. The Governor offered five hundred dollars for the arrest of the robber. The pedler's wagon had a cover that spanned the large base of the wagon, and was locked by a padlock on its side. The wagon stood empty, unlocked in the hotel shed. The pedler, in hearing of the tramp, ordered his supper, saying he was going that night to a village some ten miles distant. It was a rough road, and no house on the way. The pedler, on going over a rough place, heard something heavy roll in the wagon base. He had a toggle he sometimes put in, when he did not lock his wagon. Suspecting mischief, he put the toggle in. When some miles on the way, a man yelled out in his wagon base, "Where are you going with me?" "Who are you?" "A poor man who laid down for a nap. Let me out." "No; I will carry you up to the village." "I have a six shooter, and I will shoot you if you will not let me out." "Fire away," said the pedler, dropping down in front of the seat. At the sixth shot, he jumped to the ground, saying, "You wretch, you've killed me." Then stepping on to the wagon, he punched the horse with his cane, and put him on rapid speed. As the cover and base were strongly ironed, he could not get out, and he went so fast he could not reload. He drove up to the hotel and called for instant help. Four strong men, one of them the sheriff, stood by the wagon as he threw open the lid, and Bushhead leaped into the arms of two of them, who bound him, and left him with the sheriff. The thefts were proved to have been committed by him. The pedler recovered his goods, and the five hundred dollars offered by the Governor.

To make us more thankful to God that we have not the perils to meet that our forefathers had, I record one more tragic story : Near the banks of Lake Sunapee, in New Hampshire, in early times, lived an Indian and his wife and daughter, Penelope. The father killed moose, bear and deer, and caught fish from the lake, and his daughter carried them to the village, some half a mile distant, and exchanged them for family necessities. Two men went to this lake with rifles and fish tackle to catch eels. It was about one hundred rods from the Indian's cabin. They heard a piercing scream between them and the Indian's cabin. Said one of them, "It is Penelope returning home, attacked by some deadly animal. Let us hasten to the rescue. She is too good a girl to be destroyed." Dropping his fish rod and seizing his rifle, his companion following him, they went to the place where they heard the shrieks. "Is any one in trouble?" No reply. The leaves had fallen, and they were standing under a huge oak tree. It was starlight. They heard a rustle overhead. On looking up, they saw two large catamounts ; one on a large limb, preparing to jump, the other near the top of the tree. "I will fire at the lower one, and you shoot the other." "I left my rifle by the lake." "Then," said his comrade, "we are dead men." He fired and killed the lower one. Down came the other to the same place and jumped for the man. He struck at him with his rifle, and it glanced off and struck his friend, and knocked him down senseless. How long ere he came to, he could not tell. There lay the rifle. He looked for his friend, and some two rods from the body of the tree, he saw something that looked like a man and a catamount. He hurried to the Indian's wigwam and awakened him. He told the Indian why they came, and he was very thankful. He seized his rifle, put his hatchet in his belt, and taking a pine-knot torch, lighted it and said, "Hasten to the place." On coming to the tree, the Indian gave the rifle to the white man, and proceeded with torch and hatchet. They found both dead. The catamount had throttled the man, and while sucking his blood, the man had fatally dirked the catamount. This wonderful story was told me near the spot where it occurred. This lake is said to be about nine miles long. My agency for foreign missions for the North led me to other places around the lake. All the old settlers I asked told the same story, so I did not doubt its truth. I know of no animal of its size, that has no poisonous fangs, so terrible to encounter.

The following, taken from a Mr. Hunter's life among the Western Indians, shows the manner of his attacks: "In one of my excursions, seated by a large tree, I was surprised by a mighty rushing noise. I sprang up, and saw a herd of hundreds of buffaloes coming directly towards me on a full run. I stood behind the tree, and they passed me within a few feet. On the rear buffalo, a huge panther had fixed himself, and was voraciously engaged in cutting off the muscles of his neck. As he was near me, I shot and killed the panther." I have many other exciting facts, but let the above, for the present, at least, suffice.

SHIPWRECK AND WONDERFUL ESCAPE.

A story is told of a vessel wrecked in the Bay of Bengal. As sharks were seen around there, and the natives hostile, they durst not go ashore, though near it. Finding they must perish with thirst and hunger, a bold sailor said, "I will swim ashore; possibly the natives will befriend us. I will take a dagger, and you follow me with a telescope, and if a shark is in pursuit, give me warning." When he was within some twenty feet of the shore, they shouted, " A shark! a shark!" He saw the shark very near him. Then looking on the shore, he saw a huge tiger crouching in the bushes near the water. He plunged under the water, and swam thus for the shore. The tiger leaped into the water, where he saw the man dive under, and was caught by his paws, and went down with the shark, never to rise. The natives befriended them, and they all in due time escaped.

TRAGIC ENCOUNTER WITH A LION.

One of our missionaries, as the story was told me, wished to visit another section, some five miles distant by land, and over seventy by water. To go by land, one must pass through a dense forest infested with lions. He asked advice, and was told there was a native who would pilot him safely through. He hired him. He was armed with a double-barrel rifle and a three-foot steel spear, fixed in a strong handle. He gave a rifle to the missionary, and told him to follow him and all would be well. Ere they passed through the forest, the native touched the missionary, saying, "See that lion. He is going to give us fight. Keep behind me, and do not fire upon him." The native sought a clump of bushes as high as his head, and put the missionary behind him, and told him not to move till ordered. The lion stealthily approached the bushes. The native fixed firmly the handle of his spear in the ground, and sighted at the top of the bushes, and when the lion made a desperate leap, the spear went through his vitals and entire body, thus throwing the lion over them on to his back. "Jump aside," said the native. "Now fire on him, if you wish, but he has already a mortal thrust."

MIRACLES.

In the time of our Civil War, a church was examining a colored man for admission. He was asked if he believed in miracles. He said, "What am a miracle?" "Daniel was cast into a den of lions, and came out safe. That is a miracle." "Had dem lions just been fed? and were dey chained?" "It is not said so." "Well, I guess I does." They told him of Jonah. "Was Jonah clear down in de fish's belly?" "Yes. Do you believe he was there three days and lived?" "Well — I rather tinks I does, if it is in de good Bible." They next told him of Shadrach, Meshech and Abednego cast into Nebuchadnezzar's furnace, heated seven times hotter than usual. "Were dey clear in de middle of dat furnace, and not burnt a bit at all?" "Yes. Do you believe that miracle?" "Well — I don't believe I does; and now I don't tink dat I believes dat ar fish story."

CHAPTER XI.

STATESMEN OF MY DAY.

MY field, as agent of the Bible Society, embraced all the Baptist churches in Massachusetts, Connecticut and Rhode Island. My duty was to preach to as many churches as I could on the Sabbath, and on week days collect what I could. In some of the cities, I could address three churches on the Sabbath. It was laborious, but the hearty welcome, and the thought of the good it was doing, made it a delightful work. I was accustomed to gather together groups of children in the evening, and tell them Bible stories and historical anecdotes. In some cases I was asked to rise before daylight and tell them facts on the same themes. I never failed of addressing Sabbath-schools where I could. I worked in this way over the above States for ten years, raising more and more money each year. The tenth, or last year, I raised more than three times as much as I did the first year. Had not the Society been merged into the Publication Society, I would gladly have worked longer. The Rev. Geo. B. Ide, D. D., was then pastor in Springfield, Mass. I presented the mission cause before his church on the Sabbath, and they gave their offering on cards. On Monday, he said, "I will do by you what I have never done by an agent. We will go over the parish, collect the cards, and call on some who were not present on the Sabbath." The first family on which we called was a rich one. The wife, only, was at home. Said the doctor, "I find no card from your family. Are you not going to give anything to the cause?" "I

236

think we cannot afford to." "I am astonished," said Dr. Ide. "It reminds me of a case in Philadelphia. When pastor there, I made my own collections. I called on a wealthy man who I knew had made over a thousand dollars the day before, and said, 'What are you going to give for missions this year?' 'What ought I give?' he said. 'Ten dollars,' I replied. 'No.' 'Five.' 'No.' 'One, then.' 'I think I must be excused this year.' 'Dr. Ide,' he said, 'do you not think we are going to have a revival?' 'I do not think it looks much like it,' I said. 'Will you pray with us before you go?' 'No, I cannot while you so treat my Saviour's cause. I shall pray for you.' We had to exclude that man before the year was ended, for covetousness." I said, "My dear brother, how did you dare to talk so severely?" "Because she is so selfish, she deserves it." Dr. Ide was one of the ablest preachers of his day, of any denomination, but he could not cover up sin. Reporting the cards Sabbath evening, he said, "We found over one hundred and forty dollars on cards. Some had ten dollars and some had ten cents. But the smallest offering was a three-dollar card from a rich man." I was asked if I knew who the doctor meant. I said, "Yes." "Well, who?" I said, "Ask him."

AGRICULTURAL.

Wishing to benefit those that succeed me all I can, I record a few thoughts on the treatment of the grape and peach, two of our choicest fruits. I took the way to treat the grape from an Englishman by the name of Clough, who had the care of the gardens of the president and professors of Williams College. He was an illiterate man, but an oracle on fruit. I give his formula, in his own spelling, which I never could forget. "Dig a hole six foots in diameter, and three foots deep. Fill it with rich compost, mixed with wood ashes, so pliable you can stick a spade down to its hilt. Get a root of the grape, put some roots down deep to suck the moisture when it is a dry time, and some roots near the surface to get the sun when it is cold and wet. Let it grow up nine eyes, and coot it off and keep it coot off for the season. Always coot off close by a bood." "Why?" "Because a bood is like the tete of animals; the sap comes to the bood, and if you coot it off half-way between, it may die down several boods (joints), and get disease into the limb. This is vitally important in all tree pruning. The third year laterals will shoot out, and when the grapes are as large as bird's shute (shot), coot off the limb, one or two eyes above the outer sprig, and keep it coot off. When the grape vine thaws out in January, coot off the limb till there is music in your knife (that is, solid wood), and you will have perfect sprigs, with from eighty to eighty-six grapes on them, and much larger than those not treated so." While settled in Westfield, Mass., by following this rule, I took the first prize in Hampden County, on three kinds of grapes, three consecutive years. I found in my garden, connected with the parsonage, several peach trees ; and I was told the early frosts in the spring gave only a crop once in three years. By taking the snow away from the tree, so that the ground would freeze deep, I then put a quantity of sawdust around the trees, which kept the frost in, so that the trees blossomed too late for the frost, and I had a good crop every year.

Some years since a farmer gave me the following fact: "I hired an Irishman for the season, well recommended for farming work. We took out the manure from the yard, except the scrapings. I said to the Irishman, 'I think you can fill the cart by thoroughly scraping the yard. I have business that calls me away. You may gather all you can, and manure my orchard of about twenty apple trees.' On my return I asked him if he had treated all the trees. 'I gathered a heaping load, just enough for one tree, and dug it all in out nearly as far as the limbs reached.' I was so angry I dismissed him. It was in vain that he asserted that was the way they did in Ireland. What he did was worth a hundred dollars to me. He happened to select the best tree in the lot, and it has borne mightily for over twenty years, and taught me how to treat my orchard."

I would that I had room for a score or more of humorous Irish anecdotes, for which the nation is so famous. Let one suffice :

A farmer hired an Irishman for trial ; and to learn his pluck, he told him he might cross a little pasture, and bring home a borrowed cultivator. He knew there was an ugly bull there. When near the middle of it, the bull sighted and, bellowing, ran for him. He ran for home ; and just as he was climbing over the fence, the bull thought he did not go fast enough, and he helped him over with his horns. As the fence was very strong, he only stood pawing and bellowing. The Irishman lay quietly looking at him. Soon he burst out, " Stop your apologies, you lying baste! You know you did it on purpose !"

GLEANINGS FROM THE WORLD'S HISTORY.

A sentiment uttered by Cleobulus is worthy of note ; " Do good to your friend that he may be more wholly such ; and to your enemy tha the may become your friend." It was the motto of the great Cicero : " Speak well and act better. It is a pure heart that makes the tongue impressive." " Show mercy. Do good to all. Dispute not with the ignorant. Seek him who turns you out ; give to him who takes from you ; pardon him who injures you, for God would have you plant within your souls the seeds of his perfections." " The joys of heaven are begun here. They cannot be made to consist of gloomy misanthropy, or sullen renunciation of every pleasure and wholesome recrea. tion."

A philosopher of antiquity, when asked what is a true friend, replied, " One soul in two bodies."

Love feels no burden. It is the connecting chain between heaven and earth.

Reason, judgment, memory, and the strong passion of self-perservation were given us the better to avoid, and the better to resist, and overcome evil.

The Jewish nation, when Christianity was introduced, had the records of their race for four thousand years, and yet they had few eminent men, and they had made little progress in the arts and sciences. Christianity is truly the "handmaid of science." Office seeking, and seeking the good opinion of all sorts of people, will drawf rather than elevate mankind. Ice and petrifaction will preserve bodies forever.

In digging the foundations in the city of Quebec, the body of a petrified Indian was found. The remains of marine animals are found in our high mountains, which once came from the ocean. Capt. Allen was master of the ship Jupiter, that sailed into Cicily, where Homer describes the Cyclops of fabulous size. In digging many feet below the surface, they found a large marble coffin, with human bones in it, lettered with hieroglyphics. He says he saw a human skeleton over nine feet long.

Professor Hitchcock, of Amherst College, found on the banks of Connecticut river tracks of birds made in the mud, hardened to a rock, whose claws measured eighteen inches. Such a bird could have carried a wolf on the top of Mount Holyoke, and eaten him there.

Dr. Comstock, a reliable traveller, says he saw the skeleton of a mammoth within whose ribs thirteen men dined

Twenty thousand square miles of coal have been found in Pennsylvania alone. "Mounds," says Bishop Madison, of Virginia, "are frequent on the Canhawa river." He describes one four hundred and twenty feet in circumference, and forty feet high. It is supposed they were built for cemeteries, as layers of skeletons are found. Hon. W. Campbell, of Ohio, tells of one on Point Creek, enclosing two hundred and fifty acres. He tells of several others on the Miami. President Jefferson had a mound opened on the Rivoni river, and a thousand skeletons lying one above another, were taken out. It is generally thought there was once a race superior to the present Indian race.

It is said that all Illinois was once under water, and that the lakes were once one hundred feet higher than they are at present. The falls were on the Mississippi, which in time gave way.

America has its pyramids; one in Cholula, it is said, is one hundred and eighty feet high and fourteen hundred and sixty feet at the base. Baron Humboldt calls it the largest base in the world, built of stone. It was found here by Columbus. It was used for burial purposes.

One of the Mexican pyramids is seven hundred feet square, and two hundred and twenty feet high. It is near Vera Cruz. Baron Humboldt states that, in visiting Mexico and South America, he found palaces resembling the Roman order, and the hieroglyphics resembled the Egyptian.

On the Sciota, about three miles from Chilicotha, O., is an enclosure one mile in circumference, with twelve mounds in it. Williams, in his history of Vermont, says the Indians were rarely guilty of falsehood.

"Would you remember a dream," says a philosopher, "do not change the position of your head until you have fixed it firmly in the mind."

In Algeria is a river of ink. Two streams meet. One runs through a peat swamp; the other runs through an iron deposit. The gallic acid of one unites with the iron of the other, and makes very good ink.

Benjamin Franklin captured lightning, and Samuel Morse sent it over the world.

POLITICAL.

DANIEL WEBSTER.

Among the great men of England and America, I can make a selection of only a few. I will begin with Daniel Webster, probably the most talented man America ever produced. He was said to be very fond of fishing, especially trout fishing, and often put his fly rod in his carriage when he rode out. Once, as he approached a meadow, he observed a mill stream. A little down the stream he saw a man, to whom he said, "Good morning, sir. Do you own this meadow?" "I do; but that is not the worst of it." "It is a nice meadow." "Yes; but that is not the worst of it." "This is a very charming brook that runs through the meadow." "Yes; but that is not the worst of it." "Are there any trout in this brook?" "I guess not; but that is not the worst of it." "What beneath the heavens is the worst of it?" "There never was a trout seen in it."

When Mr. Webster was plenipotentiary to England, being in company with some Englishmen, one of them asked him if the Yankees were as shrewd as they were reported to be. "I cannot say how you regard us, but I will tell you how a Yankee served me. I commenced practicing law in New Hampshire, my native State, but after a few years I removed to Boston. A man from New Hampshire called on me, requesting me to plead his cause. I told him my business was worth five hundred dollars a week, and I might be delayed a week. 'Will you come up and respond to my call during a week, for that sum?'" Mr Webster assented. "I went," said Daniel, "and found myself on the docket for every case for the week. I made him a thousand dollars, and he promptly paid me five hundred, and pocketed the rest."

Though Henry Clay and Edward Everett could deliver a speech more impressively, yet, on reading their speeches, Mr. Webster's surpasses them in logic and true eloquence. Whoever reads Webster's speech in the United States Senate, versus Col. Haynes', may almost feel like quoting Bible: "Never man spake like that man." I have been accustomed to read this speech nearly every year. Taking all things into consideration, I think it the greatest speech made by an uninspired mortal. The first speech of Mr. Webster's I ever read was that delivered at the laying of the corner stone of the Bunker Hill Monument. Portions of it have ever been fresh in my memory. I will make from memory only one quotation. After covering a page or so, of the reasons why it should be erected, he culminates in the following beautiful strains: "For this let the monument rise. Let it be the last object the American sees as he leaves his native shore, and the first that shall greet him on his return. Let it rise till it meets the sun in his coming. Let the earliest rays of the morning gild it, and parting day linger and play on its summit."

On the death of Presidents Adams and Jefferson, which occurred on the Fourth of July, some twenty eulogies of the great statesmen were delivered, and published. I think no one equalled that of Mr. Webster's. The following extract is, I think, the finest in the English language: "Adams and Jefferson are no more. These suns, as they were gradual in their ascendancy, so they have not sunk suddenly in the west, but, like the mildness, the serenity, the continual benignity of a summer's day, they have gone down with slow, grateful, long-lingering light. And now that they are beyond the visible margin of the universe, good omens cheer us from the bright track of their fiery car." He thus closes the eulogy: "Washington is in the clear upper sky. Adams and Jefferson have joined the American constellation, and our heavens beam with new light. Beneath this divine illumination let us walk the path of life, and at its close commit our country to the benign Benignity."

Edward Everett was a contemporary with Daniel Webster. For grace in delivery, perfection in diction, few orators, if any, ever equalled him. He was the idol of his fellow-men. Had Webster had the charming and expressive delivery of Everett, who could have withstood his eloquence? Mr. Everett was seven years governor of Massachusetts. During that time I had the privilege of hearing him several times. It was a rich treat. I will quote a little from his oration at Bloody Brook, over the dust of the seventy-six, called the flower of Essex. These were all slain by King Philip's forces. Such were the robberies and murders, that the whites sent for aid to their friends in Essex County. I have given a full description of this sad massacre in another place. Suffice it to say, ninety-two men stopped their teams at Bloody Brook to feed and dine. They stacked their arms against the trees, and, after dining, climbed the trees for grapes, which were very good and plenty. Philip was on their track with nine hundred indians, who took the white men's guns, and killed seventy-six of them. At a celebration of this tragic event, over ten thousand, it was thought, were present. I can never forget the oration Edward Everett gave on that occasion. I was just eight rods from the platform in open air, and yet so distinct was his enunciation, I heard every word.

"Gathered together beneath the weeping heavens, with the everlasting hills around us, let us turn our thoughts reverently to Him who created them, and never forget He was the sole stay of our afflicted sires in the mournful days we commemorate." After an affecting description of the sufferings of the primitive adventurers, he exclaims, "Yet no white man ever saw Philip. He did not sleep twice in a place. And yet they had seen him in the distant council fires. They had seen him in the conflagration of the white man's cottage. They had seen him in his trail of blood."

After a glowing description of Philip's career down to the time he was surprised with a few followers in a cavern, at the base of Mount Hope, in Bristol, R. I., from which he attempted to escape through a swamp, where he was shot by a friendly Indian, Mr. Everett says, "And what became of Philip's wife and son? She a princess, and he a young prince! They did not hang them! No; they were sold into West India slavery! Sold from the free breezes of Mount Hope! Bitter as death; aye, bitter as hell!"

HENRY CLAY.

As an advocate, few men, if any, surpassed Henry Clay. His delivery was inexpressibly thrilling; probably superior to any of our American orators, though his speeches, when read, are inferior to many of our best orators. I will give only one illustration, given me by a clergyman who heard him. Mr. Clay was then in the United States Senate. The papers in Washington announced that Mr. Clay would speak at twelve o'clock, the next day, on a subject postponed. "I was very anxious," said he, "to hear him, and positioned myself in front of him. As the clock struck twelve, Mr. Clay arose in a very graceful and dignified manner, and said, 'Mr. President, the time has arrived when we voted to discuss the subject laid over for to-day.' A drunken senator, much the worst for liquor, arose, saying, 'I think we have done business enough for one day, and I move we adjourn.' Mr. Clay replied, 'We have published our programme, and as men of honor, I think we ought to redeem our pledge.' The inebriate arose and said, "There are men in this Senate, who, for their long continuance in this honorable body, and the many honors showered upon them, love to control this Senate.' Mr. Clay gave a sudden jerk of his body and flash of his eyes, and I feared he would dirk his assailant. He soon settled back, and quietly listened a long time to the drunkard's rant, until it was too late to resume. He then arose, folded his arms on his breast, looked some moments on the senators, and then gracefully dropping his hands, said, 'I appeal to the honorable president of this Senate,— I appeal to this honorable Senate itself, who acts as if he wished to control this Senate?' advancing toward his opponent, with his finger pointing at his head, and his eyes flashing fire." The clergyman said, "He sent a thrill from the crown of my head to the soles of my feet, such as I never felt before or since."

LORD PITT, EARL OF CHATHAM.

Mr. Pitt has generally been considered, I think, the greatest orator England ever had, though she has had, as well as Ireland, many famous orators. Mr. Pitt was tall, of a very commanding form, with a black, piercing eye. He tried his utmost to prevent the colonies of America from separating from their mother country. "Sunder the American colonies from the British crown, and it will scarce be worth the wearing."

Let one illustration of his power in oratory suffice. A subject of great importance was up before the English Parliament. An opponent made an able but sophistical speech. Mr. Pitt followed him, and exposed his sophistry to his shame. He then exclaimed, "Having thrown your deceptions and falsehoods to the winds," advancing toward him with a look Pitt only could give, "and now I have a few words to say to you, but they shall be daggers!" His opponent was so agitated that he let fall the papers from his trembling hands. Mr. Pitt paused a moment, then calmly replied, "Judge Felix trembles; I will spare him for another day."

I have ever regarded Clay and Pitt much alike in their expressive delivery. I know not the man that has ever equaled either of them in that all important thing in oratory.

I shall now notice a few of the excellent Presidents we have had.

Washington, for amiableness of disposition, soundness of judgment, energy of character and firm truthfulness from his childhood, has never been surpassed.

The Adamses were ever famous for their erudition, patriotism and eloquence.

Andrew Jackson was famous for his firmness and integrity. I give the following illustration: When South Carolina, instigated by the talented and eloquent John C. Calhoun, sent a committee to President Jackson, announcing that she had passed a vote of nullification, and would no longer pay tribute to the United States. The President listened calmly, and then said, "Gentlemen, have you finished your message?" "We have." He arose with his right arm akimbo, and said, "It seems you are instructed to say, if I send a vessel to collect revenue from your State, it will be fired on from Fort Sumter. Tell your constituants I shall send a vessel to collect revenues from South Carolina, and the first man that fires on that vessel, I will hang him higher than Haman hung, by the Eternal!" bringing down his arm with a rush. Mr. Calhoun was awaiting secretly in Washington for the result, and learning that the President had written an arrest for treason, he left suddenly, and had the vote rescinded.

Abraham Lincoln was, in many respects, a remarkable man, just the right man to be President in the perilous times through which our nation was passing. His honesty, his foresight, his candor, sympathy and benevolence, have immortalized his name.

President Garfield, for his wonderful valor as a soldier, and for his many virtues, will ever be held in pleasing and grateful remembrance.

With such an array of illustrious Presidents, ever illuminating our political heavens, can we wonder why our nation has been so prosperous?

GOVERNOR BRIGGS.

I cannot deny myself the privilege of recording a tribute to the Hon. G. N. Briggs, one of the best men I ever knew. As I had his eldest son for a pupil in the Franklin Academy, who, like himself, became an eminent lawyer, I had the privilege of meeting him at my home, which ever gave me great pleasure. He early united with the Baptist church in his native place, South Adams, Mass. He commenced the practice of law in Lanesboro, Mass. A more honest, benevolent and perfect man I never knew. Few ever surpassed him in the legal profession. He made it a principle never to plead a case where his client was in the wrong. In such cases he would say, " Give your assailant a peace offering to let you alone." This I know was often done. A friend said to him, " You can never get a living so." " Then," said Mr. Briggs, " I will die poor." But he did not die so. He was reported as dying well off. He began practice at about twenty-two years of age. A trial about this time, in which an aged judge had, in his opinion, sworn falsely, brought him applause by the public. He questioned and cross-questioned the judge until those in the Lenox Court were satisfied the judge had testified falsely, though it could not be proved. In making his plea, he said, " It becomes a young man to be modest and pay all due reverence to age, yet it becomes his duty to be just. Before the Judge of the Universe I am satisfied you have perjured yourself." The judge trembled and turned pale.

He carried his Bible into the court-room, and would often bring in a passage that helped his cause, and often corrected other lawyers if they quoted wrong. Being known as a man of superior talent, judgment and honesty, and that he would not plead for a client unless he thought him inno- cent, he generally carried the jury with him. At the age of thirty-five, he was elected representative to Congress, and nobly filled his place for twelve years. He was then chosen governor of Massachusetts, and served seven years. He was then chosen judge, and held that office until his death, at the age of sixty-six. He was one of the most amiable, kind and benevolent of men. He was often seen carrying food to the houses of the poor and the sick.

His choicest recreation was trout fishing. Says his biog- rapher : "He often took his wife in his carriage, drove to the Hoosac river, that ran near the highway, then taking his rod, he would fish down the stream, leaving his wife to ride along, and rejoice at his captures. On his return, he would divide the spoil among the sick. It was in an act of benevolence he lost his life. Seeing two ladies in trouble with their horse in front of his house, he sprang to the closet for his coat. In taking it, he pulled over a gun that discharged its contents in his throat. He lived only a few days." I will now quote from the funeral sermon of his pastor, Rev. Dr. Foster: "For forty years he was a firm advocate of temperance. The two places he loved most were his home and the church of God. His submission to God's will and his longing for heaven were constantly man- ifested. 'Why do I linger here? It is to prepare me to die. It is calm and joyful below, but how much more so above! Oh, that this poor, frail, unworthy one was there!' He said to his daughter, 'I love you all, but I want to be in heaven. I do not see how I can be saved from dying. I do not wish for it. God and Christ are my all.' His spirit gently ascended to his Saviour and his longed-for home. 'Mark the perfect man, and behold the upright, for the end of that man is peace.'"

HON. FRANCIS GILLETTE.

When my father married his mother, he came with them to Ashfield, at the age of ten years. He was two years younger than I was. We became strongly attached to each other. We worked on the farm together, hunted and fished together when we could get a chance. As we came into our teens, we attended the Sanderson Academy in Ash- field together. He fitted for Yale College there, and I fitted mostly at Amherst Academy for Amherst College.

He early showed a great fondness for oratory, and became a first-class writer and orator. An address on Temperance, that he published soon after his graduation, immortalized his name. It has been read and reread, and can never be lost. He studied law, but did not practice long, choosing to be a writer on moral reform topics. His writings were ever marked with signal ability and faithfulness. He married Miss Eliza Hooker, of Farmington, Conn. They had three sons and one daughter. The eldest son, Robert, was an able and brave officer in the Union Army. He was killed in taking Fort Fisher. The next son, Edward, has been a representative in Congress from Iowa. The youngest son, William, is a famous dramatist. He has written some very popular pieces for the theatre, in which he is the chief actor.

His daughter Lillie is the excellent wife of Hon. Charles Dudley Warner, of Hartford. They live in the homestead with their mother, made charming by the taste of the once cheerful devoted owner, now, we doubt not, dwelling in more splendid mansions, not made with hands, "eternal in the heavens." I must content myself with describing one of the many scenes of his Congress life. He happened to see a mother, near the Capitol, sold on the block and dragged off amid the agonized cries of her children. As he was ever a strong abolitionist, his soul was stirred in its depths. He took a copy of the slave laws for the District of Columbia, and came out in one of the most scathing speeches I ever read. It roused the South. Jeff. Davis and Tombs interrupted him. In every case he came out ahead. If they had known him as well as I did, they might have expected it. Mr. Davis said, "I presume the member is quoting from some abolition, spurious work." "Mr. President," said Gillette, "What firm prints your laws?" He named the firm. "I am happy to see their names, as publishers," he replied, "of the book I quote from." Bob Tombs spoke out in a loud and passionate tone, "Gillette, why are you at the North so mad with God Almighty because he made the niggers black?" Very calm and dignified he replied, "We at the North are not displeased with God for making Africans black, but we are displeased with you at the South, and disgusted too, that you make them white." They interrupted him no more.

CHAPTER XII.

RELIGIOUS ANECDOTES.

N the year 1834, two neices of mine, Nancy and Lucy Lyon, daughters of Aaron Lyon, Esq., of Cassadaga, N. Y., parted with their father in Buffalo, on their way to the Franklin Academy, at Shelburne Falls, Mass., then under my care as principal. They were to take the packet boat, which has its terminus in the Niagara river, at Buffalo. To keep the boat from swinging off into the river, strong piers were driven down for some distance. As it was in early spring, the ice so damned the river that its water quite overflowed the piers, and the boat swung over them into the current of the mighty Niagara. As it was drawing the horses that propelled the boat into the river, the captain cut the rope which was attached to the boat, and thus they were at the mercy of the Niagara. In the boat were three ladies and a number of men.

The men, to save life, leaped into the river and swam ashore. The captain promised not to leave the boat, headed for Niagara Falls, twenty miles distant. One of the ladies, who had been giddy at the starting, now screamed, tore her hair, throwing herself upon the cabin floor, exclaiming frantically, "I am going to hell!" Nothing could calm her. The Misses Lyon were both very devoted Christians, one of whom became a good missionary to China, and the other the devoted wife of the excellent Jesse Purrington. They told me their experiences of that terrible hour. "At first," they said, "it seemed solemn

251

and mysterious that we should be suddenly hurled into eternity, for the captain said there could be no hope for us. We knelt together and prayed until we felt calm and resigned to our fate. Ever and anon a huge cake of ice would strike our boat, which seemed our funeral knell. To add to the danger of our position, a dark night was shutting down upon us at our departure. A sloop was immediately started on our track. The wind was adverse, and at times it seemed impossible to overtake us. It was too dark to see them, unless they were very near. Just as the packet boat was near an island, a little above the fatal rapids, the hoarse strains of a speaking trumpet, an angel of mercy, rung out, 'Where are you? Where are you?' The captain attached a cable to the boat just in time to reach the island."

The boat was made fast for the night. The next day, with much difficulty, owing to great cakes of ice floating down the river, they reached the mainland. When this Christless, thankless girl put foot on terra firma, laughing, she said, "We have had a fine ride!" This shows what the Christian's hope is in time of trouble.

A TRAGIC EVENT.

In Ashfield, my native town, in Franklin County, there is a beautiful lake, on which, in my youthful days, I have often sailed and fished. This has been a solemn, memorable place for about sixty years. Deacon Lyon and son, two grandchildren and a neighbor, went to said lake, in company with Capt. William Bassett, my brother-in-law, to wash their sheep. They carried the sheep over a deep place to a shallow, gravelly bottom, suited to their work. They were returning with a load of washed sheep, the son, the two grandsons and the neighbor, supposed to be the worse for liquor, for he was an intemperate man, and he rocked and upset the boat in deep water. The eldest grandson could swim, and as he struck for the shore, his brother sprang for him, seized his ankle with both hands, and both went down. The neighbor made little exertion, and soon sunk. The son swam near to the shore, and became entangled in lily pads, where the water was about a dozen feet deep. The deacon, his father, a corpulent man of about sixty years of age, attempted to swim and rescue his son, but failed, and they both went down in death. Thus the whole five were drowned. The captain hastened for aid.

Soon all the bodies were put in a suitable carriage and driven to the deacon's, about two miles distant. The deacon's wife, a very pious but feeble woman, must be prepared, it was thought, for such terrible news. Two Christian friends of her acquaintance were delegated. They began by talking of the providence of God, and that we ought ever to be prepared to meet them. She soon said, "I think something has happened. If so, tell me all. God has ever been my supporter, and I am sure he will be." One of them pointed to the window, and said, "The carriage is in sight that brings a dead husband and son and two grandsons and a neighbor." She said, "Is it so? Is it so?" and knelt down by her chair and continued in prayer till the carriage rumbled up slowly to the door. She hastened to the carriage, took off the spread that covered their pale faces, then went into the house, and, after another season of prayer, calmly listened to the sad tragedy. I saw them all buried. They were my neighbors. Six months or so after, I heard Mrs. Lyon say, in a covenant meeting of the First Baptist Church in Ashfield, "The last six months of my life have been the happiest I ever enjoyed. True, my house is lonely, so far as my family is concerned. I have lost one of the best husbands God ever gave. He never gave me an unkind word. I have lost a dear, lovely son, and two dear grandchildren, but God has more than made it up by the precious influences of his spirit." This beautifully illustrates God's word: "It is good for me that I have been afflicted." "All things work together for good to them that love God." "These light afflictions work out a far more exceeding and eternal weight of glory."

In the First Baptist Church, in Ashfield, over seventy years ago, there was a powerful revival. On the south side of the Bear river, some two miles from the church, lived two neighbors of mine, very pious but illiterate. The man was ever famous for his honesty and cowardice. On returning from a very spiritual evening meeting, on horseback, in company with a sister of the church, they had to pass through a ravine made very dark and gloomy by evergreen trees. Said Mr. E. B —— to the sister riding by his side, "Don't you think it makes Christians very bold when they are revived?" "Yes," said the good sister, "the Bible says, 'The righteous are bold as a lion.'" This brother B—— had a very long nose, and when he would make a sentence expressive, he would touch his finger on each side of his nose, making a very emphatic twang. This he did as he said, "I feel awful bold! I do not think I should be afraid if I should meet the Devil." "I think I feel just so," said the sister. Soon they emerged from the dark forest, out into the starlight. As they reached near the summit of a place called Bellows Hill, a large white object appeared in the middle of the road. Both horses sheered and whinnered, and came to a sudden halt. "The Lord have mercy on us!" said Mr. B——. "We have been too presumptuous, and the Lord has sent the Devil to punish us." "What shall we do? Oh, what shall we do?" said the sister. "We had better go right back, and take the road that leads by the plain; it is only a few miles farther,—and learn never to be so presumptuous again," said Mr. B——. They went gladly. On his return, he told his son, A B——, what had happened. "It is nothing, father, but a cap sheaf of rye that fell from a load of grain that passed over the road yesterday." "Oh, my sceptical son, don't be blasphemous." "How did it look?" "It was white, a terrible looking object. Both horses seemed alarmed. It seemed threatening to approach us. I think, my son, we

escaped a terrible judgment for our daring presumption."
The son took his father in the wagon, and rode down to
the place, something like half a mile, and found a cap sheaf
of grain, lying bottom side up, just where they thought
they had seen the Devil. There is somewhat of an apology,
as it was near the time of the Salem Witchcraft, when so
many were so terribly befooled.

DR. DODRIDGE'S DREAM.

Dr. Dodridge was one of the most profound and thorough commentators of the Bible the world ever had. He
was asked if he thought the human soul would increase
eternally. The query gave rise to the following dream:
He saw in a dream an infant in a cradle under a large tree,
in distress, and an angel breathing into it strength and life.
On the cradle, written in small letters, was Dodridge. As
he looked on the body of the tree, Dodridge was written
larger and more and more brilliantly as they appeared farther up. The tree had a vast amount of branches; on
them all, Dodridge was written in letters more resplendent,
extending outward and upward in a flood of light and glory,
culminating in indescribable effulgence in the upper sky,
beyond the reign of mortals. "This dream," said Dodridge,
"illustrates my views of the endless progress of an
immortal soul."

JOHN LELAND.

The celebrated John Leland, who died about half a century ago, was one of the most talented ministers the Baptists ever had. He was very eccentric. It was often said
he would tell an anecdote that would make an assembly
laugh, and use it so as to make them weep the next minute.
He preached the last sermon for me he ever preached,
when I was pastor in North Adams. He died the same

week, aged eighty-six. Where he preached, the house would be packed, with only a short notice.

He told an anecdote that caused a burst of laughter throughout the house. He paused a moment, and so used it that most of the assembly were in tears. He did not make me weep; but in all my life, I never had such a thrill of excitement that convulsed my nerves. With me, it was too deep for tears. He was the pastor of the Cheshire Church over fifty years. In the winter months, he often travelled over Virginia and the Carolinas, and, in all, he baptized sixteen hundred. It fell to my lot to preach his funeral sermon. As I intend to print it in my book, I will not quote from it. I hardly know where to stop telling anecdotes of this wonderful man. They had a good spiritual design, though they might not always seem so at the first.

Mr. Leland, in his travels South, had his appointments daily some miles apart. He was to preach in a populous town in Virginia. Some two miles ere he reached the centre of the town, he came into a village where there was a hall in which there was a dancing school. He stopped his horse in front of the door. Soon a lad came out and asked him what he wished. He replied, "I want to know what instrument is used up in the hall?" "It is a fiddle." "Will you ask the player to bring it to the door?" The boy did his errand. "Tell the man to come in and see it if he wishes to." That was just what Mr. Leland wanted, an excuse to get among the dancers. They gathered around him, expecting some fun from the eccentric stranger. He said, "Ladies and gentlemen, are you sure you are serving God by dancing?" One replied, "The Bible says, 'There is a time to dance.'" "Yes; and it says there is a time to kill. Does that make it right for me to kill you?" All were silent. He then drew his Bible from his pocket, which he was wont to carry there, and read, "Whatsoever is not of faith is sin." "If you are sure you are serving God in the dance, dance on." They did not do it. "If you will not worship your God, will you let me worship mine ? " " He wants to pray," said one. " I would like to hear that man pray." Before he finished his prayer, he found he had more than he had bargained for. I have heard many mighty in prayer, but I never heard a mortal come near equalling him. At one of the anniversaries in Boston, Dr. Howard Malcolm presided, and was informed that Elder Leland was in the assembly, and his friends wished him to invite him to preach. Dr. Malcolm replied, he preferred not to do it, as he had been informed Mr. Leland did not think our mode of missionary operation was apostolical. The next presiding officer asked Mr. Leland to pray. When he closed, Dr. Malcolm was in a flood of tears, as well as many others. He arose, asked pardon of the audience for what he had done, saying, " A man who can pray so, I wish to hear preach." And he had the privilege. When he arose from his knees in the dancing hall, many were in tears. Mr. Leland said, " I am to preach in the centre of the town to-night, and if any of you see fit to come, I shall be happy to meet you. Good afternoon, ladies and gentlemen." The managers said, " Now let us go on with the dance." Most of the company were seated at the back part of the hall in tears. Before the figure was through, many filed off, and took seats with the convicted ones. Soon the number of dancers became too small for success, and they voted to adjourn and attend the meeting. After describing the scene, he added, " Nearly all of that company were converted in the power- ful revival that followed." He adds, " I tried the same thing in another town, and none were converted. The cause was, God was in the first trial, and only John Leland in the second."

Mr. Leland usually went dressed very plainly. He was anxious to spend the Sabbath in a large church in Virginia, where he had preached some years before. He arrived late Saturday evening. He called on the young fashionable min- ister, a stranger to him, and introduced himself as a Baptist minister, not giving or being asked his name, saying, " I would like to spend the Sabbath with you." The stylish pastor looked him over, perhaps thinking a man is known by the coat he wears, asked him sundry questions, among which was, "How many commandments are there?" "Eleven, I believe." "Well," said the pastor, "you can stop with me for this night; but please excuse me, as I have two important sermons to preach to-morrow," and went to his study. He said very little more to him. They walked together to the sanctuary, and the pastor seated him in his pew, and went into the pulpit. At the close of the morning service a number of the leading men of the church rushed up to the pew, saying, "Elder Leland, we are truly glad to meet you again; and you must preach for us this afternoon." The pastor, horror-stricken, came among them, and invited him to preach. His fame at this time was wonderful in the South. He came out fearlessly against wrong. They would bear the most severe sermons against slavery from him. In the afternoon he entered the pulpit, told the audience of the reception he had, "and among other things was asked how many commandments there were, and I told him eleven, and the eleventh is my text. 'A new commandment give I unto you, that ye love one another.'" We presume ever after he was careful how he entertained strangers, for God has given some direction on that important duty.

Mr. Leland was to preach in a Southern village at one o'clock, P. M. He had preached in the region, so that they knew no house would hold his assembly. A platform was erected under an elm tree in front of a hotel. A venerable man called at the hotel, and asked for some bread and cheese. The landlady, a fashionable, ambitious woman, said to the stranger, "I am preparing a dinner for the celebrated John Leland and suit, who is to preach here to-day, and if that is all you want, you can get it in a store opposite here." "Will you let me smoke my pipe?" "Not in the hotel, as ladies may come in." So he went out into the shed, lit his pipe, and sat on a log and smoked it. He then walked across the way and took a lunch of bread and cheese.

Before the hour of preaching arrived, hundreds, many of them ministers who had heard him elsewhere, had gathered together. The query became general, "Have you seen Elder Leland?" "No," was the reply. As the village clock struck one, a tall, venerable man came out of the store and walked toward the platform, on which no one had ventured. The aforesaid landlady, with her husband, was standing by their hotel, and on seeing the man going straight for the platform, said to her husband, "Look there, that old tramp that asked me this morning to give him some bread and cheese, knows no better than to go right up into Leland's place. Do go and tell him not to go there." As he mounted the platform, he beckoned to this and that minister in the throng to come up with him. They came, exclaiming, "Brother Leland, we are right glad you have come." "Mercy on me," said the woman, "that is Leland, and I have treated him shamefully. Do ask him to come to the hotel, that I may apologize," said she to her husband. After the services, he went to the hotel, and the woman said, "Had I known you were the famous Leland, I should not have treated you so. We want you to dine with us." "Thank you, I have no desire to do so; besides, I am pledged at another place. I am afraid your heart is not right in the sight of God. You wanted to glorify your hotel by entertaining me and my friends, but when a poor man came, you turned him hungry away." Mr. Leland was to preach some ten miles from there, the next day, and the hotel lady prevailed on her husband to go and tell Mr. Leland that his wife was in agony, and felt she could never rest till he had forgiven and prayed for her. The husband did his errand, and Mr. Leland said, "Oh, yes, I will go now." The result was, that both husband and wife, and a part of the family, were converted.

Mr. Leland's labors were greatly blessed in Cheshire, and in many other towns in Western Massachusetts. He baptized over two hundred in one revival in Cheshire. He was sound in doctrine, a Calvinist of the old school, not like the Indian's tree, straight and more too.

The Congregationalists of that day were not awake to revivals as they are now. Hence they called the Baptists "New Lights." Twelve miles, or so, from Cheshire, in the town of Savoy, was settled a Rev. Dr. Alexander, who had the town for his parish. Many of his hearers, who had heard Mr. Leland, desired their pastor to make an exchange with him. He refused. So many of his parish insisted upon it, that he had an appointment given out at 5 P. M. The church was crowded. Mr. Leland met with a casualty on the way, and could not get there till a little after the time. The doctor went into the pulpit, and, thinking it a good chance to put out the New Lights, he picked in upon them without much mercy. Mr. Leland arrived soon after he began, sat down near the door, and, putting his head down, was not perceived. When Mr. Alexander had finished his debut, Mr. Leland walked up the aisle to the pulpit stairs. "Walk right up," said the doctor. He explained why he was delayed, and then said, "You have heard a discourse from your pastor, and I do not wish to preach unless you wish it." A very unanimous vote was taken. Mr. Leland took for his text, "Alexander, the copper-smith, did me much injury; the Lord reward him." An old man, who had heard him, said he never heard a man so completely used up as the doctor was. The result was, that a good Baptist church was soon formed in the village, to which I often preached, when agent for the Bible Society.

Mr. Leland was preaching in Lanesboro, Mass., in sight of a large deep lake. His subject was "The Doctrine of Election," of which he was a firm believer and very able defender. In the midst of his sermon, he paused, put his hand on his heart, looked reverently toward heaven, and said, "Oh, my God, how little do I know! Oh, the heights both of the wisdom and knowledge of God!" Throwing his eyes toward the lake, he said, " There is a bottom in that lake, but I cannot wade it."

Preaching a funeral sermon of a man killed by a pile of wood falling on him, in South Adams, in the midst of his sermon, he paused, and said, " Could this man have died at any other time, or under any other circumstances ?" and then went on with his sermon.

In his last sickness, in North Adams, he was helped into a chair to be shaved. When well lathered, he said to Mitchell, the barber, " Hold a moment, I want to tell an anecdote." This he always loved to do, and was famous for. " In Europe, many years since, it is said, in a time of great drought, the king ordered all the Catholics to pray for rain. It did not rain. He then ordered all the Protestants to pray for rain, and it came abundantly. The Catholics said the Lord did not answer their prayers because they came up as a sweet odor, and he wished to hear more of them ; but when the Protestants prayed, it came up in such a jargon, he answered as quick as he could to get rid of their noise."

When he visited North Adams, he usually came in the afternoon, and by giving notice at two hotels, and at three of the twenty factories, that he would preach, the house would be crowded. I was very anxious to hear him. As soon as the doors of the church were opened, though it was a very warm summer night, the house was crowded. His text was John 2 : 20 : " Ye have an unction from the holy One, and ye know all thirgs." I can never forget that sermon. He said unction was performed by oil. He should spiritualize the text.

" I. Oil makes a lamp burn brightly." He then took up the enlightening influence of true religion. He soon carried me out of myself into the full blaze of divine illumination. I felt as though I could listen to him an hour on that strain. " II. Oil makes the skin soft." No less charmingly did he show the melting, soul-subduing, enrapturing and heaven-directing influence of the Holy Spirit. " III.

Oil makes the cistern wheel of machinery turn easily."
Such a contrast I never heard drawn of a backslider and a
Christian in the spirit. "Brethren," said he, "when the oil
of Divine grace moves completely the cistern wheel of my
soul, it would take a greater salary than any man has in
Berkshire County to keep me from preaching." He closed
with a most solemn address to the impenitent, causing
many a tear to fall.

After the sermon, sitting with a few Christian friends, I
said, "Father Leland, I have long wished to see you. I
have wanted to make your acquaintance for many reasons.
One is, to have you untie some Gordian knots in theology."
"What are they?" said he. "One is, 'Did God create
man in such a condition, as a free moral agent, that he
might fall, in order to glorify himself before the universe
in the gift of his Son, and cause a greater joy of the redeemed than could have been otherwise possible, and yet
make the sinner a guilty party?" He replied, "I don't
know. I don't know but little." He said the same to
some other queries.

I then gave him a question that I expected he would answer in a Calvinistic spirit: "If God created man perfectly
holy, and he could fall into sin by the self-determining of
his will, has he, or has he not, the same power to return?"
He replied instanter, "If I fall over a stone wall, and break
both of my legs, I do not think I have the same power to
return. Now," said he, "I will ask you a question. 'What
was the condition of Adam, compared with redeemed
men?'" I replied, "I considered Adam and the angels
placed on a covenant of works, and Adam and a part of the
angels lost their holiness. This was enough to ring down
the eternal ages, and he placed man on a covenant of grace,
established on better promises, that is, they shall be kept
by the power of God through faith unto salvation." "Yes,"
said he, "that is all very well, but it is not just what I
meant. If God," said he, "had lifted Adam up twelve feet
from the earth, and let go of him, which way would he

have gravitated? Which way will the redeemed soul gravitate?"

Of the strength of his intellect, his life and writings give ample proof. The late Governor Briggs, after a long service as representative in Congress, enjoying frequent intimacy with the great men of the world, was asked, "Who was the greatest or most talented man you have ever personally known?" and replied, "Rev. John Leland."

He wrote his own epitaph: "Here lies the body of John Leland, who labored years to promote piety, and to vindicate the civil and religious rights of all men." This epitaph is inscribed on his obelisk, in Cheshire, Berkshire County, Mass.

CHAPTER XIII.

CELEBRATED DIVINES.

REV. DR. CHALMERS.

REV. DR. CHALMERS was one of the most eminent divines Scotland ever had. He was a large,
corpulent man, of a very cheerful, happy spirit,
and fond of the humorous. When on an exchange, as he
arrived at the parson's house, he was met at the gate by
his honest servant, John, who had been in the employ of
his master some twenty years, to whom the doctor said,
"You have been with the minister so long, John, that, if
needed, you could preach, could you not?" "I do not
think I could." "Could you not draw some good infer-
ences from a passage of Scripture?" "You can try me."
"What inference would you draw from this passage, 'He
feedeth them on ashes?'" "I should draw the inference
that they would not be so fat as you are."

Dr. Chalmers often wrote very splendid sermons, spend-
ing much time over them. He preached one of these, and
wishing to know how it took with an illiterate farmer, he
called on him the next day, and asked him how he liked the
sermons. "I liked one of them very much," he said. "I
spent three weeks on that forenoon sermon, and only threw
out some plain, practical remarks in the afternoon." "It
was the afternoon sermon that I liked so. There were
some words I did not understand, and I have no dictionary." "What were some of the words?" "'Catastrophy'
was one." "Catastrophy is the sequence of events, or

2 d

what follows, or, to make it more plain, it is the tail of things." The doctor called on him some time after, saying, "How are you all, my dear brother?" "We are all very well, but I find I have an enemy." "How do you know?" "Why, he cut off the catastrophy of my cow last night."

WHITFIELD AND TENNANT.

Both of these clergymen were very talented, eloquent and spiritual. They roused the churches of New England from their moral lethargy, and brought them up on higher and holier ground.

Revivals followed them wherever they went. The amount of labor they performed was truly marvellous; and their influence is felt yet, and will be to all eternity. Mr. Tennant, as he met Mr. Whitfield, said, "I long to leave this world of sin and sorrow, and be with Christ, and rest from my labors." "Mr. Whitfield said, "My dear brother, you may be wrong in that wish. What would you say of the man you put in the field or store who should say, 'I long to have the day ended, that I may go home and rest with my family?' Would it not look as if he was dissatisfied with you, or the work, or both?" "I stand corrected," said Mr. Tennant. "This, I think, is the right feeling: 'All the days of my appointed time will I wait till my change comes.'"

"It will come just at the right time, under the right circumstances," said Montgomery, who never wrote us enough of his spiritual and doctrinal hymns. "A Christian cannot die before his time; the Lord's appointment is the servant's hour." Like Lord Chatham and Henry Clay, Mr. Whitfield had a most impressive delivery. It has been thought that no divine in America has ever equalled him in that respect. Yet many have written more able sermons. More than fifty years since, a Rev. Mr. Robinson, then pastor in western Massachusetts, told me the following fact: When a young man, he said, he heard Mr.

Whitfield preach on the sufferings and death of Christ. The assembly was wrought up to a high state of feeling, bending forward to catch every word. Mr. Whitfield exclaimed, in a loud tone of voice, "What sight is that I see? Blood! blood!" at the same time putting his hand over his face. Nearly all the assembly did the same. In all, Mr. Whitfield preached over eighteen thousand sermons.

REV. DR. A. B. EARLE.

We have long been blessed with faithful, efficient evangelists, many of whom I have personally known, and worked with them; but I think no one has been more prudent, affectionate, and spiritual than Brother Earle, whose pleasant home is now in the city of Newton, Mass. We always expect blessed results where he labors. Many thousands will, I doubt not, meet him in heaven as their spiritual father. I quote from his book of "Incidents," where he inserts the following facts:

"I have travelled over three hundred and fifty thousand miles; held thirty-eight thousand, four hundred and sixty public meetings; have preached in three of the British Provinces and thirty-six of the States; worked with twenty-three different denominations; have preached from three to five times a day for months together, and met with no serious casualty. One hundred and sixty thousand have united with different denominations, and four hundred have entered the ministry. I have published nine books; and over two hundred thousand have been sold in this country, and many in England.

"The principal joy of the faithful minister is in the Beyond, when he passes within the pearly gates. Then, oh, then, when the glories of that wondrous world fully burst on his enraptured vision, when his feet have just pressed the golden-paved streets and the bright, beautiful banks of the flowery river, when the music of harps of gold and of angel voices have thrilled his soul, when he has really seen and bowed before the Saviour ; when he has just begun to realize the blessedness of such a home, who can describe the joy of his heart, as, from that white-robed throng, there come many thousands gathering around him, grasping his hand in gratitude and love, and lead him to the Redeemer, saying, 'Jesus, we have believed on thee, and been led to this beautiful world, through this one, whom thou didst appoint to do the work of an evangelist on earth.' Oh, the joy of such an hour ! "

Said Paul, "What is our crown of rejoicing in that day ? Are not ye in the Lord at his coming under inspiration of God?" Paul wrote this, and it is one of the many proofs of recognition in heaven. What, oh, what is a spiritual child, viewed down the rolling ages of eternity, when it shall have passed far beyond the loftiest angel in heaven in their present blissful knowledge, still rising in ecstatic bliss, until it enjoys more in an earthly hour than all the redeemed have enjoyed since the morning stars sang together, and the sons of God shouted for joy over the birth of this infant world. Oh, the blessedness of being instrumental in saving even one soul, thus preparing it to enjoy more than men or angels can comprehend.

REV. LYMAN BEECHER, D. D.

When laboring in Boston, his labors were richly blest. ·He was a mighty champion in every good cause. Whoever read his book of sermons on the Temperance reform, could but feel his power. He was very faithful and successful as a pastor. Among others he was accustomed to visit, was a member of his church laboring as a servant girl in the family of Rev. Hosea Ballou, then a pastor of a Universalist church, in Boston. He made his calls in the kitchen, though invited into the parlor. One day, Dr. Beecher met Mr. Ballou and said to him, "I dreamed lately that I went to heaven, and looked all around, but could not find you there." Mr. Ballou, who was famous for an apt retort, replied, "You went only into the kitchen ; if you had gone into the parlor, you would have found me there."

Dr. Beecher was very fond of fishing and hunting. When pastor in Connecticut, he was returning home with a string of fish, and was surprised as he neared his church to hear the bell ring for his afternoon lecture. He threw aside his fish rod, put his trout in his sack pocket, and went into the pulpit and preached a powerful sermon from the text, " I will make you fishers of men," much to the amusement of those who saw him pocket the fish. He was greatly blest in his labors in the West. He always exercised much,— shovelling a load of sand from one side of his cellar in the morning and shovelling back at night, while in Boston. His exercise gave him vigorous health. When about eighty years of age, a brother minister called to see him, and was told he was in the woods hunting. He went into the woods, and, on hearing the report of a gun, went down to the place where he heard the report, and called Dr. Beecher's name. He was answered up about seventy feet in a tree, where he was pulling out a gray squirrel lodged in a crotch of the tree.

HENRY WARD BEECHER.

Henry Ward Beecher was in Amherst College with me. Though not in my class, yet I was intimately acquainted with him. He was very popular in college, and ever, so far as I know, was a consistent Christian. He applied himself very closely to everything pertaining to oratory and debate. In debate it was said he stood a whole atmosphere above his class. The faculty would often be present when they knew he was to speak, it was said. His wonderful success as a pastor and lecturer has immortalized his name. He was a very benevolent man. When the South sent Mason and Slidell to England, to seek aid, by promising them that the South would come under them as a protecting power, if they gained their independence as it was then understood, fearing the South would bargain away their birthright and thus bring future trouble to our prosperous nation, Mr. Beecher, to save our nation, at a great sacrifice and risk of his life, visited England. No better man, for the purpose, it was thought, could have been found. When he arrived, for many days he could find no place to plead his cause. At last a vast turbulent audience assembled. When he commenced, he was hissed down again and again. He took it calmly. No man could better meet an emergency. It is said he met it thus : " Ladies and gentlemen, will you please be silent while I tell a short anecdote ? " " Hear ! hear ! " was the response. " I had a grandfather," said he, " who learned the blacksmith trade of himself, and he took it into his head to make an axe. But he so burned up the steel, that he said, ' I can make a hatchet.' Failing in that also, he said, ' Anyhow I can make a hammer.' Not liking its looks, he threw it into the water-trough, saying, ' I have not failed entirely ; I have made a perfect hiss.' I have done more ; I have made three tremendous hisses ! " After that the English style, " Hear ! hear ! " rung through and through the many thousands present, and he held the vast assembly spellbound for more than an hour.

"On another occasion, Mr. Beecher was pledged to speak in Elizabeth City, N. J., in favor of the Union. The Copperheads in the city threatened to kill him if he spoke. He began thus, ' I am informed if I attempt to speak here to-night I shall be killed. Well, I am going to speak, and therefore I must die. But before you kill me, there is one request I have to make. All of you who are going to stain your hands in my blood, just come here and shake hands with me before you commit the crime, for when I die I shall go to heaven, therefore, I shall never see any of you again.' A burst of applause followed this sally, and for two hours Mr. Beecher swayed the minds of his audience as the wind moves the sea." [H. Grant, D. D., New York.]

" From the first this American divine gave up his whole being for the purpose of making man more pure and happy. No man can aim higher. For this purpose God has won- derfully endowed him with all the requisite qualifications found in a vigorous, keen, versatile intellect and a glorious heart." [Thomas Armitage, D. D., New York.]

Of Mr. Beecher's " Lectures to Young Men," Hon. Mr. Barstow, of Providence, R. I., says, " This book put me in sympathy with a young, vigorous mind, whose thoughts were uplifting, whose style was pictorial and captivat- ing, and whose spirit was morally and spiritually mag- netic."

" Of these lectures to young men, I can cheerfully say, no others of the kind I ever read equal them. In no place was there more decided opposition than in Liverpool and Glasgow, because the Clyde and the Mercer furnished blockade runners. On the day of his lecture in Glasgow, the city was emblazoned with large posters of what he had said, and what he had not said, in Great Britian. He com- menced, but such was the uproar of the audience he sat down. When there was a lull, he sprang to the front of the platform and so depicted the sublime beauty of our Scottish scenery, the heroism of our Scottish warriors, and the wide- world fame of our lords and poets, that a burst of applause followed. He then made a long and eloquent speech against slavery and rebellion. Some one cried out, ' The South are beating the North !' ' Yes,' said Mr. Beecher, ' And when we bring them back to allegiance, we shall think more of them for their pluck.' ' But you can never bring them back.' ' We can ; and this war will never cease as long as there is a slave in America upon whom the sun of heaven can shine.' " [Potter McCloud, Esq., Glasgow.]

MR. BEECHER AS AN ORATOR AND PREACHER.

I might quote from over thirty of our best divines who

have given their hearty praises, found in his memoirs. I have not room to quote all I could wish. I will quote from the following only:

"I remember to have heard him, in his church, deliver a preparatory lecture, which so glowed with the love of Christ I shall never forget it. It made an impression on my mind and heart which has remained ever since." [Rev, R. Storrs, D. D., New York.]

"I believe there has not been such eloquence in the world since Demosthenes." [Rev. Dr. Taylor, New York.]

REV. JABEZ SWAN, OF NEW LONDON.

Mr. Swan was one of the most devoted and successful ministers of the Baptist denomination. It is said that he baptized over five thousand, which is more than any other Baptist minister in America baptized, it is believed. Like Mr. Leland, he was very eccentric. He was the means of greatly increasing the denomination in New London. I wish I could record more anecdotes of him than I can put in this book.

When pastor in New London, he had a rich butcher, a deacon, in his church, who killed his beeves Sabbath evenings. He requested him to desist. He did not. He preached on keeping the Sabbath to no avail. He took the text, "Remember the Sabbath day to keep it holy." This deacon, Harris by name, was in the habit of responding in a loud voice as the truth fell from his pastor's lips. Mr. Swan began to illustrate his text, for which he was remarkable. "One brother thinks he will keep the Sabbath holy; but he has vessels on the waters, and ere he is aware his mind is roving over the ocean, or on the last nautical news." Deacon Harris exclaimed, "That means you, Deacon Benjamin!" "Another, who has houses to let, thought he was heeding the text in reading of the rise and fall of real estate." "That means you, Deacon Weaver!" "Another, to please his customers, breaks in upon the Sabbath in slaughtering his beeves." "That means me!" said Harris. Still it did not reform him. Brother Swan came up in another broadside more severely. "What would you say of a man who should meet one of the best of men, and rob him of seven hundred dollars. He begs for one hundred to pay for his journey home, and he gives it back ; but avarice conquers, and he takes again." "He ought to be hanged!" said Deacon Harris. Turning upon him with a look few could imitate, pointing directly to him, in a tone he was wont to pierce the hearts of the hardest sceptics, said, "Thou art the man! God has freely given you six days to do all your needful work, and you rob him of the seventh." This thoroughly reformed him.

In the time of a great revival in the First Baptist church of New London, of which he was pastor, a sceptic would rise up and dispute the doctrine preached. It was in vain that he was urged to desist. One evening, as he was praying for the anxious (whoever heard him pray, I think never could forget it), he prayed that God would either convert that man, or remove him by death. The man went home, and in a short time died, and I was told no physician could tell the disease. This caused great excitement in the city, and gave a new impulse to the revival. This fact was told me by many persons who were knowing to it. Every year of the ten I collected there for the Bible Society.

Though he was sometimes awfully severe, he possessed one of the kindest of hearts. So faithful was his preaching that he often roused opposition. A very tall infidel kept constantly opposing him. Among other things the infidel said he did not prove his sermons. To meet this, one night he took a text, backing it up with a long array of texts, asking his assembly, "Is that head proved?" At the close he asked all to rise who thought he had proved his text. All arose. As the infidel was some like Saul, king of Israel, "a head and shoulders taller than the people," he saw multitudes gazing at him. So he sat down on the arm of the pew, when the rest sat suddenly down and he was left. Mr. Swan turned on him, and said, "Who in all the history of time ever saw a sheep sit on his haunches? Dogs will do it. Beware of dogs and sorcerers."

In the time of the War of the Rebellion, a church near New London, composed of a large number of Democrats, who did not sympathize any too much with the war, having dismissed a Republican pastor, asked Mr. Swan to supply them. They finally invited him to settle with them on condition he would not preach politics. "Politics!" he exclaimed, "if I come I shall preach the everlasting gospel, hit whom it will." They settled him and a glorious revival followed, as was generally the case wherever he preached. I visited that church when agent of the American and Foreign Bible Society. I desired him to make some remarks. After expressing his approbation and enjoyment of the sermon, he said, "I hear a great deal about heavy taxes. Jesus Christ lays taxes on his servants, and they had better pay them, I tell you. Jonah thought best to follow his own will, and God put him through salt water, and then he chose to pay up. Jesus Christ and his servants were taxed, and though he thought rather high, he paid them up like a man. He had no money. He told Peter to catch a fish, and he would find money enough. It showed his divinity. How did he know he would catch one? Did any one tell him a fish had swallowed a miser's gold to put it in circulation?" His speech had a mighty effect, and we took the largest collection I ever raised in that church.

J. B. GOUGH'S GOD-MADE AND MAN-MADE MINISTERS.

I heard John B. Gough, in one of his lectures, illustrate a God-made and a man-made minister.

Some fifty years ago, a Western minister (I am happy to think there are none such there now) said he was thankful to God he never rubbed his back against college walls, and his preaching told it. "I am about to preach to you on a very solemn subject. Ah! 'He that believeth not shall be damned.' Ah! Now there are a great many dams in this world. Ah! There is mildam, and Amsterdam, and Rotterdam, and don't-care dam. Ah! But this is a more terrible one than all those are. Ah! It is 'he that believeth not shall be damned.'" One self-made minister never studied his sermons, but read a chapter till he came to a verse that interested him. He began a psalm, "Awake, O psaltery and harp!" He read it, "Awake, O pleasant tree and harp." "This is a good text, 'Awake, O pleasant tree and harp?' David was very fond of music, you know. What kind of tree this was I hardly know, but I think it was some like our fir-tree. Now see how devout David was. Early he goes up on that tree, and as he sits on its branches with his harp, swinging to and fro, hear him sing, 'Awake, O pleasant tree and harp'"

A man in England called on a D. D., and offered to preach his evening lecture, introducing himself as Dr. Bartholomy. The offer was accepted. The visiting parson was very loquacious on worldly themes. "What is your text?" "Please give me one." "'God is love,' is a good one." "Yes; I will take it," and then he kept on talking on other themes. The bell began to ring, and he asked where the text was. As he began to look for it, "Do not try to find it; it is perhaps better not to know." As he arose to preach he said, "I am to preach on one of the best texts in the Bible: 'God is love.' I shall not tell you where it is, as I want you to search the Scriptures. Oh, what a charming, glorious text! The angels love to think of it. All the good men, apostles, patriarchs and martyrs gloried in it. Yes, and there was good old Jacob, who had twelve sons and every one of them was a boy, could say in all his trials, 'God is love, God is love!'"

He then illustrated a God-made minister, who sought out every way he could to save the lost. "I knew him," said Mr. Gough, "and learning he was to preach in one of the halls of London, I went to hear him. At the front of the door that led to the filthy cell, where all sins named or nameless were committed, there was a dirty yard. Into that yard I followed the godly man. He sang a precious hymn. A few miserable, ragged men and women listened. He made a fervent, melting prayer. They nearly all went back into their filthy den. His text was, 'God so loved the world, that he gave his only begotten Son, that whosoever believeth in him, might not perish, but have eternal life.' As he waxed eloquent beyond all description, they came into the yard around him. The preacher brought his text so directly and feelingly to every one, that many trembled and wept. 'That "whatsover" means you, in all your drunken and licentious habits; you, in all your profanity and blasphemy; you, in all your poverty and squallidness; you, in all your hatred to God and holiness; even you can be saved and made happy.' A large, red, rum-faced woman burst into a flood of tears, sat down on the ground, threw her dirty apron over her head, and cried, 'God be merciful to me, a sinner.' It was an affecting scene. I think a number were savingly converted."

ROWLAND HILL.

Mr. Hill was a very pious, able and successful minister. He was ever noted for his eccentricity. He went down into a very wicked section of London. His faithfulness roused up opposition. As he was going into the hall to fulfil an appointment, some Christian friends advised him not to enter the hall, as there was a plot planned to put him out. "Who is the leader?" said he. "It is that great, rough-looking man near the desk." Mr. Hill started immediately to see him. "How do you do, sir?" said Mr. Hill. "How are you?" he answered roughly. "I am told, my friend, that some persons are intending to put me out of the house if I attempt to preach. I am very sorry, as I have a sermon on the love of Christ that I want to preach. Now, as you look like an able, resolute man, I want you to agree to help me." "I prefer that you should get some other one." "No," said he; "I do not see one I think so able." He held on to him until he promised to aid him. As he did not start, no others ventured, as they all were waiting for him. He preached, and in the sequel, a good evangelical church was formed there, and the whole region was blest by it.

Mr. Hill had a very pious, benevolent wife, but she was often gloomy and despondent. Mr. Hill could not keep her from an impression that she would finally be lost. One morning, he came to the breakfast table, saying, "My dear, I dreamed I went to hell last night." She looked up sadly, and said, "Who did you see there?" "I saw you there." She dropped her knife and fork, saying, "Now I am sure I shall go to hell. That is a providence." "Hold a moment. What do you think I found you doing?" "Well, what?" "It was a very singular place. It looked like volcanic mountains, the fire in places burning. I saw in the distance a grove, and, as I thought, I saw a female form kneeling there. I approached carefully, and found it was you praying. Soon a little devil came out from the burning cave, and said, 'Woman, stop that praying here. It is not allowed.' You did not hear him. Soon old Beelzebub came toward you, in wrath, stamped on the ground so it trembled, and said, 'Woman, stop that praying here in hell.' You looked up, and said, 'Dear sir, are there any poor folks here that I can help?'" It was so much like her, it is said, that it broke up effectually the hallucination. "Once," said Mr. Hill, "when I was returning in a boat from Ireland, I was much amazed by the swearing of the captain and his mate. 'Stop! stop!' I said; 'it is my turn. Let us have fair play.' 'At what is it your turn?' said the captain. 'At swearing,' said I. They waited a long time. 'Perhaps,' said the captain, with a laugh, 'you do not mean to swear.' 'Just as quick as I find it is right, and does not break the law of God and man, that it will not hurt or grieve the feelings of the good, and be of any use whatever.' I heard no more swearing."

An infidel called on Mr. Hill, wishing to discuss tenets. Said Mr. Hill, kindly, "Do you believe the Bible?" "No, sir." "Do you believe there is a God?" "No, sir." Said Mr. Hill to his son, "Conduct this man kindly to the outer door, and lock it after him."

CHAPTER XIV.

FUNERAL SERMON OF JOHN LELAND.

"And I heard a Voice from heaven saying unto me, Write, Blessed are the dead which die in the Lord from henceforth : Yea, saith the Spirit, that they may rest from their labors; and their works do follow them."—REV. 14 : 13.

IT is a solemn thing to live, forming as we do a character for that eternity, in comparison of which a hundred earthly ages are as nothing; while at the same time we are making impressions upon immortals around us that will spread like the circular wave onward — onward toward infinity. It is solemn, under ordinary circumstances, to expound the word of life ; it is more solemn to preach with the enshrouded dead between us, seemingly rendering that eternity nearer whither they have just departed.

The solemnity is increased, on the present occasion, by the age, the calling, and the usefulness of our venerable father in Israel, as the present and past seem to meet, presenting him performing similar solemn duties in this sacred desk for half a century, as well as other solemn offices during the sixty-eight years of his ministry. The shades of departed ages rise before me, and I almost seem standing by the urn of some patriarch or prophet of Old Testament times.

The solemnity is still heightened by the text before us, for it is a universal epitaph that the Almighty God hung out of heaven, visible to the inspired vision of the beloved disciple on the Isle of Patmos, who eighteen centuries ago penned by Divine direction, to stand as an imperishable memorial on the tomb-stone of the pious dead to the end of time.

"Blessed are the dead which die in the Lord:" that is in a vital union to him through faith and repentance. "From henceforth," or from this time forward, "that they may rest from their labors." It seems clear that reference is had to the immediate happiness in reserve for the pious, when the soul leaves the clogs of mortality. The same sentiment is taught in the twenty-third chapter of Luke: "To-day thou shalt be with me in paradise." This Jesus spoke to the malefactor on the cross. He asked to be remembered when Christ came into his kingdom. But Jesus seems to say, "I will not delay your wishes so long. To-day shalt thou be with me in paradise." Lazarus departs and is immediately comforted. This text, as well as many others, seems to have been designed to prevent the world from mistaking the state of the soul after death, or between death and the final judgment. What a reproof upon all those who believe in an imaginary purgatory, or offer prayers and masses to relieve their departed friends.

On this portion of the text, then, we are taught that the benevolent Jesus will not delay his humble, faithful follower of his reward when his toils are over, but he shall be immediately with him in paradise. This most clearly shows the blessedness of all the faithful servants of God, both in their death and after their dissolution. They are blessed, for

I. They rest from all heart-rending anxieties and responsibilities.

I speak not of the thousand anxieties of a name among men, or such as arise from disappointed ambition, the neglect of friends, or from any of the "whips and scorns of time," except so far as they pertain to the Christian as such.

The Christian has often a great anxiety to know positively whether he is a child of God. Sometimes he reads his "title clear to mansions in the skies," and then unbelief and doubtings roll a double night of darkness upon his soul. If he has but little love to God in exercise, he has cause for much anxiety, and if he loves much, heavenly things seem so valuable that he is tantalized by fear lest he may lose them. Like a parent, who has a much beloved child on the treacherous deep, disturbed with forebodings, almost breathlessly perusing the nautical news to hear, if possible, one word of that bark that bears so dear a treasure, and all because love is so strong that the parent cannot rest till all is visibly safe.

Is the Christian a parent? No language can tell the anxiety he feels that those eyes, so dear to him, may see the salvation of God, and that that tongue, whose every note is music, while the child is dutiful, may sing the praises of Immanuel. He often looks off into eternity, and says with Esther, "How can I endure to see the destruction of my kindred." He wraps himself up in the scenes of the last day, and stands with his children before the everlasting throne, and asks, "Shall any of these go away into everlasting punishment?"

Is he a faithful minister of Christ? None but a faithful minister can know his spiritual anxieties. Driven almost to despair for want of success, distressed with pride when successful, carrying the whole church and his own wicked heart, a still heavier burden; feeling each impenitent sinner around him has a soul of more value than the whole material universe, and from their awful neglect and impiety constantly fearing that it will be lost; again and again distressed that one is gone without hope, whose priceless soul must forever wail under the vengeance of retributive justice; trembling under its own responsibility in a station probably unsurpassed in its weal or woe beneath the skies, affecting three worlds in every movement, he cries out with Paul, "Who is sufficient for these things?" And might he not do it had he Gabriel's intellect and a seraph's tongue?

Something of the deceased's feelings I here give you in his own language. "Strange to relate, one hour I would entertain a comfortable hope that my sins were pardoned; the next hour nearly give up all hope, fearing that all my exercises were self-earned, and that I had not been taught of God. The third hour be impressed I must preach or perish. This conflict wore off my flesh and made me irresolute about any thing."

Moses was not a stranger to heart-rending anxieties. At one time, such were his feelings for the spiritual welfare of Israel, and seeing her given to idolatry, he exclaims, "Oh, this people sinned a great sin, and have made them gods of gold, yet now, if thou wilt, forgive their sin ; and if not, blot me, I pray thee, out of thy book which thou hast written."

What language can describe the contrast between the scenes Moses had just witnessed on Sinai and those in Israel's camp? God had come down amid thunderings and lightnings upon Sinai and the mountain trembled to its base beneath the foot-steps of a God. The holy moral law is about to be let down from heaven by hands unseen ; and Moses, wrapped up in the bright visions of Jehovah, is made so spiritual as to come within the halo of glory that surrounded the summit, and carry down the decalogue to a lost world. With a heart filled with the love of God, with a soul made erect by the majesty of Jehovah, with a heart ready to burst with joy at the scenes he had just witnessed, he hastens at the voice of God to meet his brethren waiting at the foot of the Mount, as he supposes, to hear the sublime and heavenly message : but ah ! what sound is that which falls on his ear? Is it a shout of praise from all the mighty throng, that their leader is made the honored instrument of God in bringing to a needy, dependent world, heaven's best, everlasting love? No; it is idola· trous music and dancing even in Israel's camp. His soul is chilled with horror and shrinks back aghast ; his heart, just rendered doubly tender for Israel's welfare, throbs with the keenest anguish ; his spirit groans within him — wonder not, despairing of aid from all created things, he breathes the plaintive language above quoted into the ear of his Maker.   Many a minister of Christ has had similar feelings, coming from communion with God in secret before his people, when he saw their hearts wedded to the fading things of earth.

Who can describe Elijah's feelings, when, like many a herald of Christ, he yielded too much to the "fear of man that bringeth a snare," and fled far into the wilderness to escape the vengeance of Ahab and Jezebel? It was there, beneath a juniper tree, discouraged and disheartened, trusting not enough in Jehovah, he desires death to release him from an opposing world.   It is thus he bemoans himself : "Lord, they have killed thy prophets, and digged down thine altars ; and I am left alone and they seek my life."

Jeremiah, "the weeping prophet," felt such anxieties for the spiritual good of his people, that tears told the inmost workings of his troubled soul.   "Mine eye," he says, "runneth down with rivers of water for the destruction of the daughter of my people."

Does any one ignorant of piety, catching the spirit of Cain, "Am I my brother's keeper?" say, this is human weakness and folly to thus weep and sigh over the sins of earth.   We reply, it is just such weakness as actuated Him at whose name all heaven rings with hosannas; Him in whom the Father delights ; Him before whom Cherubim bow at humble distance ;   Him at whose feet the redeemed cast their crowns and cry, "Worthy is the Lamb."   Such were his anxieties for a lost world that Jesus wept.

Often has our venerable father given vent to an aching heart in tears over the lost, but we have every satisfactory reason to believe that his weeping is turned to everlasting joy.   That heart will throb with anguish no more ; it is now cold in death.   Impenitent hearer, have you not often seen the tear roll down that venerable visage for you ? You will see it no more, for he rests from his labors.

II. They rest from all persecution, directly or indirectly practiced.

The Christian conformed to the world so much that he meets with little or no opposition, may think the day of persecution has gone down with Nero's, Domitian's and Caligula's, and that the day of martyrdom is over. He reads, " They were stoned ; they were sawn asunder, were tempted, were slain with the sword," together with the suffer ings of martyrs of a later date, under the Sharps, the Lau derdales, the Scottish Clavers, the sanguinary Bells, anc other ringleaders of iniquity who have taken the lives of the faithful in various forms invented by infernal malice, as a thing never to be acted over again. But a similar bloody tragedy is now going on among the faithful missionaries of the cross. There is no truce in Satan's heart towards the children of God.

God has said, " All that will live godly in Christ Jesus shall suffer persecution." The Christian finds everywhere hearts at " enmity against God," and if faithful as Master or his apostles, he will suffer persecution. Though the judgments of men tell them the religion of Jesus is necessary, the pride of the heart in an unrenewed state rises against the humbling doctrine of the cross, and against those who faithfully preach it. Oh, if the Christian were as faithful as Paul, how much more fierce and successful the combat. If as plain as Elijah, how many a Jezebel would seek his life.

Our friend was not a stranger to persecution. Take an example in his own words. A captain, the son of a man at whose house he had been invited to preach, forbid his entering the house of his father with severe threatenings. " After I arose to open the meeting by singing, the captain came rushing into the house, sprang upon the bed, took his sword and drew it out of its scabbard, and stepping off from the bed with his arm extended and sword glittering, exclaimed, ' Let me kill the d —— d rascal.' As he made a stroke towards me, the point of the sword hit the joists, and he behaved like an awkward soldier. The case was this : My wife, who was seated near the head of the bed, when she saw the captain step from the bed with his drawn sword, and drawing back his arm to give the thrust, sprang like the lightnings of heaven, and clasped her arms within his elbow around his body, and locked her arms together and held him like a vice, till the men took away his sword. We then took a lantern and went into the road and carried on our meeting." But now persecution and all the dangers of earth with him are over forever. He will be disturbed no more in the worship of his God, for nothing that "worketh abomination or maketh a lie" can enter that peaceful abode, whither, we trust, he has gone. He rests from his labors.

III.   They rest from all temptations.

I shall illustrate this head by an extract from his five hours' conflict, which he published several years since, abridging it occasionally, and slightly altering some sentences. After a powerful revival under his labors in Cheshire, he was attacked with a violent disease, which shocked his whole nervous system, depriving him partially of both hearing and speech. "When first seized," said he, "I had an impression riveted in my mind that I should be given up of the Lord to pass through a doleful conflict. The God whom I addressed and in whom I confided; the Mediator through whose blood and righteousness alone I hoped for pardon; the Gospel of salvation, which revealed the only foundation of trust, and the spirituality of prayer, which I preferred to all riches, were removed from my grasp, nor could I conceive that there was any happiness in the universe.

"How did my poor heart tremble. It was ten o'clock at night. All was dark without and within. On entering the contest, I felt like a feeble child cast into a pit to combat with dragons. The first question propounded to me was, 'Is there a harmony in the universe becoming a God?' Among rationals were war, famine, pestilence, earthquakes, plagues, personal slavery, despotic oppression, sickness, pain and death. Among beasts were fear, hunger, cruelty, and the bearing of the abuses of men. Why did the Almighty make creatures subject to all this? If he is the parent of all, why does he suffer one of his children to inflict so much injustice and cruelty upon another? Could he not have made things otherwise? If not, why create at all? Could he not have prevented so much misery? If so, why did he not? On reflection, I found I could not tell why water run down hill — or why the wind blew — that I could not account for the voluntary or involuntary motions of my own body; how, then, could I expect to understand the whole system, if I could not the least part.

"The next thing that arrested my mind was, there is no God. If so, who is he? If there is a Supreme Deity, he must increate himself uncaused, and this seemed impossible. But if there is no God, whence arose all creatures and things which exist? Of course, then, to escape the greater dilemma, I must believe there is a God. Surely 'Jehovah he is God! The Lord he is God!' Still there were some scruples. Various passages held me up a little, while the horrors of atheism and black despair, like billows, were dashing around my trembling soul.

"The following thought next rushed upon my mind: Jesus Christ is not God nor the Saviour of men. In health I had given up the point to attempt a reconciliation of the mystery of God manifest in the flesh. Can I prove it? I searched and found the same name applied to Jesus as to God, and that he performed the same works. All began to appear clear; but it burst into my mind like a torrent, that I was bringing my evidence from the Bible, and that was a fictitious book, and the history of Jesus was not true. This sunk my spirits. The only prop that my feeble soul had to rely upon was taken away. Upon this point I reasoned thus: The New Testament is in existence. It was written by good or bad men. To believe that bad men would write so good a book, required a faith more marvellous than to believe the truths contained there. The presumption then was, that the Bible was written by good men, and good men were not liars, therefore they spoke the truth. Still I wished to know without a doubt.

"On musing on this state of misery, of which I could see no end, the plaintive language of Jesus came to me : ' My God, my God, why hast thou forsaken me. Now is my soul exceeding sorrowful, even unto death. If it be possible take away this cup from me.' Never before did I have such a sense of the agony of Christ, — never such fellowship of his sufferings. But he agonized and resisted unto blood ; I did not. He bore his afflictions for others ; I for my own sins. Indeed, his sufferings appeared so much greater than mine, that my own, severe as they were, scarcely deserved a name. This text cheered me : 'Believe on the Lord Jesus Christ, and thou shalt be saved.'

"Another attack was the following : Man is all mortal, and has no soul that survives his dissolution. Notwithstanding the Scriptures prove the contrary so abundantly yet a spirit had been fluttering around me, that the complexity of man was chimerical. My judgment and reason told me better, but I could not stop my thoughts, though sensible, they greatly impaired my health. But I did not long continue in this train of thought before this query came up, Will the dead ever be raised? It then struck my mind that the way great events were perpetuated was by history. The resurrection of Christ was handed down by history ; and if the history were no more authentic than other histories, yet it deserved equal credit. No man disputed but what Augustus Cæsar and Tiberius Cæsar reigned in Rome. Now, as it is said, that Christ was born in the days of one of them, and rose in the days of the other, why not believe in the resurrection of Christ, as well as in the reign of those emperors? To me it appeared unaccountable. If Christ's resurrection was a forgery, why had an empire it overturned in three hundred years never denied it. And if Christ's resurrection was true, that of his followers was at once settled. The words of Jesus then

occurred to me : ' Him that cometh unto me I will in no
wise cast out.' The end of the beam loaded with doubts
was down ; my belief in the truth of the gospel and medi-
ation of Christ was up. My heart was drawn out to my
Saviour and I felt him my friend. A voice proclaimed,
' Here is one Saviour Jesus for one sinner Leland.' Nor
had I at this time any thought of another creature in the
universe. Christianity then appeared to be the religion for
sinners."

These and many similar temptations often assail the
Christian ; permitted, it may be, to show him his weakness
and complete dependence on God. These temptations
oftener come after signal blessings. So was it with Heze-
kiah, David and the unsuspecting Peter. And so was it
with him who lies in that urn in the garb of the grave; but
now he " rests " from all temptations forever.

IV. They rest from all the troubles of indwelling sin.

Man in his fallen state is a depraved sinner. No favored
clime, no royal descent, no vigilant parental watch-care,
have changed the corrupt heart. They may have softened
the roughness of his character, but they have never produced " holiness, without which no man shall see the
Lord."

Every faculty is corrupted by the fall. Man's understanding, once clear, is darkened. He is constantly
harassed in deciding between right and wrong, truth and
error. Love, that once blessed tie that bound him to
Jehovah, is turned to enmity, for "the carnal mind is enmity against God." This, by renewing grace, is but partially restored. This is the mainspring of moral action,
and, when retarded, disturbs the whole wonderful machinery of the human soul. The Christian feels himself under
infinite obligations to his Saviour, and failing of perfection
in all things, he often goes forth weeping under self-con-
demnation. For the want of perfect love, his memory is
beclouded upon all that is good, and his faith is weakened,
which gives rise to fears, doubts and unbelief. Conscience,

that blessed memory of the heart, being corrupt, breeds in-surrections, sometimes accusing and sometimes excusing to our injury. The imagination that once revelled on all that was delightful in heaven and earth, is circumscribed in its operations, and often seizes upon forbidden objects, thus disturbing the peace of the soul. Whatever view the Chris-tian takes of himself, whether physical, mental or moral, present, past or future, he often cries out with Paul, "O wretched man that I am, who shall deliver me from the body of this death;" or, in the language of another, "I abhor myself, and repent in dust and ashes." "Wash me thoroughly from mine iniquity, and cleanse me from my sin." The brighter the visions of Deity, the more dis-tressing the conflict with indwelling sin. When Isaiah had the clearest conceptions of his maker, he exclaims, "Woe is me for I am undone, I am a man of unclean lips." True there are other exercises. The Christian rejoices that he shall be satisfied when he awakes in the likeness of his God. Sometimes his soul rises on the wings of faith, and rejoices that the rest that remaineth for the people of God is so near. Yonder world of light and purity is my home. I have not long to dwell in a foreign land, in dust and tears. A glorious heaven, God my eternal father, saints and angels, await me. The warfare is short; a throne and an undying crown are ready; the heavenly hills are almost in view; the resurrection is hastening.

"Lo! I behold the scattered shades,
The dawn of heaven appears,
The sweet immortal morning spreads
Its blushes round the spheres."

Few have had a clearer view of their own sinful hearts than the deceased. Take his own language: "The sins of childhood, the vices of youth, the improprieties, the pride and arrogancy of riper years, with the presumptuous and blasphemous suggestions of my mind, up to the present time, lay heavy on my mind and sink my spirits very low."

Being with him in his last illness more or less every day, I think I may say that I never saw a Christian feel more deeply his own unworthiness. "Bury me," said he, "in a humble manner." "I want no encomiums ; I deserve none. I feel myself a poor miserable sinner, and Christ is my only hope. " Being asked, very near his end, what were his views of the future, he exclaimed, with both hands extended upward and a smile I can never forget, "My prospects of heaven are clear." He seemed already to feel the everlasting rest laying its sweet influences over his soul, and bearing it up, taking away the "sting of death."

The last clause of our text will now be considered : "Their works do follow them." The works of the Christian follow ; they do not go before as a merit, to purchase salvation, but they follow as an evidence of having lived and died in the Lord. We shall apply this :

I. To works of a private kind.

All efforts after personal holiness, evinced by self-examination, secret devotion, a faithful study of the Word of God,— all conquests over sinful self, exhibited by denying ourselves of all worldly lusts, bridling our tongues, governing our tempers, subduing our wills, mortifying our pride, and using every effort in our power to grow in grace, will follow us in their influence on the soul. Have we any reason to believe that death will essentially alter the faculties of an immortal soul ? If not, then all our spiritual attainments enlarge the soul, and fit it for more consummate joy when it arrives at heaven. Thus our works do follow us.

We are taught that we shall be rewarded according to our works, not for them. The parable of the talents is in accordance with this. The reward was according to the improvements made upon the talents given. By this, then, we are taught that the rewards of heaven will be accordingly as our works of obedience "fellow" us. Reason teaches the same from their permanent influence on the soul itself.

Suppose God should reward with pecuniary treasure, as man rewards, and one who has been more faithful, his works following him, should have one farthing more reward than the less faithful, that put at usury for eternity would soon amount to more wealth than ever Omnipotence created in this vast world. But God's rewards are infinitely more valuable; they are spiritual, with the permanent stamp of eternity upon them. And the time may come in eternity, in consequence of our works following us, that the Christian may enjoy more in consequence of his fidelity here, compared with what he had enjoyed if he had been less faithful, than all the happiness of heaven and earth, God excepted, have enjoyed since the "morning stars sang together, and all the sons of God shouted for joy" over the birth of this infant world. Oh, if so, how important that we exert every power in this cradle time of existence for additional faithfulness.

II. We shall apply the subject to works of a social and public kind, and under this head consider it solely in reference to the deceased.

Solemn and important truth: all his works will follow him. Could he now speak from that coffin, would he not say, "Let my virtues follow me, and my frailties die with me."

The Rev. John Leland was born in the town of Grafton, Mass., May 14, 1754. Few men that have ever lived possessed a more gifted intellect. His powers of reasoning were strong, accurate and peculiarly forcible; his mind highly original, and somewhat eccentric. From a child he was a lover of learning, and made rapid proficiency for the age and the advantages it afforded.

At the age of eighteen, his attention was arrested with what he said seemed a voice from heaven, "You are not about the work you have got to do." This conviction was more than ordinarily pungent. He was brought to give up all the foolish amusement of youth in disgust, he has told us, and fall at the feet of sovereign mercy as a lost, perishing sinner. After his conversion, he says, "My heart was greatly attached to the Holy Scriptures. I have not yet forgot the burning desire, the soul-longing, I had to know what was the mind of God contained in his Word. I would read, then pray, then read and pray again, that I might know the truth as it is in Jesus." He was frequently accustomed to hold meetings in company with a young convert, and, as he said, "preach two or three of our sort of sermons at each meeting." From the date of his spiritual birth, he seemed imbued with a spirit to preach, though self-distrusting on account of conscious unworthiness. "The number of sermons (such as they were) that I preached alone by myself was very great;" and he adds, "both saint and sinner said, 'John will be a preacher.'" He was very deeply sensible that no man should preach until called of God to the work.

In 1774, he united with the Baptist church in Bellingham, Mass., and by that church was licensed to preach at the age of twenty. In 1774, he journeyed to the State of Virginia, and labored there as a minister eight months. After his return he was married, Sept. 30, 1776, to Miss Sarah Devine, with whom he lived sixty-one years. He repaired with his companion to Virginia. His labors were itinerant, confined chiefly to Virginia, Pennsylvania and South Carolina. He was ordained in 1776. His meetings were often in a circuit, sometimes one hundred and twenty miles in length. In the month of October in this year, he was much revived in his mind, in view of which he said, "Souls appeared very precious to me, and my heart was drawn out in prayer for their salvation. Now for the first time I knew what it was to travail in birth for the conversion of sinners." The result was, in a short time he baptized one hundred and thirty as the seal of his ministry. For some time revivals almost constantly followed his labors. In about two years he baptized four hundred. In

1790, after a stay of fourteen years, in which time he baptized precisely seven hundred, he removed to New England with his family, then consisting of eight children. After preaching for a season in Connecticut, and about a year in Conway, in this State, he removed to Cheshire in February, 1792, which has been his residence chiefly for almost half a century.

About this time it pleased the Lord to bless his labors in adjacent towns. Lanesborough, Adams, Phillipston, Canaan, Gore and Conway successively enjoyed revivals under his ministry. He continued to preach in New England and New York until 1797, when he journeyed again to Virginia, preaching as formerly to and from the State. He remained there eighteen months. After his return, he was adjusting his concerns to go thither again, when he received an impression that it was his duty to preach day time and evening for the space of two weeks. The time had then arrived when his appointments must be met on his way to the South.

He says these words forced themselves again and again on his mind: "The Lord will work." On his way he appointed a meeting, and the people of Cheshire followed him in great numbers, and wept under the pungent truths that fell from his lips. He was absent only twenty days. On his return, he found the work of grace, like a torrent, was bearing all before it. After his return, which was early in the fall, he preached every day until the March following, when he baptized two hundred. Find for us the minister of Christ that has performed in his own parish an equal amount of preaching in a given time, that we may embalm his name forever in grateful remembrance.

In the year 1800, he made a tour of four months in New York, Connecticut, Rhode Island and Massachusetts. In November, 1801, he journeyed as far south as Washington.

In 1808, his labors were blessed in Pownal, Vt., where he baptized about sixty. In 1811, he enjoyed a revival in this town, and baptized forty.

In December, 1813, he again, for the last time, visited Virginia. The joy was indescribable, both to him and his spiritual children, in being once more permitted to meet this side of the grave. He was absent six months; travelled eighteen hundred miles, and preached one hundred and fifty times.

In the fall of 1817, he enjoyed here, under his ministration, a precious revival, and baptized thirty-one. In the March following, a revival in Adams brought seventy into the fold of Christ. In this revival his labors were much blessed, and twenty-seven of the above number were baptized by him. We have given but an imperfect description of his labors. He has stated that since he began to preach, he has travelled distances, reckoned together, nearly sufficient to thrice circle the earth, or about seventy-five thousand miles, and preached about eight thousand sermons.

The number of Baptist ministers he tells us that he has personally known is nine hundred and sixty-two; three hundred and three of whom he has heard preach. Three hundred of the above have gone before him into eternity; two hundred and seven have visited him at his own house. He has baptized one thousand, five hundred and twenty-four persons, and preached in four hundred and thirty-six meeting-houses, several capitols, and in various other kinds of buildings, as well as in the streets and groves. He has written about thirty pamphlets, some valuable pieces of poetry, and much from time to time for the public papers, both political and moral. So much did he love his Bible, that he numbered all its chapters, one thousand, one hundred and eighty-nine, its verses, thirty-one thousand, one hundred and eighteen, and even its words, seven hundred and eighty-six thousand, six hundred and eighty-three.

He has written us his own epitaph in the following words: "Here lies the body of John Leland, who labored sixty-eight years to promote piety and vindicate the civil and religious rights of all men."

Yes, there lies the noble, venerable dust, and is that all the epitaph he has left us? No. He has been writing one more durable and extensive on the imperishable tablet of thousands of hearts; and there it will remain when the cold marble over his dust has crumbled away. His name, his virtues, his success, and his melting eloquence will never be forgotten. We can present no man a perfect character. In sentiment and doctrine I can give him, in common with thousands, a hearty welcome; but I am constrained by a sense of duty, to speak with regret, that in three respects he differed somewhat from the denomination as a body with which he stood connected. I allude to his views of the Sabbath, Sabbath-schools, and the mode of benevolent operations. If in an error, I am confident it was one of the judgment rather than of the heart. Knowing his honesty and sincerity, and the age in which his impressions were formed, we will do all in our power to make an apology, and let the subject rest with his ashes.

Great and good man, he is gone! The tender and affectionate father, the kind husband, the wise counsellor, emphatically the peace-maker, the social, warm-hearted friend, the sage patriot, the lover of sound doctrine, the eloquent and unusually successful minister of Christ, is no more! Is no more? He still lives, we doubt not, where his intellect has found congenial spirits, and a wider range in the upper empire of Jehovah. He lives below in the affections of thousands, and "his works do follow him." The influence which he has exerted upon the world will never be lost. It will follow him, widening through successive generations, until the final judgment, when thousands, we trust, will meet him as their spiritual father, and in rapturous hosannas praise God together forever and ever.

Dying mortals, hastening to eternity, there comes a voice deep-toned and solemn from the associations of this day. The labors, the sacrifices, the kindnesses, the fidelity, the fearless presentation of truth, the sympathies in troubles and bereavements, the philosophic maxims, the sublime and soul-stirring strains falling from this sacred desk for a long succession of years, the clear elucidation of truth, the solemn warnings, the tender invitations, the heart-searching appeals, yea, everything in which the character of your venerable father in Israel was seen, have now found mysteriously a thousand tongues to speak on this solemn occasion.

There comes a voice from the distant past and the present, from the lifeless corpse, from the coffin, the pall, the bier, the grave and the eternal world, "Prepare to meet thy God." Inspiration tells us of the contrast of the righteous and the wicked. "Some men's sins are open beforehand, going to judgment," while those who die in the Lord "rest from their labors and their works do follow them." Hearer, are you of the former class, "condemned already," your sins having gone before you as witnesses? Is there no occasion for alarm, standing between two eternities, while the all-sweeping deluge of time is bearing away particle after particle of your sandy foundation, and for aught men or angels know, the last sand may give way during this solemn hour? One less Christian is left to pray for you, one less faithful herald of the cross to preach to you.

In all the mighty monarchy of God, I hesitate not to say, "There is no peace," no substantial happiness, no safety to the impenitently wicked. By the awful solemnity of eternity, then, I beseech you to flee to the city of refuge ere the avenger of blood overtake you.

Afflicted friends, the numbers that have assembled here on this occasion, from different towns, to "weep with those who weep," show you that you have a share of public sympathy. After all, their sympathies are unavailing to comfort the troubled heart. Turn, then, your thoughts reverently to Him who was the stay and the support of your much loved friend in dangers and toils through a long and useful life. Gather around that Bible, that your affectionate father and relative so long loved, studied and expounded, and make it your constant companion. It will tell you that "afflictions spring not from the dust;" that though "clouds and darkness are around about him, righteousness and judgment are the habitation of his throne;" that amid the trials of life "He will find out a way of escape;" that you should "remember the rod, and who hath appointed it;" that "the Lord gave and the Lord hath taken away, blessed be the name of the Lord."

The disciples of old took up the body of one they most dearly loved and buried it, and went and told Jesus. Go ye and do likewise. Tell the compassionate Redeemer all your sorrows. He still lives to intercede for his followers. He still lives to make afflictions the richest means of grace here below to his faithful servants, for they "work out for them a far more exceeding and eternal weight of glory."

Could the gate of heaven open, and he, who, we trust, has just begun the everlasting song, stop a moment from the sweet immortal strains, and drop a word through the yielding air to you, methinks it would be, "Weep not for me, but weep for yourselves and your children." Have you not rather occasion to bless God that he gave you such a friend to lose, and spared him so long, and brought him at last to the "grave in a full age, like as a shock of corn cometh in in his season?" Why should we mourn that the soldier, after a hundred conflicts on the "cannon ploughed field," amid the clangor of arms and groans and wailings and "garments rolled in blood," is permitted to hear the shout of victory, and go home in safety to his dearest friends? To live like him, is to mourn over the sins of earth, and hold up God's everlasting truth to a dying world. To die like him, is to stand on the confines of earth, looking off into eternity, and depart with the "prospect of heaven clear." To rest, at last, like him, is, we doubt not, to rest forever in the Paradise of God.

CHAPTER XV.

EXCITING AND TRAGIC STORIES.

MASSELLON, THE GREAT FRENCH CATHOLIC PREACHER.

MASSELLON was a great and noble man, and a very eloquent and spiritual preacher. Louis XIV. paid a good tribute to his eloquence. " When I hear other preachers, father, I am well pleased with them ; but when I hear you, I am dissatisfied with myself." When his King Louis met him as he came down from the pulpit, he said, " How do you dare to preach so heart-searching before your Sovereign ? " " I durst not preach otherwise, sire, in the presence of the Sovereign of the Universe." When the king died, his urn was brought into the cathedral, which was ornamented with many trophies of the king's victories. Daylight was excluded, but innumerable tapers supplied its place. Massellon rose slowly and solemnly, surveyed the scene, and in a solemn tone exclaimed, " My hearers, God only is great." The audience all arose and bowed assent.

Baron, the great actor, on hearing Massellon preach, said to a brother actor who accompanied him, " Here is an orator ; we are only actors." His sexton went over his residence with some visitants, telling of his virtues and many charities, and when he came to the room where he died, exclaimed in tears, " Here is the place where we lost him ! " I have two volumes of his sermons, and I think them as spiritual and heart-searching as any I ever read. When he was preaching on the fewness of the elect, so searching was the sermon, his audience trembled in fear lest they should be found on the left hand, to be cast into everlasting misery.

Wesley, the great Methodist divine, was one of the most spiritual, able, laborious and successful ministers of his time. In fifty years' preaching, he delivered over forty thousand sermons, and travelled over two hundred and twenty-five thousand miles, besides writing many excellent hymns. He died in triumph, saying, "Victory! victory! through the blood of the Lamb."

Rev. Dr. Payson was one of the ablest and most spiritual men of his day. He died a most happy and triumphant death. "His dying words were, "The celestial city is full in view; its glories beam upon me; its breezes fan me; its odors are wafted to me; its music strikes on my ear, and its spirit breathes in my heart; nothing separates but the river of death, now only a narrow rill, which may be crossed at a step by God's permission."

Some thirty years ago, I heard an excellent lecture given in Westfield, by Bayard Taylor, on Arabia. He gave them a high compliment for their kind hospitality. I think he said they would not take any pay at any place where he stopped. But they were the most notorious liars he ever found. He scarcely met a man or woman who did not exaggerate. He said he had an interview with their king, and asked him why his subjects so falsely colored things. The king said he did not know, unless the old legend was true, that Satan once came up to visit his subjects in Spain, where he brought nine packs, five of them were on lying, and he put them in the hotel where he quartered. Before the Devil arose, some Arabs stole all the five on lying, and carried them up into Arabia. I asked the king what was the wealth of his nation. "It is a very rich nation. I have the control of it. I have one hundred houses full of gold, and three hundred full of silver, and a dozen men come each with a horse for me to ride out for my health. After conversing a while, the king said, "What is the king of your country worth?" I told him my country was so large, if the whole of Arabia was put on it, it would be only a little speck; and it was very rich. The king of my country had a thousand houses full of gold, and seven thousand full of silver, and two hundred thousand soldiers as his body-guard, and all the horses and waiters he wanted. I was satisfied he would not respect me without I told a bigger lie than he had. He smiled and said, " A very nice country is yours, Mr. Taylor."

ARABIAN EXAGGERATION IN DESCRIBING A GIANT.

"A giant stood behind the highest pyramid of Egypt, looking over its top into the Nile. His shoes were of wood. They had been once two large canoes. They just fitted his feet. His cane was the mast of a seventy-four gunship, which he had hauled ashore in the harbor of Alexandria. His course from the pyramid was towards the Nile, which he was about to cross. I queried whether he would swim or sail over. He did neither. He jumped over from the eastern to the western shore with a single leap, but split both his shoes in the effort."

All this shows to what a state of falsehood and sin mankind may be plunged if they have no Bible. The Koran is their guide.

When pastor in North Adams, I baptized in our great revival an apothecary merchant and some of his good children. His name was Salmon Burlingame, one of the most cheerful and agreeable men I ever knew. He was very fond of trouting. We were accustomed to go up once a year to the trout brooks in Reedsboro. One year we decided to go up to Bear Swamp, where some feared to go. We left our team at Canada's hotel, and ordered our breakfast by candle light. Our direction was to walk up the old Bennington turnpike five miles, turn to the right by a marked tree, and go in a northwestern course two miles in a spruce forest, guided by marked trees. The sun had just risen, clear and beautiful. Unfortunately, we had no pocket compass. I said, "Can you keep the point of compass?" He was of the humorous make, stuttering some. "I can keep it from my store home," he said. "If the trees are not marked all the way" (which we soon found was the case), "we may get into serious trouble. If the sun continues to shine, one thing will save us. The sun will shine on our right shoulders all the way." "Yes," he said. We had not gone far before he said, "We are going west." "No; the sun does not shine on our backs," and he quietly followed. But soon he said, "We are going southwest." Again I quieted him by pointing to the sun, so illuminating the forest it told us where it was. Soon he said, "We are going right back, and I came for a good time of fishing." "So did I, so come right on." "No," he said. He was completely turned. Though he could see where the sun was, it made no difference. "Besides, we have been more than two miles, I think." No wonder he thought so, as we had to go over logs and rocks. I said, "Will you sit on that rock as long as you can hear my voice?" "Yes." I said, on leaving him, "This forest is said to be eighteen miles long, infested with bears and catamounts. It would be fearful to be lost here, and perhaps fatal." I kept calling, and he responding, and not a hundred rods from where I left my dear brother, I came to the stream, running through a natural pond, and ere he arrived, I had twelve fine trout, all jumping up and down in a safe place. I put them in my basket, and thirty-eight more ere I left that spot. He had gone to the head of the pond, and was catching larger ones, and called me there. We fished there till nearly noon, ate our lunch with happy, thankful hearts, and then followed down the stream until we filled our baskets and sack pockets full, and then went to the hotel.

We arrived at the hotel before night, and, with Canada's help, dressed over three hundred trout. While doing this,

I asked Mr. Canada for a fresh bear or catamount story, as they killed such large game in that region. He told us one of the most novel and interesting bear stories I ever heard. Pointing up north, towards the woods, he said, " A little beyond them I have a pasture. I was in those woods in pursuit of my cows, when I heard at a short distance, a strange series of noises. On approaching, I found the noise was over the opposite side of a large fallen tree. I looked over, and saw a bear lying on her back, and three fat cubs jumping alternately on to her. She tossed each up three times, and then threw the cub over her head and took another. It so tickled them, it was their laughing I heard. Thinking a cub would make a fine treat in my tavern, I sought a club, and found the motherly frolic still in progress. I struck the log with my club. The bear sprang up, putting her paws on the log, giving an angry growl. I had heard that a bear would ward off a blow, so I raised my club perpendicular, and brought it down a little, and then nearer, when I brought it down with all my might upon her head. She fell prostrate. The club broke, and with a part of it I sprang upon the log to finish up the work, and, the bark being rotten, gave way, and I fell into the paws of the bear, as she was on her back. It was the first time I remember being scared all over. I sprang out of her clutches. She sprang up, rubbing her head with her paws, and retreated, and I followed her. I knew she could not go far without coming to a ledge of rocks. She came to the ledge, and finding a hole just large enough, she went up, and the cubs followed her. When the last one came to the top, I caught him by his hind leg, and ran for home, and the bear after me. I soon came to another ledge some six feet high. There was mud and leaves on it, and they gave way, and I slid to the bottom of the ledge, and the bear came headlong on to me. I suddenly rolled her off, and shot the cub in her face. She seemed satisfied, and undertook to ascend the ledge. When the cub was at the top, I caught him again and ran for life; and when I came into the clearing near my tavern, I stopped and faced the bear, and gave her most savage yells. The bear stopped, and whining tenderly for her child, began to circle me at a little distance. I kept my eye on her, backing toward my house. I had a non-compos boy digging potatoes back of my barn. I said, "Sam, do not say a word, but get my rifle and shoot this bear." He raised his head. I repeated it. "What did you say?" The bear looked up and saw all my buildings and ran for the woods. Then began the trouble in good earnest with the cub. I had him by his hind legs. He bit me and scratched me. I tried to strike his head on a rock, but ere I brought him down, he was up biting my arm. I hurried home, and said, "Sam, you blockhead, bring me a flour barrel." I threw him in, put a cord on his leg, weighed him, and found he weighed forty pounds. Our sheriff came along the next day, and I sold him to him. The last I heard of him, the sheriff sold him to Galusha, Governor of Vermont, for his pet bear.

A SUCCESSFUL STRATEGEM.

Bayard Taylor travelled over most of the civilized world, and has immortalized himself in his lectures and writings. In a book entitled 'At Home and Abroad," I read a strategy he recorded. I have not seen the book for over twenty years, but I think I can give the story very correctly, such was the impression it made. In a battle between France and Prussia, in 1808, France conquered. The dead of both armies, sixty thousand in number, lay on the battle-field, near the village of Waldorf, in Prussia. The French generals were Lasure and Lamot, who quartered in a village near by. In the evening, Lamot went to the headquarters of Lasure, commander-in-chief, and said, "General, I have good evidence that our soldiers have been insulted in the village of Waldorf; what shall be done?" Lasure, fired by victory, said, "Take a portion of your army, and go at early dawn, and shoot ten men in the village of Waldorf, and return to camp. In the meantime, the citizens of Waldorf had spent the whole night in caring for the sufferers of both armies, being near the battle-ground. They had erected rude tables over the Common, loaded with food, surrounded by hundreds of kind men and women, rejoicing that the cruel war was over. To their surprise, martial music is heard, and lo ! a band of soldiers, headed by General Lamot, approach them. He breaks the seal of a letter and reads :

"GEN. LAMOT, COMMANDER OF THE SECOND DIVISION OF THE FRENCH ARMY :

"Sir, go with a portion of your army to the village of Waldorf, and shoot ten men for insulting the French soldiers last night."

A peal of thunder in a clear sky could not have been more astounding. A young clergyman, colleague of a good old parson, stepped forward and said, " General, I have been here with my friends all night, caring for the sufferers of both armies, and I assure you that no French soldiers have been here, except the wounded we are aiding. There are three villages called Waldorf ; it might have been there, but not here." "We have evidence it occurred, so bring on the ten men." The good parson so moved the general as he showed how unjust it was to punish the innocent for the guilty, that he said, " I will send a message to Lasure, and await his answer. In the meantime, will you give us a breakfast ? " The kind Prussians brought on the toast and coffee prepared for the sufferers. A lady said to her pastor, "We are feeding our murderers." "Hush," said he, " Let us be Christlike, whatever they do." Soon the answer came. By this time many hundreds had assembled in breathless suspense. Lamot broke the seal and read :

"Do as I command you.
"LASURE, COMMANDER-IN-CHIEF OF THE FRENCH ARMY."

Then was heard weeping and wailing. The young par·
son said, " General, I have made my plea to you, and now I
ask permission to pray to God, that you may be prevented
from doing such an unjust and cruel thing." The prayer
moved Lamot and many of the soldiers to tears, and led
him to say, " I can save you only by a strategem. Bring
forward your ten men. I will order the executioners to fire
over their heads, but they must all fall and remain quiet till
my soldiers are out of sight." The first that came was the
young minister, followed by a young man just married,
struggling to get from his bride. The next was the father
of a large family, his weeping wife and children trying in
vain to restrain him. The number was soon complete.
General Lamot stood silently looking now at the doomed
men, and then at the anxiously gazing throng, then turning
to the executioners, rifles in hand, said, in a loud, distinct
voice, "Soldiers! ready, aim at their heads," when many
fell on their knees in prayer, seeing death a sure thing.
" Fire ! " They all fell, sure enough, with scarce a
struggle. " Right about, forward, march!" As the music
began to die away, they all sprang up, amid embraces and
shouts of joy. Lamot had secretly told the soldiers to
elevate their rifles when they fired. He knew full well
his soldiers would never tell Lasure the strategem, and he
probably never knew it. Thirty years after, the village of
Waldorf invited Lamot, an old gray-headed man, to visit
them in a universal Jubilee of gratitude for what he
had done.

There was a river called Bear river, about sixty rods
from my home, which ran through a forest abounding with
gray squirrels, and the river was alive with nice trout. I
do not think my father let me hunt or fish, unless it rained
so hard we could not work. I often gained a day by taking
a stint, which I spent in hunting or fishing. I once came
home with nine gray squirrels. At other times I came
home with about a hundred trout, as wet as the trout were
before they were caught. The trout and the squirrels have

nearly all disappeared, unless it may be now and then one
that comes to get a history of the happy home of his beautiful fathers.

LITTLE HELEN IN THE LIGHT-HOUSE.

Many years ago, I heard this interesting story, and it is
good for many thousand years to come. On the coast of
Cornwall, Eng., there lived a man and wife, and a little
daughter, Helen. The father lived in the light-house, and
cared for it. Both father and mother prayed night and
morning. At the age of nine, Helen was converted, and
prayed also. Soon her mother died, and gave Helen her
large Bible, and told her to study it well and meet her in
heaven. The father and Helen kept the light-house, and
prayed together as before. One afternoon, the father said,
" Have the table ready by five o'clock. I am going to the
village on the causeway for provisions, and shall be back by
tea time." Around in the region were many robbers, or
wreckers, as some called them. He said, " It is important
to light the light-house to-night, as there are three large
vessels to pass us from the East Indies." Helen looked at
the causeway, but no father was in sight. She looked till
the sun set, and the tide and high winds drove the waters
into such commotion that he could not come. She feared
the robbers had killed him, so he could not light up, and
the vessels would be wrecked, and they could rob them.
She prayed that God would tell her what to do. She felt
impressed it was her duty to light up the light-house. She
went up the circular stairs, but found she could not reach
the lamp. She carried up a stand, and touched a match to
the wick, and the flaming light shone on the rocks in the
channel lashed by the turbulent waves. She felt happy
that she had saved many lives. She gazed off on the sea,
and soon saw a vessel coming. She stood in the light-
house tower. As the vessel came in front, men, women
and children came on deck, and a sailor took off his cap,

and swinging it, cried, "Hurrah for the girl in the light-house!" followed by many others, and on the vessel went for Liverpool. The second vessel did in like manner. They did not know then that the little Christian, thoughtful girl they cheered had saved their lives. She waited for the third vessel, but it did not come. She became more distressed about her father, fearing the robbers had killed him. She opened the good Bible her mother left her and read, " When father and mother forsake thee, then the Lord will take thee up." She prayed and went to her couch. She awoke early. All was calm. The causeway was clear. There was a little village on the beach. She hastened there, and rapped earnestly. "I am Helen ; my father did not come home. Can you tell me where he is?" She hastened to every house. No one had seen him. She ran down to a little grocery under the hill. They said he left there with a basket of provisions, and went up through the woods. They tracked him till they found tracks where he had been forced off into the forest. Seven men started to find him. Helen wanted to go, but the rocks and briers forbade it. She went on to a large rock, and waited. At night they came back without him. They cared kindly for Helen, and went the next day. Helen was on the rock, and some other girls. The men went some miles, and in a deserted house, in a rear bed-room, they found Helen's father lying on the dirty floor, nearly dead, his limbs tied, and a gag in his mouth. He opened his eyes as they approached. They removed the gag, and cut his bonds. He could but just stand. "Water! give me water!" he said. They had none. They put their arms under his, and marched him homeward. About sunset, they came in sight of the little village. Helen was on the rock with some of her mates. "They have found him, I think. Seven went out, and eight are coming back." She left the rock upon the run. The wind blew off her bonnet, but she never halted. As she approached them, she leaped up and down, saying, "It is my father! It is my father! The robbers did not kill you." "Not quite," he said. "I lit up the light-house," she said. Right there they both knelt and prayed. He thanked God for so good a child, and she that her father was spared to her.

In the early times of England, there is a curious story whether true or not, the readers must judge. It is said that two plenipotentiaries were sent from Italy to England. As Rome was the early seat of science, they supposed themselves more learned than the English. To test the case, they took a letter of introduction to the president of Oxford Collge, for the purpose of measuring heads with said president. When they had entered the kingdom, they asked a workman by the wayside to direct them to Oxford College, and he did so in Latin. Proceeding on their way, they asked a farmer for further directions, and he gave it in Greek. Surprised at the knowledge of the common people, they began to fear the result. The next man, dressed as a gentleman, of whom they made inquiry, answered them in Hebrew. They both agreed it was a hopeless case for them, as the president would be, of course, far more learned than the common people ; so they changed their programme and agreed to try him in deaf and dumb signs, which they proposed to do, after a little time subsequent to their introduction.

The president said he had never given his attention to that form of converse, but he had a brother who was an adept in that line. He was a miller and had but one eye. He sent his son, requesting him to come to the reception room, as two gentlemen wished to see him. Supposing it was for trade, he hastened to meet them. On entering, one of the gentlemen rose, waving his hand in a dignified and graceful way, pointed one finger to the miller. He pointed two toward the Italian.

The other plenipotentiary arose in dignified eclat, and pointed three fingers at the miller. He closed his hand suddenly and left the room, but soon called his brother out.

They said to each other, "These English people have been misrepresented to us. How quick the miller understood us. I put out one finger, signifying there was one God. He put out two fingers, signifying there were two persons in the Godhead." "I put out three fingers," said the other official, "and he closed his hand, signifying they were united in one." Not so did the miller understand it. He said to his brother, "Why did you introduce me to those saucy rascals? One saw I had but one eye, and he pointed at it. I thought I would treat your guests more politely, and pointed to two fingers, signifying they were more blest. But the other man carried on the insult by pointing three fingers at me, meaning that each of them and myself made out three eyes, and I doubled up my fist, signifying I would give them a terrible flogging if they insulted me more."

JUDGE HALE.

Some years since, I read a trial instituted by Judge Hale, one of the most pious judges that ever sat on the king's bench of England, who never let business keep him from family prayer, and who never, it is said, pronounced the name of God without a solemn pause. There were two brothers in England who inherited a large fortune together. They took their possessions, and settled in Europe among strangers. The younger brother went on a speculating tour and was gone many months. His older brother published his death. But he returned. The older brother disowned him, and took all the large legacy. The younger brother sought his rights by law. It went against him in two trials. He appealed, and laid the case before Judge Hale, as the place was under the jurisdiction of England. The judge, thinking there was bribery, consented to go to the trial disguised in a miller's dress. "When the jury is impanelled," the judge told him, "he had a right to object to one juryman, and you can put me in his place, and I can see the workings." The trial went on. When the jury were closeted, a man came in, and put a ten-dollar gold piece in the hands of all the jurymen but the old miller, to whom he gave five dollars. The foreman said, "We have decided the case against the younger brother." Judge Hale arose, and said, "I object to this decision for various reasons. One is, there was partiality used. Only five dollars were given me, and the rest had ten each. Your honor knows this bribery makes the trial invalid." He then made such an able speech on the subject of law that he astonished every hearer. The presiding judge said, "Will you please give me your name?" "My name, sir, is Matthew Hale, the chief judge of the king's bench, and I order you to leave that seat immediately, which I shall take, and have a fair trial." He did so, and gave the young brother his rights in the legacy, and compensation for all the expense caused him.

THOUGHTS ON VISITING NIAGARA FALLS, JUNE 20, 1842.

BY JOHN ALDEN.

Proud Cataract! around thy form
The thunder's peal; the howling storm
  Thou mockest in thy might;
As erst Creation's work was o'er
No sight like thine from shore to shore
  The sun beheld in sight.

On centuries rolled; nor mortal ear
Thy thunderings heard, or quaked in fear
  While bending o'er thy fall;
Wild beasts and echoing forests' roar
Howled mournful on thy desert shore,
  And angels heard thy call.

An Indian, roaming o'er the plain
In rural sports, heard thy hoarse strain
  In nature's anthems wild;
Then laid his deadly weapon by,
A savage yell shook earth and sky
  From nature's wandering child.

Ages rolled on; white man at last
Trod Erie's strand, and hastened past
　　Adown Niagara's stream;
Islets of green before him stood
Like Delos pinned amid the flood,
　　Of cataract did not dream.

But rumbling sounds assail his ear;
The rapids leap; "God, God is here,"
　　A deafening peal resounds.
Outlet of all creation, why
Trembles the earth, the air, the sky,
　　On these enchanted grounds?

He comes at last upon the verge,
Looks down upon the awful surge
　　Where tortured waters bound;
O God of wonders, not in sky,
Thou roll'st like an eternity
　　Unceasing thunders down.

The present throngs that come and go,
The rich, the poor, the high, the low,
　　May never bide thee more;
But thou wilt hymn God's awful praise
To men of other times and days
　　As thou hast done before.

Come, then, all nations, far and near,
God's voice unceasingly to hear,
　　And see his rainbow throne.
He speaks — a listening world is still,
All other streamlets seem a rill;
　　This wonder stands alone.

North Adams, July 25, 1842.

CHAPTER XVI.

STORIES FOR SABBATH SCHOOLS.

T is truly a wonder that Sabbath-schools were not sooner established in the Christian world. Scores of thousands have been saved through their influence. By far the most conversions have occurred in the Sabbath-schools. Almost everything depends on the piety and fidelity of the superintendents and teachers. "Faith cometh by hearing, and hearing by the word of God." I will give a few illustrations:

A pious teacher in Central New York faithfully taught her class, and the wonder was that no more were converted. After her death, her diary read: "Resolved, I will pray every day for the conversion of my class." None were converted. Some time after it read: "Resolved, to visit and faithfully converse with each pupil, and pray for them, respecting their conversion." Most of them were soon converted. The prayer of faith is always heard.

Some forty years ago, I visited a brother, deacon of a church in Central Illinois. I arrived at his house just as he was starting, with a span of horses hitched to a long wagon full of joyful children, bound for a Sabbath-school celebration, some twenty miles distant. He said, "You love to address Sabbath-schools; please get in the wagon and go with us." "Nothing could suit me better," I said. The way was filled with loaded carriages. When we reached the place, to my surprise, we met an army of little and great, just ready to march up into a burr-oak grove, escorted by a number of bands of music, with the great-

311

est throng of children and youth I ever saw in any one gathering.

Many of them had come more than forty miles. They floated to the breeze many scores of banners, with good, suggestive mottoes. We entered a vast, beautiful grove. There were tables, some two hundred feet long, laden with food. In front of these was a large platform, capable of seating nearly a hundred, which was well filled, where they could see the vast throng. It was one of the most inspiring scenes, by far, I ever witnessed. Who that love the souls of men could fail to be eloquent then. The bands struck up a stirring strain that echoed through the wilderness, cheered by happy thousands. I seem to feel that inspiration yet, while trying to describe it. After prayer, the speeches began, and lasted nearly two hours. Two of the many anecdotes related I will record. A clergyman said one Sabbath morning he went out into the woods to meditate and pray. He soon heard the scream of two parent robins. They had a nest with little birds in it, about ten feet from the body of a burr-oak tree. The robins flew rapidly toward the body of the tree from the limb on which their nest rested, uttering their shriek of fear and anguish, to drive away a large black snake, crawling up the tree. When he put his head on the limb where their nest was, they flew into the woods and returned each with a leaf in its bill. The little birds raised their heads in fear. The parent bird made a shrill command, and every head was down, and the leaves drawn over the nest. The children of the lower order of families obey without asking any questions.

They continued to fly rapidly, bringing leaves, and soon covered the nest, ere the snake came to it. Intent on a feast, the snake attempted to remove the leaves. The moment his head touched a leaf, he sprang back, perhaps as quick as he would if it had been a red hot cylinder. He tried the nest on every side, darted out his tongue in anger, and came down, and was executed on the spot as a murderer. He then climbed up and took some of the leaves that proved to be a species of the ash, long known to be poisonous to the snake, but not to any other animal. God taught them by instinct what to do. The inference that may be drawn is, that God has given us the Bible, figuratively called "Leaves for the healing of the nations." The Bible says, "The old serpent, the Devil, goeth about like a roaring lion, seeking whom he may devour." He is striving to enter the hearts of all, as much as the serpent did the bird's nest. What will keep him out ? He will try to destroy by making all tell lies, curse and swear, steal, rob, get drunk and commit murder and all kinds of sins. Fill the mind with God's holy word, the healing leaves, and if it is blest to the conversion of the soul, if he tries to enter the heart, he will draw back. Nothing does Satan hate like holiness. He felt the holiness of Christ so much, he cried out, "Hast thou come to torment us before the time !"

The next anecdote was of a youth, who, on the gallows, said, "There were just five steps that brought me here: I. Disobedience to parents. II. Sabbath-breaking. III. Stealing. IV. Drunkenness. V. Murder." I requested, all to repeat over these steps several times. Near the close of the speaking, as quite a number had gone some ways into the woods, the marshall requested me to have them repeat over the five steps of the murderer in the story I had told, and when the fifth step was repeated, he requested it to be repeated "murder" as loud as possible. This brought the wanderers back on the run, and had the desired effect to keep them from straying more.

In 1835, a very pious young lady came into the village of Hamilton, N. Y., and asked the superintendent of the Sabbath-school if any teachers were wanted. "Not now," he said. "Please hold yourself ready, if there is an opening." "Would there be any objections to my gathering a class if I can ?" "Certainly not ; but a thorough canvass has been made." She went to work in the highways and hedges, and obtained a number, which a benevolent society clothed up for her, and brought them into the school. Soon she had a pew full. She visited them at their homes, talked and prayed with them. When any were converted, she put them in another class, and filled their place with others. In a little over twenty years of such labor, just thirty were brought under her instruction, and twenty-nine were hopefully converted. When this good teacher was on her dying bed with consumption, she said, " I have a good hope for twenty-nine of my pupils, that they will be gems in the Saviour's diadem, and my eternal source of rejoicing. But there is one girl of my class so vain and so sceptical, I never could make her feel her lost condition so as to ask for mercy." The door was ajar, and this girl heard her teacher's mournful utterance. She had come to have her sick teacher pray for her. She could wait no longer, but rushed into the sick room, threw her arms around her teacher's neck, saying, " Pray for me ; your prayers have been answered for all the class but me." Then and there, amid sobs and tears, she gave her heart to God. Her teacher, in a dying condition, said, " Now I can die in peace, with the hope of meeting all my dear pupils in heaven, as so many jewels in the Saviour's diadem and my crown of eternal joy."

MISCELLANEOUS FACTS.

A good practical anecdote for ministers, which I heard many years ago, I will relate. Two theological students studied with a devout clergyman ; we will call their names Peter and John. After many years, they met their good old teacher at his house. " Well," said the old minister, " I am happy to meet you here. Will you please, Brother Peter, to tell me what has been your success in the pastorate ? " He replied with downcast eyes, " Scarcely none at all. I have ransacked the universe for strong expressions, and terrific illustrations. I have reiterated the awful thunderings of Sinai, and the eternal wailings of the lost soul. My hearers have come, listened, and gone away unconverted, with few exceptions. I am greatly discouraged." "Well, Brother John, how have you succeeded?" "Far better than I expected," said the meek John. "I have preached faithfully the law, and Christ, the end of the law for righteousness. I have dwelt much on the boundless love of Christ and the precious rewards he gives his children. I have a large, loving, harmonious church, into which I have received scores of happy servants of the Lord. We have very frequent additions." "Well," said the good teacher, "you are both fishermen. You, John, have gone out with your long, slender rod, silken line, and hook well baited, cast the hook with care, hardly making a ripple. The fish, attracted by the bait, have seized it, and you have gathered a great number. But you, Peter, went out as with a ten-foot pole, and cod-hook, and thrashed it into the water, and said, ' Bite, or be damned!' and you have scared the fish away."

Several years since, I read the following story in the *Christian Secretary*, of Hartford, Conn., which I shall try to repeat as well as memory will do it. In one of the countries of Europe, a portion of the standing army was paid off at the close of their time of service. The captain said to one of the soldiers, "Give me a ten-dollar gold piece, and I will give you advice worth more to you than the money." Having full confidence in his captain, he did it. The advice was: "I. When you travel, go straight ahead as far as possible. II. Mind your own business. III. Never do anything in anger." As they parted, the captain gave the soldier a loaf of bread, saying, "When you are perfectly happy, eat it." A fellow soldier left with him. They soon came to a steep hill. The soldier said, " Here is a level road. Let us take it, and avoid the hill." " No," said the other ; " my advice was, 'go straight ahead.' " "Well, I am going the level road, in the woods." He was robbed and murdered. The surviving soldier concluded to stop on his way home with a rich man, once a class-mate. At their supper, he was astonished to see the wife of his friend drink her tea out of the skull of a human being. Being very happy in their mutual meeting, they sat up to a late hour. He was very curious to know the cause of such a strange act, but remembering the advice, "Mind your own business," he asked no questions. Ere they retired, his friend said, "You may wish to know why my wife had such a strange teacup. One of her old lovers was a little too familiar with my wife to suit me, and I killed him, cut off his head, threw his body into a cavern on my farm, and I have made her drink her tea out of his skull. If you had been too familiar, I might have served you in like manner." In the morning he left for home, glad he had followed the advice of his captain. He reached his home in early evening. The curtains were down, yet he saw, through an opening, his wife in the rear part, sitting in the lap of a man, whom she was hugging and kissing. In anger, he raised his rifle to shoot them, but thinking of the advice, "Do nothing in anger," he sat down his rifle, walked to the rear door, and, on entering, to his inexpressible joy, he found his son in his mother's lap. He had just been admitted to Cardinal honors, which so pleased the mother, she could not so well give relief to herself as to hug and kiss her honored boy. He then felt "perfectly happy," and calling for a knife, he cut open the given loaf, and the ten-dollar gold piece fell on the floor.

A tragic event occurred to me when I was settled at Shelburne Falls, which I will describe as it occurred to me, as nearly as I can remember.

A man at the Falls, as I was going to Greenfield, wished me to take out one thousand dollars in money from the bank. I was delayed in getting it, so as to lose the public conveyance. Fearing that the stable-man might rob me, I concluded to walk home, as it was only nine miles. As I came to the base of the Shelburne hill, where a brook crosses the road, at about sunset, I saw three rough-looking men on horse-back, coming down through the woods, two abreast and the other in the rear. I saw him take a pistol from his pocket, examine it, and put it back. As the two passed me, the rear ruffian dismounted, drew out his pistol, saying, "Give me the thousand dollars you took at the bank." I replied coolly as I could, "I have no money for you. You are in bad business, and had better ride along." Cocking his pistol, and presenting it to my heart, he said, "Your money or your life." The other two roughs headed their horses towards us, ready to aid. One cried out, "Make quick work with him, if he does not hand over." I was standing on the culvert. The water that ran through it fell off down the rocks, covered with staddles and briers. I said, "If you are going to kill me unless I give up the money, I had better lose the money." The fashion then was wide-brim hats and tight pants. I had in my mind what to do, but I did not want to do it while a cocked pistol was pointed at my heart. So I was slow in getting out the money. "Hurry up," he said. I replied, "They make pants so that it is hard to get anything in or out of them," and went to unbuttoning my vest and waistbands, keeping my eyes on the pistol.

When, as I expected his arm would tire, he pointed the pistol down, I drew my fist from my pocket, and struck him in the throat with all my might. He dropped the pistol, and I sprang to catch it, when one of the men said to the other, "Hold my horse!" and he sprang for the pistol, about as near him as me. To avoid being shot, I leaped from the culvert or bridge, and went into the bushes and briers, sinking down, down, when my wife cried out, "Husband, what are you kicking so for?" "Why, to get away from these robbers." "What robbers?" "Here, at the foot of Shelburne hill." "You are not there; you are here in the nursery." "Merciful heaven!" I exclaimed. I trembled over the shock, which seemed perfectly real. I then told my wife the dream, when she burst into a laugh, saying, "These are your non-resistent principles carried out."

A REAL ROBBER STORY.

Soon after my settlement at Shelburne Falls, I visited, during a vacation, Boston and Providence, and raised over one thousand dollars to build us a church. I took my wife with me, and left her at her father's in Cambridgeport. I had agreed to spend a night on our return at a Mr. Piper's, eight miles from Ervings Grant. I arrived at Ervings Grant, ordered supper and horse fed, and about sundown left for Piper's. I had the bills, just as they were given, in a large pocket-book. I put some in a wallet, to pay as I went, but had to take out all the money. Two men in the bar-room saw that pile of bills, and left, and were harnessing a horse to a wagon as I passed the stable.

My course was down the Miller's river, for nearly three miles. It was then mostly woods, and not a house on the way. Before I entered the woods, I saw these two men in an open wagon coming, driving their horse upon the run. Fortunately I had a horse, owned by Deacon Alden, my brother, given for the occasion, that he said had trotted fifteen miles in an hour, and a new chaise and harness. Having heard a robbery was attempted on that road a few months previous, I was pretty sure what was the object. Having travelled the road, I knew down a mile or so was a little cleared spot, and that there they would try to head me. My wife knew nothing of their seeing the money, to whom I said, "Put your hand strong in the guard, as I mean to go through these woods quickly." As we neared this opening, they whipped their horse and yelled to him. I had a whip that I had not drawn from its socket on all my way till then, and touched my horse but lightly. She sprang furiously, and they failed. There was one more opening farther down, and the last one on my way. A most desperate effort was there made, and their carriage came up

to the side of mine. I snapped my whip, with a most emphatic phrase. She bounded like a deer out of their reach.
Only one more dangerous spot. It was where the road
left a bend in the river and went up a steep hill. There I
knew the power of the horses would be tested. I simply
snapped my whip with a cheer, and she never broke her
lightning trot until I heard the wagon rumbling no more.
I stopped my horse, and heard one of them say, " D — t ; it
is of no use. They have a race horse in their chaise."

All this time Mrs. Alden had not said a word. When
she found the chase was over, she said, "What did those
men mean to chase us so for?" I said, " They were in a
hurry, I suppose." "What made them stop at the bottom
of the hill?" "Because they had gone as far as they
wished." I heard them cramp their wagon and turn back.
"You can't make me believe you was not afraid of being
robbed." "If you are sure I cannot, then I will not try."
Soon we passed two houses lit up for the evening. She
exclaimed, "I never was so glad to see a house." She
never knew the whole story until we were safely
home.

This good Mr. Piper had a saw mill, and a large amount
of lumber. The mill was near his house, so if one burnt the
other would. We were awakened about daylight by the
roar of fire among the pines near his house. The wind was
driving the fire towards his buildings. It was then about
twenty rods distant. "What shall I do?" he said. "It is
all I am worth, and there is no insurance on either building." The fire would strike the mill first. "Set a counter
fire," I said instantly. "Set it a rod or so from the mill."
"That will surely burn it." I said, "If I set fire in three
places, will you agree to stop my fire from going to the
mill?" "Yes," he said; "we can do this." And we did.
Soon the fire we set met the other, and it was joyous to see
Vulcan fight Vulcan, throwing fire at each other. "My dear
brother," said Mr. Piper in tears, "you have saved me
over three thousand dollars."

More than fifty years ago, I learned a fact that perhaps has saved me several thousand dollars. A lawyer in Rochester, N. Y., had a watch stolen from him in a theatre. He advertised for it, " I will give fifty dollars for it, and no questions shall be asked. The watch is not worth half that, only as it was a present from my deceased father." A man called as he was alone in his office, saying, " Is that your watch?" "Yes." "Are you ready to redeem your pledge?" He paid the fifty dollars, and put the watch in his pocket. " I said, 'no questions should be asked,' yet I am very anxious to know how you took my watch." "Do you remember a man approached you in the theatre, saying, 'Let me snap that spider off your brow?'" "Yes." "It was then I took your watch." "Well, I am glad I have it safe in my pocket." "Good-day," said the thief, and passed out of sight. The attorney thought he would look at the watch, but lo! in showing him how he took it, he departed with the watch and fifty dollars.

In my agency for Foreign Missions, in Northern New England, and for the Bible Society, for Southern New England, I have travelled many thousand miles, and carried many thousand dollars, and have never lost a dollar, though several attempts were made. When an agent, I was about taking the cars at Hartford for Providence. It was an occasion that brought many on the platform for tickets. I noticed two men hurrying up others to get tickets, but got none themselves. Mistrusting their game, I thought I would wait till the crowd were served, and avoid them. On approaching the ticket-office, I felt a hunch under my arm, done to avert attention from my pocket. I turned very suddenly, and one of these men drew his hand from my pantaloons pocket. Nothing was in his hand. I went up to the ticket-office, and feeling for my pocket-book, I found it was gone, and seventy dollars in it. I could then in no way account for the mystery. I left a full description of the contents with the treasurer of the railroad, and my address. Very soon a letter came, saying, "Your pocket-book and contents were found. The man that clears the track, seeing a piece of coal, as he supposed, turned it over, which proved to be your wallet of black morocco, with the metalic clasp on the underside." I can think of no solution, except that he brought the purse, so that as I turned, being nearly balanced, I threw it against my overcoat, and it fell beside the rail.

I am desirous of presenting such anecdotes as give practical instruction, as well as amusement. I have ever admired the trait in President Lincoln, leading him to bear up under care and trouble, by relating some humorous story that kept up his own healthful cheerfulness, and aided others as well. Many anecdotes that I have, and expect to record, have added much to my happiness during a long life, and kept me a whole atmosphere above gloomy land and the slough of despondency. I truly hope they may harm no one, but aid them as they have aided me.

The letters inserted are numerous, but they are from friends greatly beloved, and we want to keep them choicely where we can ever find them.

CHAPTER XVII.

EARTH'S LAST SON.

BY REV. JOHN ALDEN, PROVIDENCE, R. I

[The venerable and beloved author of the following poem was formerly pastor of the Central Baptist church, Westfield, Mass., and for ten years agent of the American and Foreign Bible Society, and is favorably known to many of our readers. He informs us that the subject of the poem was assigned him while in Amherst college, so it was written more than fifty years ago. It is certainly a creditable production.]

GES on ages rolled! when lo, a scourge
Of direful pestilence swept to the verge
Of an eternity all living mould
Save one, of spirit fearless, dauntless, bold.
Earth wore a solemn stillness: not a breath,
Nor breeze, nor voice, nor sound was heard, for death
All living had destroyed, save this one man
On earth's sepulchral ball her scenes to scan.
Backward in gloom the wheels of time he rolled,
To break his revery and communion hold
With nations past, that lately peopled earth
Intent on scenes of life, of joy and mirth.
The shades of ages past rushed on his mind,
His spirit sank within him thus to find
All had gone on to judgment. He alone
Was left on earth to grieve, to weep and moan,
The double night of ages he'd beheld,
Passing from earth away, by truth dispelled.
Old Juggernaut, and heathen fane and shrine,
Fired on one pile, made morn millennium shine.
Far back that glorious era, yet a light
Refulgent shines, its annals still are bright.
But now funereal gloom broods o'er the world;
Earth, thou art desolate, to judgment hurled

Are all thy sons save me, alas ! he said;
Would I were mingled with the mighty dead.
Where now Columbia's glorious name ?
Proud rival Albion, too, equaled in fame ?
Both raised a world to life — themselves no more ;
Gone, gone to oblivion's peaceful shore.
Where Asia's thousand tribes, and Afric's hordes ?
Mute are they all. Alas ! the *earth* affords
Naught but a scene of mourning. Every dome
Is silent as the grave, and none a home.
What now are earthly honors ? What a name ?
The loftiest station and the brightest fame ?
All now promiscuous sleep the dreamless sleep,
And not a friend on earth survives to weep !

As fancy, oft by superstition led,
To roam the mansions of the sainted dead,
Has viewed by shadowy eve's unfaithful gloom
A weeping seraph on a martyr's tomb,
So a bright choir of angels from the skies
Looked down upon the scene, then turned their eyes
And back retired far in the realms of light,
Grieved here on earth to see the dismal sight.
Why stopped all nature for awhile to moan ?
Why wept the heavens, and uttered forth a groan ?
Why shrank appalled the sun and moon from sight,
And left the world in one chaotic night ?
Man, *man* had died, the mighty and the brave,
And none were left to lay them in the grave !
Roll, waves of ocean, roll ! no more a tomb
To trembling mariner, e'en now in gloom
Of horror shrouded, on thy restless bed
Ships wildly float, all freighted with the dead,
To shores where all is death ! Burst, fires that burn
In earth ! burst your eternal flames, an urn
Of fiery death; 'twould harmless deluge be ;
For none on earth to be destroyed but me.
Earth, thou art desolate — oh, horrid gloom,
Worse than the pall, the bier, the knell, the tomb.
Ah, what is man on nature's awful waste
Without a friend, deep of the cup to taste
With sorrow mingled ? Ah, me ! —ah, me !
Let down, ye heavens, an arm of charity,
And take me up where morn eternal shines,
And seraphs' burning lay all heaven refines.

Earth, thou art ripe for judgment — this be thy doom,
That God Almighty lay thee in the tomb.

Roll, judgment thunders ! shake the vaulted sky ;
Sound, Gabriel's trump ! sound from on high,
That earth shall be no more ! But, ah ! no sound ;
Silence instead reigns undisputed round.
Go, sun, proud light, when from thy station driven,
Thrown into chaos from thy seat in heaven,
Go, tell, as thou art falling, loud and clear,
A listening universe what thou sawest here.
Tell thou hast seen a lonely mortal stand,
Of earth sole tenant, whose uplifted hand
On heaven fixed, feared not a burning world,
Or falling universe to chaos hurled !
Tell that in me a spark will brightly shine
When cold thy face, and not a ray is thine.
Bright starry gems, that crown the ethereal blue,
Look down on me alone, yet I, when you
Are dark, will shine a seraph far above,
Where all is glory infinite, angelic love :
Awhile I mourn alone, yet soon shall be
An heir to angels' joys eternally.

— [From the *Christian Secretary*, S. D. Phelps, D. D., Editor.

I feel that I should leave undone a pleasant duty, should I fail to pay a slight tribute to my dear wife in these pages, and I hope none will consider it inappropriate. Delicate in structure, sensitive in temperament, reared among surroundings of culture and refinement, protected from all harsh things of the world in a Christian home, it would not seem strange had she failed to meet the requirements of the life of care and responsibility to which I introduced her immediately following our marriage. On the contrary, her natural capacities soon developed themselves, and she at once entered upon a career of usefulness, with dignity and uncommon adaptation. In our work at Shelburne Falls Academy, she was my right-hand helper, and many a soul was brought to the Saviour through her instrumentality. At North Adams, and all through our mutual labors, she has ever been an invaluable aid to those who were striving for a better life ; cheering the despondent, encouraging the despairing, speaking words of strength to the weak, and rejoicing with the joyful, always firm and unflinching in the right, and allowing no compromise with wrongdoings. She is still my most trusted and faithful helpmeet, and it is my hope and prayer that the gates may open for us both not far apart.

"When the spring of life was in its bloom, and hope gave zest to youth,
We at the sacred altar stood, and plighted vows of truth.
And since, though changeful years have passed, with joys and sorrows rife,
Yet never did I see a change in her, my faithful wife.

"Her gentle love my cares have soothed, her smiles each joy enhanced,
As fondly, through progressive years, together we've advanced;
Though calmly now the current flows, we've known misfortune's strife.
Yet ever did she cheer my woes, my faithful, loving wife.

"And ever since that joyous day I blessed her as my bride,
In joy or sorrow, calm or storm, I found her at my side;
And when the summons from above shall close the scene of life,
May I be called to rest with thee, my true and faithful wife."

AULD LANG SYNE.

DEATH OF HON. GEORGE C. ALDEN.

I gave a tribute in this book to this worthy nephew, and I regret to announce the following from the Greenfield *Gazette and Courier:*

"The funeral of George C. Alden, Esq., took place at the residence of his mother on Mechanic street, at three o'clock, Monday afternoon, Rev. A. M. Crane officiating. The Grand Army Post, Alethian Lodge of Odd Fellows and Mountain Lodge of Masons, with whom he always fraternized when here, each furnished two bearers. The body was brought from Fort Collins, Col. He was interred in Arms cemetery, in accordance with an often expressed wish, by the side of his father and only brother, one of the most beautiful country cemeteries in the State, where the near surrounding grand old hills and the murmuring of his favorite river makes everything so restful. He was born in Ashfield, Aug. 5th, 1829, being directly descended from the old Mayflower John Alden. At an early age he moved to this village, which was scarcely more than a hamlet, and his father dying when he was quite young, he began the serious part of life without property. But he was no laggard. He did what his hands found to do cheerfully and thoroughly, always dividing with his sisters, brother and mother. He was one of the pioneer workers in the cutlery. He fitted for college here, and earned the money for his tuition, board and clothes by working out of school hours. He was familiar with the haunts of the game on the hill-sides and the hiding places of the largest trout in the mountain brooks. He was full of life, with a remarkable memory, and always relished a joke, even at his own expense. He graduated at Colby University in Waterville, Me., studied law, and was admitted to the bar there, and soon after opened an office in Buffalo. He was soon recognized as a man of mark, and was quite successful. There he married the accomplished wife who survives him. He next removed to Annawan, Ill., where he built up a

large practice for that section, and became an extensive
land owner.

"Early in the war he made great sacrifices to enlist, and
was chosen quartermaster of his regiment. While foraging
for supplies for his almost famished regiment, which was at
the front, he was surprised and captured. For many long
months he was incarcerated in rebel prisons, and came very
near dying. During the bombardment of Charleston, he
was placed in the top of the post-office building, with other
prominent Unionists, for the purpose that they might prevent the shelling of the city, or be the first to be killed.
But they never tamed him. They were as afraid of his
tongue as they were of bullets, and, no doubt, felt a great
relief when he was exchanged. After the war, he returned
home and resumed his law practice, but very soon after received an appointment from President Grant, as special
agent of the Treasury Department, which he accepted, dis-
charging the difficult and many times dangerous duties of
the office with singular fidelity to the interests of the Government for a period of nearly eight years.

"He was shrewd and uncompromising in his defense of
a client, and untiring in his attacks upon an opponent, yet
he was always warm-hearted and generous. He lived for
many years in Galesburg, practising law, and dealing in real
estate and stocks. For the last few years he has resided in
Fort Collins, Col., being interested in several large ranches
near by, which were heavily stocked with horses and cattle.
When he died, he was at one of his ranches, about twenty
miles from Fort Collins. He was confined to the house
about a fortnight, and was not considered dangerously sick
but a few days. One year ago, he delivered an eloquent
memorial address at Fort Collins, and this year presided at
the exercises, and delivered a short stirring address. When
the body arrived at Fort Collins, the Grand Army boys
took it in charge and paid it all possible honors. In the far
West he leaves a widow and son. In this village, a mother
over ninety years old, and three sisters, besides many sor-

rowing friends wherever he has resided. When stricken down in the midst of his usefulness and many plans, he was just getting ready to develop a valuable mining interest in Boulder City, Col. He was always so cheery and friendly, none of his friends thought of his dying first. He will be greatly missed, and his near and dear relatives will have the heartfelt sympathy of all."

I clip a few lines from an article in the Fort Collins *Courier:*

"Died, July 17, 1888, at Box Elder Canon, Col., George C. Alden, a good man, a useful citizen, and much loved, has fallen on the highway of life, and many hearts are laden with sorrow. Judge Alden was summoned from earthly scenes when it was hardest to part with him. Physically, mentally and socially, there were few men his equal. None knew him but to admire him. Though having given up the practice of law as a profession, he frequently allowed his sympathies to enlist his active efforts in behalf of a friend, and in this way has appeared at the bar of our courts on several occasions. No man in Northern Colorado was held in higher esteem by all classes, and no man had more friends than Judge Alden. His was a generous, sympathetic nature, and a plea for deserving charity was never made to him in vain. He was ever ready to contribute liberally and freely to all worthy objects, and was recognized as a generous, public-spirited citizen. He leaves a large estate to be shared by his widow and only child, William C. Alden."

PART III.

——o——

CHAPTER XVIII.

THE PILGRIM FATHERS.

HE reign of England's Virgin Queen, Elizabeth, was characterized by many changes and reforms, among which that relating to the church was one of the most important. The reformation, under Henry VIII., and the ecclesiastical changes during the succeeding reigns of Edward and Mary, had proved very unsatisfactory. The corruptions and abuses existing in the church of Rome led many of the clergy and people to rebel against it ; and resulted, during Elizabeth's reign, in the year 1559, in an act of Parliament, abolishing Mass, adopting the thirty-nine articles as the religion of the State, and recognizing the queen as the head of the church. Thus the religion of England was changed in a single day from Roman Catholic to Protestant.

This change, however, did not prove satisfactory, there being many who objected to what they called the half-way policy of the new church ; and these people set about to introduce a form of worship more consistent with their own views.

In 1564, they were given the name of "Puritans," a term of derision, because they sought a purer form of worship, and insisted upon a purer life. They were mostly commoners, men of sterling character, and loyal to their queen. They believed in a State church, but sought to form that church after a higher pattern. This they were not allowed to do, and those who persisted in using forms differing from the established church were punished.

Thinking men among them were thus led to question the justice of the authority of the State in religious matters, and finally came to the conclusion that a body of men might band themselves together and form a church, which should be independent. The putting in practice of these doctrines caused them to be named Separatists, or Independents, afterward called, in New England, Congregationalists. They claimed the perfect independence of each congregation, answerable to no Bishop or council, acknowledging but one head of the church, God.

They were subjected to much persecution, and for this reason, about the year 1610, a congregation of these people sought a refuge from their persecutors in Holland, where they had heard every one was free to worship God according to the dictates of his own conscience. Their first place of residence was at Amsterdam, from whence they removed to Leyden,* a university town of considerable popularity. Here were educated many men of note. Their sojourn in Leyden covered a period of about ten or twelve years, during which they were blessed with the ministry of the Rev. John Robinson, a wise leader in civil as well as religious affairs. His name has been handed to us as the able and loving pastor, the wise counsellor and faithful friend, true to the interests of his flock on both sides of the Atlantic, and who, if he had been allowed, would have joined the exile band in the New World. He died in 1625. His family succeeded in reaching the Plymouth Colony, in 1630, and many of his name in New England trace back their ancestry to the beloved pastor of the church at Leyden.

The life of the Pilgrims in Holland was one of trial and hardship, not, however, without compensations ; for

* "The university of Leyden was established in 1575. It has been at times one of the most celebrated in Europe, and from its reputation the city was called the 'Athens of the West' and the 'North Star of Holland.' Arminiers, Grotius, Lepsius, Junius, Vossius, Descartes, Scaliger, Salmasius and Booerhave were among its distingushed professors and scholars." — [Morton's New England Memorial.

although they were compelled to follow vocations for which they were unprepared, and were subject to many privations and discouragements amid a strange people, they kept the bond of Christian fellowship unbroken, and took great comfort in the "freedom to worship God" after their heart's desire. From the few recorded details of their life there, we believe them to have exerted an influence for good in the community, and that they maintained their high character for integrity, industry and fidelity, we cannot doubt, if the small number who migrated to America was a sample of the majority who remained behind.

The customs and manners of the Dutch people, together with their irreverence for the Sabbath, with its baneful effects upon their youth; the fear that they would in time lose their identity as English men; the impossibility of educating their children as they themselves had been educated; and, more than all, the desire to be the means of spreading the religion of Christ, led them to look about for another home, where they would be freed from the contaminations and restrictions of the Old World.

At first, they thought of Guiana, which had been described in glowing colors by Raleigh, but afterward turned their attention to the new colonies, and decided to seek a settlement in Northern Virginia. For this purpose agents visited England, and after much delay, obtained a grant of land from the Plymouth Company.

Funds were raised to defray the expenses of emigration, and two vessels were hired, the "Mayflower" and the "Speedwell," to convey a pioneer company of these brave people across the sea.

Their last meeting in Holland, at the sea-port of Delft, has been pictured on canvas, and a copy hangs in Pilgrim Hall, at Plymouth.

The "beloved pastor" is represented as invoking the Divine blessing upon the little band. Sad, tearful faces cluster around, and the grief of parting, mingled with the hope of better things to come, is depicted in the countenances and attitudes of all.

The Pilgrims sailed from Delft Haven, July 22, 1620, for Southampton, Eng., where they remained two weeks, laying in such stores as were necessary for their voyage. They were here joined by several friends who desired to accompany them. At the end of this time they again set sail, but after a few days the Speedwell proved unsafe, and they were obliged twice to go back to port, and were finally compelled to abandon her, and transfer her passengers to the Mayflower, thus crowding the little craft to its utmost capacity.

On the 6th of September, 1620, they once more put to sea, this time bidding a final farewell to old England; and after a long, tiresome and boisterous voyage, reached the shores of Cape Cod. This was not the point intended as their destination, as their grant of land lay near the mouth of the Hudson. They, however, after making an unsuccessful attempt to pursue their voyage, came to anchor, November 11 (O. S.), in Provincetown harbor.

This is one of the best harbors on all the Atlantic coast, and it seems providential that they were guided to it. One may imagine the relief and sense of thankfulness that must have been theirs to look once more on the solid earth, after this dreary voyage of over four months. Four months' imprisonment in the close quarters of the little Mayflower was quite different from a trip across the Atlantic in these days. That the spirit of thanksgiving was uppermost among them, is evidenced by their first act after casting anchor, which was to "fall on their knees and bless the God of heaven, who had brought them over the vast and furious ocean, and delivered them from all the perils and miseries thereof." When we think of the prospects of these wayfarers at that time, we cannot but wonder at the courage and faith that sustained them. Winter coming on; no shelter on land, and soon to be none on the sea, as the captain of the Mayflower was impatient to return to

England ; short of provisions ; weakened in body by long confinement on ship-board ; an unknown country before them, perhaps infested by unknown foes. We who enjoy the benefits so dearly bought by them cannot admire enough the sublime fortitude, the unconquering courage, and the unquestioning faith which ennobled these grand heroes of the Mayflower, and made them the loved and honored " Founders of New England."

The next thing to be done was to fix upon a place of settlement, and with this object in view, a series of exploring parties were soon started, which finally resulted in the settlement at Plymouth, Dec. 20, 1620. During this search, the members of the company, with the exception of those on the expedition, remained on board the Mayflower ; and while thus detained in the harbor, four of the number died. To help fill the vacant places, two children had been born, one at sea, named Oceanus, in honor of his place of birth, and the other, Peregrine White, so named in token of the pilgrimage then in progress, and who is distinguished as the first white child born within the limits of New England.

The third, and last exploring party, consisted of fourteen men, including Carver, Bradford, Winslow and Standish. They set sail on December 6, intending to make a circuit of the bay. The first day they ranged along the shore, but found no place to satisfy them. Next morning occurred the first encounter with the Indians, but fortunately with no serious results. A severe storm of snow and rain, the following afternoon, drove them to harbor, and a landing was made at night on Clark's Island, so named from the mate of the Mayflower, who first stepped ashore. The next day proved warm and pleasant, and daylight showed to them their situation, which, by comparing with the map of Capt. John Smith, they found to be named thereon " Plymouth." This being Saturday, they remained on the island, putting their shallop and arms in order, and preparing to keep the Sabbath.

Sunday, we have every reason to believe, from the character of the voyagers, was kept as a day of rest and worship. An immense granite boulder on this island is to-day called " Pulpit Rock," from the supposition that the first service on shore was held here. Some one has inscribed upon it these words (recorded in Mourt's *Journal*) : " The Sabbath-day we rested." The Monday following was destined to become a day long to be remembered and honored by a grateful people, as the beginning of New England history ; for on this day the first landing was made on Plymouth Rock, a name now known to all the world as emblematic of the men who first stepped upon it, and the government which they established to withstand the shocks of all subsequent time securely "founded upon a rock."

The day's discoveries confirmed the impressions made before landing. They found a country provided with all necessary advantages. A good harbor, natural fortifications, plenty of clear water, wood of numerous kinds, and, best of all, much cleared land which had been occupied and cultivated by the Indians. A few years previous, a terrible scourge had visited this region, carrying off thousands of the native population, thus leaving for these exiles lands ready prepared for them.

In considering all these varied experiences, who can doubt the agency of a higher power in directing these Pilgrims to the landing place at Plymouth !

The return to the Mayflower, after a week's absence, proved a sorrowful meeting. The sad fate of Dorothy, the young wife of Bradford, who fell overboard during his absence and was drowned, and also the death of James Chilton, the day after, cast a gloom over the ship's company, and gave the returning explorers a sorrowful welcome. Many others were suffering from disease, and the condition of all was most deplorable, so that there was no time to spend in mourning for the dead. Their anxiety now was to prepare a place for the living as speedily as possible.

Accordingly, the next day saw the Mayflower on the way to her destination, coming to anchorage on Saturday, December 16, in Plymouth harbor, where they remained until Monday. Four days later, they decided upon a location, and commenced preparations for building.

For the ensuing three months the little colony endured great trials and privations. Sickness and death was a constant guest among them. Nearly one half of the number died during this time, while many more were prostrated by disease, there being at one time only seven well persons to provide and care for the sick. The scarcity of provisions, and the eating of food prepared with sea salt, together with severe cold and exposure, were instrumental in producing this devastating sickness.

The dividing into families and apportioning land, resulted in establishing nineteen families, each to build its own house, casting lots for choice of location. These house lots were very small, being only three rods long by one and one-half rods broad. The houses were placed on each side of the street now called Leyden street. They were built of hewn white oak logs, cemented together with mortar, and contained but one room. The roofs were thatched with dry swamp grass, after the style of many houses, even of the better class, in England, at that time.

A large building for storage was also erected, and as fast as possible goods and families were transferred from ship to shore, though fully eight months passed from the time they first embarked from Delft Haven before the last passengers were provided with houses on shore, and then scarcely more than one half the original number were left to occupy them.

A fort was also prepared ; and Captain Standish formed a military company, and placed five cannon upon Fort Hill, this precaution being taken to insure the safety of the village in case of a possible attack by the Indians.

The month of March seems to have brought in warm, pleasant weather, quite unlike the March of the present day in New England, for we read in Bradford's journal of the "singing of birds," and the first thunder-storm.

The visit of Samoset, chief of the Mohegans, about this time, was an event of great importance to the colony. His ability to speak English enabled him to furnish much desirable information relating to the country, its inhabitants and its resources.

He introduced to them Tisquantum, or Squanto, as he was commonly called, who became a most valuable friend and aid. He had been kidnapped by a Captain Hunt, and taken to England, but was afterward returned, only to find his tribe exterminated and himself alone.

From associating with white men, he had come to adopt, in a measure, their ways of living, and so gladly became a member of the little band at Plymouth, sharing their privations and dangers, and proving an invaluable help to them as a guide and interpreter. On this visit of Samoset with Squanto, he brought notice of the near approach of Massasoit, the great Sachem of the Wampanoags, accompanied by sixty warriors. This news created intense excitement, for the coming interview was fraught with interests vital to the safety of the colony.

When the Indian chief and his retinue appeared at the top of the hill, Squanto was sent to inquire his wishes, returning with the request from Massasoit, that a messenger be sent to confer with him.

Edward Winslow was the man appointed, and at once set out to meet the savage chief. He had not neglected to provide himself with gifts with which to insure his welcome. A pair of knives and a copper chain with jewels attached were presented to the chief, and to a brother of the chief he gave a knife, an earring, a pot of strong waters, some biscuit and some butter, the latter of which they ate and drank, much pleased.

Winslow then addressed them in substance, as follows : "That King James saluted the Indian ruler with peace and love, accepting him as a friend and ally, and that the Governor desired to see him, that he might confirm a peace with him, establish neighborly relations, and open a trade for mutual benefit."

Massasoit was much pleased with this speech as it was interpreted to him, and leaving Winslow with his brother as a hostage, and taking twenty warriors with bows and arrows, started for the village. During the absence of Winslow, the people had made such hasty preparations as were possible for meeting and entertaining their visitors, and as the great chief marched down the hill with his followers, he was met by Captain Standish and Mr. Allerton at the head of a company of musketeers, and escorted with military pomp to one of the houses which had been prepared to receive him. Governor Carver then advanced with a guard, attended by drum and trumpet, and, after formal greetings had been exchanged, they joined in partaking of food and drink.

A treaty was then drawn up and concluded between them, which was never broken by this child of nature, and was kept for many years after his death by his descendents.

The attitude of the Pilgrim colonists toward their Indian neighbors was characterized by the same adherence to Christian principles which distinguished them in all their dealings, and, according to their own records, their good faith was amply repaid in an unexpected fidelity and devotion. And yet we call them savages! These noblemen of nature, who were the friends and protectors of our early homes, and, until imposed upon by the white man, maintained a friendly relation towards them.

This treaty with Massasoit cannot be over-estimated in its subsequent results among the colonists, for we have to consider that they were in the midst of a native population of at least twenty-five thousand, notwithstanding the fact that nearly ninety-five per cent. of their number had been swept away by the great plague.

Let us, in imagination, go back to a bright day in April

this spring of 1621, and picture to ourselves, if possible, the scene before us.

A group of sad-eyed women gazing longingly at the white sails of the Mayflower spread for a long flight over "old ocean's gray and solitary waste;" and as they look through blinding tears, the little bark floats away in the distance, weighted with a freight of loving messages to dear ones on the other shore, and, as she disappears, one long sob breaks from their trembling lips as they bid farewell to the last link that binds them to their native land.

The little Mayflower never came back to Plymouth, but twice revisited the shores of Massachusetts Bay. In 1629, she landed a company of Leyden people at Salem, bound for Plymouth, and, in 1630, she was one of the fleet that brought John Winthrop and his company to Boston.

It was now time to commence planting the corn which had been procured from the Indians. Here again Squanto proved a great help to them, by instructing them in the mysteries of this corn planting, which was unknown to them. As there were no beasts of burden, the labor must be performed by men. Squanto taught them to drop three or four ale-wives into each hill with a handful of corn, and that the field must be guarded night and day, for two weeks, to prevent wolves from digging up the fish.

During this first planting, occurred what seemed the greatest calamity that had yet befallen them, in the death of Gov. Carver. While at work in the field, he was taken suddenly sick and died in a few days. William Bradford was appointed to succeed him, and the work went on. Twenty acres of corn and six acres of wheat, rye, barley and peas, together with vegetable gardens, attested to the industry of the few workers fit for active service.

The season of planting over, there came a time in mid-summer when the work of the colony was not pressing. With New England farmers of to-day, haying time presses close upon the time of seeding. But with the colonists no hay was needed, for there were as yet no horses or cattle to eat it, and if there had been, there was plenty of native grass, without the need of cultivation. For four years the children of the Mayflower ate their hasty pudding (a favorite old-time dish) without milk, and of course fresh beef and mutton were impossible dishes. The place of draught horses and cattle was supplied by bone and muscle of finer texture, backed by some of the best quality of brains that ever thought out the problems of society.

This resting time afforded an opportunity to make a long anticipated visit to the headquarters of Massasoit, on the shores of Narragansett Bay. Two men were detailed to undertake the journey, Edward Winslow and Stephen Hopkins, accompanied by Squanto, as guide and interpreter. As before, they provided themselves with such gifts as they considered would be most acceptable. A tunic, or coat of red cotton trimmed with lace, and a copper chain with medal attached, the latter to be used by the messengers of the chief as a token of good faith in going and coming between him and the English.

This expedition started in July, reaching the Namasket village (now Middleboro), fifteen miles distant, in the afternoon, where they were entertained by the villagers in royal style. The fare consisted of corn bread and shad-roe. The same night they lodged at Weir, where they found more of the same tribe engaged in fishing for bass, of which they made their supper.

In this vicinity lived thousands of the native population who died in the great plague, and whose bones lie scattered around, as there were not enough of the living left to bury the dead. Next morning, they follow the course of the river to a shallow place which they ford, and reach the lodge of Massasoit same day, where they are made welcome. He points out to them the home of the great Narragansett tribe across the bay, the strongest of all the confederations.

Here they remained over night, these two undaunted travellers, amid a company of savages, far from friends, and wholly at their mercy. This trip of Winslow and Hopkins shows of what stuff these men were made, and must have filled with anxiety the hearts of those left at home, awaiting their return. Next day, they turned their faces homeward, and arrived there in safety the second day after.

About this time, Hobomak, one of Massasoit's chief captains, came to live in the colony, probably in the family of Capt. Standish, to whom he attached himself, accompanying him on all his subsequent expeditions, and remaining a faithful friend to him and to the colonists through all the remainder of his life. His death occurred in 1642. He embraced the Christian religion, and died in hope of the Christian's heaven.

The remainder of the year 1621 was marked by several most interesting events. In July, the escapade of young John Billington, wherein he ran away and got lost in the woods, and wandered around for five days, suffering greatly from hunger, until he chanced to fall into the hands of a tribe of Indians, located near Buzzards Bay, twenty miles distant from Plymouth. His absence caused much uneasiness, and a company of men started out to find and bring him home. A report had reached them of his whereabouts, but not feeling sure of the sentiments of this tribe, they were somewhat in fear for his safety. On arriving at the place, they were received and entertained with great cordiality, and the boy was returned to them safe, and happy in the possession of a quantity of Indian ornaments. Thus the freak of the "scape-grace" of the colony, though causing considerable anxiety and inconvenience, ended most agreeably.

In August, a rumor was circulated that trouble was brewing between Massasoit and Corbitant.* Squanto and Hobomak were immediately dispatched to learn the truth regarding it.

* Corbitant was chief of the Pocassets, and for a while unfriendly to the English.

On reaching the village of Namasket, they were seized by Corbitant, and threatened with death. Hobomak escaped, and fled with all haste to Plymouth with the news that Massasoit and Squanto were both prisoners; whereupon Captain Standish

> " Took from the nail on the wall his sword with its scabbard of iron,
> Buckled the belt round his waist,"

and with ten picked men, started to the rescue. They marched all day in the rain, and at night lost their way in the woods, and wandered around for hours, but finally reached the village, and beseiged the house where they supposed Corbitant to be. The inmates attempted to run away, and were fired upon, and two or three were wounded. Corbitant, however, had fled. Massasoit was at liberty, and Squanto was found all right in one of the houses. Next day they all returned home, taking with them the wounded Indians, who were carefully treated by Dr. Fuller until well.

The prompt and determined action of the English in this instance so impressed the natives, that they were anxious to conciliate them; accordingly, soon after this, a treaty, or oath of allegiance, was drawn up and signed by at least seven of the principal sachems.

A trip to Massachusetts Bay in the month of September, for the purpose of advancing trade with the tribes located at different points thereon, and to promote a feeling of friendliness, as well as to become better acquainted with the country round about, proved successful in every partic- ular. They were everywhere made welcome, and found the Indians most anxious to trade.

The remainder of the summer was spent in getting in their harvests and preparing their dwellings for winter. Sickness and death had departed from among them, and health and hope had returned. Food in abundance could be had; plenty of game, such as deer, wild fowl, both land and sea; fish in great variety, with clams, oysters and quahaugs abounded in the waters ; and great quantities of wild fruit was found in the woods and fields ; luscious straw-berries of uncommon size ; wild plums, grapes and berries, probably kept the children busy gathering them.

The arrival of the " Fortune," in November, a small ves-sel of fifty-five tons, bringing thirty-five passengers, was a joyful event, bearing, as it probably did, several relatives and friends, besides innumerable messages from friends in Holland and England.

She remained two weeks, and when she set sail on the return voyage, went with a full cargo of beaver skins and clap-boards, estimated at about five hundred pounds value. A pretty good record considering the difficulties met and overcome.

So ended the first year of the settlement of New England.

> "O ye, who proudly boast
> In your free veins the blood of sires like these,
> Look to their lineaments. Dread least ye lose
> Their likeness in your sons. Should Mammon cling
> Too close around your heart, or wealth beget
> That bloated luxury which eats the core
> From manly virtue, or the tempting world
> Make faint the Christian purpose in your soul,
> Turn ye to Plymouth rock, and where they knelt,
> Kneel, and renew the vow they breathed to God."

CHAPTER XIX.

PASSENGERS IN THE MAYFLOWER, 1620.

HIS list is according to families. The time and place of death is given as far as known. The †
shows those who left wives, who came afterward.
The * shows those who died the first year.

NAMES.		DIED.
1. Mr. John Carver.*		Plymouth. April, 1621
2. His wife, Katherine.* (Robinson?)		Plymouth. 1621
3. Desire Minter.		England.
4. John Howland.	Employes.	Plymouth. 1673
5. Roger Wilder.*		Plymouth. 1621
6. Wm. Latham.		Bahama Islands of Starvation.
7. A Maid Servant.		
8. Jasper More.* (A child.)		Plymouth. December 6, 1620
9. Mr. William Bradford.		Plymouth. 1657
10. His wife, Dorothy May.*		Plymouth Harbor, Dec. 7, 1620
(Their son John came afterward.)		
11. Mr. Edward Winslow.		At Sea. 1655
12. His wife, Elizabeth Barker.*		Plymouth. March 24, 1621
13. Geo. Soule.	Employes.	Duxbury. 1680
14. Elias Story.*		Plymouth. 1621
15. Ellen More.* (A child.)		Plymouth. 1621
16. Mr. William Brewster.		Duxbury. 1644
17. His wife, Mary.		Plymouth. Before 1627
18. Love Brewster.		Duxbury. 1650
19. Wrestling Brewster.		——— Young.

345

	NAMES.		DIED.	
20.	Richard More.	Children.	Scituate.	1656
21.	——— More.*		Plymouth.	1621

(Richard More was afterward called Mann. The four More children were "put out" to the families with whom they came.)

22.	Mr. Isaac Allerton.	New Haven.	1659
23.	His wife Mary Norris.*	Plymouth.	February 25, 1621
24.	Bartholomew Allerton.	England.	
25.	Remember Allerton.	Salem.	After 1652
26.	Mary Allerton.	Plymouth.	1699
27.	John Hooke.* (Employee.)	Plymouth.	1621

(Mary Allerton married Thos. Cushman, who came in the Fortune. Remember Allerton married Moses Mavrick.)

28.	John Crackstone.*	Plymouth.	1621
29.	His son, John Crackstone.	Plymouth.	1628

30.	Capt. Myles Standish.	Duxbury.	1656
31.	His wife, Rose.*	Plymouth.	January 29, 1621

32.	Mr. Samuel Fuller.†	Plymouth.	1633

33.	Mr. Christopher Martin.*	Plymouth.	January 8, 1621
34.	His wife.*	Plymouth.	1621
35.	Solomon Power.*	Plymouth.	January 8, 1621
36.	John Langmore.*	Plymouth.	1621

(35, 36: Employes.)

37.	Mr. William Mullins.*	Plymouth.	February 21, 1621
38.	His wife.*	Plymouth.	1621
39.	Joseph Mullins.*	Plymouth.	1621
40.	Priscilla Mullins.	Duxbury.	After 1680
41.	Robert Carter.* (Employee.)	Plymouth.	1621

42.	Mr. William White.*	Plymouth.	February 21, 1621
43.	His wife, Susanna.	Marshfield.	1680
44.	Resolved White.	Salem.	After 1680
45.	William Holbeck.*	Plymouth.	1621
46.	Edward Thompson.*	Plymouth.	December 4, 1620

(45, 46: Employes.)

47.	Mr. Stephen Hopkins.	Plymouth.	1644
48.	His wife, Elizabeth.	Plymouth.	After 1640

NAMES.	DIED.	
49. Giles Hopkins.	Yarmouth.	1690
50. Constance Hopkins.	Eastham.	1677
51. Damaris Hopkins.	Plymouth.	After 1666
52. Oceanus Hopkins.	Plymouth.	1621
53. Edward Doty.	Yarmouth.	1655
54. Edward Lester.	Virginia.	

(53, 54 bracketed: Employes.)

(Constance Hopkins married Nicholas Snow, of Eastham. Damaris Hopkins married Jacob Cook.)

55. Mr. Richard Warren.†	Plymouth.	1628

(His wife and five daughters came in 1623. Two sons probably in 1621.)

56. Francis Cooke.†	Plymouth.	1663
57. John Cooke.	Dartmouth.	After 1694
58. John Billington.	Executed at Plymouth.	1630
59. His wife, Eleanor.		
60. John Billington, Jr.	Plymouth.	Before 1630
61. Francis Billington.	Yarmouth.	After 1650
62. Edward Tilly.*	Plymouth.	1621
63. His wife, Ann.*	Plymouth.	1621
64. Henry Sampson.	Duxbury.	1684
65. Humility Cooper.	England.	
66. John Tilly.*	Plymouth.	1621
67. His wife, Bridget Vander Velde.*	Plymouth.	1621
68. Elizabeth Tilly.	Plymouth.	1687
69. Thomas Rogers.*	Plymouth.	1621
70. Joseph Rogers.	Eastham.	1678
71. Thomas Tinker.*	Plymouth.	1621
72. His wife.*	Plymouth.	1621
73. His son.*	Plymouth.	1621
74. John Rigdale.*	Plymouth.	1621
75. His wife, Alice.*	Plymouth.	1621
76. James Chilton.*	Plymouth.	December 6, 1620
77. His wife.*	Plymouth.	1621
78. Mary Chilton.	Boston.	1679

(Mary Chilton married Gov. Winslow's brother John.)

79. Edward Fuller.*	Plymouth.	1621
80. His wife.*	Plymouth.	1621
81. Samuel Fuller.	Barnstable.	1683

	NAMES.		DIED.	
82.	John Turner.*	Plymouth.		1621
83.	His son.*	Plymouth.		1621
84.	His son.*	Plymouth.		1621
85.	Francis Eaton.	Plymouth.		1636
86.	His wife, Sarah.*	Plymouth.		
87.	Infant son, Samuel	Middleboro.		1684
88.	Degory Priest.*†	Plymouth.	January 1,	1621
89.	Moses Fletcher.*	Plymouth.		1621
90.	John Goodman.*	Plymouth.		1621
91.	Thos. Williams.*	Plymouth.		1621
92.	Edmund Margesen.*	Plymouth.		1621
93.	Richard Bitteridge.*	Plymouth.	December 21,	1620
94.	John Allerton.*	Plymouth.		1621
95.	Richard Clark.*	Plymouth.		1621
96.	Thos. English.*	Plymouth.		1621
97.	Peter Brown.	Plymouth.		1633
98.	Gilbert Winslow (Bro. to Edward.)	England.		
99.	Richard Gardner.	England.		
100.	John Alden.	Duxbury.		1687
101.	William Trevor. } Seamen.	Returned to England.		
102.	—— Ely. }	Returned to England.		

SIGNERS OF THE COMPACT IN THE CABIN OF THE MAY-
FLOWER.

"In the name of God, Amen. We, whose names are
underwritten, the legal subjects of our dread Sovereign
Lord, King James, by the grace of God, of Great Britain,
France and Ireland, king, defender of the faith, etc., having undertaken for the glory of God, and advancement of
the Christian faith, and honor of our king and country, a
voyage to plant the first colony in the northern parts of
Virginia, do, by these presents, solemnly and mutually, in
the presence of God and of one another, covenant and com-
bine ourselves together into a civil body politic, for our
better ordering and preservation, and furtherance of the
ends aforesaid, and by virtue hereof, do enact, constitute
and frame such just and equal laws and ordinances, acts,

constitutions and offices from time to time as shall be thought most meet and convenient for the general good of the colony, unto which we promise all due subjection and obedience.

"In witness whereof, we have hereunto subscribed our names at Cape Cod, the 11th day of November, in the year of the reign of our Sovereign Lord, King James of England, France and Ireland, the eighteenth, and of Scotland the fifty-fourth, Anno Domini, 1620."

The compact was subscribed in the following order :

	No. in Families.		No. in Families.
MR. JOHN CARVER.†	8	*JOHN TURNER.	3
MR. WILLIAM BRADFORD.†	2	FRANCIS EATON.†	3
MR. EDWARD WINSLOW.†	5	*JAMES CHILTON.†	3
MR. WILLIAM BREWSTER.†	6	*JOHN CRACKSTONE.	2
MR. ISAAC ALLERTON.†	6	JOHN BILLINGTON.†	4
CAPT. MYLES STANDISH.†	2	*MOSES FLETCHER.	1
JOHN ALDEN.	1	*JOHN GOODMAN.	1
MR. SAMUEL FULLER.	2	*DEGORY PRIEST.	1
*MR. CHRISTOPHER MARTIN.†	4	*THOMAS WILLIAMS.	1
*MR. WILLIAM MULLENS.†	5	GILBERT WINSLOW.	1
*MR. WILLIAM WHITE.†	5	*EDWARD MARGESON.	1
MR. RICHARD WARREN.	1	PETER BROWN.	1
JOHN HOWLAND (of Carver's family).		*RICHARD BITTERIDGE.	1
		GEORGE SOULE (of Edward Winslow's family).	1
MR. STEPHEN HOPKINS.†	8		
*EDWARD TILLEY.†	4	*RICHARD CLARKE.	1
*JOHN TILLEY.†	3	RICHARD GARDINER.	1
FRANCIS COOK.	2	*JOHN ALLERTON.	1
*THOMAS ROGERS.	2	*THOMAS ENGLISH.	1
*THOMAS TINKER.†	3	EDWARD DOTEY } (of Stephen	
*JOHN RIGDALE.†	2	EDWARD LEISTER } Hopkin's family).	1
*EDWARD FULLER.†	3		

* Denotes that the names thus marked died the first winter, the victims of the cold climate and lack of provisions.

† Denotes that these had families.

CHAPTER XX.

PILGRIM LEADERS.

JOHN CARVER.

OVERNOR JOHN, the first signer of the compact, was one of the oldest members of the colony, being between fifty and sixty years of age. He was deacon of the church in Holland, and was the principal agent in collecting funds with which to emigrate to America. He was much relied upon as a leader by Rev. Mr. Robinson, the pastor of the Leyden church, and had a reputation above reproach for ability and Christian character, which he fully sustained to the day of his death. His family consisted of eight persons, his wife and several servants. He died about five months after landing. He was in the field helping to plant corn, when he was taken suddenly sick and died in a few days. All through the trying winter months he had been untiring in his labors, administering to the sick and dying, and providing for the bereaved, besides attending to the arduous duties incident to the establishment of a new settlement. The lack of strong arms rendered it necessary for him to undertake tasks too severe for his age and strength ; and so, bowed down with toil and care, he at last laid aside his implements of labor, and sought rest in the sheltering arms of death. They laid him in the burying-ground on Cole's Hill with as much ceremony as was possible, firing a volley of musketry over his grave. His wife, Katherine, died soon after, and was laid beside him.

350

WILLIAM BRADFORD.

The second Pilgrim governor was born in Austerfield, Eng., a small village about two miles from the post town, Scrooby. He was a farmer's boy. At an early age he was left an orphan, and was brought up by his grandparents and uncles. He was a thoughtful, studious boy, and acquired an excellent education, being able to speak six different languages. At the church in Babworth, six miles distant, he was a constant attendant until their minister, Clifton, was silenced by the authorities. He then joined others in forming the Scrooby Church, and with them went to Holland, when but eighteen years of age. He there married Dorothy May, Nov. 30, 1613., who sailed with him for America, but failed to reach the land of promise, being drowned in Cape Cod Harbor, in the absence of her husband on an exploring expedition.

He married, for his second wife, Alice, the widow of Edward Southworth, who came from England in the Anne, accompanied by her two boys. He was chosen governor after Carver, and continued in office, with the exception of three years for Governor Winslow, and two for Governor Prince, until the year of his death, serving thirty-one years as governor. He has since been called the "Washington" of the infant colony. His numerous writings have proved of great value to chroniclers and historians. These writings were lost, and for years no trace of them could be found. But finally, the Bishop of Oxford discovered his "History of Plymouth Plantation" hid in the Fulham Library, in England.

His eldest son, John, died childless. Two other sons and one daughter were born to him by his second wife. The oldest, Major William Bradford, inherited his father's books and his father's love of them. At his death, in 1704, he requested to be laid beside him. The blue slate slab, which marked his resting place, was the guide to the grave of Governor William when, years after, his descendants

erected a monument to his memory on Burial Hill.   He
died at Plymouth in 1657, aged sixty-nine years.

BRADFORD'S TOMBSTONE.

EDWARD WINSLOW.

The third governor of Plymouth Colony was a native of
Droitwich, England.   He belonged to the gentry and was
an educated and accomplished man; the second in the
colony in point of wealth.

He married, in Holland, Elizabeth Barker (the bride of
Weirs painting "The Embarkation," a copy of which hangs
in Pilgrim Hall), who came with him in the Mayflower,
together with two servants and a little girl.   His wife died
the first spring, and he married Susanna, widow of William
White and mother of Peregrine, the first white child born
in New England.   Winslow was the ambassador to the
Indians for the colonists, and also to the king.   His famous
visit to Massasoit, the Great Sachem of the Wampanoags,
has become a part of history.   He settled in Marshfield, on
a farm since owned by Daniel Webster.   He was several
times governor of Plymouth Colony, and always faithful to

her interests. In 1654, he was appointed by Cromwell, commissioner of a military expedition against the Spanish powers in the West Indies. While on this trip, he died and was buried at sea, May 8, 1655.

In Pilgrim Hall, may be seen a portrait of Gov. Edward Winslow, the only authentic original portrait of the Mayflower company. It was painted in England, five years before his death, and portrays a gentleman of culture and refinement, of firm moral character and high intellectual attainment. In Pilgrim Hall are many other relics said to have been brought by him in the Mayflower.

Two other paintings, one of his son, Gov. Josiah Winslow, and a grandson, Gen. John Winslow, can also be seen there.

WILLIAM BREWSTER.

Elder Brewster was born at Scrooby, in Nottinghampshire, Eng., in 1560, at the Manor Hall of the village. Scrooby Manor was an ancient possession and occasional residence of the Archbishop of York. He was educated at Cambridge College, and afterward became confidential friend of William Davison, Queen Elizabeth's secretary, with whom he visited Holland, and became familiar with the lives and surroundings of royalty. He was possessed of an ample fortune, which enabled him to live in a style befitting his station. He was for several years post-master at Scrooby, a position of great responsibility in those days.

Espousing the Puritan faith, he was subjected to persecution, and at one time imprisoned. The Separatist church at Scrooby was begun in 1606, with William Brewster, Elder, Richard Clifton and John Robinson, pastor and teacher. Here, at the large Manor Hall, Brewster entertained the despised adherents of this sect, and from here he fled to Holland, in 1607, where he became a teacher of the English language, and a publisher of religious books, especially those advancing the doctrines of the "Independent church, or the "Separatists," as they were called. He was a faithful co-worker with Pastor Robinson in the Leyden church.

In the year 1619, the British government requested that Brewster be handed over to them for trial on the charge of selling his prohibited books in England. An attempt was made to arrest him, but he escaped and went to London, where he remained until the sailing of the Mayflower.

He was the oldest member of the Pilgrim Band, being about sixty at that time. For twenty-four years he served the infant colony in the capacity of elder; for several years acting as preacher as well. He was their spiritual staff through all the sad and trying scenes of the early days of the colony, by his cheerful spirit and firm faith in God, upholding the weak, comforting the sick and dying, and probably speaking a word of exhortation or promise at the grave of the dead. No funeral sermon was preached by the Puritans, or prayer offered. The burial was silent. Prayer at funerals in New England was first offered in 1685.

Elder Brewster early settled in Duxbury, near Captain Standish. His wife died here in 1627. He died in 1644, and his son Love succeeded to the homestead. The first apple tree in New England is said to have been planted by Elder Brewster, on this farm.

MILES STANDISH.

The celebrated captain of the Pilgrims was born in Lancashire, Eng. He entered the service of Queen Elizabeth as a soldier, and took part in the war of the Netherlands. At the end of that war, he settled in Leyden, among the English refugees, and, with them, embarked in 1620 for America. He was of small stature, but had a large heart, great powers of endurance, indomitable courage, and superior military ability, and was always held in great respect and confidence by the Plymouth colony. It is unnecessary to recite here his numerous adventures with the Indians, his military exploits, or his deeds of valor. These are recorded in history, and familiar to every boy and girl of New England. It is well known that he was the first commissioned military officer in the New World, and had command of the first military company here. It has often been said that his judgment and executive ability, joined to his military powers, many times saved the colony from destruction. In 1631, he removed to Duxbury, and settled on Captain's Hill, a high eminence overlooking the harbor and the country for miles around. On the summit of this hill were built the watch fires that signalled danger to the early settlers. Here Captain Standish could look across the bay to Plymouth, and, if aught there was amiss, a warning shot would crash out from the old fort on Burial hill, which had been built under his directions.

OLD FORT, BURIAL HILL.

The town was named in honor of the English home of the Standish family, "Duxbury Hall." He died in 1656, about seventy-two years of age. His eldest son and heir, Alexander Standish, inherited the estate, and built the house now standing in 1666. He married Sarah, the daughter of John Alden and Priscilla. A beautiful monument on Captain's Hill perpetuates the name of the Pilgrim soldier. It will be, when finished, one hundred feet high, the tallest structure in the United States erected to the memory of any individual excepting Washington. The interior will be fitted up as a museum. The monument will be surmounted by a stone statue of the Captain of Plymouth, in full uniform, fourteen feet in height. From this high eminence the old soldier will again look out, after two hundred and fifty years, across the bay and over the country around, but a vastly different scene will greet his eyes. The little hamlet at Plymouth has been changed to a beautiful village. The shores around Duxbury are sprinkled with cottages, where, in the hot season, the city dweller comes to get a breath of salt air. The woods have been swept away; the humble homes of Brewster, Howland, Eaton and Soule, are gone. Only the Alden house remains; the only one on which his living eyes rested. The grave of his " beautiful Rose" may be revealed to him, but hidden from us as well as those of his other kindred.

John and Priscilla lie within range of his eye, but we know not where. Could the statue take on life for a while, like Pygmalion's, we might learn many things which will probably ever remain a mystery, at least in this life.

STEPHEN HOPKINS.

One of the honored names in the history of our country is that of Hopkins. Stephen Hopkins, the Pilgrim, joined the Mayflower company on its final departure from England. He had previously attempted a voyage to this country with Governor Gates, of Virginia, but was wrecked on the passage. He was a venturesome and an enterprising man, and entered into all the interests of the Plymouth colony with zeal and ability. He was governor's assistant for several years, and was associated with Standish in military affairs and companion of Winslow on his expeditions among the Indians. His family consisted of wife, four children and two servants. These two servants are made conspicuous by the fact that they were the first in New England to fight a duel.

A great-grandson of the Pilgrim, Stephen Hopkins, of Scituate, R. I., was governor of the Rhode Island colony for nine years, and one of the first on the list of incorporators of Rhode Island College, now Brown University, and was a signer of the Declaration of Independence. His brother, Esek Hopkins, was, in 1775, commander-in-chief of the American Naval Forces, the first commodore of the United States Navy.

CHAPTER XXI.

JOHN ALDEN.

HE Hon. John Alden was born in England in 1599; in what part is not known. There were but few of the name of whom we have any record.

A Mr. Alden, a scholar of St. John's College, is mentioned as one who suffered from the tyrannical Bartholomew act. There is also mention of one "John Alden of the Middle Temple" as having a coat of arms assigned him in 1607. He belonged in Hertfordshire, and from the similarity in names, we conclude that the Pilgrim John Alden was a member of the same family; distinctive family names at that time and for a century later, at least, being the rule. That he was hired at Southampton as a cooper, we know from Bradford's Journal.

Whether he belonged to the Independent church in England, is not told, but the probabilities are that he was one of them in sentiment and by association, and that if not a member on joining the expedition, he became one soon after. The character of the man as evidenced by his subsequent life, leads to this inference. A stern adherent of justice and morality, unswerving from the straight line of duty as he understood it; yet, at the same time, modest and unassuming in all his ways, showing tenderness and mercy to the weak and forgiveness to the penitent, were qualities which combined to make him an example for all future generations.

He embarked with the Mayflower band, probably with the intention of joining his interests with theirs in the new world, and no doubt this desire was strengthened and confirmed by his association with Priscilla Mullins during the long voyage, and afterward, while waiting in the harbor for the older members of the company to decide upon a place of habitation. He was probably one of the seven well persons left at one time to care for the sick and dying in that terrible first winter. The death of the father, mother and brother of Priscilla, leaving her an orphan in a strange land, together with the beauty and grace that distinguished her, led the young John from sympathizing with her sorrows, to cherish a tenderer feeling in his heart for the fair young girl thus left alone in the world.

One other sincere love seems to have taken root in the heart of John Alden at this time, which was destined to exert a great influence upon his after life, and to become known in every New England home for all time. This was the affection of the youth for the middle-aged Captain Standish, which commenced in the Mayflower and ended only at death.

The popular legend connecting these three has been beautifully preserved by Longfellow in his poem, " The Courtship of Miles Standish." Whether all that is related ever really occurred, is doubtful, but there is no doubt that some of the principal points mentioned were true. That Captain Standish did turn his eyes toward "the loveliest maiden in Plymouth," after the death of his " beautiful Rose of love," is probably a fact. But for the most part we must consider the poem a creation of the poet's brain, rather than a truthful narration of the courtship and marriage of the real John and Priscilla.

Tradition represents him as the most comely youth of the Mayflower company, and possessed of a superior education and agreeable manners. Upon the division into families he was assigned to the household of Standish, in consideration of the friendship existing between them.

His marriage occurred in the spring of 1621. Where he commenced housekeeping is not recorded. The first houses of the Pilgrims in Plymouth were built of hewn logs, intersticed with mortar, with roofs thatched, and surrounding the tiny cottage was an acre of land allotted to each family for cultivation ; and history says that women and children worked cheerfully in these gardens. So we may imagine the Puritan wife, Priscilla, with her little ones by her side, employed in not only the household avocations, including spinning and weaving, but also assisting the husband and father in work outside, in the ground allotted them. Several of their children were born in Plymouth, probably the first five of the eleven born to them, according to the account in Bradford's Journal. The names of only eight are recorded; probably the other three died very young.

In 1624, the "Charity" brought the first cattle to the Plymouth colony. They were owned in common, until 1627, when they had increased sufficiently, with the addition of others imported, to allow of a distribution in lots, which was accomplished by dividing the people into twelve groups of thirteen each, and allotting to each group the use of one animal for ten years, at the end of which time it was to be returned with one half its increase. John Alden and his family now numbering four, himself and wife and two children, John and Elizabeth, were joined to the company of John Howland, to which was given one of the four heifers which came in the "Jacob," Raghorn. John Alden's family of four, John Howland's family of four, and five single men were thus made sharers in "Raghorn."

About this time, a number of the settlers desiring to extend their domain, determined on a settlement at Mattakeeset, the Indian name of the territory now included in Duxbury, Marshfield, Pembroke, Hanson, and the Bridgewaters ; and of the twenty signers of the compact who survived the first winter, six removed their families to Duxbury: Elder Brewster, Captain Standish, John Alden, John Howland, Francis Eaton, and Peter Brown. They were, however, obliged to return to the village of Plymouth in the winter season for several years. This removal was rendered necessary from the need of combining all their forces in case of an attack from the Indians, and to better facilitate their meeting in council and at religious gatherings. The early settlers on this side included quite a number of the principal men who could not be spared for a permanent absence.

In the colony records we find the following entry :

Ano. 1632, Aprill 2.
{ The names of those which promise to remove their families to live in the town in the winter time, that they may the better repair to the worship of God.

JOHN ALDEN,
CAPT. STANDISH,
JONATHAN BREWSTER,
THOMAS PRINCE.

In the first part of 1628, another division of land was made, by which each purchaser was given twenty acres additional for cultivation. There being one hundred and fifty-six purchasers, there were allotted at this time, three thousand, one hundred and twenty acres of land.

The poor land was used at first in common for pasturage, and was called "commons" or "salt meadows." Later on these lands were leased to parties for a small consideration.

It is probable that Alden's allotment in this land division was part of the farm owned and occupied by him, and still retained by his descendants. A marble slab on the site of the first house, gives the date 1627, which is the supposed time of the erection of the summer cottage. This does not exactly agree with the date of the division, but it is not unlikely that the place was selected and buildings put up the summer before, as the land allotment occurred in January.

In 1633, John Alden was appointed assistant to the governor, which office he held for nearly the whole remainder of his life, serving in this capacity, Edward Winslow, Bradford, Prince, Josiah Winslow and Thomas Hinckly, all of whom, excepting the last named, he survived.

From 1666 to his death, he held the rank of first assistant, and was frequently called the Deputy Governor, and acted many times as Governor in the absence of that official.

During ten years succeeding 1640, he served the town of Duxbury, as deputy to the colonial council. Public office was not as desirable then as at the present time, if we may judge from the fact that a law was passed in 1627, fining any person who should refuse to serve in that capacity. Salaries were small, and the duties and responsibilities, great. The compensation for magistrates was a mere trifle. In 1665, the court gave each old magistrate twenty pounds per year and the expenses of their table; but the newly elected had the expenses of their table only. In 1667, all were paid fifty pounds each per year.

Mr. Alden having devoted the greater part of his time for a number of years to the public business, to the detriment of his own private affairs, the court passed the following order as appears in the colony records:

"In regard that Mr. Alden is low in his estate and occasioned to spend time at the courts on the country's occasions, and so hath done this many years, the court have allowed him a small gratuity, the sum of ten pounds, to be paid by the treasurer."

In the year 1625, a settlement was begun at Salem. In 1630, John Winthrop arrived in Boston harbor, and laid the foundation of the great city, which points with pride to the noble statue now standing in Scollay Square, inscribed, "John Winthrop, the first governor of Massachusetts." John Cotton and John Wilson came to preach the gospel to the people; and next year came John Elliot, the apostle to the Indians, a man reared and fitted to fulfil an uncommon mission, which he faithfully accomplished. A little

later appeared Anne Hutchinson with her band of followers.

The breaking out of the Pequod War, in 1637, called for
prompt action on the part of the colonists. The cause of
education was advanced by the erection of buildings for
Harvard College in 1639. Four years later, the Narragansett Indians became uneasy and threatening, and the people were counselled to prepare for war. At this time there
were in the town of Duxbury eighty men who were able to
bear arms, of whom three were Aldens, the Hon. John,
John, Jr., and Joseph. This year, the confederation of the
four colonies was effected to insure their co-operation in
the event of war with the Narragansetts. The first regular
military company was formed. A council of war was appointed, including Winslow, Prince, Standish, Alden, and
others, with power vested in either three to act in time of
need.

Trouble between Holland and England broke out, and
was communicated to the colonies, resulting in orders being
given to raise money, troops, arms and ammunition.
Alarm signals were decided upon, and one man in every
three was ordered to carry arms to meeting on the Lord's
Day, a failure of so doing was punishable by a fine.

In all the important measures connected with the events
enumerated, the name of John Alden is conspicuous. As
adviser and executor he ever had an active share in the
management of the affairs of the colony and of the town.
From Justin Winslow's history of Duxbury, I quote the following tribute to his character .

"Holding offices of the highest trust, no important measure was proposed, or any responsible agency ordered in
which he had not a part. He was one of the council of
war, many times an arbitrator, a surveyor of lands for the
government as well as for individuals, and on several important occasions was authorized to act as agent or attorney
for the colony. He was possessed of a sound judgment and
of talents, which, though not brilliant, were by no means

ordinary. Writers who mention him bear ample testimony to his industry, integrity and exemplary piety, and he has been represented as a worthy and useful man of great humility, and eminent for sanctity of life, decided, ardent, resolute and persevering, indifferent to danger, a bold and hardy man, stern, austere and unyielding, and of incorruptible integrity. He was always a firm supporter of the clergy and the church, and everything of an innovating nature received his determined opposition."

This last mentioned trait was shown in his attitude towards the Quakers during the years 1657-8. Candor compels me to condemn the action of the Plymouth court in banishing this sect and refusing entertainment to individuals belonging to it. Any man harboring a Quaker was subject to a whipping or a fine. This seems a very strange proceeding on the part of the Mayflower Pilgrims, themselves exiles on account of religious persecution.

About the year 1653, the house now standing was erected by his son Jonathan. It is situated on the south side of Blue Fish river, near Eagle Tree Pond, so called from its being a favorite resort for eagles. The farm of Mr. Alden originally comprised over one hundred and sixty-nine acres, and was then, as now, one of the best in town. The present house, an aged and venerable structure, fit companion to its neighbor on Captain's Hill, is an object worthy of veneration. For more than two centuries it has been owned and occupied by the same family, and could it speak could relate much that would be of interest to their descendants.

As can be seen from the following picture it is a two-story square house, in its day one of the finest residences in the town. The front faces the south, as was the custom in those days. The windows were originally the small diamond shaped panes, but these have been replaced by a more modern style.

On the ground floor are four rooms. The front or "Great Room," as our forefathers called the best room in the house, is a large, square room, 25x25, with fireplace to match ; over the fireplace the walls are panelled. The ceilings are eight feet high and crossed by heavy, wooden beams.

A cupboard in one corner still stands where it was placed two hundred years ago.

The upper part of the house contains four sleeping rooms including the great guest chamber, wherein is found the usual high four-post bed-stead, with canopy top, and other

OLD ALDEN HOUSE.

old style furniture. Above all is the old attic room, fit receptacle for dust and cobweb-covered wheels for spinning wool and flax, cards for combing and reels for winding, besides a multitude of other accumulations. The table seen in the picture is of English oak, and came in the May-flower probably, as the property of the mother of Priscilla. Upon it are some account books of the first John Alden, and beside it sits the present occupant, John Alden of the eighth generation.

This is the oldest dwelling existing in New England,

with three exceptions. The "Old Fort," at Medford, which dates back to 1634, the "Old Fairbanks House," in Dedham, built in 1636, and the "Old Stone House," at Guilford, Conn., in 1640.

Here the "Pilgrim John" passed the remainder of a life well filled with labors both civil and religious. His name appears as one of the original company who suggested and traced a route for the now famous prospective Cape Cod Ship Canal; and we find him mentioned many times, even up to the last year of his life, in connection with State and church affairs.

He was a man whose unselfish interest for the general good resulted in pecuniary loss to himself, so that at his death he left but a small estate. In his early days he was possessed of considerable property, but later divided most of it among his children, giving the farm in Duxbury to Jonathan, a piece of land in Bridgwater to Joseph, and land in Middleboro, Taunton, Monument and Duxbury to his other children. He died in Duxbury, Sept. 12, 1686, aged eighty-seven. As he was the youngest signer of the immortal compact, so he lived to the greatest age, and out-lived every member of the Mayflower company, with one exception, Mary Allerton, who died in 1699, aged ninety.

It has been affirmed that Priscilla was living at the time of his death, but I can find her name mentioned no where as among the living later than 1680. In that year, Gov. Josiah Winslow died, and at his funeral was present "the venerable John Alden with Priscilla upon his arm."

His life embraced a wonderful history; eventful, thrilling, grand, sublime; his death completed an example worthy of imitation. A grand life; a triumphant death. An "elegy," written by John Cotton, voices the sentiments of his compeers, a portion of which I transcribe.

> "God give me grace to mourn most heartily
> For death of this dear servant of the Lord,

Whose life God did to us so long afford.
God lent his life to greater length of days,
In which he lived to his Redeemer's praise.
He came one of the first into this land,
And here was kept by God's most gracious hand
Years sixty-seven, which time he did behold,
To poor New England mercies manifold,
All God's great works, to this his Israel,
From first implanting that to them befell;
His walk was holy, humble and sincere,
His heart was filled with Jehovah's fear;
He honored God with much integrity:
God therefore did him truly magnify.

The heart of saints entirely did him love,
His uprightness so highly did approve,
That whilst to choose they had their liberty,
Within the limits of this colony,
Their civil leader him they ever chose.
His faithfulness made hearts wish him to close.
With all the Governors he did assist;
His name recorded is within the list
Of Plymouth's pillars, to his dying day.
His name is precious to eternal ay.
He set his love on God and knew his name;
God therefore gives him everlasting fame.
So good and heavenly was his conversation,
God gave long life, and showed him his salvation,
Seeing the death of what he saw the birth
His work now finished was upon the earth,
His gracious Lord from Heaven now calls him home
And saith, my servant, now to Heaven come;
Now shalt thou live in bliss eternally.
On dying bed his ills were very great;
Yet verily his heart on God was set.
He bore his griefs with faith and patience,
And did maintain his lively confidence,
Saying to some, the work which Christ begun
He would preserve to its perfection.
His mouth was full of blessings, till his death
To ministers and christians all; his breath
Was very sweet by many a precious word,
He uttered from the spirit of his Lord.
He lived in Christ, in Jesus now he sleeps,
And his blest soul the Lord in safety keeps."

There are very few relics in existence known to have belonged to him. His Bible is in Pilgrim Hall, Plymouth. It is in old English print, and is inscribed thus : " Imprinted at London by Robert Barker, printer to the King's most excellent majesty, *Anno Dom.*, 1620, *Cum Priuiligo.*" His autograph can be seen there affixed to a deed dated 1661, and two other instruments there bear his signature. A snuff-box, which came from Holland, is in possession of a relative of Rev. Timothy Alden (author of " Alden's Epitaphs "). These with the few preserved in the old house at Duxbury, comprise all existing relics known to the writer.

Among the descendants of John Alden have been many noted military and professional men. Two Presidents of the United States trace their ancestry to him. In looking over the " Alden Memorial," compiled by Dr. Ebenezer Alden, I find mention of thirty-four soldiers, seventeen clergymen, thirteen physicians, eleven mariners and eight lawyers. Doubtless there are many more at this time following a professional life.

In literature there has been good work done by many of the Alden name ; beside these there are many of their posterity now bearing other names who occupy high stations in almost every department of life.

The race has ever been famed for learning, ability, integrity, decision of character, and have been blessed with an unusal number of days. During the first six generations, we find one hundred persons who lived to the age of seventy and upwards ; fifty-four who reached eighty ; thirteen who attained to ninety, and two who completed a full century of life.

A few words relating to some of the individuals belonging to the Alden family may be of interest to my reader. It is hard to select from the many deserving notice, and as the number increases with each succeeding year, I have chosen a few representative characters from the earlier generations.

CHILDREN OF THE PILGRIM JOHN ALDEN.

CAPTAIN JOHN

Was born in Plymouth, in 1622. Removed to Duxbury when very young. He was admitted a freeman in 1648. Removed to Boston in 1649, and lived in Alden lane, now Alden street. He was at one time the tallest man in Boston. He was twice married. By his first wife he had one child. He was married in 1660, to Elizabeth Everill, widow of Abial Everill, by Governor Endicott. Captain Alden was a mariner, and had command at different times, of several of the Massachusetts armed vessels. He accompanied Col. Benj. Church on his expeditions to the East against the Indians, and in 1696, commanded the Brigantine "Endeavor." He was of great service on these expeditions on account of his knowledge of the coast, and skill as a mariner. His manners were characteristic of his calling, and his language at times somewhat blunt, but he was held in great esteem by his associates for his bravery, sound judgment and unexceptional moral character. He was an original member of the Old South Church, in Boston, at its organization in May, 1669.

In the wall of the new church edifice on Boylston street, a descendant of the Alden family has placed an ancient slate slab, originally erected to his memory in King's chapel burying-ground. It bears this inscription: "Here lyeth the body of John Alden, senior, aged seventy-five years. Deceased, March, 1701." It can be seen in a side wall of the central archway, facing Copley Square.

During the witchcraft delusion in 1692, he was present at a court in Salem, where several persons were being tried for this offense, whereupon a girl pointed her finger at him and cried out that he was the one who had bewitched her. He was seized by the authorities, tried and committed to prison, where he remained fifteen days, when he escaped by some friendly aid, and made his way to Duxbury, arriving there late at night. On being questioned he said "he had come from the devil and the devil was after him."

It seems that many in the church at that time believed him guilty, which so exasperated him that he absented himself from them for a long time. His death occurred Mar. 14, 1702, at the age of eighty. His will was dated Feb. 17, 1702. His estate amounted to £2,059, 11s. 7d., and included one wooden and one brick house. There were also debts due the estate of £1,259. He was the father of thirteen children.

JOSEPH

Inherited land in Bridgewater and Middleboro. He settled in Bridgewater. Married Mary Simmons, daughter of Moses Simmons, of Duxbury, who came in the "Fortune," in 1621. Five children are attributed to him.

ELIZABETH

Married William Pabodie, son of John Pabodie. He was a man of influence in the town, and possessed of considerable property. Was town clerk for eighteen years. Was deputy to the General Court several times, and acted as attorney for the town and for individuals.

About 1684, they removed to Little Compton, R. I., then a part of Plymouth colony.

Their residence while in Duxbury was east of Eagle Nest creek, and near Brewster and Standish. They had thirteen children, all of whom were born in Duxbury, and ten married in that town.

They had only two sons, one of whom, John, died from an accident in 1669, aged twenty-four. While riding on horseback under a tree, his head came in contact with a bough, and fractured his skull.

Of the daughters who married in Duxbury, Elizabeth married John Rogers, Mary married Edward Southworth,

Mercy married John Simmons, Martha married Samuel Seabury, Sarah married John Coe, Ruth married Benjamin Bartlett, Jr., Rebecca married William Southworth, and Priscilla married Rev. Ichabod Wiswall; the latter a pastor of the Duxbury Church at the time of her grandfather John's death. It is likely that all these marriages were executed by John Alden, as he was a magistrate.

Elizabeth Pabodie died at Little Compton, May 31, 1717. A granite monument to her memory stands in the old burying-ground there. It is inscribed: "Here lyeth the body of Elizabeth Pabodie, who dyed May ye 31st, 1717, and in the ninety-fourth year of her age."

The following is from the *Boston News Letter* of June 17, 1717:

"Little Compton, 31 May. This morning died here Mrs. Elizabeth Paybody, late wife of Mr. William Paybody, in the ninety-third year of her age. She was a daughter of John Alden, Esq., and Priscilla, his wife, daughter of Mr. William Mullins. This John Alden and Priscilla Mullins were married in Plymouth, New England, where their daughter, Elizabeth, was born. She was exemplarily virtuous and pious, and her memory is blessed. She has left a numerous posterity. Her granddaughter Bradford is a grandmother. Elizabeth Alden is said to have been the first white woman born in New England.

DAVID

Was a resident of Duxbury. A prominent member of the church and town. Served as assistant to the governor, was Town Treasurer and Selectman. Also deputy to the court. He inherited land in Middleboro, and was appraised 20 May, 1719. He married Mercy or Mary, daughter of Constant Southworth, who was a son of Governor Bradford's second wife, Alice. They had two sons and two daughters. He died in 1719.

CAPTAIN JONATHAN

Was born about 1627. Made freeman in 1657. He was the youngest son of the Pilgrim, and resembled him in many ways, and seems to have been a favorite with him. He inherited the homestead where he spent his whole life, and which inheritance he handed down in a direct line to the present occupant, John Alden, of the eighth generation, who has a son John, also living in the old house, and a daughter, Priscilla. Captain Jonathan was administrator of his father's estate, and made a final settlement with the heirs, June 13, 1688. He lived a bachelor until he was about forty-five years of age, when he married Abagail Hallet, of Barnstable. He was selectman of his town for several years, and engaged in military duties from 1658 to his death. He was first appointed ensign in the Duxbury company, then promoted to lieutenant, and afterward captain. He died February, 1697, and was buried under arms. An address was delivered at his grave by Rev. Mr. Wiswall, which was contrary to the usual custom, and occasioned much comment. Funeral services were not general until after 1700. From "Alden's Epitaphs" I copy a portion of the address of Mr. Wiswall:

"Neighbors and friends, we are assembled this day in a posture of mourning, to solemnize the funeral of the present deceased, to pay our last tribute of respect to a person well known among us. I need not enlarge upon his character, but in brief, am bold to say this much. He stepped over his youth without the usual stains of vanity. In his riper years he approved himself a good commonwealth's man; and, which is the crown of all, a sincere Christian, one whose heart was in the house of God, even when his body was barred hence by the restraints of many difficulties, which confined him at home.

"He could say, in truth, 'Lord, I have loved the habitation of thy house.'

"As to his quality in our militia, he was a leader, and, I

dare say, rather loved than feared of his company. Fellow
soldiers, you are come to lay your leader in the dust, to
lodge him in his quiet and solemn repose. You are no
more to follow him in the field. No sound of rallying drum
nor shrillest trumpet will awaken him, till the general mus-
ter, when the Son of God will cause that trumpet to be
blown, whose echoes shall shake the foundations of the
heavens and the earth, and raise the dead.

"Fellow soldiers, you have followed him into the field,
appeared in your arms, stood your ground, marched, coun-
ter-marched, made ready, advanced, fired, and retreated;
and all at his command. You have been conformable to
his military commands and postures, and it is to your
credit. But, let me tell you, this day he has acted one posture before your eyes, and you are all at a stand! No man
stirs a foot after him! But the day is hastening wherein
you must all conform to his present posture. I mean, be
laid in the dust."

SARAH

Married Alexander Standish, oldest son and heir of Capt.
Miles Standish. He was admitted freeman in 1648.
Served the town as deputy, and was town clerk for several
years. It was during this service that his father's house
was burned, and as is supposed the town records burned
with it as they were lost about this time. He owned land
near the Alden estate, but lived at the Standish farm, two
miles distant. The house now standing on Captain's Hill,
was built by him in 1666. It is a small, gambrel-roofed
building, shingled on two sides, and is in a good state of
preservation. Here the son of Miles Standish and the
daughter of John Alden and Priscilla lived many years.
He died in 1702. The date of his wife Sarah's death is
not recorded. By her he had seven children. He married
a second wife, who died in 1723.

RUTH

Married John Bass of Braintree, and from this union descended John Adams and John Quincy Adams, presidents of the United States. She died in 1674.

MARY

Married Thomas Delano of Duxbury, son of Philip Delano, (or De La Noy) who came in the "Fortune," in 1621. He was an influential man in the town. By her they had one son, Thomas, Jr. She died young.

Ye Old Time Aldens

Combined Ages 455

Rev. Timothy Alden
Age 92

Maj. Judah Alden
Age 94

Rev. John Alden
Age 103

Col. Briggs Alden
Age 74

Dr. Ebenezer Alden
Age 92

CHAPTER XXII.

DESCENDANTS OF THE ALDEN FAMILY.

COL. BRIGGS ALDEN,

SON of Col. John and Hannah Briggs Alden, was born at the old homestead, Duxbury, June 8, 1723, where he lived and died. His wife was Mercy Wadsworth (who belonged to the family of Wadsworth ancestors of the Poet Longfellow, on the maternal side). He was father of nine children. He died at the age of seventy-four. His son Samuel was mortally wounded in an expedition to the Penobscot river against the British, in 1778, under command of Gen. Lovell. The second officer in command was Gen. Peleg Wadsworth, who built a beautiful mansion in Portland, Me., afterward occupied by his son-in-law, Stephen Longfellow, father of the poet.

Briggs Alden was youngest son of Col. John. He early developed the military tastes inherited from his father and grandfathers, and became an officer in the local military company. In 1762, he was major, and in 1776, elevated to the office of colonel.

The passage of the Stamp Act, in 1765, called forth an indignant protest from the colonists. Major Briggs Alden was at that time a representative to the General Court, and went thither with instructions from his towns-people to oppose the passage of such act —"with all the eloquence and address you are master of; and that you use your utmost endeavors to vindicate our precious rights and privileges — these privileges for which our forefathers bled;

for which those heroic spirits bid adieu to the tyrannical names of the Stuarts, traversed the vast Atlantic, and sat down in these then deserts of America ; and which, sir, we their descendants, esteem dearer to us than life."

In 1773, the growing feeling of dissatisfaction toward the mother country, led to much correspondence between the colonies. From a letter written by a committee of the town of Duxbury to the Boston authorities, I quote a few sentences as an illustration of the spirit that animated their leaders.

"We inherit the very spot of soil cultivated by some of the first comers of New England, and though we pretend not that we inherit their virtues in perfection ; yet hope we possess, at least, some remains of that Christian and heroic virtue and manly sense of liberty, in the exercise of which, they in the very face of danger, emigrated from their native land to this then howling wilderness, to escape the iron yoke of oppression, and to transmit to posterity that fair, that amiable inheritance — liberty, civil and sacred. We glory in a legal, loyal subjection to our sovereign ; but when we see the right to dispose of our property claimed and actually exercised by a legislature thousands of leagues off, in which we have no voice, and many things of a like nature take place — shall it then be deemed disloyalty to complain ? By no means ; we esteem it a virtue, and a duty which people of every rank owe to themselves and posterity, to use their utmost exertions to oppose tyranny in all its forms, and to extricate themselves from every dangerous and oppressive innovation."

It is said that not a single Tory was known to live in the town of Duxbury, and when troops were called for to resist the requirements of the English Government, the descendants of the Pilgrim John Alden were among the first to volunteer.

All through the war, Col. Alden was an active and valuable worker for his country, resisting her wrongs, and earnestly laboring to sustain her liberties. For years he was a magistrate, a member of the General Court, selectman of the town, and an active and consistent member of the church. A portrait in Pilgrim Hall, from which the picture in this book is taken, is said to be a striking likeness of the original. He was a man of large stature and commanding bearing. The flowing silver hair and white cravat gives him an air of dignity almost ministerial, but the small piercing eyes, Roman nose, and firm set mouth, betoken the soldier. He died Oct. 4, 1796, and his son, Judah, succeeded him in the paternal home.

MAJOR JUDAH ALDEN

Was but twenty-six years of age at the breaking out of the Revolutionary War, and, following in his father's footsteps, joined Col. Bailey's regiment as captain. He had for three years previous, conducted the drill of the military company of his town. In 1773 the first minute company was formed, of which he was clerk and ensign.

He was a brave, skilful and prudent officer, and soon rose to the rank of major. In 1776, he was stationed with his regiment in Roxbury, and at one time accompanied Col. Leonard to the headquarters of the English, with a flag of truce. He inquired of their colonel why they did not come out to Roxbury and make the troops a visit. 'Ah,'' replied he, "we shall have to think of that some time first." He was an intimate friend of General Washington, and with him at one time in New York. A letter written by Washington I transcribe here:

HEADQUARTERS, 23 Nov., 1780.

SIR, — I impart to you in confidence that I intend to execute an enterprise against Staten Island to-morrow night, for which reason I am desirous of cutting off all intercourse with the enemy on the east side of the river. You will therefore to-morrow, at retreat beating, set a guard upon any boats which may be at the Slot or Niack, and not suffer any to go out on any pretense whatever till next morning. Towards evening you will send a small party down to the Closter landing, and if they find any boats there, you will give orders to have them scuttled in such a manner that they cannot be immediately used; but to prevent a possibility of it, the parties may remain there till towards daylight (but not to make fires or discover themselves), and then return to your post. I depend upon the punctual observation of this order, and that you will keep the motive a secret.

Acknowledge the receipt of this, that I may be sure you have got it.

> "I am, sir, your most obedient servant,
>
> GEORGE WASHINGTON."

"CAPT. ALDEN."

This letter is directed to "Captain Alden, or Commanding Officer, Dobbs' Ferry."

A house built by him is still standing in Duxbury, about two miles from the old homestead. His wife was Welthea Wadsworth. They had ten children, the youngest of whom, Samuel, graduated at Harvard College at the age of nineteen, and from Dartmouth Medical College four years later.

Major Alden lived almost a century. Born in 1750, he was, at an early age, familiar with all the troubles terminating in the War of the Revolution. He was fifteen years of age when the odious Stamp Act was thrust upon the people, and he was present the following year at the jubilee on Captain's Hill, celebrating its repeal. The "Boston Tea Party" and the "Ride of Paul Revere" were fireside topics in his father's house. His ear caught the echo of the "shot heard round the world," and his noble spirit shared in the enthusiasm and patriotism that greeted the "Declaration of Independence." He saw the thirteen colonies emancipated from the English rule, and the framing of that grand "Constitution" that has made the United States the greatest nation on earth. Would that he might have tarried yet a little to behold the final act in the great drama of Freedom, which culminated in the Emancipation Proclamation, Jan. 1, 1863.

He died Mar. 12, 1845, aged ninety-four, in the full possession of his intellectual powers. His great physical strength and excellent health remained to him until within a few years of his death. His oldest son, John, inherited the original homestead in Duxbury, and was great-grand-father to the present occupant, John Alden of the eighth generation. Two hundred and thirty-five years ago, Priscilla Mullens Alden lived here, when this old house was new. To-day, a little child of this John, two years of age, is called Priscilla Mullens, the first namesake to occupy the home of her great ancestress.

The old gray walls again resound
　　To sweet-toned childish laughter,
And gentle voices speak the name
　　Still dear, two centuries after;
　　　　The old time name Priscilla.

Two summer's roses tint the cheeks
　　And kiss the lips to redness,
Two summer's blue is in the eyes,
　　And gold gleams in the tresses
　　　　Of little maid Priscilla.

The "fairest maiden Plymouth knew,"
Comes here again to greet us,
Arch, loving, tender, grave and true ;
Her ancient grand-dames loveliness
Renewed in child Priscilla.

COL. ICHABOD ALDEN,

Son of Capt. Samuel Alden, of Duxbury. From Justin Winsor's History of Duxbury, I glean the following regarding him :

He was appointed lieutenant to Col. Theophilus Cotton, and was part of a detachment ordered to throw up entrenchments on Dorchester Heights, in 1776. Was soon after promoted to the rank of colonel, and after the capture of Burgoyne, was stationed at Cherry Valley, sixty miles west from Albany. A fort had been constructed here for the protection of the frontier, and Colonel Alden was made its commander. On the evening of Nov. 11, 1778, he was surprised by the enemy, numbering seven hundred Royalists and Indians, led by Brant, a celebrated Mohawk chief. A large portion of his officers and men were killed. He, with his lieutenant, Stacia, were lodged at the house of Mr. Robert Wells. The house was attacked and the inmates massacred. Colonel Alden escaped, but was pursued by an Indian who demanded his surrender. Upon his refusal, the Indian threw a tomahawk, killing him instantly.

"As an officer, Colonel Alden was brave and persevering ; as a gentleman, he was accomplished and agreeable ; and in all his relations of life, he formed around him lasting and steadfast friends, and in his intercourse with others was honorable and just, and his untimely death could not but be lamented by all who knew him."

JOHN ALDEN, THE CENTENARIAN,

Son of John and Hannah Alden, was born in Bridgewater, Mass., in 1747, and died at Middleboro, March, 1821, in the one hundred and third year of his age. The Christian Watchman of April 14, 1821, gives the following:

"In Middleboro, died the venerable John Alden, in the one hundred and third year of his age. His great grandfather, whose name he bore, was one of the first settlers of New England, and his grandmother was daughter of Peregrine White. He was married young, and his first wife, by whom he had five children, died at the age of twenty-seven. By his second and last wife he had fourteen children.

When his century sermon was preached he is understood to have said that he had read through his Bible in course as many times as he was years old. He retained his bodily strength and mental energy to a remarkable degree. When more than one hundred years old, he would converse with great propriety upon religion, and occasionally repeat whole chapters and quote numerous passages from the sacred Scriptures. He was the oldest man in the old colony and probably the oldest in the commonwealth. He had been a professor of religion and connected with a church upwards of seventy-eight years, and was probably the oldest church member in the United States."

In 1835, there were living of his descendants one hundred and seventy-three persons. He had nineteen children, sixty-two grandchildren and one hundred and thirty-four great grand-children.

An oil painting of him, said to be a correct likeness, hangs in Pilgrim Hall.

DR. ENOCH ALDEN,

A native of Ashfield, Mass., and uncle of the writer, was a man of uncommon ability, and made himself famous by performing a difficult surgical operation.

A man's leg had become so diseased by a fever sore as to necessitate the removal of the bone. Dr. Alden extracted about six inches, and inserted in its place the corresponding bone of an animal. The experiment was a success. He settled in Rome, N. Y., and was often called hundreds of miles in his practice. He was of a genial, social nature, and possessed of marked literary tastes. His library contained the whole of Ree's Encyclopædias, about one hundred and fifty volumes. The writer well remembers the impression this collection made upon him the first time he saw them together on the shelves of Amherst College library. He lived to old age, respected by all.

REV. TIMOTHY ALDEN,

Of Yarmouth, Mass., was born in Bridgwater, Nov. 24, 1736. He was a graduate of Harvard College, and afterward pastor of the Congregational church in Yarmouth, where he remained nearly fifty-nine years. He was much loved by his people, a man of exemplary piety, great humility and cheerful disposition. He married Sarah, daughter of Rev. Habijiah Weld, of Attleboro, whom he outlived. He died at the age of ninety two.

DR. EBENEZER ALDEN

Was born in Stafford, Conn., July 4, 1755, was educated at Plainfield Academy, and pursued a course of medical studies under the teaching of Dr. Elioha Perkins. He was invited and accepted the position of physician in Braintree (now Randolph), Mass, in 1781, where he remained in the practice of his profession until his death, twenty-five years later. He was a successful practioner and also an able medical teacher, having under his instruction at various times, many young men, some of whom became eminent in their profession. He was highly respected by his townspeople, and beloved by his patients and friends. He died at the age of fifty-one, "just when he was rising into special prominence as a man and a physician."

DR. EBENEZER ALDEN, 2D.

The second Dr. Ebenezer Alden was the eldest of the three children of Ebenezer and Sarah Bass Alden He was a descendant on both sides of the Pilgrim John Alden,

Sarah Bass being descended from the union of Ruth Alden and John Bass. He was born in Randolph, Mar. 17, 1788, the year of the adoption of the Constitution of the United States. He was eighteen years of age at his father's death which occurred during his collegiate course at Harvard, from which he graduated in 1808. He then went to Dartmouth, and pursued a course of medical studies, and received the degree of M. B. in 1811; afterward he attended medical lectures in Philadelphia, and received the degree of M. D. from the University of Pennsylvania, in 1812. He then settled as a physician in his native town. He married in 1818, Anne, daughter of Capt. Edmund Kimball, of Newburyport. In his chosen profession he was widely known and very successful, and not only in this, but in many other walks of life he was a man of influence, greatly esteemed for his superior judgment, high intellectual attainments and benevolent dispositon.

He was a member and an active worker in many different societies, religious and educational. For thirty-three years a trustee of Amherst College, and for twenty-five years director of the American Education Society. He became a member of the N. E. Historic Genealogical Society in the year of its organization, in 1846, and afterward contributed $500 towards the Librarian fund.

Dr. Alden was also a ready writer. His publications embrace quite a number of works on medical topics, several memoirs, and the " Memorial of the Alden Family," published in 1867. The last named has been of great interest and benefit to all descendants of the name.

Beside all these accomplishments, he was a leading singer in his town, and much interested, especially in church music. At the National Peace Jubilee at Boston, in 1869, and at the International Jubilee, three years later, he was one of the chorus singers. At this time he was eighty-four years old.

For several years before his death he was totally blind, and was cared for by his daughter, Sarah Bass Alden, at the old homestead. He died January 26, 1881, in his ninety-third year.

Two sons and the daughter above named survive him.

Rev. Ebenezer Alden, pastor since 1850, of the First Congregational Church in Marshfield, Mass. In his parish lived Daniel Webster, and in 1852, he was called to conduct the funeral services of the great statesman.

The second son is Rev. Edmund Kimball Alden, D. D., who was ordained to the Congregational ministry in 1850, and after serving for some twenty-six years as pastor at Yarmouth, Me., Lenox, Mass., and in Phillips Church, South Boston, is now one of the secretaries of the American Board.—[From Increase Tarbox Memorial of Ebenezer Alden. M. D.

CHAPTER XXIII.

REV. TIMOTHY ALDEN, A. M., PRESIDENT OF ALLEGHANY COLLEGE.

HE subject of this sketch was a son of Rev. Timothy Alden, of Yarmouth, Mass. He was the oldest of six children; was born in Yarmouth in 1771, and died at Pittsburg, Pa., in 1839, aged sixty-eight years; a useful life cut off too soon. At eight years of age he went to live with his uncle, Lieutenant Joshua Alden of Bridgewater, remaining seven years. He then decided to fit for college, and commenced a preparatory course under his father's teaching, which was finished at Philip's Academy, Andover, Mass. He entered Harvard College in 1790, where he distinguished himself by his excellent scholarship, especially in the ancient languages. At his graduation, in 1794, he delivered an oration in Syriac. In 1799, he entered upon the pastorate of the South Presbyterian Church in Portsmouth, N. H. The following year he opened there a school for young ladies. He resigned his charge as pastor in 1805, and devoted his time until 1808 to the interests of the school. He was afterward principal of a young ladies' academy in Boston, a young ladies academy in Newark, N. J., and a similar school in New York city. While a resident of Boston, he was appointed librarian of the Massachusetts Historical Society, and prepared a catalogue of its books, which was printed in 1811. He removed in 1815 to Meadville, Pa., and immediately entered upon an undertaking to establish a college in that place. A public meeting was called June 20, 1815, Major Roger Alden pre-

siding. At this meeting was laid the foundation of Alle-
ghany College by the appointment of Rev. Timothy Alden,
president and professor of Oriental languages and of eccle
siastical history. Mr. Alden then undertook to raise the
necessary funds to carry on the enterprise. Among those
who honored him by their contributions, were John Adams,
Ex-President of the United States, Hon. James Winthrop,
of Cambridge, Mass., Major Roger Alden, and many other
noted men of that time. At the laying of the corner-stone
of the college building, Mr. Alden took a prominent part as
a master mason. His son, Timothy Fox Alden, delivered

TIMOTHY ALDEN.

a Hebrew oration, and another son, Robert W., one in
Latin.

While residing in Meadville, he became interested in the
condition of the Indian tribes located in Western New
York and Pennsylvania, the Seneca's and the Mansee's, and
was appointed in 1787 by the Boston Society for "the Prop-
agating the gospel among the Indians," as missionary in
that region. A volume published by him, in 1827, gives
very entertaining details of his work in the mission field,
and contains much of interest regarding the manners and
customs of the Indians of these tribes. His anecdotes of
the Indian chiefs " Cornplanter," "Red Jacket" and "Black

Snake," and of Mary Jamieson, the white woman of the Genesee Valley, are extremely interesting. He closed his missionary labors in 1820. In 1831, resigned his connection with the college to open a boarding school in Cincinnati. In 1833 removed to East Liberty, near Pittsburgh, Pa., and took charge of an academy. Failing health obliged him to again resign his office of teacher. He retired to the residence of his daughter, Martha, wife of Patrick Farrelly, M. C., where he died in 1839. His last sermon, preached in Sharpsburg, Pa., was from this text : "The end of all things is at hand."

He was a man of rich intellectual endowment, enthusiastic in every educational and religious work, yet easily discouraged and somewhat visionary. He was founder of no less than seven schools of learning, was honorary member of the Massachusetts and the New York Historical Societies, and member of the American Antiquarian Society. His literary work was considerable. The most important of his publications being a collection of American epitaphs, issued in five volumes. Copies of this work are rare. A relative of his, Mrs. Gormley, of Sewickley, Pa., has recently donated a set to the Massachusetts Genealogical Society. Through the courtesy of this society, I have been enabled to secure the following extracts. In his preface he says :

" My original design was merely to gratify an inclination for acquiring knowledge of important chronological, biographical, and historical facts, nowhere to be found except on the mouldering mansions of the venerable dead, and on the face of monuments or corner-stones, and other parts of public buildings equally a prey to the touch of time, and on such materials, and under such circumstances as to render them difficult of access. At length, having amassed many documents, and having enjoyed much satisfaction in contemplating these interesting memorials, it occurred to me that my collection, if issued from the press, would be acceptable to my fellow citizens, and, at the same time, give publicity to a multitude of facts which ought not to be buried in oblivion, and preserve in a form more durable than marble or brass, a tribute of gratitude and respect to the memory of many, of whom the world was most worthy."

EXTRACTS FROM DR. TIMOTHY ALDEN'S COLLECTION OF AMERICAN EPITAPHS PUBLISHED IN 1814.

YARMOUTH, MASS.

Sacred to the memory of Mrs. Sarah Alden, consort of the Rev. Timothy Alden, who departed this life 28 October, 1796, in the 59 year of her age.

> Ye friends that weep around my grave,
> Compose your minds to rest,
> Prepare with me, for sudden death,
> And live forever blest.

Mrs. Alden was a daughter of Rev. Habijah Weld, of Attleboro. She died suddenly while her husband was on a long journey, and when three of the six children were at too great distance from home to receive the heavy tidings, till the last respects were paid to the remains of the deceased.

BRIDGEWATER, MASS.

Here lies buried Eleazer Alden, who died 29 January, 1773, in the 79 year of his age.

> Laid in the dust he must abide,
> Thus sleeping by his consort's side,
> Ye children living come and see
> Where both your once loved parents be.
> Then follow in the path they trod
> Till you shall rest with Christ in God.

Here lies buried Mrs. Martha Alden, the wife of Mr. Eleazer Alden, who died 6 January, 1769, aged 69 years.

> The resurrection day will come,
> And Christ's strong voice will burst the tomb;
> The sleeping dead, we trust, will rise
> With joy and pleasure in her eyes,
> And ever shine among the wise.

Joseph Alden, the second son of the Hon. John Alden of Duxbury, whose wife was Mary Simmons, was one of the original settlers of Bridgewater. The first improvements in this place, which were begun in 1654, were in what is

called the West Parish, which for a time was known as the
"Duxburough Plantation." The Sachem who deeded this
township, went with the purchasers upon a certain hill in
the East Parish, and made his conveyance in this manner,
mentioning the consideration: "I give you all the land
south, seven miles, all the land west, seven miles, all the
land north, seven miles, and all the land east to where the
white men live."

Joseph Alden departed this life 3 February, 1697, 'at the age of about 73
years, leaving a widow and three sons, Isaac, Joseph and John.

Beneath are deposited the remains of Lt. Joshua Alden, who died 21st March,
1809, in the 80th year of his age.

He led a sober and regular life, was a friend to peace and good order, a
steady attendant on public worship and a valuable member of society. In
his last will and testament, after some deductions he bequeathed a tenth part
of his property to the So. Congregational Society in Bridgewater, of which
one hundred dollars were for the use of the church of which he was a member, two hundred dollars for the encouragement of psalmody, and the remainder for the fund of said Society.
To perpetuate his memory and to express the gratitude due to an example
so worthy of imitation, it has been thought fit to erect this monument.

DUXBOROUGH, MASS.

In memory of Capt. Samuel Alden, who died 24 February, 1781, aged 92
years, 2 months and 3 days.

It is a remarkable circumstance that Captain Samuel
Alden and his sister, Alice Paddock, two of the grand-children of one of the first settlers of the old colony, should
have been upon the stage at the commencement of the
Revolutionary War. They lived to see the country peopled with three million white inhabitants, and successfully
opposing the ungenerous usurpation and tyranny of the
parent empire.

PHILADELPHIA.

In memory of Mrs. Martha Gifford, wife of Alden Gifford, who, on the 10
of June, at the age of 29 years, 4 months and 20 days, exchanged this
earth for heaven.

> Sickness sore long time I bore,
> Physicians' skill in vain,
> Till God revealed his tender love
> And took away my pain.

> And now I at my anchor ride,
> With many of the fleet ;
> Once more, again, I will set sail
> My Saviour, Christ to meet.

BENJAMIN AND DEBORAH FRANKLIN, 1790.

The body of Benjamin Franklin, printer, like the cover of an old book, its contents torn out, and stript of its lettering and gilding, lies here, food for worms, yet the work itself shall not be lost; for it will, as he believed, appear once more in a new and beautiful edition, corrected and amended by the author.

ANDOVER, MASS.

In memory of Mr. John Abbott, who departed this life 10 November, 1793, in the 90 year of his age.

> Grass, smoke, a flower, a vapor, shade, a span,
> Serve to illustrate the frail life of man;
> And they who longest live, survive to see
> The certainty of death, of life the vanity.

Several of the grandsons of Mr. Abbott are distnguished among the literati of New England.

NORTHAMPTON, MASS.

In memory of Caleb Strong, who died 13 February, A. D., 1770, in the 66 year of his age.

> Man's home is in the grave ;
> Here dwells the multitude ; we gaze around,
> We read their monuments, we sigh, and while
> We sigh, we sink.

In memory of Mrs. Phebe Strong, the relict of Mr. Caleb Strong, who died 5 January, anno domini 1802, in the 85 year of her age.

> We loved, but not enough, the gentle hand that
> Reared us. Gladly would we now recall that
> Softest friend, a mother, whose mild converse
> And faithful counsel we in vain regret.

These were the parents of His Excellency, Caleb Strong, governor of Massachusetts.

BRISTOL, R. I.

Here lies buried the body of the Hon. William Bradford, Esq., who departed this life 6th July, 1808, in the 80 year of his age.

> Peaceful
> May he sleep out the sabbath of the tomb,
> And wake to rapture in the life to come.

Benj. West, LL.D., a distinguished Mathematician and Philosopher, was born at Rehoboth in Massachusetts, and early removed to Bristol, R. I., where he was educated. From his earliest years he had a remarkable fondness for mathematical studies, and was for many years the able and esteemed professor of mathematics and astronomy at the College of Rhode Island, now Brown University. He deceased in autumn of 1813, having passed the age of fourscore years and left one son and three daughters. His love for his country expired but with the last glimmering ray of life. He left the world without an enemy in the ardent hope and expectation of the joys of heaven.

PROVIDENCE, R. I.

President James Manning, the founder of the R. I., College, which was first located in Warren, in 1765. Afterwards removed to Providence and received the name of Brown University in honor of Nicholas Brown who made a large donation to the Institution.

In memory of Rev. James Manning, D. D., President of R. I. College. He was born in New Jersey, A. D., 1738. Became a member of the Baptist church, A. D., 1758. Graduated at Nassau Hall, in 1762; was ordained a minister of the gospel in 1763; obtained a charter for a college in 1765; was elected president the same year; and was a member of Congress in 1786. His person was graceful and his countenance remarkably expressive of sensibility, cheerfulness and dignity. The variety and excellence of his natural abilities, improved by education and enriched by science, raised him to a rank of eminence among literary characters. His manners were engaging, his voice harmonious, his eloquence natural and powerful; his social virtues, classical learning, eminent patriotism, shining talents for instructing youth, and zeal in the cause of christianity, are recorded on the tables of many hearts.

He died of Apoplexy 29 July, 1791, aged 53. The trustee and fellows of the College have erected this monument.

In memory of Nicholas Brown, Esq., who departed this life 29 May, A. D., 1791, aged 62.

His ancestors were some of the first settlers of this state. His stature was large. His personal appearance manly and noble; his genius penetrating, his memory tenacious, his judgment strong, his affections lively and warm.

He was an early, persevering and liberal patron of the College in this town and a member and great benefactor of the Baptist Society. His donations in support of learning and religion were abundant. As in life he was universally esteemed, so in death he was universally lamented.

Here repose the remains of Colonel Benjamin Hoppin. Having sustained various public offices with probity and honor, by an exemplary private life endeared himself to his numerous connexions and friends and having professed and practiced the religion of Christ, on the 30 day of November, A. D., 1809, in the 68 year of his age serenely departed, in peace with all mankind, leaving his numerous descendants an example, with what tranquility a Christian can die.

Sacred to the memory of Colonel Jeremiah Olney, a patriot soldier of the Revolution, late collector of the customs in the district of Providence, and president of the society of Cincinnatti of the State of Rhode Island and Providence Plantations. He closed his honorable and useful life with Christian serenity on the 10 of November, 1812, in the 63 year of his age.

The remains of Elder Joseph Snow, the first pastor and teacher of the Pedobaptist Congregational church in Providence, lie entombed in the family cemetery. He was born in Bridgewater, Mass., on the 6th of April, 1715, and died 10th of April, 1803, having entered on the eighty-ninth year of his age, and the fifty-sixth of his ministry.

NORWICH, CONN.

In memory of Doctor Johna. Lathrop. He died, 29 October, A. D., 1807, in the 85 year of his age.

> A soul prepared needs no delays;
> The summons comes, the saint obeys;
> Swift was his flight, and short the road,
> He closed his eyes and saw his God.

MONTVILLE, CONN.

Dorathy Coffin Alden, died 29 July, 1796, aged 11 months and 1 week.

> So fades the lovely blooming flower,
> Sweet smiling solace of an hour.

MOHEGAN, CONN.

In the Rev. Dr. Holme's memoir of the Moheagans, it is said that the following lines were found on a grave-stone in their burial ground :

> Here lies the body of Sunseeto
> Own son to Uncas, grandson to Oneeko,
> Who were the famous Sachems of Moheagan,
> But now they are all dead I think it is Werheegan.

(The last word is interpreted by the phrase "all is well" or, "good news."

The island in the Penobscot river called Oldtown, has been the favorite residence of the aborigines for more than a thousand years. Here Orono, the venerable chief of the Penobscot tribe, departed this life on the 5th of Feb., 1801, aged, one hundred and fifteen years. He was greatly endeared to his tribe, and spent his life in cultivating the principles of peace. During the Revolutionary war, he formed a treaty with our government, which he faithfully kept, while some of the more Southern tribes became a scourge to our frontier settlements. The following anecdote is related of him :

On a certain time, Rev. Daniel Little, who was sent on a

mission into the Penobscot country, in a pleasant, familiar way asked Orono in what language he prayed. Orono made no reply, but assumed a very grave aspect. Mr. Little repeated his question still without a reply. After a little interval, Mr. Little clapping Orono on the shoulder, said, " Come, Orono, come, tell me in what language you say your prayers, Indian, French or Latin ? " Orono with a solemnity of countenance which delighted Mr. Little, lifted up his hands and his eyes toward heaven and said, " No matter, Great Spirit know all language."

His Epitaph reads as follows :

> Safe lodged within his blanket, here below
> Lie the last relics of Old Orono;
> Worn down with toil and care, he in a trice
> Exchanged his wigwam for a paradise.

ATTLEBORO, MASS.

> Here lies the best of slaves,
> Now turning into dust,
> Caesar, the Ethiopian, craves
> A place among the just.
> His faithful soul has fled
> To realms of heavenly light,
> And by the blood that Jesus shed
> Is changed from black to white.
> January 15 he quitted the stage
> In the 77 year of his age.

In memory of Dr. Herbert Mann, who with 119 sailors with Capt. Magee, Master, went on board the brig General Arnold, in Boston Harbor, 25 December, 1777, hoisted sail, made for sea, and were immediately overtaken by the most tremendous snow storm with cold, that was ever known in the memory of man, and unhappily parted their cable in Plymouth harbor, in a place called the Cow Yard, and he with about 100 others were frozen to death, 66 of whom were buried in one grave. He was in the 21 year of his age.

> And now Lord God Almighty, just and true
> Are all thy ways, but who can stand before thy cold?

The calamity which this inscription records, was one of the most distressing ever witnessed on the coast of Massachusetts, an account of which was published by one of the survivors, Bartholomew Downs, of Barnstable. In closing his account he says, " It is worthy of remark that the captain, and some others, by his advice, poured ardent spirits into their boots, but took none internally, which was unexceptionally the means of preserving their lives and limbs. Those who made freest use of intoxicating liquor, fell the first victims to the intensity of the cold.

The following was written by a gentleman well versed in the technical language of the navy, for a monument which was to have been erected to the memory of the Hon. Job Pray, a member of the executive council of Georgia, and during the Revolutionary war a brave, naval commander :

Sunk at his moorings, on Wednesday, the 29 of April, 1789, one who never struck his flag while he had a shot in the locker ; who carried sail in chase till all was blue : in peace, whose greatest glory was a staggering topsail breeze ; in war, to bring his broadside to bear upon the enemy, and who when signals of distress hove out, never stood his course, but hauled, or tacked, or wore to give relief, though to a foe ; who steered his little bark full fifty annual cruises over life's tempestuous ocean, and moored her safe in port at last ; where her timbers being crazy and having sprung a leak in the gale, she went down with a clear hawse. If these traits excite in the breast of humanity, that common tribute to the memory of the departed, a sigh, then traveller as thou passest this wreck, let thine be borne upon the breeze which bends the grassy covering of the grave of old Job Pray.

CHAPTER XXIV.

MILES STANDISH.*

I.

N the old colony days, in Plymouth the land of the Pilgrims,
To and fro in a room of his simple and primitive dwelling,
Strode, with a martial air, Miles Standish the Puritan Captain.
Near him was seated John Alden, his friend, and household companion,
Writing with diligent speed at a table of pine by the window.

II.

LOVE AND FRIENDSHIP.

Nothing was heard in the room, but the hurrying pen of the stripling,
Or an occasional sigh from the laboring heart of the Captain,
Reading the marvellous words and achievements of Julius Caesar,
" So he won the day, the battle of something or other.
That's what I always say; if you wish anything to be well done,
You must do it yourself, you must not leave it to others ! "

        *   *   *

Finally closing his book, with a bang of the ponderous cover,
Thus to the young man spake Miles Standish the Captain of Plymouth:
" When you have finished your work, I have something important to tell you,
Be not however in haste; I can wait; I shall not be impatient ! "
Straightway Alden replied, as he folded the last of his letters,
" Speak, for whenever you speak, I'm always ready to listen. "
Thereupon, answered the Captain, embarrassed and culling his phrases,
" Since Rose Standish died, my life has been weary and dreary;
Oft in my lonely hours have I thought of the maiden Priscilla.
She is alone in the world ; her father and mother and brother,
Died in the winter together; I saw her going and coming,
Now to the grave of the dead, and now to the bed of the dying.
Go to the damsel Priscilla, the lovliest maiden of Plymouth,
Say that a blunt old Captain a man not of words, but of actions,
Offers his hand and his heart, the hand and heart of a soldier. "

        *   *   *

When he had spoken, John Alden, the fair-haired, taciturn stripling
All aghast at his words, surprised, embarassed, bewildered,
Trying to mask his dismay by treating the subject with lightness,
Thus made answer and spake, or rather stammered than answered:

"Such a message as that, I am sure I should mangle and mar it;
If you would have it well done, — I am only repeating your maxim, —
You must do it yourself, you must not leave it to others!"
'Truly the maxim is good, and I do not mean to gainsay it;"
I can march up to a fortress and summon the place to surrender,
But march up to a woman with such a proposal, I dare not.
I'm not afraid of bullets, nor shot from the mouth of a cannon,
But of a thundering ' No !' point blank from the mouth of a woman,
That I confess I'm afraid of, nor am I ashamed to confess it !
Surely you cannot refuse what I ask in the name of our friendship!"
What you demand in that name, I have not the power to deny you.

III.

THE LOVER'S ERRAND.

All around him was calm, but within him commotion and conflict.
" Was it for this I have loved, and waited, and worshipped in silence ?
Was it for this, I have followed the flying feet and the shadow
Over the wintry sea, to the desolate shores of New England ? "

*   *   *

So through the Plymouth woods John Alden went on his errand;
Gathering still, as he went, the Mayflowers blooming around him,
" Modest and simple and sweet, the very type of Priscilla !
So I will take them to her; to Priscilla the Mayflower of Plymouth. "
So through the Plymouth woods John Alden went on his errand ;
Came to an open space, and saw the disk of the ocean,
Saw the new built house, and people at work in a meadow ;
Heard, as he drew near the door, the musical voice of Priscilla
Singing the hundreth Psalm, the grand old Puritan Anthem.
Then, as he opened the door, he beheld the form of the maiden
Seated beside her wheel; and the carded wool like a snow drift
Piled on her knee, her white hands feeding the ravenous spindle,
While with her foot on the treadle she guided the wheel in its motion.

*   *   *

So he entered the house; and the hum of the wheel and the singing
Suddenly ceased: for Priscilla, aroused by his steps on the threshold,
Rose as he entered, and gave him her hand, in signal of welcome,
Saying, " I knew it was you, when I heard your step in the passage ;
For I was thinking of you, as I sat here singing and spinning."
Silent before her he stood, and gave her the flowers for an answer.

*   *   *

" Kind are the people I live with, and dear to me my religion ;
Still my heart is so sad, that I wish myself back in Old England."

*   *   *

Thereupon answered the youth : — "Indeed I do not condemn you;
Stouter hearts than a woman's have quailed in this terrible winter.
Yours is tender and trusting, and needs a stronger to lean on;
So I have come to you now, with an offer and proffer of marriage
Made by a good man and true, Miles Standish the Captain of Plymouth ! "

Thus he delivered his message, the dexterous writer of letters —
Came straight to the point and blurted it out like a school-boy;
Mute with amazement and sorrow, Priscilla, the Puritan maiden,
Looked into Alden's face, her eyes dilated with wonder,
Till at length she exclaimed, interrupting the ominous silence:
" If the great Captain of Plymouth is so very eager to wed me,
Why does he not come himself, and take the trouble to woo me?"
Then John Alden began explaining and smoothing the matter,
Making it worse as he went, by saying that "the Captain was busy."
"Has he no time for such things, as you call it, before he is married.
Would he be likely to find it, or make it, after the wedding?
Had he only showed that he loved me, had he but waited a while,
Even this Captain of yours, — who knows? — at last might have won me,
Old and rough as he is; but now it never can happen."

*   *   *

Still John Alden went on, unheeding the words of Priscilla.
Not to be laughed at and scorned, because he was little of stature,
Any woman in Plymouth, nay, any woman in England,
Might be happy and proud to be called the wife of Miles Standish!

*   *   *

But as he warmed and glowed in his simple and eloquent language,
Archly the maiden smiled, and, with eyes over-running with laughter,
Said, in a tremulous voice, " Why don't you speak for yourself, John?"

IV.

JOHN ALDEN.

Into the open air John Alden, perplexed and bewildered,
Rushed like a man insane, and wandered alone by the sea-side.

*   *   *

" Is it my fault, " he said " that the maiden has chosen between us?
Is it my fault that he failed, — my fault that I am the victor?
Back will I go o'er the ocean, this dreary land will abandon,
Her whom I may not love, and him whom my heart has offended. "

*   *   *

Thus as he spake, he turned, in the strength of his strong resolution,
Till he beheld the lights in the seven houses of Plymouth.
Soon he entered his door, and found the redoubtable Captain.
" Long have you been on your errand, " he said with a cheery demeanor.
" Not far off is the house, although the woods are between us,
Come, sit down, and in order relate to me, all that has happened. "

*   *   *

Then John Alden spake, and related the wondrous adventure.
But when he came at length to the words Priscilla had spoken,
Words so tender and cruel; " Why don't you speak for yourself, John?"
Up leaped the Captain of Plymouth, and stamped on the floor:
Wildly he shouted, and loud; "John Alden! you have betrayed me!
Me, Miles Standish,—Your friend! have supplanted, defrauded, betrayed me!"

Alden was left alone. He heard the clank of the scabbard
Growing fainter and fainter, and dying away in the distance,
Then he arose from his seat, and looked forth into the darkness,
Lifted his eyes to the heavens, and folding his hands as in childhood,
Prayed in the silence of night, to the Father who seeth in secret.

V.

THE SAILING OF THE MAYFLOWER.

Just in the grey of the dawn, as the mist uprose from the meadows,
There was a stir and a sound in the slumbering Village of Plymouth;
Standish the stalwart it was, with eight of his valorous army,
Northward marching to quell the sudden revolt of the savage.

*   *   *

Loud over field and forest, the cannon's roar, and the echoes
Heard and repeated the sound, the signal gun of departure!
Meekly, in voices subdued, the chapter was read from the Bible,
Meekly the prayer was begun but ended in fervent entreaty!
Then from their houses in haste, came forth the Pilgrims of Plymouth.

*   *   *

Foremost among them was Alden; all night he had lain without slumber.
Then he arose from his bed, and heard what the people were saying,
Joined in the morning prayer, and in the reading of Scripture,
And, with the others, in haste, went hurrying down to the sea-shore.

*   *   *

Nearer the boat stood Alden, with one foot placed on the gun-wale,
One still firm on the rock, and talking at times with the sailors.
He too was eager to go, and thus put an end to his anguish.
But as he gazed on the crowd, he beheld the form of Priscilla.
Fixed were her eyes upon his, as if she divined his intention,
That with a sudden revulsion, his heart recoiled from its purpose,
"Here I remain!" he exclaimed, as he looked upon the heavens above him
"There is no land so sacred, no air so pure and so wholesome,
As is the air she breathes, and the soil that is pressed by her foot-steps.
Yes! as my foot was the first that stepped on this rock at the landing
So, with the blessing of God, shall it be the last at the leaving!"
O strong hearts and true! Not one went back in the Mayflower!
Then as if filled with the Spirit, and wrapt in a vision prophetic,
Baring his hoary head, the excellent Elder of Plymouth
Said "Let us pray!" and they prayed and thanked the Lord and took courage
So they returned to their homes; but Alden lingered a little.

VI.

PRISCILLA.

Thus for a while he stood and mused by the shore of the Ocean,
Thinking of many things, and most of all of Priscilla.

Lo! as he turned to depart, Priscilla was standing beside him.
"Are you so much offended, you will not speak to me?" said she.
"Yesterday I was shocked, when I heard you speak f Miles Standish,
Praising his courage and strength, and even his fighting in Flanders,
Frankly I speak to you, asking for sympathy only and kindness.
For I know and esteem you, and feel that your nature is noble,
Now that our terrible Captain has gone in pursuit of the Indians,
You may speak boldly, and tell me of all that happened between you."
Thereupon answered John Alden, and told her the whole of the story
How he had even determined to sail that day in the Mayflower
And had remained for her sake on hearing the dangers that threatened.

VII.

MILES STANDISH.

Meanwhile the stalwart Miles Standish was marching steadily northward.
" I alone am to blame" he muttered, "for mine was the folly.
What has a rough old soldier, grown grim and gray in the harness,
Used to the camp and its ways, to do with the wooing of maidens?"

THE COURTSHIP.

VIII.

SPINNING WHEEL.

Meanwhile Alden at home had built him a new habitation,
Solid, substantial, of timber rough-hewn from the firs of the forest.
Still may be seen to this day some trace of the well and the orchard.

      *   *   *

Oft when his labor was finished, with eager feet would the dreamer
Follow the pathway that run through the woods to the house of Priscilla.

      *   *   *

So as she sat at her wheel, one afternoon in the Autumn,
John Alden opposite sat and was watching her dexterous fingers.

      *   *   *

Lo! in the midst of this scene, a breathless messenger entered.
Yes; Miles Standish was dead! an Indian had brought them the tidings.
Silent and statue-like stood Priscilla, her face looking backward.
But John Alden, upstarting as if the barb of the arrow
Piercing the heart of his friend had struck his own, and had sundered
Once and forever the bonds that held him as a captive,
Clasped, almost with a groan, the motionless form of Priscilla,
Pressing her close to his heart as forever his own and exlaiming:
"Those whom the Lord hath united let no man put them asunder!"

IX.

THE WEDDING DAY.

This was the wedding morn of Priscilla the Puritan Maiden.
Softly the youth and maiden repeated the words of betrothal,
Fervently then, and devoutly, the excellent Elder of Plymouth
Prayed for the hearth and the home, that were founded that day in affection.

      *   *   *

Lo! when the service was ended, a form appeared on the threshold,
Clad in armour of steel, a sombre, and sorrowful figure!
Into the room it strode, and the people beheld with amazement
Bodily there in his armour, Miles Standish, the captain of Plymouth!
Grasping the bridegroom's hand, he said with emotion, Forgive me!
I have been angry and hurt,—too long have I cherished the feeling;
I have been cruel and hard, but now, thank God it is ended.
Never so much as now was Miles Standish the friend of John Alden.
Thereupon answered the bridegroom: Let all be forgotten between us;
All save the dear old friendship, and that shall grow older and dearer!
Then the Captain advanced, and, bowing, saluted Priscilla.
Then he said with a smile; I should have remembered the adage,—
If you would be well served, you must serve yourself.
Meanwhile the bridegroom went forth and stood with the bride at the door way.

Then from a stall near at hand, amid exclamations of wonder,
Alden the thoughtful, the careful, so happy, so proud of Priscilla,
Brought out his snow-white steer, obeying the hand of its master,
Led by a cord that was tied to an iron ring in its nostrils
Covered with crimson cloth, and a cushion placed for a saddle.
Placing her hand on the cushion, her foot in the hand of her husband,

Copyright, 1861. By J. E. Tilton & Co.

THE WEDDING JOURNEY.

Gaily with joyous laugh, Priscilla mounted her palfrey.
"Nothing is wanting now," he said with a smile, but the distaff,
Then you would be in truth my Queen, my beautiful Bertha!

         *   *   *

Onward the bridal procession now moved to their new habitation.
Happy husband and wife, and friends conversing together,
So through the Plymouth woods passed onward the bridal procession.

---

* Extracts from Longfellow's Courtship of Miles Standish (By permission of Houghton,
Mifflin & Co., Sole Publishers of Longfellow's Works.)

CHAPTER XXV.

THE AUTHOR'S LINE OF ANCESTRY.

OSEPH[2] **ALDEN*** Son of Hon. John[1] Alden.

B Bridgewater, Mass. D 8th Feb. 1697, at 73 yrs.

M —— Mary Simmons, of Duxbury, Mass., daughter
Moses, Jr., and Sarah —— Simmons.

He was a farmer, and freeman, 1659. Had his father's proprietary share in Bridgewater, Mass., where he settled in that part now known as West Bridgewater. His will was dated 14th December, 1696, and proved 10th March, 1697. Widow Mary and son John, Executors.

CHILDREN.

I. **ISAAC**[3]   B Bridgewater.   M   2nd Dec. 1685, Mehitable Allen,
                  D   daughter of Samuel Allen.
Had nine children.   C   1665.

II. ***JOSEPH**[3]   B ——   1667. M —— 1690, Hannah Dunham,
                  D 22nd Jan. 1747.   daughter of Daniel, of Plymouth.

III. **JOHN**[3]   B W. Bridgewater. M ——   Hannah White, daughter
                  D 29th Sept. 1730, at 56 yrs.   of Capt. Ebenezer, of
And as Mitchell thinks,   Elizabeth[3] and Mary.[3]   Weymouth.

NOTE.—Mr Mitchell thinks that Joseph[2] Alden had also daughters.

ELIZABETH[3] who B ——   M ——   1691, Benjamin Snow.
               D ——   1705.

MARY[3]   who B ——   M ——   1700, Samuel Allen, of
               D ——   Bridgewater, Mass.

These two are not named in the will of Joseph[2] Alden; but may have received their portions at their respective marriages.

No records of their births have been found, or baptisms.

B Denotes born. M Married. D Death. A About. The numbers 1, 2, 3 and 4 denotes the generations in their order of precedence.

*JOSEPH³ ALDEN Son of Joseph,² Hon. John¹ Alden.
Bridgewater, Mass.

B	1667.	D 22nd Dec. 1747, aged 80 years.	
M ——	1690,	Hannah Dunham, of Plymouth, Mass.,	
		daughter of Daniel.	
B ——		D 13th January. 1748, at 78 years.	

He lived at So. Bridgewater, Mass., was "Deacon" of the Church and much esteemed. His will dated 12th November, 1743.

CHILDREN.

I. **DANIEL⁴** B 29th Jan. 1691. M —— 1717. Abigail Shaw,
Bridgewater, Mass. daughter of Joseph Shaw.
Stafford, Conn.

D —— B —— D 12th July, 1755, at 61 years.
Had children.

NOTE.—He was a Magistrate. His wife was sister to Rev. John Shaw, 1st Pastor of the Cong. Church, So. Bridgewater, C. 1729, ordained 1731 and grandfather of Hon. Lemuel Shaw, C. J., Sup. Court of Massachusetts.

II. **JOSEPH⁴** B 26th Aug. 1693. M —— D 9th Dec. 1695.

III. ***ELEAZER⁴** B 27th Sept. 1694. M 1720, Martha Shaw, daughter
Bridgewater. D 30th Jan. 1773. of Joseph.
B —— D 1759, at 69 years.

IV. **HANNAH⁴** B —— 1696. M 1722, Mark Lothrop, of
Had children. D 1777, at 81 years. Easton, Mass.

V. **MARY⁴** B 10th Apr. 1699. M 1719, Timothy Edson.
Bridgewater, Mass.
Stafford, Conn.

D 14th Feb. 1782.

VI. **JOSEPH⁴** B 5th Sept. 1700. M ——
D 5th Oct. 1700.

VII. **JONATHAN⁴** B 3rd Dec. 1703. M —— D ——
D 10th Nov. 1704.

VIII. **SAMUEL⁴** B 20th Aug. 1705. M 1728, Abiah Edson, daughter of
Titicut. D 1785, aged 80 yrs. Captain Joseph Edson.
He had nine children.

IX. **MEHITABLE⁴** B 18th Oct. 1707
D 11th April, 1737, aged 30 years.

X. **SETH**[4]   B 6th July, 1710.   M 1741,   Mehitable Carver,
Bridgewater, Mass.   D 6 Sept. 1784.   daughter of Eleazer Carver.
                                        B —— D 14th Feb. 1757.
He was known as "Captain" Seth Alden, and had 4 sons.

*****ELEAZER**[4] **ALDEN**   Son of Joseph,[3] Joseph,[2] Hon. John[1] Alden.
   Bridgewater, Mass.
   B 27th Sept. 1694.   D 30th Jan. 1773, aged 79 years.
   M   1720,   Martha Shaw, daughter
   B ——   D 1769, at 69 years.   of Joseph.

CHILDREN.

I. **JONATHAN**[5] B   1721. M 1743,   Experience Hayward,
Ashfield, Mass.   D 1801 or 1805.   daughter of Nathaniel.
                                       B —— D 1809, at 90 years.
See "Thayer Memorial" and History of Bridgewater, Mass.

II. **ELEAZER**[5]   B   1723. M —— Sarah Whitman, daughter
                      D   1803.   of Nicholas.
                      aged 80 years.   B 1726. D 18th April 1818, aged
                                                92 years.

III. **ABSALOM**[5]   B   1725.
                       D   1727.

IV. *****DAVID**[5]   B   1727. M ——   Lucy Thomas, his
Ashfield.   D   1807.   cousin.

V. **JOSHUA**[5]   B   1729. M 1786,   Mary Carver, daughter of
Bridgewater, Mass. B 19 or 21 March.   Eleazer Carver.
                    1809. No issue. B —— D 1811, at 63 years, and she
                    was a widow of Seth[5] Alden, son of Seth[4] Alden.

He was "Lieutenant." He was a farmer, and from 1756 to 1809, kept an
accurate bill of mortality in So. Bridgewater. He left a legacy to the South
Parish, and in gratitude they erected a monument to his memory.

VI. **CALEB**[5]   B   1731. D 1733.

VII. **EZRA**[5]   B   1734. M ——   Miriam Richardson
Stafford, Conn. [daughter of Uriah, of Stafford, Conn., and grand-daughter
Greenwich, Mass.   of Rev. Jacob Green, of Hanover, N. J.
"Deacon" in 1775   D   1818, aged 84 years.

VIII. **TIMOTHY**[5] B 24th Nov. 1736. M ——   Sarah Weld, daughter of
   Yarmouth, Mass,   Rev. Habijah Weld of
                    D 13th Nov. 1828.   Attleborough, Mass.
                    aged 92 years. B —— D 28 Oct. 1796, at 59th yr.

He was pastor of the Congregational Church of Yarmouth, Mass., ordained 13th December, 1769, and was graduated from Harvard College in 1762. He was, as has been given, " a faithful and devoted pastor."

*DAVID⁵ ALDEN Son of Eleazer,⁴ Joseph,³ Joseph,² Hon. John¹
Ashfield, Mass.   Alden.

    B   1727. D 1807, aged 80 years.
    M ——   Lucy Thomas, his cousin, daughter of ——
    B ——   D ——

    I. **ISAAC**⁶   B ——   M ——   Irene Smith, daughter of
    Warren Co. Penn. D ——   Rev. Ebenezer Smith.
                     aged 80 years. Warren Co. Penn.
Had nine children.

    II. **DAVID**⁶   B ——   M 27th May, 1783,   Susanna Ward,
    Middlefield, (O). D ——   daughter of John and Mary (Torrey)
Had nine children.   Ward of Buckland.

    III. ***JOHN**⁶   B   1761. M ——   Nancy Gray, daughter of
    Ashfield.   D ——   Jonathan G. of Pelham, Mass.

    IV. **LYDIA**⁶   B ——   M ——   Jonathan Gray.
                D ——
Had eight children.

    V. **ENOCH**⁶   B ——   M ——   Lucy Elmor.
    Rome, N. Y.   D ——
    Redfield, N. Y.
                Physician and Surgeon.

*REV. JOHN⁶ **ALDEN** Son of David,⁵ Eleazer,⁴ Joseph,³ Joseph,²
Ashfield.   Hon. John¹ Alden.

    B   1761. D 1842, aged 81 years.
    M ——   Nancy Gray, of Pelham, Mass., daughter of
                         Jonathan and   Gray.
    B 23d Dec. 1771. D March, 1813, at 42 years.

Rev. John⁶ Alden of Ashfield, Mass., Minister of the Baptist persuasion, and inherited the paternal estate. A man of piety and respectable attainments, and had a large family of sons and daughters, as below enumerated.
    He had fourteen children.

CHILDREN.

OF JOHN⁶ AND NANCY GRAY ALDEN.

    I. **ARIAN**⁷   B ——   M ——
                D ——

II. **ELIZABETH**[7] B 5 March, 1789. M —— William Ranney.
        D 7 May, 1870.   B 30 June. 1785,
  aged 81 years, 2 months and 2 days.   D 9 Sept. 1857,
                      aged 72 years, 2 months and 9 days.

CHILDREN OF William and Elizabeth[7] [Alden] Ranney.

   1. BETSEY RANNEY.   B A 1808.   M F. C. Annible,
                         D 9 May, 1881, D 2nd Oct. 1886.
Had two children.

       1. HELEN, who   M John Williams [California.]
       2. EDWARD, Prominent Lawyer, Paw Paw, Van Buren
           County, Michigan.

   2. JOHN RANNEY.   B 8 Oct. 1812. M ——
                    D 29 Sept. 1863.

   3. LUKE RANNEY.   B 8 Nov. 1815. M Rebecca Lyon.
                    D ——
Had children.

       1. FRANK.   B 13 Feb. 1846. M ——
         Has two children.
       2. WM. CYRUS.   B 29 Oct. 1847. M ——
         No children.
       3. ALDEN S.   B 8 Oct. 1850. D 3 Oct. 1859.
       4. CHARLES.   B 17 Oct. 1852. D 12 Sept. 1855.
       5. EDWARD L.   B 11 Nov. 1858.
         Had children, William, Edward, Charles.

   4. MARTHA RANNEY.   B 21 Mar. 1821. M ——

   5. MARY RANNEY.   B A Jan. 1824. M Edward Whitney.
                  D 7 Feb. 1873.
Had three children.

       1. ——   M ——   Mr. Shaw. Van Buren
                        Co. Michigan.
       2. CORA.   M ——   Fred Munro.
       3. Boy who died young.

III. **EUNICE**[7] B 12 Sept. 1790. M 6 Jan. 1811, Luther Ranney.
            D 5 Sept. 1882. B 6 Sept. 1785.
                      D 5 March, 1871.

CHILDREN OF Luther and Eunice[7] [Alden] Ranney

1. NANCY G. RANNEY.   B 24 Oct. 1811, M   30 Jan. 1839,
                        D 18 Aug. 1879,   Elijah Field.
                                        D 17 Aug. 1871.

Had children.

      1. AMELIA S. FIELD. B 5 Nov. 1839.

      2. FRANK H. FIELD. B 19 Sept. 1850.

2. FLAVILLA RANNEY.   B 3 March 1813. M ——
                        D ——

3, HARRIET N. RANNEY. B 8 Sept. 1814. M   2 Nov. 1856,

                    Lorenzo Metcalf.   No issue.

4. RACHEL H. RANNEY. B 11 May, 1816. M   25 Apr. 1855,
                                        Charles S. Guilford.

5. SOPHIA A. RANNEY.   B 23 Aug. 1819. M   12 Nov. 1851,
                         D 23 July, 1885.   Lyman Goodwin.

No children.

6. LUTHER B. RANNEY.   B 16 Oct. 1821. M   30 May, 1843.
                                          Mary A. Putney.
                                    M   20 Feb. 1882.
                                    Mrs. Mary J. Millett.

Had children.

      1. LUTHER Z. RANNEY, B 4 Apr. 1845,

      2. ELLEN J. RANNEY, B 25 Mar. 1848.

      3. EARL G. RANNEY,   B 21 Jan. 1851.

7. JOHN A. RANNEY,   B 6 Feb. 1827. M   5 Oct. 1846,
                         D ——   Caroline Belding.

Had children.

      1. DURWIN D. RANNEY, B Sept. 1850.

      2. CARRIE E. RANNEY, B 8 Feb. 1854.

      3. JOHN A. RANNEY,   B 1 Dec, 1859.

8. DAVID F. RANNEY.   B 21 July 1830. M   Margaret Hill.

Had children.

      1. KATE E. RANNEY,   B 22 Aug. 1859.

IV. **NANCY**[7]   B 10 Feb. 1792   M 23 Jan. 1823. William Bassett.
                     D 8 Apr. 1840.   D 21 Sept. 1857.

CHILDREN OF William and Nancy[7] [Alden] Bassett.

1. JOHN BASSETT.   B 11 Apr. 1824. D 8 Aug. 1825.

2. WILLIAM F. BASSETT.   B 11 July 1825 M 26 Sept. 1860.
                                           Lizzie C. Leonard.
Had children.

    1. ELLEN M. BASSETT, B 26 July, 1861.

    2. FRANK L. BASSETT, B 3 Feb. 1864. M 24 Nov. 1884.
                                            Lillie R. Vanscent.

And had ALICE VANSCENT BASSETT,   B 17 Nov. 1886.

    3. WILLIAM H. BASSETT,   B 23 May, 1866.
                                            D 26 Sept 1866.

    4. ALICE L. BASSETT, B 26 June 1867. D 11 Sept. 1867.

    5. J. MURRAY BASSETT, B 9 Sept. 1869.

    6. GEO. WM. BASSETT, B 1 Nov. 1871.

3. NANCY A. BASSETT,   B 23 Aug. 1828. M 26 May, 1847.
                           D 8 Mar. 1876.   Asa Guildford.
Had children.

    1. LUCY M. GUILDFORD, B 16 Sept. 1848. M 26 Nov. 1873.
                                            George B. Church,
And had children.

        1 ISABEL B. CHURCH,   B 29 Oct. 1874.

        2. FREDERICK R. CHURCH,   B 23 Jan. 1879,

        3. HELEN L. CHURCH, B 23 Aug. 1880.

    2. WILLIAM B. GUILDFORD.   B 2 Apr. 1853.
                                            D 23 Nov. 1853.
    3. HATTIE B. GUILDFORD.   B 17 Oct, 1854.
                           She married 8 Jan. 1882, Charles Lilly.
    4. MARY L. GUILDFORD.   B 8 June 1860.
                           She married 12 Jan. 1881, Isaac C. Bassett.

V. **ARMILLA**[7] B 3 Dec. 1793.   M Nov. 1812, Aaron Lyon.
  Cassadaga,   B 1 July, 1789.
  Chautauqua Co., N.Y. D 7 Feb. 1867.   D 20 June, 1870.

FAMILY OF LYON.

1. AARON EZRA[8] LYON. B 23 Aug, 1813. M 26 Aug. 1840,
    Mary Ann Kidder,   B 23 Nov. 1812.
Children as follows :

1. FRANCIS KIDDER[9] LYON,   B   27 July. 1841
     M   24 Dec. 1866.   Anna M. Heath
And had children as follows, viz :

    1. JESSIE MARY[10] LYON,   B   27 Oct. 1867.

    2. JENNIE ADELLE[10] LYON,   B   19 May, 1870.

    3. LUCY JANE[10] LYON,   B   7 Nov. 1873.

2. MARY JANE[9] LYON. B 16 Mar. 1843   M   8 Mar. 1860.
                                    Royal E. Park.

    1. FRANK ERNEST PARK.   B 1 Apr, 1862.

    2. MARY ADELINE PARK.   B 12 Nov. 1864.

    3. ELLEN ANNETTE PARK.   B 21 Nov. 1867.

    4. ROYAL WILTON PARK.   B 13 Oct. 1878.

    5. RAYMOND LYON PARK.   B 13 Feb. 1887.

3. MARCUS EZRA LYON. B 9 Sept. 1845. D ——
   M 28 Mar. 1870.   Rhoda A. Skinner.

4. SAMUEL KING LYON. B 4 Feb. 1848. D 8 Dec. 1849.

5. ARMILLA ANNETTE LYON,   B 5 Mar. 1849.
               D ——   M 24 Dec. 1866.
                                    Loren H. Park.
Had children.

    1. LEEMAN EUGENE PARK,   B 20 Feb. 1872,

    2. JOHN EZRA PARK,   B 24 Jan. 1879.

6. AARON MASON LYON,   B 6 Dec. 1850.
             D 9 Mar. 1851,

7. FLORA MARIA LYON, B 27 July 1852. M 15 Feb. 1881.
                              Dr. Sidney E. Ford.
And had these :

    1. MARY[8] FORD,   B 14 Jan. 1883.
            D same day.

    2. EDWARD LYON FORD,   B 10 Mar. 1885.

8. EUGENIA PATIENCE LYON.   B 11 May, 1854.
           M 16 Nov. 1886.   Francis E. Dow.

2. NANCY ALDEN LYON, B 2 July, 1815. D ——
    M 29 Apr. 1846.   Rev. Jesse Martin Purington.
             B 12 Aug. 1809. D 17 June, 1869.
Had children as follows :

1. EDWARD LORD PURINGTON.   B 10 Aug. 1847
                                D 22 May, 1862.

2. DANIEL BOARDMAN PURINGTON.   B 15 Feb. 1850.
    M 6 July, 1876.   Florence Abbey Lyon.
Had children.

    1.   EDWARD EARLE PURINGTON.

    2.   MARY LYON PURINGTON.   B 3 Nov. 1879.

    3.   JOHN ALDEN PURINGTON.   B 27 July, 1884.

    4.   JESSIE PURINGTON.   B 14 July, 1886.

3. AARON LYON PURINGTON.   B 11 Feb. 1854.
                         M ——

4. GEORGE DANA PURINGTON.   B 1 Oct. 1857.
    M 23 Aug. 1878. Helen Blanche Fordyce.
Had these children.

    1.   ADA MAY PURINGTON.   B 15 Apr. 1879.

    2.   ROBERT LAWRENCE PURINGTON.   .
                                B ——

3. LUCY THOMAS LYON. B 15 Feb. 1817. D 3 May 1853.

    M 14 Sept. 1846, Rev. Edward Clemens Lord.
        B 22 Jan. 1817.   D ——
And had children.

    1.   EDWARD CLEMENS LORD, JR.   B   14 Jan. 1848.
                                D 6 Oct. 1849.

    2.   ROSINA LYON LORD.   B 6 Oct. 1850.
                                D same day.

The Rev. Edward Clemens Lord married for his second wife, November 1853, Freelove Althena Lyon, born 31st Jan. 1831. Younger sister to Lucy Thomas Lyon, herein named. See pages following.

4. FRANKLIN SMITH LYON.   B 27 Feb. 1819.
                                M 25 Aug, 1853.
                                Harriet Amanda Johnson
                                B 25 Apr. 1829.

CHILDREN OF Franklin Smith Lyon.

    1.   FLORENCE ABBY LYON.   B 26 Aug. 1855.

    2.   HARRIET ELIZA LYON.   B 31 Jan. 1862.

3. MARY AMANDA LYON.   B 6 Oct. 1866.
      M 6 Aug. 1884.   George B. Foster.
    And had

            1.   RAYMOND LYON FOSTER.   B 29 May 1885.

5   MARY MASON LYON.   B 11 May, 1821,
                      D 16 Oct. 1871. M 23 Nov. 1870,
                                       Henry Grevie.

6   ROSINA LYON.   B 6 Oct. 1822.   D 26 Aug. 1869,
        M 9 May 1850.   Rev. Peter Carpenter Dayfoot.
    Had children as follows:

        1   ROSA MARIA DAYFOOT.   B 16 Apr. 1851.

        2. CARRIE MARILLA DAYFOOT.   B 10 Dec. 1854.

7.   ELECTA MOORE LYON, B 4 Aug. 1825   D ——
          M 31 Aug. 1846,   Horatio Warren Green.
                      B 29 Aug. 1825.
     Children as follows:

        1.   LUCY SOPHRONIA GREEN.   B 10 July, 1847,
             Kansas.   M ——   Sidney Holt.
     Had three children.

        2.   HORATIO FRANK GREEN.   B 22 Apr. 1849.
                      D 10 Mar. 1864.

        3.   SEVELIA CASSA GREEN.   B 4 July, 1851,
                                        D 21 Dec. 1852.

        4.   SYLVANIA EMMA GREEN.   B 4 July, 1851,
                                        D 21 June, 1852.

        5.   HORATIO FRED GREEN,   B 16 Dec. 1866.

        6.   FANNY ELECTA GREEN.   B 21 June, 1870.

8.   SOPHRONIA MINER LYON.   B 2 July, 1828.
          M 7 Apr. 1852.   Rev. Thomas Freeman Thickstun.
                                     B 3 July, 1824.
     Had children as follows:

        1.   FLORA ELLEN THICKSTUN.   B 13 May, 1854.
                                        D 13 July, 1865.

        2.   HATTIE EVELYN THICKSTUN.   B 8 Feb. 1856.
             M 4 July, 1876.   Orville Maurice DeKay
             And had

1.   MAURICE THICKSTUN DeKAY.

B 1 Jan. 1881.

2.   MESSINGER EARLE DeKAY.   B 3 Aug. 1887.

3.   CARRIE LILIAN M. THICKSTUN.   B   25 Feb. 1861.
M 25 Dec. 1884.   Harvey Augustus Ballanger.
And had

1.   FRANCIS LILIAN BALLANGER. B 3 Jan. 1886.

4.   WILLIAM LYON THICKSTUN.   B 7 July 1867.

5.   THOMAS FRANK DUANE THICKSTUN.
B 4 Oct. 1869,   D 25 Feb. 1873.

9.   FREELOVE ALTHENA LYON.   B 31 Jan. 1831.
D 31 Jan. 1860.
M Nov. 1853.   Rev. Edward
Clemens Lord.
B 22 Jan. 1817.
Who previously married her sister.   D ——
And had these children :

1.   LUCY L. LORD.   B 10 Aug. 1854.   D 10 June 1871.

2   FRANKLIN LYON LORD.   B 27 Aug. 1856.
M 1883, M. Josephine Brown.

3.   WILLIAM DEAN LORD   B 27 Aug. 1856.
M 25 Dec. 1879, Delle Wilcox.
Had children.

1.   EDWARD H. LORD.   B 27 June, 1882.
D 23 Oct. 1884.

2.   BESSIE LORD.   B 27 Aug. 1886.

4.   FANNY ARMILLA LORD.   B 17 Feb. 1859.
M 21 Aug. 1885,   William H.
Had :   Bansum.

1.   JENNIE BANSUM.   B 26 June 1886.
5.   MARY LORD.   B 19 Jan. 1661.

10.   FANNY MARTHESIA LYON.   B 17 Apr. 1836.
D ——
M 2 Aug. 1866, Alvin J. Van Fleet.
B 9 Mar. 1839.
Had :

1.   JOHN EDWARD VAN FLEET.   B 8 Oct. 1867.

2. MAGGIE ARMILLA VAN FLEET.   B 29 June 1872.

3. FRED ALVIN VAN FLEET.   B 12 June, 1874.

VI. **CYRUS**[7]   B 15 Aug. 1795.   M 20 Oct. 1819, Eunice Bacon.
Ashfield, Mass.   B 10 Oct. 1801.
                       D 24 Nov. 1842.   D 12 May, 1821
                                         M 6 Nov. 1823, Lura Flagg.

CHILDREN BY FIRST WIFE.

I. **FLAVILLA**[8]   B 23 June, 1820.   M   20 Dec. 1840,
                       D ——   Sylvester N. Whitney.
                                   B 24 Aug. 1815.   D 26 Sept. 1880.
Children :

    1. LURA FLAVILLA WHITNEY.   B 26 Feb. 1844.
                                                    D 2 Apr. 1846.

    2. CYRUS ALDEN WHITNEY.   B 3 Dec. 1855.
                                                    D 4 Dec. 1859.

    3. LIZZIE MUNRO WHITNEY.   B 18 Oct. 1865.
                                                    D 20 Dec. 1865.

II. **EUNICE**[8] B 20 Mar. 1821.   M ——   D 24 Oct. 1825.

BY SECOND WIFE.

III. **ELIZABETH FLAGG**[8]   B 3 Dec. 1824.   M   6 June, 1858,
                       Squire Munro, B 19 Nov. 1805. D 7 Mar. 1880.

IV. **EUNICE BACON**[8]   B 11 Sept. 1827. M   28 Feb. 1877,
                       D ——   Chester C. Tolman. B 13 Nov. 1819.

V. **GEORGE CHANDLER**[8]   B 5 Aug. 1829, M Susan A. Boss.
                       D 17 July, 1888.   B 16 May, 1831, had child, Wm,
                                   Cyrus Alden, B Anawam, Henry
                                   Co. Ill., Mar. 1, 1862.
                                   M Inez May Mitchell, Oct. 28,
                                   1885, at Friendship, Me. They
                                   have one child, Susan May
                                   Alden.   B Bristol, Col.
                                   Jan. 1, 1887.

VI. **CHARLES FLETCHER**[8] B 27 Apr. 1832.   M ——
                             D 29 Apr. 1882.
VII. **LUCY**[7]   B 5 July, 1797.   M ——
                             D ——

VIII. **WILLARD**[7]   B 24 Apr. 1800.   M 27 Sept. 1832.
Cazenovia, N. Y.   Corintha Wilcox.
                                  B 10 Mar. 1807,   D 27 Dec. 1886.
                    D 25 Feb. 1878.
CHILDREN :

          1. THEODORE CLERMONT[8]   B 30 Oct. 1833.
                                           Cassadaga, N. Y.

          2. THEODOSIA AUGUSTA[8]   B 6 Apr. 1835.

IX. **MINERVA**[7]   B 1 June, 1802.   M ——
              D ——

X. **HABILLA**[7]   B 3 June 1804.
              D ——

XI. **JOHN**[7]   B 10 June, 1806.   M 23 Nov. 1833,   Ann Maria Cham-
Providence, R. I. D ——   berlain, daughter of Ephraim C.
   1888.
And whose life we continue.

XII. **SOPHRONIA**[7]   B 20 Sept. 1809.   M 19 Apr. 1834,
              D ——   Edward Griffith Miner,* " Banker,"
                                           Winchester, Ill.
                              B Jan. 21 1809.   D ——
Children as follows :

          . JAMES MINER.   B 16 Jan. 1835.   M 17 Apr. 1861,
              Physician and Surgeon, 101 Regiment,   Ellen Thomas.
                 Illinois Volunteers.

          2. HENRY MINER.   B 10 Jan. 1837.

          3. ANNA JUDSON[8] MINER.   B 5 Sept. 1839.
                 M 22 May, 1866.   Chas. B. Hubbard.

          4. LUCY ALDEN[8] MINER.   B 30 Oct. 1841.

          5. JOHN HOWARD[8] MINER.   B 24 May, 1844.
                 D 14 Sept. 1862. Killed in U. S. Army in Mississippi,
                                           14 Sept. 1862.

          6. MARY ELLEN[8] MINER.   B 19 Aug. 1847.   D 28 Aug. 1848.

XIII. **LUCY THOMAS**[7]   B 23 Aug. 1810.   M 16 Jan. 1834,
Coleraine, Mass.   in Ashfield, Mass., Dr. Chenery Puffer,
                                 of Shelburne Falls, Mass.
                              B 22 Jan. 1804, in Sudbury, Mass.
                                           D 6 Mar. 1877.

---

*These items were furnished by E. G. Miner.

CHILDREN OF Lucy Thomas [Alden]Puffer.

    I. HENRY MERVIN PUFFER[8]   B 21 Jan. 1835.
Graduate Rochester U., 1860, studied law.
                   M 20 Sept. 1866, in Fenelon, Mich.
        Mary Field, B 28 Jan. 1840, LeRoy, Mich.
Had these children:

        I. CARRIE LAMSON[9] PUFFER.   B 18 May, 1872.
                             Shelburne Falls, Mass.
               D 25 Aug. 1872, in Shelburne Falls.

   2. SAMUEL WILLIS[8] PUFFER.   B 8 Jan. 1837,
               M 22 May, 1866, in Winchester, Ill.
               Mary Catherine Powell.
               B 6 Nov. 1842. Winchester, Ill.

CHILDREN OF above Samuel Willis[8] Puffer.

        I. STARKEY POWELL PUFFER.   B 16 July, 1874.

        2. CHENERY PUFFER.   B 31st Mar. 1878.

        3. WILLIE PUFFER. B 29 Jan. 1880. D July, 1880.
                             All in Winchester, Ill.

   3. CHARLES CHENERY[8] PUFFER.   B 15 June, 1841.
               M 1 May, 1865, in Avon, N. Y.
Graduate Rochester U., 1863.
               Susan Emma Markham.
           B 2 Feb. 1843.   Avon, N. Y.
Children as follows:

        I. ISABELLA[9] PUFFER. B 4 March 1867. Elizabeth, N. J.

        2. LINDA DANA[9] PUFFER.   B 10 Oct. 1868.
                             Avon, N. Y.

     LUCY MARIA[8] PUFFER. B 5 Dec. 1842, in Coleraine, Mass.
            D 10 Feb. 1846,   "   "

NOTE.—Dr. Chenery Puffer has been President of the Franklin Dist. Med. Society, and in 1863, Representative to General Court of Massachusetts.

   IV. **DAVID**[7]   B 10 Feb. 1812.   M 19 Feb. 1839.   (1) Tirza Maria
               D 24 Nov. 1864.   Hunt, who   D 16 July, 1840,
He was a teacher and farmer,   Kalamazoo, Mich.
graduated from Brown University, in   M 29 Aug. 1842.   (2) Esther Wells
1838, resided in Ashfield, Mass., and   Blackington, North Adams, Mass.
Kalamazoo, Mich., Shelburne Falls,   who D 3 Jan. 1845.
Mass.   M 27 Aug. 1846.   (3) Mary Bliss

Ingraham, daughter of Asa Ingraham of No. Adams, Mass.

Styled of "Kewanee, Illinois, teacher and farmer." Held office of "Deacon" seventeen years, was a Justice of the Peace and much employed in public business. He was killed by his carriage, coming into collision with the engine in crossing a Railroad.

CHILDREN:

    1. ISABEL MARIA[8]   B 12 July, 1844.   D 6 Feb. 1848.

    2. FRANCIS HEARSAY[8]   B 18 May, 1847.

    3. JAMES WILLIE[8]   B 3 Nov. 1849.

    4. MARY ISABEL[8]   B 10 Jan. 1852.   D 23 Sept. 1854.

    5. CHARLES DAVID[8]   B 16 Aug. 1855.

    6. EDWARD MINER[8]   B 15 Mar. 1857.   D 13 Oct. 1859.

    7. HARRY BARTLETT[8]   B 14 Sept. 1859.   D 13 Aug. 1862.

    8. FREDERICK F.[8]   B 14 Nov. 1861.   D 2 Sept. 1862.

    9. FLORA GRACE[8]   B 23 Nov. 1864.

* REV. JOHN[7] ALDEN Rev. John,[6] David,[5] Eleazer,[4] Joseph,[3] Joseph,[2]
Providence, R. I.   Hon. John[1] Alden of D.
(See Part 1.)

B 10 Jan. 1806.   D ——   M 23 Nov. 1833,
Ann Maria Chamberlain, daughter of Ephraim
and Anna [Hovey] Chamberlain.
B 17 Mar. 1812.   D ——

CHILDREN OF Rev. John[7] Alden of Providence, R. I.

I. **AUGUSTUS EPHRIAM**[8]   B 22 Feb. 1837. M 2 Oct. 1859.
Ella Blake, daughter of Charles and Sarah Carter
Abbott, and daughter by adoption of Ezekiel
B 24 July, 1841.   Blake, of Chicopee Falls, Mass.

Had children.

    1. MATTIE BLAKE[9]   B   28 Feb. 1862, at Chicopee
                                                        Falls.
    M 22 Nov. 1880, at Providence, R. I. Walter L. Clarke.

And had

    1. HELEN RUTH.   B 15 Nov. 1883.
    2. RONALD BLAKE.   B 13 Sept. 1885.

2. LILLIE ANNA⁹.   B   13 Apr. 1866, at Providence,
                                                R. I.

3. JOHN AUGUSTUS⁹   B   23 Nov. 1867, at Providence,
        D ——   R. I.

4. EDWARD DANA⁹   B   15 Sept. 1870, at Providence,
                                                R. I.

II. **FRANCIS HOWARD**⁸   B 7 Jan. 1839, at Shelburne Falls,
                                                Mass.

                            D 19 July, 1844, at North Adams,
                                                Mass.

III. **ADONIRAM JUDSON**⁸ B 21 Nov. 1844, at North Adams,
                                                Mass.
              M ——   Eliza Cornell.

Had children.

> 1. } JOHN HERBERT. B 1 Apr. 1885.
> 2. } MILES STANDISH. B 1 Apr. 1885.

FAMILY OF MOLINES OF ENGLAND.

The surname has been written "Molines" and also "Mullens," and from the English Records we have the following :

2D APRIL, 1621.

In the name of God, Amen. I comit my soule to God that gave it, and my bodie to the earth from whence it came. Alsoe, I give my goodes as followeth : That fforty poundes in the hand of goodman Woodes. I give my wife tenn poundes, my sonne Joseph tenn poundes, my daughter Priscilla tenn poundes, and my eldest sonne tenn poundes. Alsoe, I give to my eldest sonne, all my debtes, bonds, bills, (onelye yt forty pounds excepted in the handes of goodman Wood) given as aforesaid with all the stock in his owne handes.

To my eldest daughter I give ten shillinges, to be paied out of my sonnes stock.

Furthermore, that goodes I have in Virginia as followeth : To my wife Alice halfe my goodes, & to Joseph and Priscilla the other halfe equallie to be divided betweene them.

Alsoe I have xxj dozen of shoes and thirteene paire of

bootes wch I give into the companies handes for forty poundes at seven yeares, and if they like them at that rate. If it be thought too deare as my overseers shall think good. And if they like them at that rate, at the divident I shall have nyne shares where I give as followeth : Twoe to my wife, twoe to my sonne William, twoe to my sonne Joseph, twoe to my daughter Priscilla, and one to the Companie.

Allsoe, if my sonne, William will come to Virginia, I give him my share of land. Furdermore, I give to my twoe overseers, Mr. John Carver and Mr. Williamson, twenty shillinges apeece to see this, my will, performed desiringe them that he would have an eye over my wife and children, to be as fathers and friendes to them.

Allsoe to have a specialle eye to my man Robert, which hathe not so approved himselfe as I would he should have done.

This is a coppye of Mr. Mullen's his will of all particulars he hathe given.

In witness thereof I have sett my hande. John Carver, Giles Hale, Christopher Joanes.

Vicessimo tertio ; die mensis Julie Anno Domini Millesimo sexcentessimo vicesino primo Emanavit Commissio Sare Blunden als Mullinsg felie naturali et legiteme dicte defuncti administrand bona iura et credita ciusdem defuncti iuxla benorem et effectum testamente suprascripti co quod nullum in codem testamento nominavit executorem de beue es Iurat.   68 Daler.

MENSE JULY ANNO DOMINI, 162J :

Vicesimo tertio die emanavit comissio Sara Blunden als Mullens filie urali et ltime Will mi Mullens, nus de Dorking in com Tuvr sed in parte bus ultra mavinis def hentis es ad administrand bona iuva et credita ejus dem def iuxta benorem, et effcum testamenti ipsius de functi co quod nullum in Codem nominavit exrem de bene et iuvat.

PROBATE ACT BOOK, 1621 AND 1622.

William Mullins, the testator, was one of the passengers in the Mayflower, and the father of Priscilla Mullens, the heroine of Longfellow's poem, "The Courtship of Miles Standish."

The will was evidently drawn up at Plymouth, New England, which was then considered a part of Virginia. The date of the will is not given, but it must have been on or before Febuary 21, 1620 – 1, for on that day Mr. Mullens died according to Gov. Bradford's Register, as quoted by Prince in his Chronology, Part II, p. 98. The date of April 2, 1621, was probably that on which the certified copy was signed.

Gov. Bradford in his list of passengers in the Mayflower has this entry :

"Mr. William Mullens and his wife and two children, Joseph and Priscilla, and a servant, Robert Carter." In the margin he gives the number of persons in Mr. Mullen's family, " 5."

In Bradford's memoranda of changes that had occurred in these families in the course of thirty years, we find this entry :

"Mr. Molines and his wife, his son and his servant died the first winter. Only his daughter Priscilla survived, and married with John Alden, who are both living, and have eleven children, and their eldest daughter is married and hath five children."

This will gives the names of Mr. Mullens' two children who were left in England. William, the eldest son, and Sarah, who married a Mr. Blunden. The Probate Act Book supplies the English Residence, Dorking, in the County of Surrey.*

Mr. Williamson, who is named as an overseer of the will, I take to be " Master Williamson," who, according to Mourts Relation, p. 36 — Dexter's Edition, p. 927, was present March 22, 1620 – 1, when the first treaty was made with Massasoit. Rev. Alexander Young, D. D., finding no person of the name of Williamson among the signers to the

---

* Bradford, New Plymouth, Boston, 1856, pp. 446 – 452.

compact, concludes that the name of Williamson was probably an error of the press, and suggests that of Allerton instead and Dr. Young's conjecture has been generally adopted by later writers.—*Chronicles of the Pilgrims*, 1841, p. 192.

Christopher Jones may have been the captain of the Mayflower, whose surname we know was Jones. Rev. Edward D. Neill, however, in the N. E. Historic Genealogical Register, XXVIII, p. 314, gives reasons for believing that his Christian name was Thomas.†

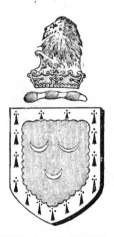

ARMORIAL BEARINGS OF ALDEN OF ENGLAND.

1. Gu. Three Crescents within a Bordure Engrailed Erm.

CREST.

Out of a Ducal Coronet Perpale Gu, and Sa, a
Demi-lion Or.

2. Gu. Three Crescents within a Bordure Engrailed Erm. (sometimes ar.)

3. ALDEN OR ALDON.

Gu. A Mullet Ar. between three Crescents, Erm, with a Bordure
Engrailed of the second.

CREST.

4. Out of a Ducal Coronet Or. a Demi-lion Gu.

† N. E. Historic Genealogical Register, Vol. XLII (1888) pp. 62, 64.

5. OR.   a bats wing Gu. surmounted of another Ar.

CREST.

Out of a Coronet Ar. two wings as in the Arms.

The *Arms* of the *English Family* of *Alden.* These various "*Armorial Bearings*" of the "Family of Alden" are taken from "*Burke's General Armory*," and correspond in most particulars in the Heraldic Emblems on the Shield.

IN EXPLANATION OF THE ARMS.

1. THE SHIELD.

    The tinctures — the charges placed thereon, are represented as made of metal or fur, or as painted in colors.

    (In the Arms of Alden.)

2. "GU." (gules) Means red.

3. "THREE CRESCENTS." Mean half moons with the horns uppermost.

4. "BORDURE ENGRAILED." A "Bordure" is a border extending around a Shield one-fifth of its width, and "Engrailed" *curved lines as* follows : ∿∿∿∿∿ at the edge of border.

5. "ERM." (ermine) Consists of a white field with black spots.

6. Of the "CREST." The Crest is a common adjunct of the Shield, and consists of any object or objects placed above it.

7. "CORONET." A form sometimes called "*Ducal* Coronet," more properly a "*Crest* Coronet," of various forms, and can only be described by plates or drawings.

8. "A DEMI-LION GU." Means half a lion painted red, and issuing from the Coronet.

9. TERMS "PERPALE, GU AND SA." Mean red and "*sa.*" (sable) black, equally divided in the Coronet.

10. "OR." Means Golden.

11. "AR." Means Silver. Abbreviation of *Argent.*

The Arms of the Aldens of England would seem to indicate considerable of civil service and respectability, and some military exploit.

This coat was assigned the 8th Sept. 1607, by Wm. Camden Clarencieux to John Alden of the Middle Temple, and was borne by the Aldens of Hertfordshire, London.

See "*Elements* of Heraldry."

See Plates, "Edmonson's Herald."

CHAPTER XXVI.

PLYMOUTH. — 1888.

THE oldest New England town affords rare attractions for the searcher after antiquities, or for the sight-seeing tourist. A pleasant, quiet village, with shady streets, comfortable dwellings, and many points of historic interest. The main street of the Pilgrims has since been called Leyden street. Here can be seen the spot where their first buildings were erected for the living, and near by rises the hill where the first permanent rest-

NATIONAL MONUMENT, PLYMOUTH.

ng-place for the dead was located. A visit to Burial Hill will show the traveller the graves of many of the early settlers, and the spot on which was placed their stronghold of defense. Here stood the Old Fort, erected by Standish and his followers; and from here, the old soldier sallied forth on his expeditions among the Indians. It was also used as a meeting-house, and up this hill on Sunday mornings might be seen the whole settlement marching in military order, with their muskets and firelocks; the governor, preacher and captain in the rear.

Across the brook to the south rises Watson's Hill, the scene of the treaty with Massasoit

To the north towers up the magnificent memorial, "The

PILGRIM HALL.

National Monument to the Pilgrims." It consists of an octagonal granite pedestal, forty-five feet in height, on which stands a statue of Faith, thirty-six feet high. This statue is said to be the finest specimen of granite statuary in the world. It is a most beautiful work of art. In her left hand she holds an open Bible; her right is raised and pointing heavenward. Her feet are planted on Plymouth Rock. The statue is two hundred and sixteen times life size, and is composed of fourteen blocks of granite, weighing in all one hundred and eighty tons. Four other statues adorn the pedestal; Morality, Education, Law and Liberty. Below these, in panels, are alto-reliefs in marble, representing the Departure from Delft Haven, the Signing of the Compact, the Landing of the Pilgrims, and the Treaty with Massasoit. Other panels extend to the top of the shaft, and on these are engraved the names of the Mayflower passengers.

Pilgrim Hall was built in 1824 by the Pilgrim Society. In 1880, J. Henry Stickney, of Baltimore, a liberal and patriotic friend, expended a large sum in enlarging and improving the building and grounds. A day spent here would be too short a time to satisfy lovers of the antique and historical in studying the relics contained in the building.

PLYMOUTH ROCK CANOPY.

The walls of the large hall are hung with rare and interesting pictures, many of which are portraits of the early settlers.

Cases around the room contain articles once belonging to Bradford, Standish, Winslow, Brewster, Alden and others.

Chairs owned by Carver and Brewster, the cradles of Peregrine White and Samuel Fuller, and a model of the Mayflower, are among the objects of interest here preserved.

Enclosed in an iron railing near the building, is a tablet bearing a copy of the "Immortal Compact," and on the fence surrounding it is inscribed the names of the forty-one signers.

"Plymouth," or "Forefathers' Rock" is the point toward which the tourist turns with the greatest eagerness. Here beneath a granite canopy is the identical rock upon which the Pilgrim feet first touched as they came ashore from their little shallop. It is protected from the hand of the spoiler by iron gates fitted to the arches of the canopy on each side. Above, in the chamber, are deposited the bones of some of the little band who died the first winter. They were exhumed while digging near Cole's Hill, a few years since. To the west of the rock, a flight of stone steps leads to the plateau on top of this hill, where can be seen a slab sunk in the ground, which marks the place where the first burials were made in 1621.

The Plymouth Rock House is located on the summit of the hill, and is one of the best in town. The view from its windows across the harbor is very fine.

Another hotel in the village is called the Samoset House in memory of Samoset, the Indian friend of the colonists.

Plymouth County court house, a large, handsome building, should not be passed without notice. Here the earliest records of the colony are preserved, and many legal documents in the Registry of deeds bear the signatures of the Pilgrim Fathers.

ALDEN NAMES.

———o———

The covers of this book are too narrow to bind in all the notable descendants of the family of Alden. I would be glad to record the good, brave, and noble deeds of many whose names are unknown to the public; and I would delight to enrich these pages with the biography of scores who have built for themselves memorials in the history and literature of their country. It is impossible to do justice to all. I would, however, call attention to the following :

The ancestors of John Adams and John Quincy Adams, Presidents of the United States, were John Bass, of Braintree, and Ruth Alden, daughter of the Pilgrim John Alden.

Henry Wadsworth Longfellow was descended from the union of the Alden and Wadsworth families of Duxbury.

Alden Bradford, historian, biographer, clergyman and Secretary of State, was a descendant of Gamaliel Bradford and Sarah Alden, of Duxbury.

Duncan Bradford, son of the above, was a scholar of note.

His son Gamaliel was a political writer. All three were graduates of Harvard College.

Henry Mills Alden, a native of Vermont, graduate of Williams College and Andover Theological Seminary, was in 1869, managing editor of Harper's *Magazine*. He was an author with Guernsey, of Harper's Pictorial History of the Great Rebellion.

James Alden, born in Portland, Me., was in 1871, Rear Admiral of the United States Navy. He died in San Francisco in 1877.

Joseph Alden, of Cairo, N. Y., was professor in Williams and Layfayette Colleges, and president of Jefferson College. He wrote over seventy volumes, mostly Sunday-school books. He was editor of the New York *Observer*, and Philadelphia *Christian Library*.

William Livingstone Alden, son of Joseph, was a graduate of Jefferson College. Studied law, wrote for New York *Times*, mostly humorous. In 1885, was United States Consul General at Rome. Founded the New York Canoe Club in 1870; was author of several works illustrating popular recreations.

Maj. Roger Alden was a soldier in the Revolutionary War, and served as aide to General Greene. He spent the last years of his life at West Point as Ordnance Storekeeper. His son, Bradford R., was a graduate of West Point, and afterwards an instructor and commandant there. He served two years as aide to General Scott, and was in the frontier service, where he was severely wounded. He was an accomplished and literary man as well as a good soldier. He died at Newport, R. I., in 1870.

Timothy Alden, of New York, was inventor of a typesetting machine.

Henry W. Alden, his brother, made many improvements on the invention.

John Goodwin, of Lowell, Mass., author of the "Pilgrim Republic," a work of great interest and merit, was descended from the family of Alden and of Bradford.

His son, Wm. Bradford Goodwin, a resident of Lowell, Mass., is an accomplished scholar. Dr. Jeremiah Taylor, of Boston, holds an honorable and responsible position as Secretary of the American Tract Society.

Oliver Alden Taylor, and his brother Rev. T. A. Taylor, were Congregational clergymen of note, Rev. E. K. Alden, of Boston, is the honored Secretary of the American Board of Foreign Missions. John B. Alden, of New York, publisher, has done the world good service in disseminating a high grade of literature at prices within the means of all.

General Alonzo Alden, of Troy, N. Y., won distinction in the Civil War.

Dr. Wm. H. Alden, of Portsmouth, N. H., is a clergyman of high standing in the Baptist denomination.

Hon. Geo. C. Alden (elsewhere spoken of), was a successful jurist.

Henry M. Puffer, Esq., of Shelburne Falls, Mass., is a practicing lawyer, and a man of noble heart and mind.

Wm. H. Gillette, son of Hon. Francis Gillette, of Hartford, Conn., is a dramatist of note.

Rev. Marcus Alden Tolman, of Mauch Chunk, is an Episcopal clergyman, and an accomplished scholar.

Mrs. Isabella M. Alden (Pansy) is a popular writer of Sunday-school books.

Mrs. D. Lothrop (Margaret Sydney) is also a very popular writer for the young.

ALDEN C. H.	Millinery.	Providence, R. I.
" C. T.	"	"
" Mrs. E. H.		"
" Emma T,		"
" Erastus C.		"
" Eva V.	Bookeeper.	"
" James	Insurance Agent.	"
" John A.	Clerk.	"
" Mary A.	Widow.	"
" Nellie		"
" Ada F.	Bookeeper.	Boston, Mass
" Adelbert U.	"	"
" Amherst A.	Clerk.	"
" Augustus	"	"
" Augustus D.	Organ Finisher.	"
" Augustus E.	Photographer.	"
" A. Judson	"	"
" Bartlett R.	Carpenter.	"
" Charles A.	(Marshall & Alden.)	"
" Charles	Shoemaker.	"
" Charles A.	Clerk.	"

ALDEN	Charles A.	Clerk.	Boston, Mass
"	Charles E.	Bicyclist.	"
"	Charles E.	Clerk.	"
"	Charles E.	Salesman.	"
"	Charles H.	"	"
"	Charles H.	Woodworker.	"
"	Charles C.	Carpenter.	"
"	Charles T.	Scale Maker.	"
"	Charles W.	Insurance Agent.	"
"	Charles W.	Manager.	"
"	Mrs. C. A.		"
"	C. S. & Co.		"
"	Dana K.		"
"	Darius G.	Fancy Dry Goods.	"
"	David A.	Accountant.	"
"	Rev. Edmund K.	Sec'y Am. Board.	"
"	Edward A.	Foreman.	"
"	Edward M.	Clerk.	"
"	Edwin	Piano Maker.	"
"	Elisha C.	Clerk.	"
"	Elizabeth		"
"	E. Hyde	Stenographer.	"
"	Francis	Salesman.	"
"	Frank D.	Clerk.	"
"	Frank E.	Machinist.	"
"	Frank E.	Architect.	"
"	Frank W.	Foreman.	"
"	Fred. T.	Clerk.	"
"	Geo. A.	Clerk.	"
"	Geo. A. & Co	Rubber Com. Merchant.	"
"	Geo. C.	Carpenter.	"
"	Mrs. Geo. C.	Magnetic Physician.	"
"	Geo. E.	Clerk.	"
"	Griffith	Salt Bottle Mfr's.	"
"	Gustavus F.	Bookeeper.	"
"	G. Edwin	Clerk.	"
"	Harry B.	Draughtsman.	"
"	Henry D.	Clerk.	"
"	Herman S.		"
"	H. B.	Sec'y India Mutual Ins.	"
"	Ichabod		"
"	James B.		"
"	James C.		"
"	James E.	Jig Saws.	"
"	John	Carpenter.	"
"	John	Music Teacher N. E. Conservatory.	"
"	John C.	Coal Dealer.	"
"	John E.	Clerk.	"

ALDEN	John H.	Furniture Repairer.	Boston, Mass.
"	Joseph D.	Painter.	"
"	J. Henry	Clerk.	"
"	Louis T.	Civil Engineer.	"
"	Lucius F.	Boot and Shoe Mf'r.	"
"	Martha S.	Widow.	"
"	Mary E.	"	"
"	Mary S.		"
"	Morton	Clerk.	"
"	O. W.	Grocer.	"
"	Richard B.	Salesman.	"
"	Samuel S.	Caulker.	"
"	Silas A.	Teacher of Oratory.	"
"	Mrs. Susan C.		"
"	S. A.	Clerk.	"
"	Egbert S.		"
"	Thomas	Bookbinder.	"
"	Walter J.	Steward.	"
"	Walter M.	Carpenter.	"
"	Wm. A.	Electrician.	"
"	Wm. E.		"
"	Wm. H.	Conductor B. & P. R. R.	"
"	W. S.	Clerk.	"
"	Adelbert H.	Sec'y.	New York
"	Amelia D.	Widow.	"
"	Annie C.	Widow.	"
"	Arthur B.	Straw Goods.	"
"	Carl C.	Sec'y.	"
"	Charles H.	Carpenter.	"
"	Cyrus A.	Dentist.	"
"	Edwin	Advertising Agent.	"
"	Frances	Widow.	"
"	Frank G.	Broker.	"
"	Fred C.	Clerk.	"
"	Geo. A.	President.	"
"	Henry		"
"	Henry		"
"	Henry H.		"
"	Henry N.		"
"	Henry W.		"
"	J. Wager		"
"	James	Sec'y.	"
"	James G.	Insurance.	"
"	John B.	President Publishing Co.	"
"	Percy R.		"
"	Thomas J.		"
"	Wm.	Manager.	"
"	Wm. H.	Real Estate.	"

ALDEN Samuel G.	Mason.	Malden, Mass.
" Geo. N.	Sec. Fire Ins. Co.	New Bedford, Mass.
" Maria O.		"
" Silas		"
" Christopher	Painter.	Fall River, Mass.
" Geo. F.	Steward.	"
" Myra		Pawtucket, R. I.
" Adeline		Chelsea. Mass.
" Edgar	Clerk.	"
" Frank	Painter.	"
" Fred S.		"
" Mrs. Hepsey		"
" Isaac	Grocer.	"
" C. W.	Merchant.	"
" Geo. H.	Moulder.	Newton, Mass.
" Hiram		"
" Nancy A.		"
" Arthur P.	Grocer.	Brockton, Mass.
" Charles C.		
" Fred S.		"
" George		"
" George W.	Stoves.	"
" Frederick	Confectioner.	"
" John	Foreman.	"
" Lucus W.		"
" Lucius F.	Shoes.	"
" Sandford		"
" Mrs. S. F.		"
" Thomas J,	Freight Agent.	"
" Clara A.		Manchester, N. H.
" Daniel		"
" Zenas P.		Pennacook N. H.
" M. E.	Widow.	New Haven, Conn.
" Harriet C.	"	"
" Horace E.		"
" L. A. J.		"
" Mary J.	Teacher.	"
" Wm.	Machinist.	"
" Fred C.	Painter.	Lewiston, Me.
" Miss Oxa E.		"
" Stephen C.		"
" Wm. A.		"
" Hiram R.	Dentist.	Portland, Me.
" Wm. O.	Apothecary.	Old Orchard, Me.
" Darius	Pres. Granite Nat. Bank.	Augusta, Me.
" Darius	Carpenter.	"
" Robert E.	Conductor.	"
" Alton	Teamster.	Hallowell, Me.

ALDEN	Farrelly	Agent Cleveland Stove Co.	Pittsburgh, Pa.
"	Frank E.		"
"	Harry		"
"	James	Agent.	"
"	John B.		Jamestown, N. Y.
"	Charles P.	Grocer.	Hyde Park, Mass.
"	Wm. H., D.D.		Portsmouth, N. H.
"	Elliott	Boots & Shoes.	Medford, Mass.
"	Albert		Middleboro, Mass.
"	Arthur B.		"
"	Jared F.		"
"	Arthur H.		"
"	Elijah		"
"	Andrew		"
"	Amos C.		"
"	Charles C.		"
"	Charles C.		"
"	Charles F.		"
"	Frank		"
"	Frank F.		"
"	Fred.		"
"	George L.		"
"	Apollos G.		"
"	J. Edward		"
"	James G.		"
"	James M.		"
"	John F.		"
"	Leander M		"
"	Sidney H.		"
"	Wm. L.		"
"	H. B.		Plymouth, Mass.
"	Marshall		Dover, N. H.
"	Adna W.		Norwood, Mass.
"	George		"
"	Harris W.		"
"	Horatio H.		"
"	Marcus Morton		"
"	Henry		Norton, Mass.
"	Rev. Morrison		"
"	C. E.	Machinist.	Marlboro, Mass.
"	Geo. S.	"	Waltham, Mass.
"	Mary S.	Widow.	"
"	Sarah B.		"
"	Fred C.		Taunton, Mass.
"	Geo. T.		"
"	John C.	Agt N. E. Despatch Ex. Co.	Taunton, Mass
"	Nathaniel	Prop'r Key City Spice Mills.	Dubuque, Ia.
"	James	Agent " " "	"

ALDEN	Wm. J.		Duxbury, Mass.
"	Wm. J., Jr.		"
"	Charles H.		"
"	Charles		"
"	Samuel		"
"	Samuel, Jr.		"
"	Amos		"
"	J. D.		"
"	Thomas		"
"	Mattie		"
"	Thomas		"
"	James		"
"	James, Jr.		"
"	Frank		"
"	Ezra		"
"	Arthur		"
"	Emma		"
"	Henry		"
"	Henry, Jr.		"
"	John		"
"	Mrs. John		"
"	Edith		"
"	John, Jr.		"
"	Frank		"
"	Mary		"
"	Lydia		"
"	Lyton		"
"	Emma W.		"
"	James B.		"
"	Peleg C. C.		"
"	Priscilla Mullens		"
"	Edson J.		Salisbury, Vt.
"	Julius W.		Leicester, Vt
"	Wm.		Brandon, Vt.
"	Columbus		San Francisco, Cal.
"	Oscar		"
"	Harry K.		"
"	Timothy		Brandon, Vt.
"	Wm. S.		Leicester, Vt.
"	Wm., Jr.		"
"	Burton		"
"	Loyal		"
"	Clifford		"
"	George A.		Whiting, Vt.
"	John C.		"
"	Rev. Willis		Gold Hill, Oregon.
"	H. L.	Lawyer.	Wyandotte, Kan.
"	Miss Sarah	Teacher.	Belchertown, Mass.

ALDEN	Mary C.	Widow.	Newark, N. J.
"	John	Plankinton House.	Milwaukee, Mich.
"	Albert A.	Clerk.	Minneapolis, Minn.
"	Albert M.	Real Estate.	"
"	Bertha		"
"	Charles S.	Agent.	"
"	Charles M.	Clerk.	"
"	Edgar H.	Clerk.	"
"	Gertrude C.	Embroiderer.	"
"	Herbert D.	Clerk.	"
"	John	Harnesses.	"
"	John B.	Bookkeeper.	"
"	Nancy A.	Milliner.	"
"	Robert S.	Carriages.	"
"	Wm. A.	Alden & Wilson.	"
"	Charles M.	Hardware.	Grand Rapids, Mich.
"	George W.	Agent.	"
"	Mary W.		"
"	Samuel R.	Lawyer.	Fort Wayne, Ind.
"	Miss A. S.	Clerk.	Columbus, Ohio.
"	Eugene E.	Soldier.	"
"	Frank S.	Printer.	Cleveland, Ohio.
"	Henry	Card Writer.	"
"	Sanford	Broker.	"
"	Mrs. Ella		Denver, Col.
"	Frank D.	Carpenter.	"
"	Mrs. George C.	Widow.	Fort Collins, Col.
"	Wm.	Stock Ranch.	"
"	Willis	Teamster.	Omaha, Neb.
"	Edgar F.	Printer.	St. Louis, Mo.
"	John T.	Builder.	"
"	Edward	Plumber.	St. Joseph, Mo.
"	Edward F.	Bacon House.	"
"	Rosa		"
"	Emma		Kansas City.
"	Lincoln S.		"
"	Frank E.	Bookkeeper.	Peoria, Ill.
"	Horace A.	Supt. Acme Hay Harvester.	"
"	Sidney	Bookkeeper.	Savannah, Ga.
"	Henry		Saratoga Springs.
"	Phebe		"
"	T. A.		Rochester, N. Y.
"	Charles S.	Sec. Roch. Bridge and Iron Wks.	"
"	John F.		"
"	Wm. H.	Mason.	Albany, N. Y.
"	Geo. Alonzo		Troy, N. Y.
"	Charles S.	Lawyer.	"
"	Edward M.	Grocer.	"

ALDEN	A. B.	Straw Goods.	New York.
"	Barnabas G.		Chicago, Ill.
"	Carrie	Widow.	"
"	Charles		"
"	Emmons J.		"
"	Rev. Ezra		"
"	Ezra J. Jr.	Agent.	"
"	Frank		"
"	Frank A.		"
"	Henry E,	Engineer.	"
"	R. C.	Councillor.	"
"	Warren A.	Pres. Alden Book Co.,	"
"	Wm. T.	Postal Clerk.	"
"	Charles E.	Machinist.	Philadelphia.
"	Geo. D.	Bookeeper,	"
"	Geo. W.	Machinist.	"
"	Joshua		"
"	Rev. Wm.	Librarian.	"
"	Ebenezer	Merchant.	Washington, D. C.
"	Elijah		"
"	Harry	Clerk.	"
"	Harry	Clerk.	"
"	James M.	Admiral U. S. Navy.	"
"	Lucius D.		"
"	Sadie		"
"	Thomas	Merchant.	"
"	Wm. H.		"
"	C. L.	Machinist.	Cincinnati, Ohio.
"	E. E.	Hatter.	"
"	Edwin	President Edwin Alden Co.	"
"	Ella M.		"
"	Ethel	Cashier.	"
"	F. H.	Manager Hat Store.	"
"	Frank H.		"
"	John D. Mrs.	Widow.	"
"	Mary C.	Widow.	"
"	Edmund K.		Brooklyn, N. Y.
"	Edward	Bookkeeper.	"
"	Flats		"
"	George		"
"	Harry T.		"
"	John		"
"	John B.	Telegraph Operator.	"
"	Machine Co.		"
"	Samuel H.		"
"	Fannie	Fancy Goods.	Newark, N. J.
"	James G.	Insurance.	"
"	Prof James W.	Music.	"

ALDEN	Geo. C.	Grocer.	Troy, N. Y.
"	Harry M.	Grocer.	"
"	Joseph D.		"
"	Frank	Carpenter.	Buffalo, N. Y.
"	Jacob	Engineer.	"
"	Edward M.	Express.	Holyoke, Mass.
"	Dwight I.	Bookkeeper.	"
"	Philo W.		"
"	A. O	Piano Manufacturer.	Springfield, Mass.
"	Adin	Clerk.	"
"	Charles P.	Druggist.	"
"	E. A.	Trea. Springfield Waste Co.	"
"	Merrill F.		"
"	Frank		"
"	Geo. A.	Cashier.	"
"	Mrs. J.		"
"	James		"
"	James O.	Pres. Woolson Machine Co.	"
"	Joel		"
"	John B.		"
"	Olive A. Mrs.		"
"	Orville	Farmer.	"
"	Ralph P.	Teller 2nd National Bank.	"
"	Wm. W.	Jeweller.	"
"	Charles C.		Worcester, Mass.
"	Charles		"
"	Edward	Engineer.	"
"	E. Elmer	Engineer.	"
"	Fred L.	Machinist.	"
"	Prof. Geo. I.	Free Inst.	"
"	J. Brown	Conductor.	"
"	Priscilla E.	Widow.	"
"	Samuel E.	Carpenter.	"
"	Fred S.	Conductor.	Fitchburg, Mass.
"	George W.	Clerk.	"
"	Wm. C.		Lowell, Mass.
"	John	Chemist.	Lawrence, Mass.
"	Albert N.	Musician.	Lynn, Mass.
"	David O.	Shoes.	"
"	James A.	Livery.	"
"	Oliver N.	Carriage Painter.	"
"	Otis A.	Printer.	"
"	Solomon T.	Shoes.	"
"	Wm.		"
"	Charles C.	Student.	Malden, Mass
"	Daniel A.	Accountant.	"
"	Edward	Rubber Shoe Co.	"
"	Henry A.	Wood Worker.	"

ALDEN	Frank F.	Supt. Key City Spice Mills.	Dubuque, Ia.
"	Isaac B.	Clerk. " " "	"
"	Ella		"
"	Emma		"
"	Rev. Willard		"
"	Cyrus	Mf'r Shoes.	Glens Falls, N. Y.
"	Clara M.	Music Teacher.	Cambridge, Mass.
"	Elizabeth A.		"
"	Fannie A.	Milliner.	"
"	Geo. W. A.	Manufacturer.	"
"	G. Edwin		"
"	Louise M.		"
"	Otis B.	Printer.	"
"	Sophia D.	Widow.	"
"	Susan M.	"	"
"	Wm. R.	Manufacturer.	"
"	Anna B.	Widow.	Medford, Mass.
"	A. M.		"
"	Ella L. Mrs		"
"	F. William		"
"	C. Walter		Melrose, Mass.
"	Samuel		Dedham, Mass.
"	Amasa		"
"	Abner		"
"	Herbert W.		"
"	Henry C.		"
"	Elisha C.		"
"	Frank E.		"
"	Frank, Jr.		"
"	M. Stella Miss		Salem, Mass.
"	Babcock		"
"	John Augustus		London, England.
"	George		"
"	James	Merchant Tailor.	"
"	James	Chair Manufacturer.	"
"	John	Chemist.	"
"	Wm.	Salesman.	"

TESTIMONIALS.

———o———

From Rev. Dr. Bixby, Pastor of Cranston Street Baptist Church, Providence, R. I.

"Rev. John Alden, a near neighbor of mine, has just completed his autobiography, a large part of which has been read to me in manuscript. It is a book of thrilling interest. Naturally gifted, liberally educated, a careful observer, an active worker, and living more than four score years in New England in a most eventful period of the world's history, Mr. Alden is pre-eminently prepared to write a book of this kind. It is full of facts and anecdotes, maxims and principles, so woven together by his facile pen, as to make the book exceedingly fascinating. It is also of great historic value. Ministers will find it especially helpful and stimulating, and all classes will find something in the book that will interest and profit them. I hope the book will have a large sale."

From President Robinson, D.D., LL.D., President of Brown University, Providence, R. I.

"From the table of contents of **Rev. Mr.** Alden's book I am confident it will be a book of engrossing interest, and will be wanted by many readers."

From Thomas M. Clark, Bishop of Rhode Island.

"I heartily endorse President Robinson's and other testimonies given to the Rev. **Mr.** Alden, and do not doubt but the book will prove to be of great interest."

From E. K. Alden, D.D., Congregational Rooms, Somerset Street, Boston.

"I concur in the judgment expressed by President Robinson."

From Rev. Dr. Jeremiah Taylor, American Tract Society Rooms, Bromfield Street, Boston.

"I am very glad to add my testimony to the value of the work which Rev. Mr. Alden has in hand. I have listened to the table of contents, and also have been familiar with the spirit and ability of the writer."

TESTIMONIALS.

TESTIMONIALS.

through a period of more than fifty years has passed under your observant eye, must possess elements of interest and value worthy of permanent print. The book written in the lively style which comes from personal observation and experience, will not fail to be read with delightsome interest, both of pleasure and profit.

Ever truly yours,

JOHN W. OLMSTEAD.

Boston, June 29, 1888.

" I heartily concur in the opinion of Rev. Dr. Olmstead as above stated. I am well satisfied that Mr. Alden's book will be read with special interest and profit." — R. J. ADAMS, D. D.

Boston, June 30, 1888.

From Rev. O. P. Gifford, Pastor of Warren Avenue Baptist Church, Boston, Mass.

"From my personal knowledge of Rev. John Alden, and a knowledge of his great work in Shelburne Falls, I expected a treat when told he would publish an autobiography. A study of the table of contents confirms my expectations, and quickens the desire to see the book. The length of time covered by his life, the number of eminent people he came into relation with, the large part he has played in the religious and educational life of New England, makes this work a contribution of genuine worth to the student of history."

From A. J. Gordon, D.D., Pastor Clarendon Street Baptist Church, Boston.

"Having looked over the prospectus of Rev. John Alden's autobiography, I judge that the work will be of great interest to such, especially, as would be informed concerning the religious history and characteristics of a generation now nearly passed away, to which Mr. Alden belongs. I commend his work most cordially."

From Alanson Wedge, A.M., Principal Forestville Literary Institution, New York.

"The autobiography of Rev. John Alden cannot fail to interest and instruct. It abounds in wit and wisdom. It is a faithful record of the life of one of the most active and useful men of the present century. Whoever becomes acquainted with Mr. Alden, loves him and respects him. Whoever may be so fortunate as to possess his autobiography, will not willingly part with it."

From Rev. Mark Trafton, D.D., the eminent Methodist Divine, Cambridge, Mass.

"Rev. John Alden, D. D., in the Christian ministry and different branches of religious work for over half a century, proposes to give to the world a picture of his active life, and also of the bustling world as he has seen it 'from grave to gay, from lively to severe.' I have seen the plan of the projected work, and having known him for a half century, and having been a neighbor to him, I think his book will be a success. This man of over four score years is a lineal descendant of the never-to-be-forgotten 'Priscilla' of Plymouth fame, and there is a strain of that humorous blood in his organism which is whispering: 'Speak for yourself, John;' and I incline to think he will, and will be listened to with responsive smiles."

From Rev. Francis H. Rowley, Pastor North Adams Baptist Church.

"It was my pleasure, some few weeks ago, to listen to the reading of several selections from the MSS. of the Rev. John Alden's Autobiography. Those who know Mr. Alden and are at all familiar with his long and eminently useful life, can imagine something of the richness and value of this self-told story of his more than fourscore years. The serious and the gay, the humorous and the pathetic, each is present to lend its charm. No lover of New England can fail to be interested in this record of one of its most devoted and widely-known ministers. Especially will this book, when published, be of great interest and historical value to the places in which Mr. Alden has labored. The record left behind him in North Adams well deserves publication, for under his ministry here some of the men whose lives have most shaped the church of God in this place, were converted. Most heartily do we commend its reading to all."

From Rev. A. M. Crane, Pastor Shelburne Falls Baptist Church.

Rev. J. Alden,

My dear Brother:—Your name is closely connected with the early history of our church, and is still held in pleasant memory. Any work that you might write, bringing out your own experience in years long gone by must contain much that would interest the present generation, and contain lessons of profit to those now toiling in the Master's vineyard. I shall anticipate the book, and hope you may meet with good success in its publication.

From Rev. Thatcher Thayer, D.D., an eminent Congregationalist Divine, Newport, R. I.

"My old classmate proposes to tell the story of his life. He was considerably venerable in college, and has lived a great while since. Most of his time has been spent with the Baptist persuasion, some of whom we know to be very excellent people, especially in Rhode Island. His adventures with them, by land and water, cannot fail to be interesting. Even in early times he was noted for power to discriminate what was worthy of narration and for ability to narrate. We may then confidently expect that out of his rich store of observations made during a large part of this century, he will bring forth much to edify and amuse. Most of us who were in Mr. Alden's class are dead, or are likely to die soon, but the survivors will read these memories with the kindest recollections of the author; they will recall their classmate's genial spirit; above all, they will remember his unfeigned piety, and heartily testify to the good will ever felt towards him."

CPSIA information can be obtained
at www.ICGtesting.com
Printed in the USA
BVHW071223050121
596834BV00001B/70

9 789354 029530